THE SEXUAL AGGRESSOR

Current Perspectives on Treatment

JOANNE G. GREER, Ph.D.
Office of the Inspector General
Department of Health and Human Services
Washington, D.C.
formerly, Deputy Chief,
National Center for Prevention and Control of Rape
National Institute of Mental Health
Rockville, Maryland

IRVING R. STUART, Ph.D.
Department of Psychology
Lehman College of the City University of New York
New York, New York

VNR VAN NOSTRAND REINHOLD COMPANY
NEW YORK CINCINNATI TORONTO LONDON MELBOURNE

Copyright © 1983 by Van Nostrand Reinhold Company Inc.

Library of Congress Catalog Card Number: 82-24709
ISBN: 0-442-22855-4

Manufactured in the United States of America

Published by Van Nostrand Reinhold Company Inc.
135 West 50th Street, New York, N.Y. 10020

Van Nostrand Reinhold
480 Latrobe Street
Melbourne, Victoria 3000, Australia

Van Nostrand Reinhold Company Limited
Molly Millars Lane
Wokingham, Berkshire, England

15 14 13 12 11 10 9 8 7 6 5 4 3 2 1

Library of Congress Cataloging in Publication Data

Main entry under title:

The Sexual Aggressor.

   Includes index.
   1. Sex offenders—Rehabilitation. 2. Psychotherapy.
3. Sex offenders—Mental health services. I. Greer,
Joanne G. II. Stuart, Irving R. [DNLM: 1. Criminal
psychology. 2. Paraphillias—Therapy. 3. Sex
offenses. WM 610 S515]
RC560.S47S49 1983   616.85′83   82-24709
ISBN 0-442-22855-4

Contributors

Gene G. Abel, M.D.
Department of Psychiatry
Columbia University Medical School and
Director, Sex Offender Treatment Program
New York State Psychiatric Institute
New York, New York

Judith V. Becker, Ph.D.
Department of Psychiatry
Columbia University Medical School and
Sex Offender Treatment Program
New York State Psychiatric Institute
New York, New York

Fred S. Berlin, M.D., Ph.D.
Biosocial Hormonal Clinic
Department of Psychiatry and
    Behavioral Sciences
Johns Hopkins University School of Medicine
Baltimore, Maryland

Carol Bohmer, L.L.M., Ph.D.
Department of Medical Psychology
Johns Hopkins University Medical School
Baltimore, Maryland

Emily M. Coleman, Ph.D.
Sex Offender Treatment Program
University of Tennessee Center
    for the Health Sciences
Memphis, Tennessee

Henry Donnelly
Division of Program Planning,
    Evaluation, and Research
New York State Department
    of Correctional Services
Albany, New York

C.M. Earls, Ph.D.
Department of Psychology
Queen's University
Kingston, Ontario, Canada

Jeffrey C. Fracher, Ph.D.
Sexual Counseling Service
Department of Psychiatry

Rutgers Medical School
Piscataway, New Jersey

Cynthis C. Gibat, Ph.D.
Department of Psychiatry
University of Rochester School of Medicine
Rochester, New York

A. Nicholas Groth, Ph.D.
Director, Sex Offender Treatment Program
Connecticut Correctional Institute
Somers, Connecticut

Mary R. Haynes, Ph.D.
Sex Offender Treatment Program
University of Tennessee Center
    for the Health Sciences
Memphis, Tennessee

D.R. Laws, Ph.D.
Director, Sexual Behavior Laboratory
Atascadero State Hospital
Atascadero, California

Robert E. Longo, M.R.C.
Director, Sex Offender Program
Correctional Treatment Programs
Oregon State Hospital
Salem, Oregon and
President, Sexual Assault
    Research Association, Inc.

Donald Macdonald
Division of Program Planning,
    Evaluation, and Research
New York State Department
    of Correctional Services
Albany, New York

Kee MacFarlane, M.S.W.
National Center on Child Abuse and Neglect
U.S. Children's Bureau
Department of Health and Human Services
Washington, D.C.

iii

iv CONTRIBUTORS

G. Alan Marlatt, Ph.D.
Department of Psychology
University of Washington
Seattle, Washington

Janice K. Marques, Ph.D.
Department of Mental Health
State of California
Sacramento, California

W.L. Marshall, Ph.D.
Department of Psychology
Queen's University
Kingston, Ontario, Canada

Leonard Morgenbesser, Ph.D.
Division of Program Planning,
 Evaluation, and Research
New York State Department
 of Correctional Services
Albany, New York

William D. Murphy, Ph.D.
Sex Offender Treatment Program
University of Tennessee Center
 for the Health Sciences
Memphis, Tennessee

Candice A. Osborn, Ph.D.
Sexual Behavior Laboratory
Atascadero State Hospital
Atascadero, California

William D. Pithers, Ph.D.
Departments of Psychiatry and Genetics
University of Rochester School of Medicine
Rochester, New York

Vernon L. Quinsey, Ph.D.
Director, Oak Ridge Division
 Mental Health Center
Pentanguishene, Ontario, Canada

Carl M. Rogers, Ph.D.
Associate Director, Child Protection Center/
 Special Unit

Children's Hospital, National Medical Center
Washington, D.C.

Raymond C. Rosen, Ph.D.
Sexual Counseling Service
Department of Psychiatry
Rutgers Medical School
Piscataway, New Jersey and
Chairman, Criminal and Violent Behavior
 Grants Review Group
National Institute of Mental Health

Stuart B. Silver, M.D.
Superintendent, Clifton T. Perkins Center
Maryland State Hospital
 for the Criminally Insane
Jessup, Maryland

Linda J. Skinner, Ph.D.
Department of Psychiatry
Columbia University Medical School and
Sex Offender Treatment Program
New York State Psychiatric Institute
New York, New York

Michael K. Spodak, M.D.
Clifton T. Perkins Center
Maryland State Hospital
 for the Criminally Insane
Jessup, Maryland

Joyce N. Thomas, R.N., M.P.H.
Director, Child Protection Center/Special Unit
Children's Hospital, National Medical Center
Washington, D.C.

Frank Tracy
Director, Division of Program Planning,
 Evaluation, and Research
New York State Department
 of Correctional Services
Albany, New York

Preface

According to all available published statistics, there is currently an epidemic of sexual assaults throughout all age groups. Health care providers, in physical medicine as well as in the mental health services, admit that these represent only a minor proportion of the actual number of such attacks. The stigma attached to being a victim or a revealed aggressor tends to restrict accurate records.

The increase in cases of sexual aggression over the past decade has alerted professionals to the need for better preparation of those dealing on a face-to-face basis with such aggressors, whether they appear as clients to a private practitioner or as members of a correctional institution. Aggression and its targets demand the skills and insights that can be provided by trained professionals in the health care services. In order to have a cooperative exchange of information among these professionals, whose roles are segmented by social considerations and professional barriers, a unified source of current techniques dealing with sexual aggression is required.

This book is designed to provide for such a need. It contains practical contributions by professionals in various concerned divisions of the physical and mental health services. They emphasize the requisite skills and techniques that each division brings to a particular area of service. Because of the acknowledged complexity of interrelated social, physical, and emotional factors involved in treating sexual offenders, the manner in which individuals and agencies can effectively intervene forms the basis for this book. As such, it represents a selective survey of contemporary management techniques and professional issues facing the therapist and investigator dealing with sexually aggressive clients. Although the book is primarily oriented toward the working professional in the mental health services, it should also be informative to those currently in training in disciplines associated with this area.

Where does a mental health provider search for literature on this subject when confronted with a sex offender as a client? There has been a lack of practical literature detailing how to proceed with such clients. Considering the urgency of the problem, the editors believe that this book, written by those engaged in providing services to sexual aggressors or in conducting related research, will be of great value. Much progress has been made since a decade ago when it was first suggested that the study of rape could be divided into four categories: motives, method of approach, coercion (or seduction), and past experiential history of the offender. As a consequence, the development of consistent analysis and creative therapeutic programs measured to fit particular personality profiles and offenses has been very productive.

To present a variety of programs, procedures, and conceptions of the problems involved, the book has been divided into four sections. Part I presents treatment and assessment issues with mentally retarded offenders and a discussion of forensic mental evaluation of the violent sexual offender. It concludes with a chapter on the legal considerations involved in mandatory treatment of sexual offenders. Part II contains an extensive coverage of biomedical perspectives on sexual offenders and a status report on biomedical treatments. Part III includes a number of chapters dealing with psychotherapy in a variety of settings. It begins with material on tension-reduction training in the treatment of compulsive sex offenders and continues with two chapters on treating sex offenders in correctional institutions. There is also an evaluation of treatment programs, a presentation of research conclusions on variables influential in recidivism and relapse prevention, and an analysis of the long-term sequelae of sexual assault. Part IV is concerned with building and operating behavioral laboratories to evaluate and treat sexual deviance, as well as with a detailed exposition of the technology involved in the laboratory assessment of sexual arousal patterns. An appendix lists names and addresses of prominent programs throughout the country for treating the sexual offender.

We wish to thank the contributors for taking time from their heavy schedules to write these chapters. Their patience with the editors is greatly appreciated. In addition, we are grateful for the cooperation and assistance of Ms. Susan Munger, Senior Editor, Professional and Technical Division, Van Nostrand Reinhold Company, and Ms. Alberta Gordon, Managing Editor. Their understanding of our problems did much to encourage our efforts.

J.J.G.
I.R.S.

Introduction

Joanne G. Greer, Ph.D.

THE SEX OFFENDER: THEORIES AND THERAPIES, PROGRAMS AND POLICIES

Toward a Theory of Rape

Throughout history, mankind has commonly established cultural and religious controls over the expression of the sex drive to protect the procreative function. Feminists maintain that such controls were also established because of the primitive view of women as property, but this would not explain the rules or taboos with regard to nonfemale sexual objects, such as those found in the biblical book of Leviticus against intercourse with animals, intercourse between males, and "spilling seed upon the ground." Undoubtedly, the sources of such prohibitions are multiple and reflect a complex of concerns which anthropologists delight in identifying and explicating. Cultures also evolve. What was accepted sexual behavior in one century, or even one generation, may be seen in a different light by those who come after. The slowness of this evolution is witnessed by the fact that even in modern times, bride rape and clitoridectomy have not disappeared in some remote areas. Standard psychiatric reference works from the pre-World War II era barely mention rape and incest when discussing sexual "deviations" and "perversions," but they lavish pages on homosexuality and such rare exotica as foot fetishism.

Today, serious thinkers about the nature of man, be they philosophers or theologians, would see some merit in viewing rape as more of a sexual perversion than consenting homosexuality. Current views of sexuality place a greater emphasis on consensual activity and reverence for the partner than has ever existed in the past. Deviate or perverse activity, from this point of view, is sexual activity which misuses persons, rather than sexual activity which misuses sperm or genitalia.

Even those who consider the women's movement extremist and unidimensional must concede that it is primarily the advent of feminism which has forced Western society to examine as never before the meaning of sexuality in its wholeness. Feminism raised, and is still raising, questions about sexuality, bodily integrity, and human freedom which mankind has never fully faced before. The earliest feminist answers to these questions now seem simplistic even to many feminists, but the women's movement nevertheless deserves historical notice for calling attention to previously neglected, important social problems.

Prior to the development of the women's movement, there was a tendency to view sexual assault of females in one of two ways. Either the offender, as a healthy, red-blooded man, had been driven into temporary madness by the thoughtless or perhaps deliberate seductiveness of his victim, or the offender himself was the unfortunate victim of poor heredity. Such views were moderated with regard to sexual assault of little girls, but there was still slight understanding of the pathology of the offender and much need to blame the victim. Feminists, with justifiable rage, were quick to point out that rape victims 18 months of age, or 80 years of age, were not unknown to big city emergency rooms. Such victims were, obviously, not very seductive in behavior, at least to the normal observer. Victim advocates demanded and gradually brought about a radical reorientation of lawmakers, the judiciary, the media, educators, and mental health theorists and practitioners. As laws changed and sentencing procedures were reformed, more offenders came under the control of the courts and were available for etiology and treatment research. A new image of the sex offender gradually developed. The offender, far from being infected with an excess of joie de vivre or libido, was often found to be filled with hatred or callous contempt for his victim and for females in general. This picture remains valid for many offenders, although further research has focused on elucidating subclassifications in order to more precisely serve both treatment and prevention.

Another development concurrent with the women's movement also paved the way for a serious study of the most common sex offenses: rape, incest, and child molestation. Until the 1960s psychoanalytic theory dominated the mental health field, but in the past two decades social psychiatry/psychology and biological psychiatry have become at least its equal. The dominance by psychoanalytic theory was not favorable to the development of a better understanding of the sex offender. Sex offenders were not common in the case load of the psychodynamically oriented therapist either as self-referrals or as court referrals. Court referrals were uncommon because convictions were uncommon, and those few persons convicted tended to be treated as common criminals. Self-referrals were, and always will be, uncommon because of the personal characteristics of the typical sex offender. Not only is the sex offender *not* psychologically minded, but he usually employs rigid, primitive defenses such as denial and projection, and often refuses to acknowledge his actions. The sex offender does not often refer himself to any type of therapist, but if he does, he will not knowingly choose insight-oriented therapy. For those few sex offenders discussed in psychoanalytic literature, psychodynamic writers generally view case material from a broad "metapsychological" point of view, incorporating any deviant sexual behavior exhibited by their patients into an overarching conceptualization of the patient's mental processes which would not ordinarily be useful in directly changing his mode of sexual expression. This approach, while theoretically interesting to the relatively few individuals with the background necessary to follow it, is many steps removed from the design of low-cost, rapid modes of focused remediation.

In recent decades, social psychology and biological psychiatry have taken great interest in the sex offender. Each of these disciplines has made substantial contributions to research on the etiology and the control of aberrant sexual behavior. Social psychologists, leaning heavily on behavioral theory, regard sexual assault as a learned behavior, conditioned by the attitudes and examples of the growing boy's milieu. The role of power struggles between men and women in shaping the behavior of the offender has been elucidated primarily by social psychology, as has the power of intergenerational transfer of patterns of male-female relations in influencing individual sexual behavior. Armed with ever more sophisticated laboratory techniques, the biochemical theorists have been successful in testing many interesting hypotheses about the psychophysiological substratum beneath certain types of aberrant sexual behavior, accepting some of these hypotheses, modifying some, and rejecting others. In the biochemical research area, there are many unanswered questions because of ethical constraints on the use of certain types of invasive procedures in human research.

Although sexual assault can be viewed from a variety of disciplinary perspectives, few current researchers would deny that the best picture can be obtained only by the use of a composite approach, which attempts to take careful cognizance of the relative contributions of the intrapsychic, social, behavioral, and physiological dimensions. The chapters which appear in this book are written by specialists and are, as such, relatively narrow in viewpoint. In some cases, the authors have made an attempt to integrate their own disciplines or their relatively narrow specialties into the bigger picture, but to do this extensively would make the volume as a whole repetitious and inefficient for use as a reference work. The reader is advised, however, that such an integration is at least implicit in each chapter.

Theory into Practice: Assessment and Treatment

The chapters presented here sample the most current and exciting developments in sex offender treatment at the beginning of the 1980s. They do not represent a complete discussion of all the facets of the sexual offender for two reasons. First, the research community is shaped in its endeavors, at least partially, by funding and by the needs and demands of current society. Secondly, research in a narrow specialty such as offender treatment is both limited and shaped by research developments in broader areas such as biochemistry, biometry, or psychometrics. These broader disciplines provide the tools and the original training to the specialized sex researcher. New developments in a broader discipline inevitably stimulate applications and extensions in a variety of applied, "practical" areas. For example, among many other applications, sophisticated computerized brain mapping is now being used to study the brain changes during the dissociative states common in adults who were once incest victims. Similarly, current child development observational research is raising some interesting questions about the psychology of child molestation and incest.

The explosion in development of precise behavioral shaping techniques and measurement strategies, coupled with the relatively low cost of behavioral treatment, is responsible for the dominance of behavioral approaches in current sex offender treatment. In attempting to survey and compile the best of current research, one would have to "overrepresent" the behavioral because that is precisely where the most activity is. This does not imply any judgment on the editors' part that behavioral treatment is always the treatment of choice for a sex offender. Neither does it imply that behavioral treatment has more stable long-term effects than other types of therapy. Outcome research is still in its infancy in the general field of mental health, and it has barely begun in the specialized area of sex offender treatment. Such outcome research may never isolate precisely the significant variables or variable interactions even in the seemingly "cut and dried" behavior modification treatments. Many such treatments, including those described in this volume, are conducted by persons originally trained in psycho-educational, humanistic, or even psychodynamic programs. Their manner of approach to the client is necessarily influenced not only by their present task but by their past training. Many behavioral and biochemical treatment programs also formally include concurrent supportive or insight-oriented individual or group therapy, as well as many kinds of psychoeducational adjuncts. These program aspects are described only sketchily in the present volume because of lack of space and because they are well covered in the general mental health literature. However, their presence must be taken into account before a program is labeled strictly "behavioral" or "biochemical."

Issues in Program Development and Management

Some readers of this book will be reviewing offender treatment material for the first time, perhaps as policy makers, administrators, graduate student trainees, or even patient or prisoner advocates. Depending on background, each reader may wonder why certain approaches are taken and others are not. For this reason, it is well to review and summarize here some general issues which are important in actually setting up offender treatment programs. More than in most mental health fields, the program planners and policy makers involved in this work have severe and unique constraints.

1. Their clients are considered dangerous to others and, in point of fact, often are. Any therapeutic technique which encourages regression and/or disregard of inhibitions, even for the purpose of long-term, in-depth, intrapsychic reorganization, is inadvisable for use with nonincarcerated offenders. A crucial assumption in therapies which encourage regression is the assumption that the patient has sufficient discipline to avoid generalized "acting out" of his impulses, an assumption one cannot make with a sex offender.

2. In treatment planning, options are most plentiful when the program planner can predict that the client has a strong wish to be rid of symptoms which he

perceives as ego-alien, and will offer his therapist continuous, voluntary coopera-tion and a modicum of trust. Most sex offenders meet none of these conditions. Many rapists and most child molesters deny their acts even after court conviction and sentencing. Prison-based therapists often work for long periods of time to reach a point at which the offender admits in therapy that a thoroughly documented crime actually took place. The therapist has to help the client to acknowledge his behavior as his own and to label it realistically as sexual violence before he can be helped to inhibit it. In this aspect, the treatment of sexual aggression has much in common with the treatment of alcoholism, another notoriously difficult undertaking.

3. The sex offender and the court which often has ordered his treatment need a rapid and inexpensive mode of treatment. Therefore, the purpose of treatment is quite narrowly defined as the discontinuance of the illegal behavior.

4. Maintenance of abstinence from the offending behavior after termination of treatment is a major goal. For this reason, concurrent with treatment to inhibit or extinguish the offending behavior, a treatment program may also have to provide training in such diverse matters as social skills, normal masturbation, relaxation therapy, meditation, or other methods of increasing general coping. Vocational training may be appropriate for some offenders.

5. Rapists, child molesters, and incest offenders all relate poorly to women. A "corrective emotional experience" of exposing the offender to the reserved friend-liness of an attractive but assertive female staff may be a necessary component of treatment. Group discussions with rape victims who have volunteered to partici-pate in offender reeducation can also be helpful. These program embellishments are based on the hypothesis that the offender, as a boy, has had a developmentally inadequate experience with frustrating, weak, neglectful, or abusive women. For such a man, rape is thought to be a symbolic degradation of both past and present frustrating females. The offender who assaults children or other men avoids the conflictual female object altogether. A planned and controlled reeducational expe-rience may expand his repertoire of reactions to women, particularly if he can tolerate at least a little insight into his past.

6. Countertransference problems and burnout among staff are at a maximum in a program treating sex offenders. Countertransference, or the experiencing of emo-tional responses to the client which have some natural complementarity to his characteristics and problems, is a natural phenomenon in therapists. In recent years it has been viewed in an increasingly positive light, as a means of attaining em-pathic understanding of the client for hypothesis building and hypothesis testing in the treatment hours. Although negative emotional reactions to a client are as nor-mal and useful as positive ones, most therapists would find immediate and constant reactions of fear or contempt toward the client to be both destructive to the psycho-therapeutic work and personally destructive to the therapist. Unfortunately, sex offenders are more likely than most other clients to repel, exhaust, and alienate their therapists, particularly in long-term relationships.

These factors and others must be taken into account in the design of treatment programs for offenders. In addition, programs are often residential and involve at least minimum security, another factor which increases costs. The annual cost of a good-quality, comprehensive program is, therefore, very high. Trained staff are scarce, and in-service training and specialized professional organizations are just beginning to service the field. Treatment research grant funds, always limited, are now almost unavailable. Many of the contributors to this volume received some program support or training funds from the U.S. Department of Health and Human Services, specifically from the National Center for Prevention and Control of Rape or the National Center for Study of Crime and Delinquency, both in the National Institute of Mental Health, or from the National Center on Child Abuse and Neglect in the Office of Human Development Services. Others received grant support from the Law Enforcement Assistance Administration in the Department of Justice. Still others have simply incorporated their research and writing into their daily work in state prisons and mental hospitals. Given the current shortage of research funds, it seemed particularly important to disseminate the assessment, treatment, and program policy expertise of these individuals. The editors' role has been to offer them a forum to communicate with the many individuals and groups having a personal and professional interest in the work of offender treatment and rehabilitation.

Contents

PART IV: BUILDING AND OPERATING
BEHAVIORAL LABORATORIES FOR
EVALUATING AND TREATING SEXUAL OFFENSES

Part I

Issues in Treatment and Assessment

1

Legal and Ethical Issues in Mandatory Treatment: The Patient's Rights versus Society's Rights

Carol Bohmer, L.L.M., Ph.D.

In dealing with the sex offender many different elements of society must interact. The police, the courts, the prison system, and the mental health system all may interact with the offender at various stages. Each of these represents some aspect of the interests of the society which the offender has affronted with his crime. However, the offender is also a human being and a member of that same society. As such, he too has rights which must be safeguarded. An attempt must be made to balance the interests of the individual and those of the group–an attempt which becomes particularly difficult and delicate in the matter of treatment. In this chapter, a legal sociologist discusses some of the issues which are relevant to the treatment of offenders.

INTRODUCTION

Mandatory treatment is a particularly thorny social question because the rights and interests of the patient are often in conflict with the rights and interests of the institution and society. This chapter will identify the most important areas of conflict, and discuss the legal, ethical, and practical issues involved. Needless to say, in a chapter this size, it will only be possible to outline these issues without being able to go into great detail.

In an examination of mandatory treatment, two major issues must first be addressed. On the one hand, we can examine the range of rights and interests of the person being treated (the "client" or "patient"). On the other hand, we must consider the responsibilities of the treating professionals both to the institution with which they are affiliated and to the wider society. One of the remarkable aspects of this area is the extent to which the potential conflicts and dilemmas are ignored in both the legal and the psychiatric literature. For understandable reasons, many lawyers and psychiatrists are too threatened by the issues to face them. It is nevertheless important that the patient's interests and society's interests be spelled out so that practitioners can make informed, albeit difficult, ethical and legal choices.

3

There is no simple way of setting out and separating the issues involved in these conflicts. They are complex, overlapping, and related in a variety of different ways depending on the perspective taken. Recognizing this difficulty should not, however, detract from the need and utility of identifying the most important problem areas.

This chapter will be divided into two major parts: the first covering the legal issues involved; the second, the ethical problems in this area. In the first part, we will initially discuss the status of the person being treated and then examine the issue of informed consent. The next section will cover the right of a patient to be treated and the right to refuse treatment. After a general discussion, the application of the doctrine to the two most important subgroups, mental patients and prisoners, will be examined separately; this will be followed by a discussion of the application of the doctrine to the sexual aggressives who are the subject of this book. In the third section, we will look at two special types of treatment which pose particular legal problems: surgery and behavior modification. The fourth section will examine special offender programs with particular reference to sex offenders.

Part II will deal with the ethical ramifications of the legal issues discussed in Part I. The role conflicts involved in serving both patients and institutions will then be considered. Finally, possible contractual relationships between therapists and patients will be examined.

PART I: LEGAL ISSUES

It is essential at the outset to clarify exactly who and what constitute the subjects of this discussion. Both the legal and the ethical approaches depend on clarifying just what voluntary and involuntary treatment means, as well as exactly what is involved in treatment—in both its purpose and its content. It is also important to determine the exact legal status of the patient/offender. For example, the scope of the patient/offender's rights depends on whether he is indeed a patient or an offender, or something in between. The law, as well as the professional's ethical responsibilities, can be seen to differ depending on whether someone is classified as a mental patient (voluntary or involuntary), an offender (in prison, on probation, or on parole), or an offender under some special statute (e.g., sex offender or habitual offender statutes). This may all seem rather obvious, but a careful examination of the concepts and doctrines involved will show the necessity of keeping these distinctions in mind especially when attempting to make sense out of a confusing array of recent statutory and case law.

Informed Consent

Until relatively recently, the issue of informed consent to treatment was not of major concern, despite a *legal* requirement that it be given. The general view was that if someone was institutionalized in some kind of involuntary status (either as an involuntary mental patient or as a prisoner), he had thereby forfeited the right to give or withhold consent. Thus, any treatment which was ordered by a court or by the professionals in the institution was generally administered without regard to the wishes of the subject. Recently, however, a number of factors have radically altered this perception of the rights of the subject vis à vis consent to treatment. The first major change has been the rise of the prisoner/patient's rights movement and the resultant interest of the law in the status and treatment of prisoners and mental patients, which has had the effect of drawing attention to the issue of consent. As a result of this legal and public attention to what goes on inside such institutions, a number of particularly noxious "treatments" have been discovered, along with the revelation that in many cases these "treatments" have in fact been disguised punishment and control techniques. It has also been found that some of the most frequently used treatments are neither as benign nor as beneficial as they were believed to be. In addition, there has been a public outcry against the use of captive populations as "guinea pigs" for experimental treatment methods and a considerable tightening of the rules under which such populations can be subjected to experimentation.

The patients' rights movement has also focused attention on the practice of combining the status of involuntary mental patient with that of legal incompetent so that anyone involuntarily institutionalized was automatically believed to be incapable of giving consent. Despite the fact that these two categories were never officially merged in the great majority of states, practitioners either believed their patients were incompetent or simply assumed incompetency for the sake of conveniently handling large numbers of mental patients. Modern statutes explicitly separate the civil commitment from a finding of legal incompetency. It is now increasingly necessary to deal with the question of legal incompetency on a case-by-case basis. The issue of general legal incompetency is also increasingly being separated from issues of incompetence for a particular purpose. In this case, before substituted consent can be obtained from someone other than the subject, it would have to be proven that the patient was incompetent to make decisions about the precise issues of his or her health. Factors such as the circumstances surrounding the treatment, its importance to the patient, and other variables must all be taken into account.

As a result of these changes, it is now necessary for anyone professionally involved in the treatment of clients/patients in an involuntary setting to meet the issue of informed consent head on, just as it has always been necessary to do so with voluntary patients.

Without consent from a subject, treating professionals—and, in some cases, institutions—are technically liable for the charge of battery.[2] This has always been so as a legal principle, except in those cases in which substituted consent was obtained, but now with the increased involvement of lawyers in patient/prisoner rights, the risk of prosecution is a real one.

Courts and statutes speak of the consent to be given by the subject as "informed" consent. Exactly how much information must be given to the subject before he or she is considered informed is still a matter of legal debate. According to Schwitzgebel, "At a minimum, the person should be given information about the basic nature of the treatment and the 'material risks' involved."[3] He points out that a material risk is one which a reasonable person in the patient's position would view as central. He summarizes the content of information to be given as "(1) the diagnosis or purpose of the treatment, (2) the nature and duration of the treatment, (3) the risks involved, (4) the prospects for success or benefit, (5) possible disadvantages if the treatment is not undertaken, and (6) alternative methods of treatment."[4] As will be seen, these apparently straightforward requirements are fraught with problems in cases in which it is impossible to provide detailed information about risks and benefits because enough is not yet known. Informed consent to experimental procedures (and the definition thereof) poses a difficult question and will be dealt with later in this chapter.

The subject must, of course, be competent to understand the information which is provided. Some cynics believe that if a patient consents to the proposed treatment, he or she is deemed capable of giving consent. If, however, such consent is withheld, it is because the patient is not able to give consent. It is to be hoped that with increased emphasis on the right of the patient to refuse consent, such an attitude no longer prevails. The issue nevertheless remains a difficult one, particularly for involuntary patients, as will later be seen in the examination of the recent case of *Kaimowitz* v. *Department of Mental Health*.[5] That case, as well as other authorities, divided the issue of consent into three elements: competence, knowledge, and voluntariness. With respect to the last element, the view has been expressed that since an institution is an inherently coercive environment, patients can never give voluntary consent. However, as Wexler points out, this leads to a Catch-22 situation which effectively vitiates the right to treatment in institutions. He states:

> Patients have a right to treatment. They also have a right to resist treatment in the absence of informed consent. But informed consent cannot be given by institutionalized patients because any such consent would be inherently coerced rather than voluntary. Thus, patients cannot be forcibly subjected to therapy, nor can they voluntarily submit to it, for their submission will be equated with forcible subjection.[6]

This would, as Wexler indicates, have the effect of turning our institutions into holding pens, an outcome which would appear to be as unacceptable as the other extreme in which no consent is necessary for any treatment. It seems that the appropriate solution would be to make a careful distinction between pressure and coercion.[7] Thus, a person would be able to consent, all other things being equal, even if the nature of the institution was seen as a source of pressure, for example, if consent were motivated by a desire to reduce the term of institutionalization. Only if the pressure consists of benefits or detriments promised to the patient which lead him or her to make unreasonable decisions should that pressure be deemed coercive and the resulting consent invalid.

Thus, in summary, it can be seen that it is relatively easy to list the elements of informed consent to treatment. It is, however, much more difficult to apply these elements to various patients and various situations. As this issue is taken up in other contexts, it will be seen that much depends on the legal and psychiatric status of the patient and also on the exact nature of the treatment to be administered.

The Right to Treatment and the Right to Refuse Treatment

One of the major recent legal developments in this area has been the enunciation of a right to treatment for both prisoners and mental patients. Detailed discussion of the history and nature of this concept is beyond the scope of this chapter.[8] However, a brief description of the positive right is necessary as background to the analysis of the patient's right to refuse treatment, which is germane to this discussion of enforced treatment. The right to treatment is seen as based on the exercise of the states' police power in involuntarily confining prisoners and mental patients. With regard to prisoners, this exercise of police power is justified by the proof of a crime having been committed, for which incarceration is the appropriate punishment. Accordingly, it is not at present clear that prisoners have a right to psychological treatment and rehabilitation, although they clearly have a right to adequate medical treatment.[9] For mental patients, however, the argument in favor of a right to treatment is based on the need for a quid pro quo extended by the government to justify confinement. This right has been recognized by a number of recent court decisions (although not directly by the Supreme Court) as well as by many of the more recent state statutes in the area of mental health. It may seem strange that the same decade which has witnessed the development of a constitutional and statutory right to treatment has also seen increasing legal activity in the area of a right to refuse treatment. However, the two are not logically inconsistent. The right to treatment is not merely the right to any treatment or anything which may be called treatment by the hospital staff. The terms most frequently used by the courts have been "adequate," "appropriate," "suitable," and "effective." Unless a patient is given autonomy to make decisions as to whether this treatment will help or harm him, the right to treatment becomes not a right but a justification for the imposition of unwanted treatment procedures.

The right to refuse treatment also springs from another major source which is closely related to the concept of informed consent. The general legal principle holds that a mentally competent patient may refuse treatment even if this refusal would result in the loss of his life. The only circumstance in which his consent is not required is an emergency situation in which the patient is unconscious and therefore incapable of consenting to the treatment. As discussed earlier, patients deemed mentally incapable of giving consent may also be treated without their consent. Mere commitment of a person to a mental hospital, however, is no longer a sufficient basis to abnegate this recently developed right, a right which has both statutory and judicial support.

Mental Patients.   At present, a right to refuse treatment exists for mental patients in some form in all 50 states and the District of Columbia.[10] However, the scope of that right varies tremendously and may in fact be limited to the right to refuse sterilization or the right to refuse physical restraint. Many states remain unwilling to extend the right to refuse treatment to the administration of psychotropic medication, an issue which is presently one of great controversy, and in fact two states specifically *permit* the forcible medication of patients. In some states, the right is rather empty as a patient's refusal can readily be overridden by hospital staff. Only one state specifically gives the patient the right to refuse chemotherapy.[11] Thus, to determine the extent of the relevant statutory right to refuse treatment, the treating professional would be well advised to check the details of his or her own state statute.

In the absence of a statutory right to refuse treatment, courts have used either a common law basis (i.e., that treatment without consent constitutes "battery") or a constitutional basis. It is the latter which has generated the greatest controversy in recent cases, particularly in relation to medication. In the landmark case of *Wyatt* v. *Stickney*, patients' rights were outlined in great detail.[12] In that decision, patients were protected against experimental research without consent, against major physical treatments (e.g., ECT), and against aversive reinforcement conditioning and other "hazardous treatment." They were also to be protected from unnecessary or excessive medication but were *not* specifically given the right to refuse medication in general. This reluctance to see psychotropic medication—the most frequently used treatment in mental hospitals—as similarly intrusive as other treatments, such as psychosurgery and ECT, is echoed by other state courts and is the subject of much recent legal scholarship.

Several recent cases which have addressed themselves to this issue deserve examination to identify the directions in which courts seem to be moving. These cases have used constitutional arguments of various kinds to uphold a right to refuse psychotropic medication. The first argument, and perhaps the least controversial because of the extent to which it is entrenched in the Constitution, is that forcible medication can violate a patient's First Amendment right to freedom of religion. In the case of *Winters* v. *Miller*, the patient, a Christian Scientist, was forced to take medication despite her objection and despite the fact that there was no finding of incompetency or of any emergency of dangerousness to others.[13] While this is an important recognition of First Amendment rights, it does not have very wide application to patients not similarly situated.

On a somewhat broader constitutional basis, the case of *Scott* v. *Plante* held that the forcible administration of drugs could constitute a violation of due process. It said:

> [O]n this record we must assume that Scott, though perhaps properly committable, has never been adjudicated an incompetent who is incapable of giving an informed consent to medical treatment. Under these circumstances due process would require in the absence of an emergency that some form of notice and opportunity to be heard be given to Scott or to someone standing *in loco parentis* to him before he could be subjected to such treatment.[14]

In *Rennie* v. *Klein*, the plaintiff made three further constitutional arguments. He alleged that forced medication had violated his constitutional rights because it infringed (a) his Eighth Amendment right to be free of cruel and unusual punishment, (b) his First Amendment right to freedom of thought and expression, and (c) his right to privacy.[15] The claim was unsuccessful on the first two grounds, but the court did agree that nonemergency forced medication to a committed mental patient violated his right to privacy. The Eighth Amendment argument failed because the defendant was able to show that the disputed drug Prolixin was both of proven effectiveness and an "integral component of an overall treatment program. While the side effects of prolixin are serious, they are not *unnecessarily* harsh in light of the potential benefits."[16]

The court also rejected the argument that forced medication interfered with Rennie's mental processes and thus deprived him of his right to mentation. It did this because his ability to perform on intelligence tests was not in fact impaired, and in addition, any drug-induced dulling of his senses had been proven to be temporary. The court also buttressed its argument by pointing out that Rennie had indicated a desire to be cured and had thereby in effect waived his First Amendment rights. The constitutional argument which was successful was that forced medication violated Rennie's right to privacy. The court applied the concept developed in other areas of the law to make clear that such a right does indeed survive involuntary commitment and does include the refusal of the most frequently used treatment within institutions. It is clear, however, that this right is far from absolute and that in appropriate situations (e.g., an emergency; potential danger to other patients) the state's interest in treatment can override the patient's right to refuse treatment.

The final case worth mentioning with respect to mental patients is that of *Rogers* v. *Okin*.[17] The constitutional arguments made here were similar to two of those made in *Rennie*: the right to privacy argument and the First Amendment argument. As to the right to privacy, both the District Court and the Court of Appeals had little difficulty stating that a patient has a right to preserve his or her privacy against unwanted infringements of bodily integrity. The District Court went further than *Rennie* in defining those situations in which the state's interest overrides the patient's right to privacy. It limited such emergencies to situations in which a failure to medicate a patient would result in *substantial likelihood* of harm to that patient, other patients, or staff. The Court of Appeals expanded this by stating:

> The state's purpose in administering drugs forcibly must be to further its police power interests, i.e. the decision must be the result of a determination that the need to prevent violence in a particular situation outweighs the possibility of harm to the medicated individual. Thus, medication cannot be forcibly administered solely for treatment purposes absent a finding of incompetency.[18]

Thus *Rogers* stands for the proposition that a competent patient cannot be *treated* against his will, only controlled for his protection or that of others.

The District Court in *Rogers* also went further than *Rennie* in its finding that forced medication can constitute a First Amendment violation, another important development in the law in this area. "Whatever powers the Constitution has granted our government, involuntary mind control is not one of them, absent extraordinary circumstances."[19] The opinion is not, however, clear as to whether it is considering the effect of psychotropic drugs on psychotic thinking, the capacity to think and produce ideas, or the ability to think at all.[20] Thus it is still too early to tell exactly how broad the First Amendment argument will be and what evidence would be needed to assert the state's rights over those of the patient.

Prisoners.   The "right to refuse treatment" issue is somewhat different with respect to prisoners because of their different status and the increased extent of the state's police power over them.[21] Two countervailing arguments relate to a determination of whether prisoners have a right to refuse treatment. The first view is that in the absence of any cruel and unusual treatment which would be banned by the Eighth Amendment, prisoners have no right to refuse mandatory treatment. Because the state has an interest in enforcing treatment which will bring about their rehabilitation and presumably reduce recidivism rates, it can require prisoners to participate in appropriate treatment programs. This is also the basis for requiring prisoners to work and to receive compulsory education. It is also the justification for statutes which are designed for rehabilitation of special offenders (e.g., addicts and sex offenders) whose sentences under these statutes are longer than they would have been under a regular conviction.

The argument in favor of a prisoner's right to refuse treatment is similar to that described above in relation to mental patients. "There has been growing recognition by the courts that prisoners retain all rights enjoyed by free citizens except those necessarily lost as an incident of confinement."[22] Following this argument, then, since prisoners are presumed competent, they have the same rights as other competent persons, including the right to refuse treatment based on their constitutional right to privacy. This right to privacy may, however, be limited by the fact that the prisoner has already committed a criminal act which gives the state greater rights than it has with mental patients, which could permit the state to require prisoners to participate in treatment programs.

The right to refuse treatment has been addressed in a few recent cases, although the clearest judicial statements come out of cases in which the "treatment" involved could be viewed as punishment or at least as unacceptable aversive conditioning. For example, in the case of *Knecht* v. *Gillman*, injections were administered to induce vomiting in patients who violated certain rules.[23] Because this was an experimental procedure, as well as one designed to punish rather than treat (despite any description of it as "aversive conditioning"), the court had little difficulty finding a violation of the plaintiff's Eighth Amendment rights. The case of *Mackey* v. *Procuniar* had a similar outcome.[24] There, prisoners were given "Anectine therapy" as an experimental aversive conditioning technique. Anectine can cause temporary paralysis and respiratory arrest. Here the court noted that such procedures could raise both Eighth and First Amendment questions.

Both these cases deal with experimental procedures, as well as with what can be described as extreme measures. In the case of less noxious treatment, the law is still unclear as to the extent of a prisoner's right to refuse treatment.

Sexual Aggressives.   Given the focus of this book, it is important to consider just how the right to refuse treatment applies to sexual aggressives. It will of course be affected by the variables outlined in the above discussion. First, it is clear that the right to refuse treatment is stronger and has a sounder legal basis for patients whose status is civil rather than criminal. While most institutionalized sexual aggressives are likely to be criminally convicted, it is possible that some may be in civil mental hospitals. For the majority, however, who are either in criminal mental hospitals or in prisons, the right is more limited and depends on other variables. If the procedure being used to change the sex offender's behavior is experimental, the need to obtain consent will be correspondingly greater. This will also be the case if the proposed treatment is particularly intrusive (e.g., psychosurgery or castration), as the *Kaimowitz* case indicates. Treatment which involves no physical intervention will clearly be viewed more positively by the courts, although of course one is then faced with the practical problem of the effectiveness of mandatory psychotherapy in which the patient/offender would have refused to participate if permitted. Drugs occupy a middle ground, as the cases described above show. The author knows of no cases specifically dealing with the forced use of drugs for the purpose of changing sexual behavior, for example, antiandrogens such as Depo-Provera. The right to privacy argument would be the constitutional argument most readily made in such a situation, on the basis that such drugs clearly affect a person's "bodily integrity." The First Amendment argument could also be made to the extent that such drugs do interfere with the subject's thought processes, especially in such areas as sexual fantasies. As has been seen, however, this argument has met with less acceptance by the courts in the case of psychotropic drugs.

For a cruel and unusual punishment argument to succeed in such a case, it would first have to be shown that the medication was for the purpose of punishment and not treatment. It would then have to be proved that it is disproportionate to the offense, as well as contrary to common standards of decency. While the term "chemical castration" can readily be used to inspire emotional responses, it must be pointed out that the effects of Depo-Provera are reversible and that it may also be effective in reducing the criminal behavior. In conclusion, then, it is the opinion of the author that in a case of forced administration of antiandrogen, both the right to privacy argument and the First Amendment argument have a much greater chance of being effective than an Eighth Amendment argument.

Special Types of Treatment and Their Special Problems

Two special types of treatment which have been mentioned in the discussion above deserve further elaboration both because of the special legal and ethical problems they raise and because they may be used in the treatment of sexual aggressives. The first category is that of surgery (psychosurgery and castration), and the second is the use of behavior modification techniques.

Surgery.   Surgical castration as a method of punishment or treatment has been used in the past. Because of its drastic and irreversible nature and the emotional aura surrounding it, castration is highly unlikely to be acceptable in this country to be performed on an unconsenting offender. In fact, it is even questionable whether it would be permitted today on a *voluntary* basis. Brecher describes a 1973 case in California in which two sex offenders applied to the court for voluntary surgical castration, in the hope that it would lead to eventual parole, rather than the lifelong imprisonment they faced.[25] Despite the fact that California courts had approved voluntary castration prior to 1968 and that the offenders filed waivers releasing their lawyers, the judge, and the surgeon from civil liability, they never obtained the sought-after procedure. The surgeon, on discovering that despite the waivers, he might still be liable for criminal prosecution, withdrew his consent—leaving the issue somewhat inconclusive from our point of view.

The outcome of the landmark case of *Kaimowitz* v. *Department of Mental Health* was not dissimilar to that described above.[26] In that case, the sex offender who was to have undergone the experimental psychosurgery was released from custody and subsequently withdrew his consent. However, the court gave an opinion on the issue of informed consent to such a procedure, details of which have been described above. The court made it clear that an institutionalized patient or prisoner could not legally consent to a procedure such as the type of psychosurgery contemplated in this case, because it was experimental, highly intrusive, dangerous, and irreversible. The possibility of consent to psychosurgery is still available to someone who is not institutionalized. In fact, psychosurgery has enthusiastic supporters among the medical profession who have undertaken such surgery.[27] In addition, by implication from *Kaimowitz*, if the procedure could ever be considered nonexperimental and less dangerous, the possibility that an institutionalized patient could consent still exists. There is little doubt that without consent, such a procedure (even if viewed as treatment) would be judged to be a violation of the Eighth Amendment prohibition of cruel and unusual punishment and, therefore, unconstitutional.

At present, then, it is clear that neither castration nor psychosurgery is available as a treatment option for nonconsenting patients, and that their availability to consenting subjects is extremely limited.

Behavior Modification as a Treatment Technique. The use of behavior modification techniques has grown rapidly in the treatment programs of both mental patients and criminal offenders. These techniques are particularly suited for use among offenders because such procedures (and their underlying theories) focus on behavior, and most offenses involve overt behavior. It is beyond the scope of this chapter to discuss in any detail the variety of different programs which have been used on sex offender populations, some of which are described by other contributors to this book.

While behavior modification has become an increasingly popular technique for a variety of different subjects, both within institutions and without, it has not escaped legal scrutiny, as well as some legal and ethical controversy of its own.[28] The great increase in public concern over the widespread use of behavior modification may stem from a more general concern for the extent to which it involves attempts to shape and control thoughts, behavior, and actions. The specter of mind control is one which is of increasing concern to our society. The ethical problems it evokes are serious and worthy of special consideration, which will be given later in this chapter.

Many of the legal issues raised by behavior modification techniques are similar to those we have already discussed and include treatment versus punishment, experimental versus ordinary techniques, issues of consent, and the different position of mental patients and prisoners. The two major issues which have attracted legal attention are those programs dependent on the use of aversive techniques and token economies which may involve deprivation of basic rights or privileges.

Aversive Techniques: Treatment or Punishment? As we have seen, courts and legislatures have in many cases been reluctant to intervene in the exercise of discretion by treating professionals. However, this reluctance is diminishing and is much less obvious in those cases which involve the use of aversive conditioning techniques, especially when the main purpose of the techniques is that of punishment. The Eighth Amendment has been used in a number of cases as a basis for a right to refuse hazardous or intrusive procedures which may be called "aversive conditioning" or "treatment" by the prison or hospital staff, but which in fact are punishment. This is not to say that negative reinforcement will invariably be considered unconstitutional by the courts, especially on Eighth Amendment grounds. As discussed above, the conditions for a finding of cruel and unusual punishment are rather restricted. The court will look to the program as a whole to determine whether negative reinforcement is an appropriate part of a comprehensive behavior modification program, or simply a justification for punishment or inmate control. This approach would also apply to court scrutiny of involuntary negative reinforcement on other constitutional bases, including right to privacy and substantive due process.[29] Thus, a careful treating professional, designing a program for institutionalized sex offenders, need not assume that he or she cannot incorporate negative reinforcement into it.

Rights as Reinforcers. One of the major stumbling blocks in organizing behavior modification programs has occurred when the program has used as reinforcers those things which the courts have considered to be part of the basic constitutional rights of prisoners or mental patients. Ever since *Wyatt* v. *Stickney* guaranteed patients a number of personal requirements which were considered to be so basic as to be a matter of absolute right (including, for example, food and a place to sleep, the right to have visitors and to attend religious services), due process has required that these be made available to patients.[30] There do exist a number of contingent rights which are considered by the courts to be less fundamental to a patient's needs and which remain available for use as reinforcers. In cases where the rights are less carefully spelled out than in *Wyatt*, there may, however, be conflict in determining whether a right is absolute or contingent. It should also be noted, lest behavior modification proponents come to believe that all such programs are doomed, that competent patients can consent to the waiver of rights, thereby allowing them to become available only contingently as part of the reinforcement program. In addition, legally incompetent patients may in limited circumstances have these rights waived if it can be shown that the behavior modification program is the least intrusive way of treating the patient.

The problem is particularly difficult in the case of those patients who are most seriously disturbed, for they are the very patients for whom the fundamental items involved are the only ones which are effective. It is also true that these patients are likely to be the least willing to embark on a difficult program which involves such serious deprivation.

Consent can also pose a difficult problem. In general, courts have required that a patient or prisoner who gives his consent to a treatment program should be entitled to withdraw it at any time during the program. So a patient may waive his right to food or to a bed, but when he is hungry or tired he is likely to revoke his consent to the use of this absolute right as a reinforcer, thereby undercutting the rationale of behavior modification. The only possible solution to this problem would be to allow a patient to waive the right of revocation, something the courts may not view with enthusiasm.

Other Issues. In concluding this discussion of behavior modification programs, the issue of the relative position of prisoners and mental patients remains. There is an argument to be made that the state has a compelling interest in rehabilitation of prisoners which is sufficiently great to make possible the imposition of involuntary behavior modification techniques. At present, the constitutional question remains unresolved. The issue of experimental versus established procedures is also a difficult one. Many behavior modification programs in institutions are by definition experimental, and therefore the issue of consent becomes even more crucial. It should also be remembered that a number of the cases discussed above involve experimental procedures and the courts have been unwilling to permit mandatory imposition of such programs on institutionalized persons.

Commentators on recent cases see a move away from a deferential acceptance of the discretion of treating professionals toward a more rigorous view of what can legally be included in a behavior modification program. Treating professionals would therefore do well to evaluate the program carefully before it is implemented, to avoid the risks of lawsuits. Interested professionals are referred to a set of guidelines proposed by Friedman to govern the use of such programs in institutions.[31]

Special Offender Programs

It is beyond the scope of this chapter to describe in great detail the variety of programs for special categories of offenders which exist in many states. Because many of these programs refer specially to sexual offenders, or sexual psychopaths as they are frequently called, and have as their justification "treatment" and/or "cure," a few general points should be made.[32] Such programs exist in a majority of states but vary widely in their standards of admission, length of stay, and release criteria. Some require a criminal conviction for a sex offense (or several), while in others a criminal charge is sufficient to trigger the operation of the statute. Some are essentially civil in nature; others, criminal; still others, a kind of hybrid. In general, however, these programs were initiated in the 1950s (often in response to a particularly horrifying sex crime) to provide indeterminate treatment to those who could not control their aberrant sexual behavior. There are a number of problems with these statutes, some particularly relevant for the treating professionals involved. The implication that such offenders can be "cured" by "treatment" (usually unspecified in the statutes) places a huge burden on the treating staff. The ambiguity of their legal status may lead to confusion. The statutes are also phrased in such a way as to leave huge discretion both to judges and to institutional personnel in matters of admission and release standards. In many cases, these standards are highly arbitrary, often resulting in the indeterminate institutionalization of less serious offenders. A high proportion of those in such programs are not serious sex offenders but rather chronic, minor offenders who have been caught by a technicality of the statute. A few of the statutes have been subjected to constitutional scrutiny, and while some of them have been struck down, others have been upheld despite obvious due process and equal protection arguments. Some programs have been modified, for both constitutional and practical reasons. For example, one of the most extensive of the special offender programs, Maryland's program at Patuxent, has abandoned much of its involuntary and indeterminate nature. Among the most important reasons are that the program was too expensive and that it did not furnish the treatment and cure which was promised for its participants at its inception. Such an admission has great implications for those involved in treating sexual aggressives. It is to be hoped that in the future, the law will have a more realistic understanding of the potential for treatment and cure of the sex offender. Within this more modest climate, treating professionals will be able to work more comfortably, and offenders will be benefited in terms of both their treatment and their legal rights.

PART II: ETHICAL ISSUES IN MANDATORY TREATMENT

Here we return to the problem of the rights of society versus the rights of the individual and to the awkward role of the therapist as judge. Many of the same issues which have given the courts legal difficulties also make for ethical problems for the personnel involved in treatment. For example, in the case of behavior modification programs, the ethical treating professional cannot escape from a balancing process involving the much-touted specter of mind control versus the "mental integrity" of the patient. The field of behavior modification has had its share of ethical controversy, and a variety of conflicting views have been expressed.[33]

Many of the difficulties stem from the fact that the theory of behavior modification is ethically neutral and provides little assistance in distinguishing "good" or "appropriate" programs from the many abusive techniques which have received recent publicity. The major focus of behavior modification is on ends rather than means; so the major question at issue is whether the technique works or not. It is up to the ethical practitioner to insert his or her own moral values to make the determination of whether the ends justify the means used. A further complication in institutional programs arises from the fact that the behavioral change hoped for by the patient does not always coincide with the hope of the institution. The professional is thus faced with attempting to tie together these two conflicting sets of needs. There are those who argue that behavior modification programs in total institutions are a fraud and a sham because they are actually designed not to change the patient's real-world behavior but to encourage compliant behavior within the institution, and thereby make possible the smooth running of an otherwise potentially unchangeable system. Thus, some other questions which the ethical professional must ask him or herself are, What is the purpose of this behavior modification program? Whose needs does it serve?

In the same way, a therapist or neurosurgeon involved in the decision-making process about psychosurgery must also wrestle with a number of ethical conflicts. A similar balancing process to that undertaken by the courts is at work here in a consideration of questions such as, Are the potential benefits to the patient and society worth the risks involved? On a more philosophical level, the treating professional needs to consider whether we, as a society, have a right to interfere with the bodily integrity of one of our members. If so, in what circumstances?

The final issue which provides both legal difficulties for the courts and ethical problems for the treating professional is that of informed consent. Just as the courts have shown a need to develop criteria for determining whether a subject has given his or her informed consent, so the ethical professional must be clear in his or her mind that the consent given is indeed a valid one. In most cases, this will be a less troubling issue than some of those mentioned above. Patience in explaining what is involved, and in getting to know the subject so as to determine if the procedure is truly understood, will in most cases be sufficient to satisfy these concerns. The issue of the inherently coercive nature of institutions, raised by the courts in *Kaimowitz* and elsewhere, remains. It is for this reason that a number of professionals have simply ducked this issue by working only with patients outside institutions. However, as discussed above, it is possible to determine whether a consent within an institution is coerced or whether it is given relatively freely. Much of the onus rests on the treating professional to ensure that he or she does not use the power of his/her position to extract a consent which would not otherwise be forthcoming.

Serving Two Masters: Dual Loyalties and Role Conflicts.   The problem of serving both the needs of the patient and those of the institution has been mentioned above in connection with behavior modification programs in institutions. However, the conflict of dual loyalties must be faced, or avoided, by any professional whose employer is someone other than the patient. This problem, which is particularly acute for a profession such as psychiatry whose fundamental operating principle is based on a personal, private relationship between therapist and patient, has been largely ignored by that profession.[34] The conflict is sharpened by the fact that the professional socialization of loyalty to one's patient comes first in the training of the psychiatrist. The loyalty to one's employer, the institution, and the loyalty to society in general are part of later socialization. The dilemma of serving two masters can never be resolved, merely minimized, and it is this fact which has kept many therapists out of such inherently conflict-ridden situations. The most obvious mechanism for handling such role stress, and one which can be seen in a myriad of situations, is simply to suppress the trade-offs which must be made.

For those who have remained to attempt to serve two masters, a certain introspection and ongoing awareness of potential conflicts can serve to reduce the role stress. First, there is the fundamental issue of honesty: that all parties in the treatment process (therapist, patient, and employer) are informed about the existence of the interests and needs of the others. While this may sound unduly obvious, the author has frequently been struck by the reluctance of many therapists to make their true role clear to the "client." Whether the argument against such an "antagonistic" approach is valid clinically or not (and the author has seen no evidence of its validity), the ethical duty of the therapist is clear.

The second issue with which the concerned therapist must wrestle is the constant recognition of his or her superior power vis à vis the patient. It can be argued that the power is never equal in a therapeutic relationship; however, it is in those situations where an institution stands behind the therapist that the power is most unequal. A noncooperating, mandatory patient stands to lose many privileges or even his freedom itself. In fact, in Szasz's view, the involuntary patient and the psychiatrist are adversaries at every point in their encounter.[35] Szasz's solution—that the involuntary commitment system be abolished altogether—not only may seem a little drastic to some therapists, but also does not solve the conflicts of the psychiatrist in other institutional settings. A recognition of the powerful and potentially adversary relationship between therapist and involuntary client is at least the first step toward being able to live with an unresolvable dilemma.

The ethical therapist will not be able to resolve those problems that arise in a particular situation in which serving the needs of the institution may actually harm the patient or vice versa. It may be, as Shestack suggests, that the law can be of assistance here by the provision of appropriate due process safeguards when the loss of some individual liberty is involved. As he puts it,

> What is needed is a careful identification of each conflict situation and the fashioning of the procedural safeguards appropriate to that situation. I believe that the law is moving in this direction. The progress may be slow here in view of the paucity of knowledge among lawyers and judges of the complexities of psychiatric conflict settings.[36]

This will be in the therapist's interest because it establishes outside norms which will give him or her the means to resist the administration of the institution in cases where that is appropriate.

A related problem of the therapist who must serve two masters is confidentiality. How can the psychiatrist protect the confidentiality of material revealed in therapy sessions when part of his or her allegiance belongs to a third party? This difficulty is one which must be clearly faced at the outset of any therapeutic relationship. To the extent that it is not within the therapist's power to keep matters confidential, that limitation should be made clear to the patient. This is also true for the legal concept of privilege which involves the requirement that the therapist not reveal to a court information obtained in a confidential relationship. In many of the situations which have been the subject of this chapter, the concept of privilege may not apply, thus leaving the patient vulnerable both to courts and to other third parties.[37]

Treatment Agreements between Therapist and Patient

All of the above emphasis on full disclosure of information and valid consent to treatment leads to the logical step of developing a written contract between therapist and patient. This idea has been increasingly proposed for all therapeutic relationships, irrespective of the legal status of the patient, by persons ranging from Thomas Szasz to Ralph Nader.[38] In addition to considering the provision of important information (which may be potentially detrimental to the patient), the treatment contract serves to set down the results of the negotiation of appropriate and realistic treatment goals. Both parties can then have a clear idea of what is expected of them, as well as an understanding of what is within the power of the other to provide. Even when the patient is in an institution, a treatment contract is still possible: as has been made clear above, neither prisoners nor mental patients lose their power to enter into contracts by the mere fact of their institutionalization. It is clear that courts will take into account the fact of institutionalization in interpreting such contracts rather narrowly. They would also be concerned as to the application of such limiting doctrines as fraud, duress, or unconscionability to contracts between therapists and institutional patients. However, this should not discourage the concerned therapist from viewing the contract as one way of minimizing the inevitable role conflicts inherent in his or her position.

CONCLUSION

Most of the issues dealt with in this chapter have involved rather intrusive therapies. This emphasis merits an explanation lest the reader think that the author has ignored less drastic therapies such as psychotherapy and social skills training which are crucial parts of the armamentarium of the therapist working with sexual aggressives. It is simply that the courts have not as yet extensively involved themselves in a consideration of this type of treatment, but have been willing to leave its management to the discretion of the treating professionals. The courts have been faced with far more dramatic cases to consider in which the intrusiveness and potential harm of the therapy are much more obvious. This does not mean that other types of therapy do not have a potential for harm or that the courts will not be asked in the future to consider the legal issues they may raise. It is only recently, however, that the courts have been willing to intervene in the medical discretion of therapists in even the more intrusive therapies.

The ethical issues are equally relevant to all kinds of therapy and should be weighed carefully by the therapist. It is clear that resolution of the ethical conflicts is not easy. Different points of view can be argued with merit. The real question is whether the profession itself is going to set up guidelines and a policing procedure for dealing with difficult situations, or leave it to the courts and other outside agencies to do so. To the extent that the profession fails to set up its own policing system, it invites the law to step in. We have witnessed this in a number of cases. To deny that problems and conflicts exist is to invite outsiders to intervene and attempt to resolve the profession's conflicts.

REFERENCE NOTES

1. Plotkin, R. Limiting the therapeutic orgy: mental patients right to refuse treatment. *Northwestern University Law Review* **72:** 461-525 (1977-8).
2. For a discussion of the relevant law on this issue, as well as an extensive and scholarly discussion of the legal rights of offenders, see Schwitzgebel, R.K. *Legal Aspects of the Enforced Treatment of Offenders*. National Institute of Mental Health Center for Studies in Crime and Delinquency. Washington, D.C.: U.S. Government Printing Office, 1979.
3. Ibid., p. 43.
4. Ibid., p. 44.
5. Civ. No. 73-19434 AW (Civ. Ct. of Wayne County, Mich. July 10, 1973).
6. Wexler, D. *Criminal Commitments and Dangerous Mental Patients: Legal Issues of Confinement, Treatment and Release*. National Institute of Mental Health. Washington, D.C.: U.S. Government Printing Office, 1976, p. 17.
7. Ibid., p. 18.
8. The last few years have seen a burgeoning of the literature on the right to treatment. For a brief list of recent articles and books on the subject, the interested reader is referred to Brooks, A.D. *Law, Psychiatry and the Mental Health System* (1980 supplement). Boston: Little, Brown, 1980, pp. 185-6.
9. Schwitzgebel, note 2, pp. 7-8.
10. Right to refuse treatment under state statutes. *Mental Disability Law Reporter* **2:** 241-256 (1977).
11. Iowa Code Ann. §229.23 (West Supp. 1979). For a discussion of the various state provisions, see Comment, Madness and medicine: the forcible administration of psychotropic drugs. *Wisconsin Law Review* 497-567 (1980).
12. 344 F. Supp. 387 (M.D. Ala. 1972) affirmed sub. nom. *Wyatt* v. *Aderholt*, 503 F. 2d 1305 (5th Cir. 1974).
13. 446 F. 2d 65 (2d Cir. 1971), *cert. denied*, 404 U.S. 985 (1972).
14. 532 F. 2d 939 (3rd Cir. 1976).
15. 462 F. Supp. 1131 (D.N.J. 1978).
16. Ibid., p. 1143.
17. 478 F. Supp. 1342 (D. Mass. 1979) affirmed in part, reversed in part, and vacated and remanded for further proceedings.
18. Ibid. (7th page after beginning). The issues on which the Court of Appeals reversed the District Court opinion have to do with circumstances in which a legal finding of incompetency is required, as well as other minor issues which are not relevant here.
19. 478 F. Supp. 1342, 1367 (D. Mass. 1979).
20. For a discussion of this part of the opinion, see *Wisconsin Law Review*, note 11, p. 517.
21. For a more extensive discussion of the rights of prisoners to refuse treatment, see Schwitzgebel, note 2, pp. 64-68.
22. *Pugh* v. *Locke* 406 F. Supp. 318, 328 (M.D. Ala. 1976).
23. 488 F. 2d 1136 (8th Cir. 1973).
24. 477 F. 2d 877 (9th Cir. 1973).
25. Brecher, E.M. *Treatment Programs for Sex Offenders*. National Institute of Law Enforcement and Criminal Justice. Washington, D.C.: U.S. Government Printing Office, 1978, p. 52. See also Klerman, G. Can convicts consent to castration? *Case Studies in Bioethics*. Institute of Society, Ethics and the Life Sciences, pp. 16-17.

26. Note 5.

27. The subject of psychosurgery still continues to spark much heated debate by surgeons, lawyers, and philosophers. For a bibliography of recent writing, see Brooks, note 8, pp. 260-262.

28. The literature on behavior modification is vast. For some scholarly discussions of the most important legal issues, see a special issue of the *Arizona Law Review*: Viewpoints on behavioral issues in closed institutions. *Arizona Law Review* **17**(1): 1-143 (1975). See also Schwitzgebel, R.K. *Development and Legal Regulation of Coercive Behavior Modification Techniques with Offenders*. National Institute of Mental Health, Center for Crime and Delinquency. Washington, D.C.: U.S. Government Printing Office, 1971.

29. For a detailed discussion of the constitutional issues involved in behavior modification, see Friedman, P.R. Legal regulation of applied behavior analysis in mental institutions and prisons. *Arizona Law Review* **17**(1): 39-104 (1975).

30. Note 12.

31. Friedman, note 29, pp. 95-100.

32. For a detailed discussion of the statutory standards of special offender programs, see Schwitzgebel, note 28, pp. 22-26, 69-73.

33. See note 21, especially the articles by Teodoro Allyon "Behavior Modification in Institutional Settings," and Edward M. Opton, Jr., "Institutional Behavior Modification as a Fraud and Sham."

34. The exception has been Thomas Szasz, one of whose ongoing themes has been the ethics of the psychiatrist's relationship with his patient. See, for example, Szasz, T. *Psychiatric Justice*. New York: Collier Books, 1965 especially the chapter entitled "The Psychiatrist as Adversary," pp. 56-82. For a discussion of the role conflicts of the psychiatrist who is employed by the court to evaluate offenders, see Bohmer, C. The court psychiatrist: between two worlds. *Duquesne Law Review* **16**(4): 601-612 (1977-8). For a general discussion of the issue by a lawyer, see Shestack, J., Jr. Psychiatry and the dilemmas of dual loyalties. In Ayd, F.J. (Ed.) *Medical, Moral and Legal Issues in Mental Health Care*. Baltimore: Williams and Wilkins, 1974, pp. 7-17.

35. Shestack, note 34.

36. Ibid., pp. 13-14.

37. It is beyond the scope of this chapter to go into the legal complexities of confidentiality and privilege. The interested reader is referred to Slovenko, R. (Ed.) *Psychotherapy, Confidentiality and Privileged Communication*. Springfield, Ill.: Thomas, 1966.

38. See, for example, Szasz, T.S. *The Ethics of Psychoanalysis*. New York: Basic Books, 1965. See also the discussion of treatment contracts by Schwitzgebel, note 2, pp. 48-60 and sample contracts, pp. 98-106.

2
Treatment and Evaluation Issues with the Mentally Retarded Sex Offender*

William D. Murphy, Ph.D., Emily M. Coleman, M.A., and Mary R. Haynes, M.A.

The treatment of sex offenders becomes particularly difficult if, as is by no means rare, the offender also has other personal difficulties. It is impossible to cover all the variations which may occur, but this chapter addresses one of the most common. Often the sex offender either actually is or appears to be mentally retarded, or at least deficient intellectually. Th authors note that this may be due only to the fact that less intelligent offenders are more likely to be apprehended and convicted. For whatever reason, the treatment system does have to deal with the particular needs of sex offenders who are also mentally retarded or borderline retarded. The authors conduct one of the very few programs in the country which serves this special population of offenders with a special program. This chapter describes their procedures.

Even under optimal circumstances, the treatment of sex offenders is a difficult task. When we add to this task the problem of limited cognitive ability, treatment issues become even more complex. There is a dearth of research in this area, and many treatment techniques currently employed require certain cognitive and verbal abilities that may be lacking or limited in the retarded sex offender. Further, many professionals who specialize in treating sex offenders have limited experience with retarded individuals, while professionals who treat the mentally retarded often lack knowledge regarding the treatment of sex offenders.

The present chapter will be based on a review of the existing literature on the treatment of the mentally retarded and on our limited experience with mentally retarded individuals in an outpatient treatment program for sex offenders. This chapter will examine the prevalence of sex offenses among the retarded population, review previous treatment studies, suggest a possible model from which to

Portions of this project were supported by USPHS Grant MH–34030–02 from the Center for the Studies of Crime and Delinquency and from Tennessee Department of Mental Health and Mental Retardation Research Contract ID–0783 to the Department of Psychiatry. The authors wish to express appreciation to Donna Townsend and Christy Wright for secretarial and editorial assistance.

approach such offenders, and suggest possible treatment and assessment methods derived from such a model. Much of what we will recommend will of necessity be extrapolated from the limited existing literature and our clinical impressions. As such, it must be realized that specific recommendations should be considered tentative until sufficient data are available to either support or refute our proposals.

PREVALENCE RATES AND PREVIOUS TREATMENT STUDIES

A recent review (Murphy, Coleman, and Abel, in press) indicated substantial variability in reported incidence rates of sex offenses among the mentally retarded. In an earlier report, Selling (1939) stated that 51% of a group of rapists and 43% of a group of individuals charged with indecent conduct had IQs below 70. Mohr, Turner, and Jerry (1964), on the other hand, reported that 4% of their sample of pedophiles and 3% of exhibitionists had IQs below 79, compared to an expected population rate of 9%. However, the majority of reports suggest rates in the 10–15% range (see Murphy et al., in press). Except for the early Selling (1939) study, the data suggest only a slightly higher percentage of retarded individuals among sex offenders than would be expected by population statistics alone.

Even these small reported differences may be spurious. For example, the retarded offender's limited social skills and cognitive abilities may make him more likely to be apprehended. Santamour and West (1978) have reviewed data which indicate that compared to the nonretarded defendant, the retarded offender confesses more often, pleads guilty more often, is less likely to plea bargain and to appeal the judgment, and is given parole or probation less often. These factors are more likely explanations of the elevated rate of retarded offenders than are hypotheses regarding some lack of sexual control among the mentally retarded.

Although the retarded offender represents the exception rather than the rule, such offenders do present special treatment and assessment problems. Few studies can be found in the literature to assist in treatment planning. The majority of studies (see Murphy et al. for a summary) are single case reports that describe treatment for such sexual behaviors as public masturbation in retarded children (Barmann and Murray, 1981, Cook, Altman, Shaw, and Blaylock, 1978) or public disrobing (Foxx, 1966). It appears that with these populations and these behaviors, operant based techniques are effective. Such techniques as response cost, time out, DRO procedures, facial screening, and/or overcorrection have been proven effective.

The majority of offenders we have seen clinically do not fall in the profound or severely retarded range but in the mild to borderline range of retardation. In addition, the behaviors are more like those seen in nonretarded offenders, that is, rape, pedophilia, and exhibitionism. For the profoundly and severely retarded who engage in inappropriate sexual behaviors, the operant based techniques outlined above can be employed. However, limited data are available on the mild to moderately retarded who engage in behaviors that seem clearly indicative of a sexual deviation. For this reason, the remainder of the chapter will focus heavily on the treatment of this group.

SOCIAL LEARNING MODEL OF SEXUAL DEVIATION

Because of the limited available data, one approach is to draw treatment techniques, with appropriate modifications, from the general literature on sexual deviation. One model that has generated research support is the behavioral model outlined by Abel and his colleagues (Abel, Blanchard, and Becker, 1978; Barlow and Abel, 1976). Table 2-1 is a derivation of this model with the addition of an area labeled "cognitive." This model proposes that the sex offender presents with a number of interrelated problems, and the model does not assume that all offenders have problems in all areas. It is probable that as the field develops, the areas outlined in the table will be modified and expanded.

Basically, the model suggests that sex offenders have excessive arousal to inappropriate objects (e.g., the pedophile) or inappropriate behaviors (e.g., rapists or exhibitionists). Some offenders also lack arousal to appropriate stimuli (e.g., mutually consenting sexual interactions between adults) may be deficient in heterosocial and assertiveness skills. In addition, some sex offenders have specific sexual dysfunctions (e.g., premature ejaculation) and lack of sexual knowledge. As we will discuss further, the areas of social skills and sexual knowledge are especially relevant to the retarded offender.

The cognitive area has not been explicitly stated in the behavioral model but is consistent with recent advances in behavioral theory. Bandura's social learning theory (Bandura, 1977) clearly outlines the role of cognitive factors in learning and performance. Also, this area is one that feminist writers have consistently noted as a major causal factor in male aggressive sexual behavior. Our clinical experience with both retarded and nonretarded offenders suggests that this area deserves further research attention and may be an essential component of any comprehensive model of sexual deviation. Many offenders have negative and aggressive attitudes toward women, accept rape myths, and hold stereotyped perceptions of women. We have also noted that many offenders are deficient in their ability to discriminate sexual from nonsexual behavior (e.g., the pedophile who perceives a child's affectionate behavior as sexual) and deviant from nondeviant behavior (e.g., the rapist who consistently fails to see his coercive sexual behavior as rape). Although we have listed the cognitive area as a separate area, we in fact feel that it cuts across the other areas as will be apparent in various treatment sections.

The remainder of this chapter will focus on the areas outlined which we feel are most appropriate for the retarded offender; we will suggest special considerations and possible difficulties in extrapolating data from the nonretarded to the retarded.

Where appropriate, for example, in the social skills area and the sex education area, general procedures developed with the retarded non-sex offender will be presented.

GENERAL CONSIDERATIONS

In discussing treatment of the retarded sex offender, one must first define the use of the term "mental retardation." Although intellectual level is an obvious defining characteristic, it is also important to consider adaptive behaviors when one is designing treatment programs and trying to determine possible limitations of treatment goals. Individuals who have the same IQs may be quite different in their social functioning, social knowledge, and insight into their behavioral problems. A mentally retarded individual who has spent his life in institutions may behave very differently from someone with the same level of retardation who has been raised in a normal family environment and has experienced normalization procedures in the school system. In addition, many mentally retarded individuals, like many sex offenders, present with problems other than mental retardation alone. For example, we have seen numerous subjects who also have concomitant psychiatric histories, including psychotic episodes. We have also seen individuals with handicaps such as cerebral palsy and speech deficits. In designing treatment programs and goals, these issues must be taken into account.

A second and related factor is that some mentally retarded offenders have numerous behavioral disorders in addition to their sex offense. Some may be impulsive, showing extremely poor judgment; some may behave aggressively in many situations; and there may be a range of inappropriate behaviors such as temper tantrums. In such cases, ongoing behavioral control programs may be necessary adjuncts to specific treatments for the sexual deviation. In this regard, it is important to work with family members in setting up home behavioral programs and behavioral contracts to control some of these inappropriate behaviors. Often, it is necessary to deal with these general inappropriate behaviors before instituting some of the treatment techniques that will be discussed . There is a vast literature on behavioral programming in the mentally retarded, which we will not attempt to review here.

A third area of concern is sexuality in the retarded. This is an area replete with myths, stereotypes, and misunderstanding among the general population, and often among the caretakers of the mentally retarded themselves. Such caretakers may be resistant to attempts to provide heterosocial skills training or to assign masturbatory activities to the retarded. Because it is important that family members and/or caretakers be included in treatment programming, special effort must be made to explain the rationale for such treatment and to allay any fears regarding possible increases in promiscuity or sexual acting out as a result of the retarded individual's increased social skills and knowledge of sexuality. It is important to realize that most mentally retarded individuals in the mild or borderline range are probably engaging in sexual behaviors in a fairly responsible manner (Murphy et al., in press). Those working with mentally retarded offenders should have some knowledge of the literature on human sexuality in the retarded and some understanding of the sexual behaviors in which the retarded are already involved.

A final issue is the treatment setting. Our own experience has been in an outpatient setting. Many of the considerations involved in determining whether any offender can be treated as an outpatient apply to the retarded. These considerations include frequency of acting out, past history of self-control of behavior, the seriousness of the offense, and dangerousness to others. With the retarded, an extremely important issue is the cooperation of family members. Our experience has been that if the family will cooperate and assist in monitoring the patient's behavior at home, outpatient treatment is feasible. Without family cooperation, however, patients often drop out of treatment, or treatment is a complete failure. Therapists must guard against families who want the mentally retarded individual removed from the community and attempt to use the therapist as a means of achieving this goal. Clinicians must make it very clear to caretakers that they will not take complete control of the patient and will not serve as a vehicle for the patient's institutionalization.

If inpatient treatment is required, numerous problems arise. A recent survey of institutional facilities for the retarded (Coleman and Murphy, 1980) found that very few have programs for the retarded offender. A general review of the correctional literature on the retarded also suggest problems. It has been observed that the mentally retarded individual in prison or in a correctional program tends to function at the bottom of the intelligence range of that population and is often victimized by other offenders. On the other hand, compared to residents in facilities for the retarded, offenders tend to be at the higher end of the range of functioning, and often manipulate and victimize those who function at lower levels. This is also the case in inpatient facilities, where the retarded offender may victimize the acutely psychotic patients who make up the majority of the population. In our setting, the only available inpatient facilities are a state psychiatric hospital and a private psychiatric unit. Because such facilities emphasize short-term treatment and lack programming for the mentally retarded, staff are sometimes reluctant to admit the retarded offender.

Thus, we have no satisfactory solution to the problem of optimal treatment settings. If offenders are placed on a psychiatric unit or in a facility for the retarded, strict behavioral control procedures must be instituted and they must be made to face the consequences of their behavior. It is also important for the treating clinician to try to work closely with the nursing personnel, who may otherwise feel that the patient is being "dumped" on them. The optimal solution would probably be a specialized treatment program for mentally retarded sex offenders in which individuals have similar intellectual levels. However, since most centers do not have sufficient numbers of these individuals to warrant such specialized units, we will probably continue to be limited to some of the imperfect solutions discussed above.

EXCESSES AND DEFICITS IN AROUSAL

Assessment

Within the social learning model, the major procedures for assessing arousal patterns have been self-report and penile assessment. Since the general procedures for physiological assessment will be dealt with elsewhere, we will only briefly touch on procedures employed in our laboratory and on potential problems in using these procedures with the retarded. In our laboratory, the basic procedure involves two-minute presentations of sexual stimuli (slides, audiotapes, and/or films) during which the subject's erection is monitored via a metal band strain gauge. Stimuli are chosen to represent the class of sexual behaviors or sexual objects relevant to the specific patient. All data are converted to percent full erection, and subjects also estimate their own percent erection and percent arousal following each stimulus presentation.

The literature suggests some possible problems in using penile assessment with the retarded although there are no data to substantiate this. For example, Gebhard and associates (1965, 1973) have suggested from interview data that the retarded are less responsive to visual stimuli and that their behavior is more a function of attention seeking and affection rather than a deviant arousal pattern. However, this finding is based on self-report data and, as those who work with pedophiles know, many nonretarded pedophiles report their behavior to be affectionate rather than sexual, while penile data may suggest quite the opposite (Abel, Becker, Murphy, and Flanagan, 1980). A more relevant problem is the tendency for many retarded individuals, especially those who have displayed any aggressive behavior in the past, to be placed on phenothiazines or other major tranquilizers, which can interfere with the laboratory assessment of sexual arousal. It is also difficult to obtain accurate self-reports of estimated arousal and erection from retarded subjects. However, this can usually be overcome by using various concrete descriptors. For example, rather than using the term "percent erection," we ask the subject a series of questions such as, Is it all the way hard? Is it more than half-hard? Is it less than half-hard? Similarly, in questioning percent of mental arousal, the subject can be asked, Did you like that a little? Did you like that a lot? etc. These techniques have been generally successful with mild to borderline retarded subjects.

Another problem relates to the offender's ability to discriminate deviant from nondeviant behaviors. We have noted that many offenders, both retarded and non-retarded, not only are aroused by stimuli that we label deviant but fail to label such stimuli as deviant. Offenders sometimes do not label the rape stimuli as rape or coercive. Similar problems arise among child molesters, who may be unable to discriminate affectionate behavior from sexual behavior in children and who may project onto children's behavior nonexistent sexual connotation. Originally, we speculated that the offenders were rationalizing their behavior or deliberately lying. However, we began to feel that this may represent a more basic problem, namely, a true deficit in discrimination and a resulting inability to view sexual situations as they are viewed by a nondeviant population. We are currently investigating some of these discrimination deficits but have not yet developed a clear procedure for assessing this postulated deficit. We do ask the subject to describe the stimuli they have seen in post-stimuli questionnaires and post-laboratory interviews. We attempt to determine through these interviews or questionnaires whether the subject's perceptions of the stimuli match their intended purpose. This is a rather crude measurement but one that has some clinical utility.

Figures 2-1 and 2-2 represent examples of penile data recorded from two retarded subjects. Figure 2-1 represents the responses of a 15-year-old moderately retarded male (Mr. A.) with a history of a previous psychotic episode. The stimuli employed (Abel, Becker, Murphy, and Flanagan, 1980) are six two-minute audiotape descriptions of sexual interactions with children, with increasing levels of aggression, and a seventh control stimulus of an adult mutual interaction. This patient was referred by a local adolescent unit for evaluation following a charge by his sister that he had molested her 7-year-old daughter. The patient denied this charge and accused his sister of physically abusing him. As the erection responses clearly indicate, although he denied all such arousal, this patient evidenced high

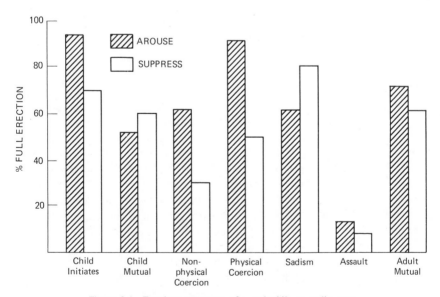

Figure 2-1 Erections responses of a pedophile to audio cues.

deviant sexual arousal to young children and to aggressive interactions with young children. It can also be seen that the patient displayed little ability to control (suppress) such arousal.

The data in Figure 2-2 are from a subject (Mr. B.) referred to our program by his lawyer after being accused of raping a woman who was eight months pregnant. Previous intellectual assessments had suggested IQs ranging from the borderline to the dull normal range; verbal IQ was extremely low and on most previous testing had fallen in the mildly retarded range. The patient also had neurological impairment which further interfered with his cognitive ability and impulse control.

As in Case 1, although this patient denied his deviant behavior, his erection data were consistent with the arousal pattern observed in rapists, and he also evidenced difficulties in suppressing his deviant arousal. Although he was able to control his arousal to purely aggressive stimuli (i.e., those depicting no sexual interaction) and to stimuli depicting mutual arousal, his arousal to rape stimuli actually increased slightly under control conditions. This lack of control is not universal among, or restricted to, the retarded. Because similar patterns are observed in many nonretarded offenders, we believe that the retarded offenders may be more similar to the nonretarded offenders than dissimilar.

As demonstrated in these two cases, erection measures can be a valuable assessment tool with the retarded offender. However, as with the nonretarded offender, some subjects do not show expected patterns and either respond normally or fail to respond to any stimuli. Whether this is due to lack of responsivity to analog stimuli, deliberate faking, or other factors is yet to be determined.

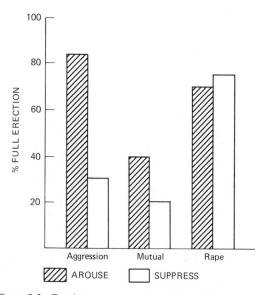

Figure 2-2   Erections responses of a rapist to video rape cues.

In addition to penile assessment of sexual arousal, our project usually employs two types of self-reports that require daily recording by the subject. The first is a frequency count of deviant and nondeviant behaviors and fantasies. The second is a card sort in which subjects rate on a scale of -3 (unpleasant) to $+3$ (pleasant) a series of brief descriptions of deviant and nondeviant sexual behavior. With the retarded, we have used pictures (e.g., adult women and children) rather than verbal descriptions, and subjects are asked to rate these simply as either pleasurable or not pleasurable. Some retarded subjects have difficulty with the frequency counts in the self-report procedure. However, this ability cannot be predicted from IQ alone and should be empirically tested with each patient. In some cases, subjects' self-report accuracy can be increased by providing specific training which uses concrete examples of deviant and nondeviant fantasies and behaviors. Another possibility is the use of indirect measures of possible deviant fantasies or behaviors. We have observed in some retarded offenders stereotyped behavioral patterns associated with periods of frequent urges. These behaviors have included increased irritability, increased distraction, and restlessness. Many times, family members are well aware of these patterns and will spontaneously report that they know when the offender is having difficulties. When such patterns are evident, it is important to have families keep track of, and record, such behavior, which can provide some indirect measure of possible acting out. In working with the retarded offender (and probably any offender), the importance of obtaining family cooperation cannot be emphasized enough.

Treatment

Table 2-1 lists treatments for reducing deviant arousal and increasing nondeviant arousal. Since some of these procedures have received limited empirical support (e.g., biofeedback-assisted suppression) and are reviewed in other chapters, we will limit our discussion to a few of the procedures.

In reducing deviant arousal, the three major procedures used by most behaviorists are electrical aversion, satiation, and covert sensitization with or without the pairing of a noxious odor. The major procedure for increasing appropriate arousal seems to be some form of masturbatory conditioning. Although there have been no published reports on the application of these procedures to the retarded, all the procedures are probably appropriate for some retarded offenders. The case of Mr. C. which follows, will detail the use of the variation of two of these procedures with a mentally retarded offender (see Murphy et al., in press, for complete details of this case).

Mr. C. was a 38-year-old mildly retarded male who came to our project in 1976. Although his IQ was estimated to be in the mildly retarded range, he seemed to have insight into his difficulty in controlling urges toward children beyond what

Table 2-1.   The Behavioral Assessment and Treatment of Sex Offenders.

	PROBLEM AREAS	TREATMENT METHODS	ASSESSMENT METHODS
Arousal variables	Excessive arousal to deviant stimuli	Aversion-suppression methods 1. Covert sensitization 2. Electrical aversion 3. Odor aversion 4. Chemical aversion 5. Biofeedback-assisted suppression 6. Satiation	Penile recordings Self-report Clinical interviews
	Deficit arousal to nondeviant sexual stimuli	Generation of arousal to nondeviant cues 1. Masturbatory conditioning 2. Exposure 3. Fading 4. Systematic desensitization	
Social skills deficits	Heterosocial skills Assertive skills	Heterosocial skills training Assertive training	Behavioral role-playing procedures Self-report inventories Clinical interviews
Sexual behavior	Sexual dysfunction Sexual knowledge	Therapy Sex education	Sexual inventories Sex education test Clinical interviews
Cognitive/social	Attitudes Perception Discrimination	?	Burt scale ?

one would expect from his intellectual level. In fact, he initiated the treatment contact and insisted that his parents seek treatment for him when he felt that his urges were getting out of control.

He had at least a 25-year history of attraction to young children and was incarcerated at age 30 for child molestation. Although he had been married briefly to a woman he described as "not liking sex," he had little heterosexual experience and almost all of his masturbatory fantasies were related to young children. Physiological assessment proved unreliable because of Mr. C.'s inability to achieve an erection in or out of the laboratory, which may have been secondary to phenothiazine administration. However, he did masturbate to ejaculation with a flaccid penis.

While in prison, Mr. C. had been treated with electrical aversion, which he felt was helpful. He requested the same treatment from our project. The use of electrical aversion with the retarded raises numerous ethical problems related to the ability to give informed consent. However, in this case, the patient requested the treatment and had found it helpful in the past, and the family was agreeable to the idea. In addition, a Patient Advocate who interviewed Mr. C. in an independent assessment felt that he was competent to consent and was under no external coercion to seek the treatment. Electrical aversion was thus employed, and the patient received 16 treatments over a three-month period. In addition, because his masturbatory fantasies were almost exclusively of children, he was instructed in a home program of masturbatory reconditioning that involved masturbating to pictures of adult women two to three times a week. He was able to follow this assignment and was very compliant with the instructions.

Mr. C. has been followed on a periodic basis since that time. He continued to report no deviant urges and increased arousal to women until approximately three months ago, at which time he noted a return of the deviant urges. These urges seemed to be associated with a stressful period in his life related to a decline in his father's health. We reinstituted electrical aversion for three sessions, with resulting good suppression of deviant urges. According to the patient's self-report and the report of his family (who monitor his behavior), there has been no incidence of deviant behavior over this five-year period.

Despite the ethical, and at times legal, questions related to electrical aversion, it is a procedure that should not be prematurely eliminated from our treatment armamentarium. In Mr. C.'s case, the availability of this procedure has probably assisted him in avoiding long-term incarceration and prevented the victimization of a number of children.

In addition to electrical aversion, other procedures including covert sensitization and/or assisted sensitization can be considered. Covert sensitization is a procedure in which all stimuli are presented in imagination. The therapist verbally describes to the patient a deviant sexual scene and then an aversive scene. The patient is asked to imagine these scenes and to place himself in the scenes as they are described. The nature of the aversive scene is determined by interviewing the patient and may include socially aversive stimuli such as going to jail or physically aversive stimuli such as vomitus or blood. We usually intertwine the sexual and aversive scenes by switching back and forth between them. Usually a scene lasts approximately 10 minutes and two scenes are presented within each session. The aversiveness of the scenes can be increased by pairing them with a noxious odor such as valeric acid (see Maletzky, 1980).

The use of this technique with the retarded may be hampered by limitations in imagery ability. However, this problem also occurs in the nonretarded, and the subject's ability to participate can only be determined empirically. To check the patient's comprehension of the scene, he can be asked to verbalize the scene following the therapist's presentation. Sexual arousal can be monitored physiologically during the verbal presentation of sexual fantasies to assess the ability to respond to this material. Reactions to aversive fantasies can be monitored by periodically checking pulse rate during aversive scenes. However, it should be noted that heart rate changes are not always reliable indices of aversiveness; some patients tend to respond in other systems, such as by decreased skin resistance. Finally, pictures may be employed to assist the patient in forming images.

Satiation can also be considered for use in reducing deviant arousal in the retarded. In our project, patients are first asked to masturbate to nondeviant fantasies until ejaculation and then are requested to continue masturbating for 30 to 45 minutes to deviant fantasies during the refractory period. Subjects are required to verbalize the fantasies, which are tape recorded. The tape recorded fantasies provide a built-in check on the subject's compliance, on the quality of the fantasies and verbal output, and on ability to use this technique. In our experience, most retarded offenders do masturbate to deviant fantasies as do their nonretarded counterparts, and this procedure seems to have some promise. Again, it may be necessary to use pictures to prompt fantasizing. We have discussed the use of masturbatory conditioning for increasing appropriate arousal; since this has been well detailed in other chapters, it will not be reviewed here.

Treatment techniques for training discrimination within the sex offender population have seldom been reported. Many programs at least imply that such treatment occurs in various confrontation models, but these are never specifically directed to discrimination. We attempt to provide subjects with various role models or behavioral descriptions of a variety of sexual behaviors and ask the subject to label these as either coercive or noncoercive, affectionate or sexual, etc. The subject is then provided feedback on the accuracy of his discrimination, and the therapist provides a rationale of why certain behaviors may be coercive or nonsexual. Also, as in other projects, we sometimes are very confrontive with subjects, pointing out to them how this behavior would be seen from the woman's perspective. Similar procedures can be used with the retarded offender although much more data are needed both on the basic aspects of this discrimination problem and on appropriate treatment techniques to remedy such deficits.

In summary, our experience suggests that many of the procedures available for increasing and decreasing arousal are appropriate for the retarded offender. It may be necessary to provide concrete explanations, to repeat explanations frequently, and to use language the patient can understand to describe the requirements of treatment. However, with all offenders, the real test of any procedure is whether the deviant behavior changes. This can only be determined through adequate assessment, including penile responses, self-reports, and family observations. If one is thorough in assessment and continues assessment throughout treatment, techniques can be modified until an effective procedure or combination of procedures is found.

SOCIAL SKILLS

Assessment

Data from our project indicate that sex offenders have deficits in social skills, although this finding is not universal. Mentally retarded offenders seen in our project are equally if not more deficient in heterosocial skills. It often appears that this deficit is a major causative factor in sexual acting out. These deficits are understandable in that many retarded offenders have spent years in institutional settings and/or have been overprotected by their families. Because they are seen as different by their nonretarded peers, they tend to be excluded from normal socialization processes. Until recently, there has been little focus on interpersonal skills in the retarded; the major focus of treatment has been on decreasing inappropriate behaviors, increasing grooming, increasing self-help skills, etc. However, with increased community placement for the retarded, workers in the mental retardation field have begun to recognize the importance of interpersonal skills for maximum functioning. Matson and his colleagues (Kazdin and Matson, 1980; Matson, 1980; Matson, Kazdin, and Esveldt-Dawson, 1978) have demonstrated that moderately and even more severely retarded individuals do respond to traditional behavioral procedures for training social skills. We suggest that the interested reader consult these references for a better understanding of social skills assessment and treatment in the retarded.

In our project, we have used our standard assessment procedures for social skills with the retarded offender. To assess heterosocial skills, the Behavioral Checklist developed by Barlow, Abel, Blanchard, Bristow, and Young (1977) is employed (see Table 2-2). Basically, this scale consists of the major categories of voice, form of conversation, and affect, with the subcategories specified. During assessment, subjects are asked to role play three 2½-minute scenes with a female confederate. The scenes are designed to increase in intimacy from an initial meeting to a date with someone they have known for a long time. All scenes are videotaped and rated at a later time in 30-second blocks for the presence or absence of the specific behaviors outlined.

The tapes are also reviewed for such behaviors as inappropriate touching of the body (i.e., touching the genitals or picking the nose), unusual body mannerisms or

Table 2-2.   Components of the Heterosocial Skills Checklist

VOICE	FORM OF CONVERSATION	AFFECT
Loudness	Initiation	Facial expression
Pitch	Follow-up	Eye contact
Inflection	Flow	Laughter
No special dramatic effect	Interest	

facial gestures that make the patient "appear odd," and inappropriate verbalizations such as asking for a kiss when first meeting someone. We observe these types of gross behavioral deficits more often in the retarded than in the nonretarded offender, and they must be targeted early in treatment or the patient will continue to experience social rejection.

Figure 2-3 presents the social skills data for Mr. A. (described previously) for baseline and for three assessments during treatment. The treatment probes followed every two treatment sessions. Figure 2-3 is presented to highlight one of the difficulties in assessing the retarded offender. First, the baseline data indicate deficits in social skills that are consistent with Mr. A.'s interview and history. Assessment during treatment showed an initial improvement, with a return to baseline for two of the behavioral classes following the sixth treatment session. As noted, this patient had both limited intellectual ability and a concomitant psychiatric disorder. On the day of the last data point, the patient was angry about an incident on his treatment unit and seemed resistant to the assessment procedure. This type of behavioral reaction to emotional states, which occurs often in retarded offenders, produces substantial variability in our behavioral data. At times, it appears that the offender has appropriate social skills in his repertoire but uses inappropriate behavior or refusal to communicate as a means of "punishing" the environment. It is

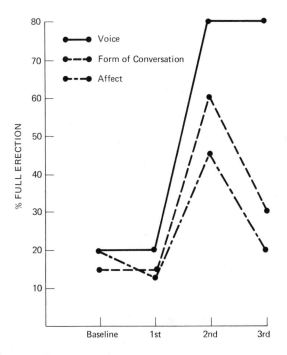

Figure 2-3   Changes in components of heterosocial skills during treatment.

important during social skills evaluation that an attempt be made to assess current emotional state and correlate this with observed behavior. When this is observed, the treatment focus must be on handling frustrations appropriately rather than training basic conversational skills.

Another problem observed in both retarded and nonretarded offenders is in the perception of women and of their reactions. Although this is present in both retarded and nonretarded offenders, it sometimes is much more obvious in the retarded and more likely to be noted by treatment staff. We have observed two major types of misperceptions in these offenders. First is their perception of the "appropriate woman." Many retarded offenders develop their ideas of women from television and books, and feel that only a "Farrah Fawcett" type will do. Retarded females may then be rejected because of these stereotypes. Because the retarded offender probably has a limited range of women to approach, these stereotypes interfere substantially with his ability to develop appropriate interactions.

A second perception problem is misinterpretation of female behavior. A female who acts in a friendly manner or just returns a "hello" may be seen by the patient as his "girlfriend." Also, unless there is a very clear rejection, the patient may have difficulty realizing that a woman is not interested in interacting with him. This leads to continued inappropriate approaches and social difficulties. An extreme example of this was Mr. D., a 23-year-old obscene phone caller with a history of one rape. This patient had an IQ of 66 and a concomitant schizophrenic disorder that was controlled with medication. The patient would continually talk about his girlfriends who were "stuck on him." On further questioning, and in checking with Mr. D.'s mother, it became obvious that he had dated none of these women. Some were women he had not even seen but to whom he had made obscene phone calls. His interpretation was that if the woman did not reject him outright, she must be interested in him and he would continue making nightly calls. There are no clear procedures for assessing such perceptual difficulties, although we have been investigating this area by having subjects rate videotapes of women role playing various reactions to male approach behavior. We have found some very small but significant correlations between intellectual level and an individual's ability to discriminate the various role-played reactions in a normal population.

Treatment

Work by Matson and his colleagues (Matson, 1980; Matson, Kazdin, and Esveldt-Dawson, 1978) suggests that the techniques used for social skills training in normal populations are applicable to the retarded. Matson's work also indicates that the retarded can self-record their social behavior when given appropriate training. Our experience with the basic techniques of behavioral rehearsal (role playing), videotape feedback, modeling, and social reinforcement is consistent with their data. In sessions with the retarded offender, the therapist tries to elicit from the patient situations from his life in which he has had the opportunity to interact with individuals of the opposite sex (or the same sex, depending on the patient's sexual orientation). The therapist chooses a simple situation initially and asks the subject to role play such a situation. This is videotaped, and after the behavioral rehearsal, the videotape is reviewed by the patient and the therapist. The therapist will point out possible problems as well as any appropriate behaviors. The therapist then models the appropriate behaviors, and the cycle starts anew.

The major difference in using these techniques with the retarded versus the nonretarded offender is that one must sometimes start at a very low level of skills, and more learning trials may be necessary. Also, some retarded offenders may engage in inappropriate physical gestures or mannerisms, or make inappropriate verbal responses during training. These need to be focused on and corrected. Basically, to use social skills training with the retarded, one must start at the individual's level, shape appropriate responses slowly, give concrete examples, use repeated practice, and provide high levels of reinforcement. For example, a mentally retarded exhibitionist with a speech deficit who had spent the majority of his life in an institution was seen by the second author for social skills training. The first three sessions all involved simply saying hello. Attention focused on eye contact, verbalizing the word "hello," and avoiding other interfering behaviors and verbalizations. As this vignette suggests, the major skill needed in providing social skills training to this population is patience.

Because of the limited attention span and easy loss of motivation of some retarded offenders, it is important to keep sesssions short and reinforcement levels high. Videotaping is very helpful in maintaining attention and increasing motivation. Many subjects are fascinated by the working of the equipment and receive reinforcement from seeing themselves on the TV screen. In addition, the video feedback allows the therapist to show concrete examples rather than try to verbally outline deficits and excesses in the patient's performance. This is particularly important with the retarded offender, who often has deficits in both expressive and receptive verbal abilities.

It is also important to avoid overwhelming the retarded patient with feedback. The therapist must begin with one or two simple behaviors such as eye contact and saying hello, and focus on achieving appropriate levels of this behavior. Once these levels are achieved, one can take the next step. Because of their limited information processing ability, the mentally retarded are easily frustrated and become resistant to social skills training if feedback is too extensive.

The training of accurate perception is a more difficult task, for which there is currently no empirically validated treatment technique. Our major approach with both retarded and nonretarded offenders is to incorporate perception training into social skills training. Initially, the therapist (who, in our project, is a female) plays various roles, and the patient is asked to identify her emotion and to indicate whether or not she is displaying interest. The roles are very clear and at times exaggerated initially, and then become more subtle, with both verbal and nonverbal cues. Once the patient shows some skills in identifying cues with the primary therapist, various female confederates will be introduced and the process is re-peated to promote generalization. Again, videotaping is used and the therapist tries to identify various aspects of the female behavior that indicate the emotion or state being role played. As we stated, this procedure has not been validated, but we have found it clinically useful with some offenders.

This section has focused on the training of heterosocial skills, with little mention of assertiveness skills and other aspects of the model. The issues and the training techniques are similar, although the role-playing situations may change. There is a wealth of information on assertiveness training, most of which can be applied to the retarded, with the modifications suggested for heterosocial skills.

SEX EDUCATION

Assessment

Unlike other areas we have reviewed to this point, there is an extensive literature on sex education in the retarded, and much of the data has been recently reviewed (Murphy et al., in press). In addition, a recent survey of inpatient facilities for the retarded (Coleman and Murphy, 1980) indicated that most of the facilities which responded provided sex education and approved of such education. Because of the extensive literature in this area, we will keep our comments brief. Our experience suggests that retarded individuals are extremely deficient in their knowledge of both biological and social aspects of sex. Many have extensive misinformation. Parents or caretakers have often taken restrictive or punitive attitudes out of fear that sexual knowledge might lead to rampant sexual acting out and promiscuity. This restrictive environment may lead the offender to experience much guilt sur-rounding sexual functioning or to totally deny his own sexuality. A prime example of this is Mr. B., discussed earlier. This patient had had one sexual interaction, initiated by a woman, approximately two years prior to his being seen by our project. He still experienced intense guilt about this incident and had similar in-tense guilt feelings about masturbation, denying that he ever engaged in such be-havior. He seemed to have repressed his sexuality completely, and it was felt that this may have been related to the acting out that occurred during the rape.

In the past, assessment of sexual knowledge in the retarded was difficult because of deficiencies in reading skills. Recently, a sexual knowledge inventory has been developed for the retarded (Edmonson, McCombs, and Wish, 1979), and in our project we have used a pretest of the EASE (Essential Adult Sex Education Curric-ulum; Zelman and Tysler, 1979). This is a well-developed sex education package including a large number of slides that can be easily tailored to the individual. This package covers four basic areas—biological, sexual behavior, sexual health, and relationships—and includes pre-post tests for each section.

By using the pretest from each area, we have a better understanding of an indi-vidual's sexual knowledge across areas. For example, Mr. B. scored 19% correct on the biological area, 44% correct on sexual behavior, 38% on health, and 85% on relationships. This indicated that he did have knowledge of male-female relationships on a social level but was very deficient in his knowledge of sexual behavior and biology. This type of information is more useful in treatment planning than tests which provide only one overall score.

Treatment

Sex education, like social skills training, is basically the same for the retarded and the nonretarded offender. The important factors are use of concrete examples, repetition, and limiting the amount of information presented in any one session. Simple terminology should be used, and expectations of the offender's learning must be consistent with his intellectual level. A number of excellent packaged programs are available such as the EASE program and the program *Sexuality in the Mentally Handicapped* developed by Kempton and Hanson (1978).

COGNITIVE FACTORS

We have pointed out how problems with perception and discrimination may play a role in sexual offenses. Another important cognitive variable is the individual's attitudes toward women and toward violence. Feminist writers have long stressed the role of these socially developed attitudes in rape. Recently, Burt (1980) has developed scales to assess sexual stereotyping, adversatively sexual beliefs, sexual conservatism, acceptance of interpersonal violence (mainly against women), and acceptance of rape myths. She found that the other attitudinal scales were predictive of acceptance of rape myths. Malamuth (1980) has shown in a college population that these scales are related to sexual arousal (measured physiologically) to rape cues, aggression toward women in a laboratory situation, and self-reported likelihood of raping.

We have been investigating the relationship of these attitudes to various arousal and social perception variables in a large-scale community sample. Although this study was not designed for the mentally retarded, our subjects have had a wide range of IQs (61–135) on the Otis Quick Scoring Mental Abilities Test, and we have therefore been able to take a preliminary look at the relationship between IQ and attitudes. Sample sizes in this preliminary analysis range from 84 to 95 because of missing data in some cells.

Before presenting these data, we must clearly state some limitations. Because the IQ test was self-administered, results represent only those subjects who could read. In addition, the test is heavily loaded for verbal ability and probably underestimates the actual IQ of a number of our subjects. Therefore, although some of the scores fell in the mildly mentally retarded range, it is probably best to assume that no subject was below the borderline range. Caution should be used in generalizing these data to more severely retarded individuals.

Basically, the data indicated moderate and significant negative correlations between IQ and the various attitude measures employed. Correlation between IQ and rape myth acceptance, sexual stereotyping, adversarial sexual beliefs, sexual conservatism, and acceptance of interpersonal violence against women were $-.54$, $-.42$, $-.42$, $-.60$, $-.46$, respectively. These findings are not surprising in view of our experience and a literature review, which indicate that many mentally retarded individuals experience very restrictive and punitive attitudes toward sexuality and get their knowledge about sexuality from television or other popular sources. If similar data were found for the mentally retarded offender, this would support our observation that many retarded sex offenders have a good deal of misinformation about sex, women, and male-female relationships. It also would support our observation that these offenders often have difficulties discriminating deviant from nondeviant behavior. However, further studies with retarded offenders will be needed to substantiate these hypotheses.

There is no readily available treatment technique for attitude change in the retarded and the nonretarded offender that has been tested. This seems to be an area where preventive procedures, such as early education and appropriate social models, are warranted. Our own approach with individuals who are already offenders has been cognitive-behavioral, with a confrontational approach challenging these belief patterns. However, we have no data to substantiate the effectiveness of these procedures. It appears that the old maxim "more data needed" must also be applied to this area.

CONCLUSION

Many of the problems we have outlined for the retarded offender are very similar to those for the nonretarded offender. Most of the retarded sex offenders we have seen have seemed to be just that, sex offenders, who have developed a deviant sexual arousal pattern and appeared to show a deviant sexual preference. It is toward this population that this chapter has been addressed. In our experience, techniques such as social skills training, sex education, covert sensitization, and satiation are appropriate for mildly or borderline retarded offenders. Further studies will be needed to determine whether our clinical impressions can be supported empirically.

Throughout this chapter, we have focused on some of the cognitive variables related to sex offenders. Many of these deficits are quite obvious in the retarded, and these variables have not been clearly presented within the behavioral model. We hope that our discussion of these issues will lead to further research in the area of perceptual, discrimination, and attitudinal problems within the sex offender population and to the development of empirically tested treatment techniques. Only further controlled clinical studies and basic research studies will provide the basis for a rational approach to this serious social problem.

REFERENCES

Abel, G.G., Becker, J.V., Murphy, W.D., and Flanagan, B. *Identifying dangerous child molesters.* Paper presented at the 11th Banff International Conference on Behavior Modification, Banff, Canada, 1979.

Abel, G.G., Blanchard, E.B., Becker, J.V., and Djenderedjian, A. Differentiating sexual aggressives with penile measures. *Criminal Justice and Behavior* **5**:315-332 (1978).

Bandura, A. *Social Learning Theory.* New Jersey: Prentice-Hall, 1977.

Barlow, D.H. and Abel, G.G. Recent developments in assessments and treatment of sexual deviation. In Craighead, W.E., Kazdin, A.E., and Mahoney, M.D. (Eds.) *Behavior Modification: Principles, Issues, and Applications.* Boston: Houghton Mifflin, 1976.

Barlow, D.H., Abel, G.G., Blanchard, E.B., Bristow, A.R., and Young, L.D. A heterosocial skills checklist for males. *Behavior Therapy* **8**:229-239 (1977).

Barmann, B.C. and Murray, W.J. Suppression of inappropriate sexual behavior by facial screening. *Behavior Therapy* **12**:730-735 (1981).

Burt, M.R. Cultural myths and supports for rape. *Journal of Personality and Social Psychology* **38**:217-230 (1980).

Coleman, E.M. and Murphy, W.D. A survey of sexual attitudes and sex education programs among facilities for the mentally retarded. *Applied Research in Mental Retardation* **1**:269-276 (1980).

Cook, J.W., Altman, K., Shaw, J., and Blaylock, M. Use of contingent lemon juice to eliminate public masturbation by a severely retarded boy. *Behaviour Research and Therapy* **16**:131-134 (1978).

Edmonson, B., McCombs, K., and Wish, J. What retarded adults believe about sex. *American Journal of Mental Deficiency* **84**:11-18 (1979).

Foxx, R.M. The use of overcorrection to eliminate the public disrobing (stripping) of retarded women. *Behaviour Research and Therapy* **14**:53-60 (1976).

Gebhard, P.H. Sexual behavior of the retarded. In de la Cruz, F.F. and LaVeck, G.D. (Eds.) *Human Sexuality and the Mentally Retarded.* New York: Brunner/Mazel, 1973.

Gebhard, P.H., Gaymon, J.H., Pomeroy, W.B., and Christenson, C.V. *Sex Offenders.* New York: Harper and Row, 1965.

Kazdin, A.E. and Matson, J.L. Social validation in mental retardation. *Applied Research in Mental Retardation* **2**:39-53 (1981).

Kempton, W. and Hanson, G. *Sexuality and the Mentally Handicapped: Nine Slide Presentations for Teaching the Mentally Handicapped Individual.* Santa Monica, Calif.: Stanford Film Associates, 1978.

Malamuth, N.M. Rape proclivity in the general population. *Journal of Social Issues* **37**: (1981).

Maletzky, B.M. Assisted covert sensitization. In Cox, D.J. and Daitzman, R.J. (Eds.) *Exhibitionism: Description, Assessment, and Treatment.* New York: Garland Press, 1980.

Matson, J.L. Acquisition of social skills by mentally retarded adult training assistants. *Journal of Mental Deficiency and Research* **24**:129-135 (1980).

Matson, J.L., Kazdin, A.E., and Esveldt-Dawson, K. Training interpersonal skills among mentally retarded and socially dysfunctional children. *Behaviour Research and Therapy* **18**:419-427 (1980).

Mohr, J.W., Turner, R.E., and Jerry, M.D. *Pedophilia and Exhibitionism.* Toronto: University of Toronto Press, 1964.

Murphy, W.D., Coleman, E.M., and Abel, G.G. Sexuality and the mentally retarded. In Matson, J.L. and Andrasik, F. (Eds.) *Treatment Issues and Innovations in Mental Retardation* (in press).

Santamour, M.B. and West, B. The retarded offender and corrections. *Mental Retardation and the Law* 25-37 (October 1978).

Selling, L.S. Types of behavior manifested by feeble-minded sex offenders. *Proceedings from the American Association on Mental Deficiency* **44**:178-186 (1939).

Zelman, D.B. and Tysler, K.M. *Essential Adult Sex Education for the Mentally Retarded.* Madison, Wisc.: The Madison Opportunity Center, 1979.

3
Forensic Mental Evaluation of the Violent Sexual Offender

Stuart B. Silver, M. D.
Michael K. Spodak, M. D.

Violent sex offenders may require mental evaluation at various times as they pass through the criminal justice system. Upon arrest, they may exhibit symptoms of acute illness needing prompt diagnosis and treatment. Later, specific legal questions may be posed. This chapter explores considerations relevant to evaluation for competency to stand trial and criminal responsibility, focusing on violent sexual offenses. A case example illustrates a defendant's movement through the pretrial forensic mental evaluation process.

Forensic evaluations are those which may be used in the public "forum" of the courtroom. The phrase mental evaluation is used in order to emphasize that any information which bears on the mental processes of the individual under examination is relevant, whether obtained from witnesses, other professionals, direct examination, or other sources. These data must be collated, scrutinized, and evaluated in specific relationship to the questions asked by the criminal justice system. This is not a "psychiatric examination" or the exclusive product of any one discipline, but rather an assessment of a particular subject's mental function using whatever techniques are appropriate and available. This chapter will focus particularly on the "violent" sexual offender—the rapist, the rape murderer, the sexual sadist—rather than those charged with less severe offenses such as exhibitionism, voyeurism, and certain fetishes.

The two offenses to be described were both committed by the same man. In the first, he threatened the victim with a shotgun; in the second, he used a knife. Police apprehended the defendant in another state and suspected him of other serious sexual offenses. Although some modifications of the history will conceal true identities, this case will form the framework of an examination of the use of mental evaluation at various stages in the prosecution of a criminal case. According to the investigative report:

The suspect armed with a sawed-off shotgun and disguised in a ski mask confronted the victim as she was exiting her laundry room and demanded money. The suspect at this point bound the victim's feet and hands and placed a washcloth in her mouth. The suspect than forced the victim to lay on the floor on her stomach, pulled down her pants and forced vaginal intercourse from the rear. The suspect then placed the victim in the storage room and fled the scene.[1]

The report of the second offense follows:

The suspect walked up to the victim as she was entering her car and asked for a light. When the suspect was denied the light, the suspect forced his way into the victim's vehicle, produced a knife and had her slide over into the seat. The suspect then forced the victim to the back seat of her vehicle and bound her hands and feet. The suspect then drove the victim to the location where he forcibly forced vaginal intercourse, anal intercourse, fellatio and then performed cunnilingus on the victim. The suspect then robbed the victim of jewelry and her purse, drove her to an apartment complex and abandoned her nude in her car.[2]

The suspect, R.R., waived his right to an extradition hearing in the remote state where he was apprehended and was returned to a Maryland county detention center. Bond was set at $100,000. The county investigator's report established positive fingerprint and other identification. That, combined with evidentiary proof obtained by medical examination of the victims, indicated beyond reasonable doubt that R.R. was their man.

Emergency Evaluation Requested as a Consequence of the Detainee's Symptomatic Behavior

Two weeks after R.R. was placed in jail, the guards noticed that his behavior was peculiar. Besides extreme introversion and what appeared to be a depressed, silent mood, he occasionally screamed out that "the demons are controlling my life." At other times he became very suspicious of all others in the jail. The sheriff informally asked the detention center's medical consultant to see R.R. No court orders were obtained; the interview was arranged by a telephone call. The detention center was a modern facility. Its medical wing was adequately staffed for the interview to proceed in relative safety for the doctor.

It is important whenever such an emergency consultation is performed that the examiner be mindful of the security arrangements before he begins interviewing. Reality-based fearfulness will thereby be minimized. The clinician then will be able to evaluate his own internal feeling states generated during the interview, while being adequately safe.

This physician's note became the first medical report following the charged offenses. The consultant had little history about his patient beyond the charges lodged against him. Not available, for example, were the police reports, the investigator's summary of the case, or the "rap sheet." There were no prior medical records nor were family members available for interviews. Fortunately, however, he was able to review the observations of the jail attendants which were recorded by each shift and which described some of the strange behaviors. R.R. had not evidenced any unusual conduct at the hearing when bond was set. In fact, the observations of the guards were the first indication that there might be a mental disorder.

In this case, as in most, the clinical information available was extremely limited. Additionally, psychological testing, x-ray, and laboratory testing were not available. The consultant, however, drew on his 17 years of experience at the facility. He knew that often patients detained for major offenses malingered, behaved boisterously in order to promote disturbance, or became unreasonably demanding. Suspected criminals are often self-centered and manipulative, and the consultant maintained an appropriate level of skepticism. He was also aware of the stresses of incarceration and the mental decompensation that often occurs in those charged with major crimes who are confined abruptly, as well as the increased risk of suicide. Finally, he was aware that there was a possibility that his report might be used in court and as a resource for other mental health professionals. Accordingly, he was careful to record his observations and the patient's statements in detail, and to avoid any premature conclusions. He was, after all, functioning largely in a triage capacity—guiding the custody officials in the correct clinical management of a possibly ill person.

"This thirty four year old man offers no spontaneous complaints. His version of the reason for his arrest is that he was standing in a pawn shop and he accidentally pressed a button bringing the police who arrested him for carrying a concealed weapon. He denies knowledge of a rape charge and claims he does not know what "rape" means. He says he dropped out of the eleventh grade because of family "problems" which he would not elucidate. He denied use of drugs and alcohol. He claims he was discharged by the marines after two years of duty as "unfit". "They told me I was a paranoid schizophrenic" at the "Navy Hospital" and later that "I was a chronic schizophrenic" at a V.A. clinic. No history of suicidal attempts was elicited.

The patient manifests no obvious physical abnormalities and he is alert and oriented. He sits quietly and is reluctant to answer questions. Adequate responses may be elicited by repeated prodding on the same issue. He speaks in a low monotone. He says he hears voices of "demons" telling him to get up and go away. "It is hard for me to concentrate because these demons are keeping my mind busy . . . people are against me and talk about me all the time . . . this makes me mad . . . sometimes a ghost chases me." His affect appears depressed, but he indicates good appetite and describes no sleep disturbance. Current suicidal thoughts were not evidenced. His intellectual functions appear intact and adequate. . . .

Impression: the history and clinical findings suggest the possibility of a major psychiatric illness, schizophrenia, but there is a component of the presentation (specifically his familiarity with and willingness to mention his illness in spite of his otherwise secretive nature) which suggests malingering. I recommend further psychiatric evaluation in a hospital setting. The suicidal risk does not appear substantial at this time and there is not an emergent need for hospital care.[3]

Evaluation of Current Competency to Stand Trial

In most jurisdictions, the test for competency for trial consists of a combination of the defendant's ability not only to understand the charges and their potential consequences, but also to assist in his defense in general and particularly to cooperate with his attorney. Competency is a "here and now" test. An opinion about competency is given for the time of the evaluation and includes a short-term prediction through the time of the trial. The evaluation is directed predominately, therefore, to the defendant's mental status at the time of the assessment. Does he appear alert and without bizarreness? Is there evidence of psychomotor retardation or excitation? Is his speech coherent, relevant, and goal directed? Is emotional responsiveness appropriate or distorted? Is his thought process logical? Does the content of the defendant's responses suggest some plausible way of answering the allegations against him? Is recent and remote memory intact?

When R.R.'s lawyer heard the results of the doctor's consultation, he requested and obtained a court order for formal evaluation of his client's mental competence to stand trial. The rules governing this question in Maryland are typical of the rest of the country. Competency evaluation may be sought at any time in court proceedings and may result from observations by the judge or at the request of other interested parties. The final determination of competency is exclusively a matter for the trial court[4] and is not a jury question. Whenever the issue is raised, the judge must determine upon testimony and evidence presented on the record, outside the jury's presence, whether the accused is unable to understand the nature or the object of the proceedings against him or to assist in his defense.[5] Both parts of this test must be established before the accused may be brought to trial.[6] Generally, testimony is sought from a psychiatrist or other mental health professional according to local court precedents, but the judge may make a determination without expert testimony if he so chooses. The alleged incompetent person is usually referred to the state mental health authority for examination and evaluation of trial competency. In Maryland, most individuals accused of serious crimes who require formal forensic mental evaluations are referred to the Clifton T. Perkins Hospital Center, the maximum security mental hospital operated by the state's health department.

One week after his examination at the detention center, R.R. was admitted to the Perkins Center pursuant to court order for evaluation of his competency to stand trial. According to the admission nursing notes, ". . . he is rather calm and quiet. . . . He is well oriented and relates that he has 'seizures' as a result of being given medications (Thorazine, Stelazine, Loxitane). . . . Cogentin relieves these reactions. He denies drug abuse and states that he has no suicidal ideation."[7] His medical and neurologic examinations were unremarkable, but he gave a good history suggesting dystonic reactions from prior treatment with antipsychotic medications.

A full psychiatric examination was performed by Dr. A.C., a staff psychiatrist at the hospital. He made sure that the patient knew the purpose of the interview and that a report would be filed with the court. He went on to recount identifying information about the patient from other sources. He made judicious inquiry about the offenses, reviewed past medical and psychiatric history, and performed a thorough mental status examination. Dr. A.C. additionally reviewed the laboratory studies, as well as the physical and neurological examinations, and finally offered a diagnostic impression. R.R. was presented before a hospital staff conference attended by three psychiatrists, a psychologist, a nurse, a social worker, and the hospital's attorney. While this level of investigation is not necessary to establish competence, double rape, combined with the history of mental hospitalization and current suggestion of hallucinations, dictated a need for extreme caution in the clinical investigation.

Standardized tests for trial competence—the competency screening test (CST) and the competency assessment instrument (CAI)—have been developed by McGarry et al.[8] Furthermore, a number of states have developed community-based screening agencies to examine defendants about whom this question has been raised.[9] Such approaches have minimized the formerly widespread use of a finding of incompetence as a means of preventive detention. Prompt reporting of competency evaluations also tends to preclude the innappropriate use of this mechanism to delay trial for tactical reasons or to empty local jails temporarily into mental health facilities. The competency order, however, remains a traditional way for lower-level courts to dispose of misdemeanants into hospitals and out of the criminal justice system. In most cases, an assessment of a patient's current clinical status will be sufficient for the clinician to render an opinion on trial competency.

When dealing with violent sex offenders, one often hears the defense of mistaken identity or complete lack of recall of the offense. Exploring with the defendant any possible alibi and the way in which he can assist his attorney in establishing such an alibi may reflect on his competence. When the defendant alleges a lack of memory, examination of whether this is part of some mental or neurological disorder is important. Although the test for competency may not specifically mention the presence of illness, a true amnestic condition may bear on the competency issue.

The Supreme Court in the *Miranda* decision of 1966 ruled that persons suspected of a crime must be advised of their rights before interrogation.[10] Occasionally, the clinician may be asked to render a retrospective opinion on a defendant's competence to have waived his *Miranda* rights. If a substantial period of time has elapsed from the arrest to the evaluation, a reconstruction of the defendant's prior condition is required. Had the defendant sufficient intellectual function to understand the words of the *Miranda* warning? Did he feel coerced? Arresting officers are becoming increasingly sophisticated in obtaining waivers, but a mere head nod or initial on a sheet of paper may not be an adequate indication that a person "knowingly" relinquished certain constitutionally guaranteed rights. Does a defendant who is so depressed that he does not care what happens, or one who is terrified by rumors of police brutality, waive his rights "knowingly"?

The findings in the case of R.R. were summarized in the following letter to the court:

Dear Judge D.C.:

The above named patient was admitted to our hospital on May 8, 1978 for an evaluation of his competency to stand trial in connection with the above case number. Since his admission, he has received a psychiatric evaluation and other pertinent studies.

Mr. R.R. was presented before a staff conference on April 14, 1978 where he was interviewed and his case reviewed. It was the unanimous opinion of the medical staff that the diagnosis is Schizophrenia, Paranoid Type associated with some attempts to malinger.

It was the further unanimous opinion of the staff that, at the present time, Mr. R.R. is able to understand the nature and object of the proceedings against him and to assist in his own defense.

In view of the above opinions, we have made arrangements to return Mr. R.R. to your custody as our evaluation has been completed.

Should additional information with regard to this case be necessary, please do not hesitate to request it of us.[11]

R.R. was found mentally ill, but not currently in need of inpatient care, and was considered to be manageable in a jail setting. It was the medical opinion that he was able to stand trial. Equally important was the absence of statements which might have been made with regard to the charged offenses, R.R.'s dangerousness, or dispositional recommendations. Such gratuitous observations were omitted in this pretrial report on "trialability" as potentially prejudicial to R.R.'s case. Not surprisingly, however, professional input on these matters was subsequently sought by a court order with a different forensic question.

Criminal Responsibility, Part I

The area which has perhaps received the most attention falls under the heading of the plea of "not guilty by reason of insanity." This plea is raised only by the defense, usually by a petition to the court that presents some preliminary rationale. Many jurisdictions have an independent panel of mental health experts who perform the evaluation and report their findings to the court. Should the case be litigated on the question of insanity, they may be called upon by either the defense or the state for testimony. Such an order was entered in the case of R.R.

IN THE CIRCUIT COURT FOR JESSUP COUNTY, MARYLAND

STATE OF MARYLAND
vs.
[R.R.]
Criminal Trials No: . . .

ORDER FOR MENTAL EXAMINATION
AND
EXAMINATION OF MEDICAL RECORDS:

Pursuant to authority contained in Art. 59, Sec. 25(b), and Sec. 9-109(e) (3), Article, Courts and Judicial Proceedings of the Annotated Code of Maryland, and an appropriate plea having been entered, it is this 5th day of June, 1978, by the Circuit Court for Jessup County, Maryland,

ORDERED, that an examination of the mental condition of the defendant, [R.R.], shall be made by the Department of Health, to determine whether he was insane at the time of the commission of the alleged crime and is competent to stand trial; and that the Department of Health report its findings to this Court within 60 days after the referral as provided by Art. 59, Sec. 26 of the Annotated Code of Maryland, and it is further,

ORDERED, that the State of Maryland, the State's Attorney of Jessup County, or his duly authorized representative, be permitted to examine and inspect any and all relevant records relative to the examination and evaluation of the defendant maintained by Clifton T. Perkins Center, and to discuss the reports and findings of said examination and evaluation with the medical and other personnel of Clifton T. Perkins Center, and it is further,

ORDERED, that the defendant be remanded forthwith to the custody of the Sheriff of Jessup County to be confined to the Jessup County Detention Center to await delivery to the Clifton T. Perkins Center, and upon receipt of notice from the Superintendent of the Clifton T. Perkins Center by the Sheriff of Jessup County of the availability of facilities and personnel for conducting such examination, the said defendant shall forthwith be delivered to said Center, and the said defendant shall remain in the custody of said Center until notification of the completion of said examination at which time the defendant shall be returned to the custody of the Sheriff of Jessup County.

[D. C.], JUDGE[12]

The order not only directs the examiner to inquire into "sanity" at the time of the "alleged crime" but also requests a repeat determination of competency (a status which may fluctuate on a day-to-day basis). The records are opened fully to the prosecutor. Finally, detailed instructions are provided for the custody and transportation of the defendant.

Although the propriety of the "medical excuse" has long been debated,[13-16] misunderstandings still cloud appreciation of certain core issues. Most prominently, it should be apparent that there is no judge, jury, lawyer, court, or psychiatrist who has the power to absolve anyone of personal responsibility for anything that person has done. Nonetheless, mental health professionals may often expend considerable effort in assisting a patient who is grappling with inner feelings of responsibility. The topic which is now being examined is "criminal responsibility," not "personal responsibility." The former is a legal determination made by a community's representatives concerning the application of criminal penalties to an offender; the latter is not an issue resolvable by court decree. While a defendant may be found not "criminally" responsible in the court for an illegal act, he may spend many years thereafter attempting to find some resolution of his sense of "personal" responsibility. This process may occur in a hospital, with the assistance of professionals in mental health fields;[17,18] it may occur in the solitude of prison if the individual is found guilty; or it may occur in other ways if he is found not guilty. Unfortunately, the issue is often ignored altogether as the general concern is with evaluation and disposition rather than resolution.[19]

In R.R.'s case, however, his return to Clifton T. Perkins Center for evaluation of criminal responsibility resulted in a far more extensive inquiry than had been undertaken thus far. Both the police report and the investigative reports were now made available. A social worker interviewed not only the family of the defendant but also, with the state's attorney's authorization, the victims of the assault. Thorough psychological testing was obtained, and detailed nursing observations were made of R.R.'s behavior on the ward. The reports of R.R.'s military psychiatric treatment were obtained. The task this time was, after all, far more complex. R.R.'s state of mind at the time of the alleged offenses four months earlier had to be reconstructed by piecing together observations reported by the victims, the family, the police, and others. Comparisons were then made with the patterns of illness characteristic of patients with similar clinical presentations, symptoms, and signs. Following this synthesis, a clinical assessment of the connection between R.R.'s mental condition and his offenses was to be related to the test for insanity required in the law.

To be excused for criminal behavior, a defendant must evidence severe illness which must be linked clearly to the offenses themselves in accordance with the legal framework supplied in the local community's "test" for "insanity." In this context, "insanity" is exclusively a legal term describing that situation of illness severe enough to satisfy the requirements of the locally accepted "test." In most of the United States, one of the following "tests" is required for a finding of "insanity." The M'Naghten test has been the traditional one borrowed from English law and in use in more than half of the jurisdictions in the United States:

THE M'NAGHTEN TEST[20]

Every man is to be presumed to be sane, and . . . to establish a defense on the ground of insanity, it must be clearly proved that, at the time of the committing of the act, the party accused was labouring under such a defect of reason, from disease of the mind, as not to know the nature and quality of the act he was doing; or if he did know it, that he did not know he was doing what was wrong.

In the twentieth century, many states and the federal courts adopted the recommendation of the Amercian Law Institute in the Model Penal Code. This formulation is usually denoted by the initials ALI:

THE AMERICAN LAW INSTITUTE TEST[21]

1. A person is not responsible for criminal conduct if at the time of such conduct as a result of mental disease or defect he lacks substantial capacity to appreciate the criminality of his conduct or to conform his conduct to the requirements of the law.

2. As noted in the Article, the terms "mental disease or defect" do not include an abnormality manifested only by repeated criminal or otherwise antisocial conduct.

While there are several variations of the precise wording of the tests from state to state and a few alternative tests have been employed, the two cited above are the most widely used. A thorough discussion comparing the meanings which have been attached to these statements is beyond the scope of this chapter. Such analyses are available in several reference works,[22-24] and the current state of the law nationwide is reported in the *Mental Disability Law Reporter*.[25]

There are, however, certain generalities worth reviewing. The defendant must have had something wrong with his mind, whether it is termed a "mental disease or defect," "defective reason," "disease of the mind," or "mental disorder"

(Maryland).[26] There must have been a linkage between what was wrong and the commission of the illegal act. In M'Naghten the focus is on cognitive understanding; in ALI there is a combination of cognition (expressed in the more complex term "appreciate") and a degree of self-control.

The evaluation of clinical data in the light of one of these tests is a complex task. The first of the several parts of ALI asks whether the defendant had "a mental disease or defect" at all. If there was none, then the analysis stops. Otherwise, the next section of ALI is considered. Was there any inability on the part of the defendant either to "appreciate" the criminaltiy of his conduct or to "conform" to the requirements of the law? If there was no inability in these areas, then the analysis stops and the report finds the defendant "sane." If however, there was "some" impairment in the defendant's relevant capacities, then was the degree "substantial"? If not, the report will find the defendant "sane." Finally, if the required elements do exist in the evaluator's opinion, then a determination must be made concerning whether a causal link (". . . as a result of . . .") exists between the defendant's mental condition and his lack of "substantial" capacity.

Each of the key words in the test requires a clear understanding in the evaluator's mind before an opinion on the totality of the test can be reached. From jurisdiction to jurisdiction there are variations in the locally accepted meaning of the words. Similarly, few examiners agree on the precise definition of these somewhat vague terms. Such cloudiness built into the test permits the expert to testify more fully about his own findings and their relationship to the legally mandated requirements for exculpation of criminal responsibility. For example, "mental disease or defect" is usually defined by, but not confined to, conditions listed in the *Diagnostic and Statistical Manual of Mental Disorders* (third edition) known as DSM III.[27] Maryland placed the word "disorder" in its version of ALI to emphasize a broadness of intent to permit application of the test even to those not considered seriously ill. Thus, in Maryland, the word "disorder" has a limited screening function. In other jurisdictions, "mental disease or defect" is interpreted more narrowly.

The phrase "lacks substantial capacity" may be the most difficult in ALI. "Substantial" may be loosely defined as a degree (i.e., more than some, but less than all; more than 70%[28]) or as a quality or depth combined with a degree (i.e., having substance, solidity, reality, meaning, etc.). The *Oxford English Dictionary* lists 18 principal definitions, extending over a page, for this one word.[29] Most of the listed definitions have potential applicability within the context of the ALI test. "Substantial" leads to great consternation and is often the crucial point in the so-called battle of the experts.

The ALI test is called "two-pronged" in that either the cognitive incapacity or the lack of behavioral control is sufficient if the test is otherwise satisfied. The cognitive element of the test demands that the defendant's impairment have been in his capacity to "appreciate" the criminality of his actions. The selection of this term rather than "know" allows the expert to consider and testify about the complex elements of human understanding and their impairment in certain mental illnesses. Under the ALI test, the expert witness is usually permitted greater latitude in presenting his reasoning than is possible under the more specific rubric of M'Naghten.

In Maryland, the ALI test has been modified ("disorder" substituted for "disease or defect"), and it was against this standard that the case of R.R. was evaluated. The case summary follows:

A thirty-four year old married appliance repairman, R.R. was born in Baltimore and has received a high school equivalency. In his earlier years he was subjected to chaotic family conditions characterized by physical fighting between his parents, parental divorce and repeated infidelity. There were step-siblings and step-parents, frequent moves about the country, and ultimately severe beatings which he sustained at the hands of his step-father. He had several set-backs in school and a suspected learning disability while in elementary school. Later, disciplinary problems subsided, but there was little interest in study. He saw himself a ladies' man by middle school and first experienced heterosexual relations at the age of twelve with a classmate. He denied homosexual relationships and declined comment on masturbation.

There was no family history of mental illness, seizure disorders, suicidal attempts, alcoholism or drug abuse, or any prior history of criminality. R.R. denied early separation from mother, witnessing of primal scene, fire-setting, enuresis, or cruelty to pets. Married for the past seven years to his present and only wife, he has functioned reasonably well on his job. There are three children. His psychiatric problems began in the military and are documented in official records. His illness has been characterized by periodic emergence of hyperreligiosity, bizarre behavior in response to hallucinated commands, and delusional thinking. The clinical picture has repeatedly been diagnosed as Schizophrenia, Paranoid Type. According to his wife, R.R. was inconsistent in taking his medications, but complied with her urgings at times when his symptoms intensified. When asked about the offenses, he denied the laundry room assault, but admitted to the second charged offense. His description of the rape was in general agreement with the police report. He recalls lying to his wife about his activities that evening and then driving out of state. ("The voices told me to flee").

"I was at a shopping center. We were sitting around (me and the demon's voice—I only saw the demon once). The voices were laughing at me for missing a bus. Something told me to be like a lion. When a lion eats human meat he desires that flavor. I found a knife handle with two holes and put it into my pocket and walked to this young lady. I asked her for a cigarette; she said 'no'; that upset the demon. A grip came over me; I pushed her to the side; I pulled out the handle; I told her it was a knife and a gun." They drove around until they parked in a deserted area and the assault took place. "I was like in a cave. There was darkness around me. I was maybe trying to scream out. It was like the lion's blood kept singing in my head. Like a story being repeated in a chanting kind of way . . . then repeating 'The blood for the lion' . . .". Walking the streets at night trying to find someone to rape he would feel "Like a lion would feel . . . the taste of human meat."

On mental status examination he presented as a short male who appeared his stated age and was appropriately dressed and groomed. He exhibited excellent eye contact and was aware of the seriousness of his charges. Though somewhat restless, he was correctly oriented and his responses were goal directed and relevant. Although he claimed that last night he heard voices and sounds "mumbling" and cursing and added that he reads the Bible daily, he did not appear to be currently hallucinating. "Lately voices have been my companion. They talk to me; they tell me when to laugh . . . it is evilness, the demon trying to destroy me. I am a slave of the voices . . . now I am fighting back." He evidenced no confabulation or perseveration. Current delusional thinking was not noted. His interpretation of the proverb pertaining to counting unhatched chickens was, "The opposite—don't believe in what you don't see"; on tears for spilled milk, "Don't weep for what is dead and gone." He gave correct responses on tests for hypothetical judgment. There was no evidence of abnormal mood elevation nor depression. Suicidal rumination was absent. Intellectual functions including memory, remote and recent, concentration, computation, and knowledge were grossly intact.

Physical neurologic examination were unremarkable and lab studies were within normal limits.

On psychological testing he was slightly depressed appearing, but cooperative, persistent, and involved in the tasks. His lethargy quickly gave way to interest and energy. Generally, his test behavior was immature. His intellectual function was in the average range, although erratic results suggested a higher potential. Several subtests showed disturbed thought associations and other signs of formal thought disorder. For example, when asked how a poem and a statue were alike, he responded, "they both stand—a poem has stanzas and a statue stands." Projective testing was characterized by distortions, bizarre content, and general impairment in reality testing. Anger and overtly expressed hostility were easily evoked by females or authority figures. Despite his obvious efforts at suppression and censoring, blatant sexual material was rampant on the Rorschach indicating a preoccupation with the subject. Sexual identity was poorly formed and confused.

Social work evaluation revealed confirmation of past illness, but no evidence suggesting bizarreness was elicited from the victims' accounts or the police reports. Nursing reports were particularly interesting in that there was no evidence of bizarreness, hallucinations, or social introversion in the patient's interactions or conduct on the ward.[30]

On June 17, 1978, R.R. was presented before a staff conference attended by five psychiatrists and other staff members who read and reviewed all reports and interviewed the patient. This conference gave all examiners an opportunity to compare their findings and to give particular attention to discrepancies in R.R.'s story. There were many. His execution of the offense showed considerable organizational skills. He lied and left the state after the offense. The staff believed him to be lying about the source of the weapon. His wife did not describe clear exacerbation of his symptoms at the time of the offenses. He had told one of the nursing attendants that he was putting on an act of "make believe" and was afraid he could not convince all the psysicians of his illness. During his interviews, he was particularly interested in the examiners's findings, and "how did I do?" questions were frequent. Most of the evidence for current illness, consisted of self-reported hallucinations. In summation, the staff was of the opinion that although R.R. was a significantly ill man, probably schizophrenic, there was little connection between the natural history of his illness for ten years and the current spree of sexual assaults. Furthermore, there was no hard evidence of a recent decompensation in spite of no medication. The final opinion was schizophrenia, paranoid type, in partial remission; competent to stand trial; responsible at the time of the alleged offense. This opinion was not unanimous, but R.R. elected to withdraw his plea of insanity and to be tried on the merits of the case. He ultimately accepted a sentence of 20 years in exchange for a guilty plea to one count of first degree sexual asaault. R.R. will be eligible for parole in 1982, four years after sentencing.

Criminal Responsibility, Part II

The case of R.R. has demonstrated the process. Now we will examine the general relationships between the insanity defense and sexual offenders in the light of the ALI framework. What sorts of mental disorders do such offenders have; what are some of their styles of presentation? What are the pitfalls in evaluating those accused of such crimes?

Sexual offenders may be viewed within several broad diagnostic categories which generally follow DSM III. The first is loosely subsumed under the heading "psychoses" including, for example, schizophrenic, paranoid, and affective disorders. With the crime of rape, psychotic disorders may manifest extreme grandiosity in which a defendant believes himself irresistible or inaccurately assesses when "no" really means "no." An individual in a paranoid distortion may believe himself righting the wrongs of the world by punishing women with sexual assault. Organic mental disorders and substance-induced disorders are infrequently found in the crime of rape or other sex offenses, since individuals with these disorders are rarely able to organize their behavior sufficiently to perform the complexities of such assaults.

Neurotic conditions, categorized in DSM III as anxiety disorders, somatoform disorders, and dissociative disorders, may also be associated with violent sexual offenses. Of the dissociative disorders, psychogenic amnesia, psychogenic fugue, and multiple personalities are sometimes associated with sexual offenses. Often a defendant, when confronted with the details of the rape, will deny memory of the incident or claim that it must have been someone else. A history of previous episodes of fugue, multiple personality, or amnesia is helpful but usually not confirmable. In any case, mere lack of recall does not alone qualify under ALI for legal insanity. Although such cases may present a dilemma, it is rather convenient for the defendant to have amnesia only while committing crimes, and such claims are to be viewed with skepticism.

It is problematic to evaluate the rare, bona fide case of multiple personality when one of the emerging personalities is that of a sex offender. Should each personality be evaluated independently, or should the predominant personality be the baseline? In this rare circumstance, one must look for at least one episode of the emergence of other personalities, in the absence of criminal charges, which was sufficiently distressing and serious to have led either to hospitalization or to treatment on an outpatient basis. Many defendants contend that "it wasn't the real me," but rarely is this claim based on a mental illness.

The "conduct" disorders (in DSM III, the aggressive and dyscontrol disorders, particularly) including episodic dyscontrol and "temporal lobe" seizures, form a third category. Here, one is considering the defendant who claims to have committed a violent sex act during a "seizure." Certainly, the presence of medically documented seizure episodes without the complication of criminality is evidence supporting this assertion. An abnormal electroencephalogram (EEG) at the time of evaluation is of some value, but not every case of dyscontrol disorder evidences an abnormal EEG and many who are without seizures have irregular EEG findings. As a rule, it is unwise to hinge an entire assessment of criminal responsibility on one or another ancillary test. Additionally, it is extremely difficult in most cases to determine when, in the course of criminal events, an atypical seizure had its onset.

A fourth diagnostic group consists of the DSM III personality and psychosexual disorders. When the defendant claims, "I did it because I couldn't help myself and have always been this way," to what extent is this considered a way of life or a "substantial incapacity"? It is useful in such cases to have confirmatory evidence that on practically every occasion the "irresistible" impulse led to the misbehavior. Then, the level of incapacity might meet the test of "substantial." In the case of a personality disorder or a psychosexual disorder, it is a rare situation in which an individual truly was unable to conform his conduct to the requirements of the law. These disorders are troublesome because they are primarily defined by the specific noxious behavior. Almost invariably, however, the assaultiveness is reserved for opportune times. Careful history will usually demonstrate relatively substantial capacity to control the offensive acts, particularly when the potential for apprehension appears high.

Another broad category of disorders includes substance abuse, whether of alcohol or other agents. "I was high at the time and didn't know what I was doing" and

"I was too drunk to know what was going on" are statements heard frequently. Here the examiner must determine whether there is objective evidence that the substance abuse warranted diagnosis as a disorder and was not simply an unverified diagnosis "by history." Furthermore, were there data proving that any substance was ingested and, if so, was it identified with assurance? Without such data, the claim of intoxication is shaky if the defendant successfully operated a vehicle around the time of the offense, if he stalked the victim, if he attempted to evade arrest, or if he exhibited other behaviors indicating relative awareness. However, occasionally the assailant has fallen asleep after the commission of a rape and been pushed aside by the victim who was able to make escape. Such instances suggest the possibility of intoxication. Once again, one must recognize that merely establishing that a defendant was intoxicated is in no way tantamount to a finding of "not responsible."

Many jurisdictions have a specific caveat excluding "voluntary intoxication" from the insanity defense.[31] Operationally, "intoxication" has been expanded to include both drugs and alcohol. Occasionally, chronic substance abuse may lead to brain damage and "substance abuse psychosis." Organic brain syndromes generally are relevant to the insanity issue. These conditions would have had to impede significantly the defendant's judgment with regard to future contact with the intoxicants—an extreme impairment with global manifestations in psychological function. The test's requirement for a linkage betwen the crime and the illness, however, would still exist.

Mentally retarded offenders present special problems in evaluation and management. Although measurement of intelligence quotient (IQ) by specific recognized psychological testing instruments[32] is necessary, the assessment of "street intelligence" may be quite relevant to the forensic task. The tests applied for determining competency and responsibility are no different for the retarded individual. While he may not be able to explain clearly his legal predicament, he may still have an adequate notion of what court process is about, what possible consequences he may face, and what defense options are available. Often patience on the part of the examiner in conducting the interview and in his choice of words will enable the mentally retarded defendant to express himself adequately. Should such an individual be found incompetent on the basis of retardation alone, he may face prolonged confinement. Assessment of educability may be relevant to the overall choice of options in these cases. A lack of social experience and poor impulse control are frequent features of retardation that may be relevant to criminal responsibility. In the case of child molestation and perhaps in other sexual crimes, the individuals may be of comparable psychological age although vastly different in chronological age. The rules supplied by the legal tests must still be applied. Immaturity of judgment may be far from "substantial" impairment in either cognition or self-control.

Having explored the issues of diagnosis, the evaluator then must relate the sexual assaultiveness to the "two-pronged" portion of the ALI test. The first question,

Did the defendant lack "substantial capacity to appreciate" the criminality? is often answerable in large part by a review of the facts of the case. Here it is important to establish whether the offense was premeditated, planned, thought out; whether there was effort at evasion, lying, concealment of evidence, avoidance of police questioning. What sort of explanation was given at the time of arrest? Rapists and other violent sexual offenders may generally be divided into two types; predators or opportunists. The former evidence considerable care in identifying a victim, stalking their prey, and attacking. They may use disguises. There may be carefully prepared escape routes and attempts to identify the victim and to ensure that she is alone. Such well-organized behavior often establishes that the defendant met the cognitive portion of the ALI test no matter what construction is given to "appreciate." One possible exception might be an individual beset with severe psychosis who believes his sexual performance satisfies some mystically higher purpose. When the predatory offender reaches the level of serious consideration for a recommendation of nonresponsibility, he usually manifests marked distortion of reality testing.

Opportunists, however, are those sexual offenders who commit crimes with little planning or on impulse. They include the man who pounces on a solitary woman in a secluded spot or the man who refuses to accept his anticipated partner's change of heart which leads to an unexpected refusal. In these cases, the short time frame before the offense often limits data on state of mind, but a consideration of the defendant's conduct afterwards should be of consequence. What efforts were made to avoid detection? Did the defendant provide an explanation which changed the facts in ways to minimize the incriminating points, thereby evidencing his awareness of wrongfulness? These cases frequently are a battle of credibility between the victim and the defendant in establishing whether the sexual acts were consensual or forced.

Whether dealing with predator or opportunist, if the examiner establishes that cognitive impairment did not meet the ALI requirements, he may move on to the section on self-control. Did the defendant "lack substantial capacity to conform his conduct to the requirements of the law"? In most cases, this part of the analysis is usually germane to those offenses which are opportunistic in nature. If a defendant explains, "I did it because I couldn't help myself," then the logical question is how often was the potential offense contained rather than committed. It often turns out that likelihood of apprehension was the deciding factor. Such cases usually fail to satisfy the second prong of ALI. It is rare to hear of a case of a woman raped in the lingerie section of a busy department store, but not uncommon for the assault to occur in a storage area out of the general traffic. The issue of behavioral control is often raised, however, in cases of exhibitionism and homosexual pedophilia. Although the former problem is not usually considered a violent sexual offense, in some cases the behavior is so persistent and overt that the question of capacity to conform to the law is seriously at issue. The pedophile whose behavior becomes ritualistic and repetitive may also present a serious question under this part of ALI.

Usually, however, it is rare to establish insanity on the second prong alone, but rather when there is also significant compromise in the cognitive sphere.

In determining "substantial," it is helpful to consider whether the impairment is global. If a defendant alleged that he was righting the wrongs of the world and claimed bizarre manifestations (viz. R.R.), yet worked full-time at his job, went to the movies the night before, and played bridge two nights earlier, one would become cautious on the question of degree of incapacity. If on the other hand, he was leading the life of a recluse, had been locking himself in his room, feared conspiracies against his world leadership, etc., then there would be support for the significance of his impairment. Obviously, the observations by family and associates of his behavior around the time of the offense can be critical in establishing a pattern consistent with severe illness. With each interview of these informants, one should attempt to reconstruct the mental status of the defendant through the other person's eyes. Questions about the defendant's physical appearance and personal hygiene, his ability to converse in a relevant and goal-directed manner, the ideas he expressed, and his mood are all vital in this retrospective construct. It is rare that a defendant's illness had the substance to render him not criminally responsible for a particular act, yet did not extend to many other areas of his life. For example, one might inquire about the overall sexual relationships of the defendant accused of rape. A finding of little impairment might argue against a finding of insanity for a sexual offense.

The last broad area to be considered in the analysis of the ALI test is the causal connection (". . . as a result of . . .") between the illness and the lack of capacity. Often the specific criminal act is linked poorly, if at all, to the mental illness. Here, perhaps more than in other areas, it is important to find out what was in the defendant's mind at the exact time of the offense. If he justifies the act with a recitation of delusional material, this weighs toward causality. Paranoid defendants often feel they are helping themselves by alleging inability to recall details when, in fact, the details might be most supportive to the defense strategy. Although in such cases collateral sources may be sufficient, it might be necessary to defer an opinion on responsibility until the defendant is able to come forward with more specific information about his thought content when the crime occurred. It may be appropriate in these cases to reconsider competency to assist defense and postpone legal proceedings until more trust has been established.

Diminished Capacity

A recent development has been the introduction of the concept of diminished capacity. This defense has been applied in cases of homicide to show that the defendant lacked the mental capacity to form the requisite intent for first degree murder. The result of its application might be conviction of a lesser included offense. While rape is not an offense for which intent is graded, as is murder, the defense of diminished capacity may still appear as the boundaries are tested for ameliorative presentations to the court. There is, at this writing, no uniformity of definition from state to state, but several agree that the burden is on the defendant to prove the fact of his mental condition.[33] Morse has argued against the concept, believing that all legally sane offenders should be held fully accountable.[34] In his view, the issue remains whether or not the offender could have controlled his conduct rather than the matter of degree of culpability. In evaluating "diminished capacity," the clinician is faced with the same task of in-depth examination as in evaluating responsibility. The pitfall to be avoided is guessing the legal issues. Since the laws and court precedents defining the concept are so variable, it is necessary to have the requestor of the examination forward the relevant legal guidance for the precise questions to be addressed. This is an important general principle for any forensic work. There will always be new areas in which the court will find the need for expert testimony in psychological matters, whether these concern "diminished capacity," "guilty but mentally ill," the death penalty, presentence or prerelease reports, or other areas. The forensic practitioner should always assure himself that the legal questions to be addressed and the precedential case concepts have been formally propounded for his review and analysis prior to the clinical interview. When he has digested this material, the evaluator can begin the process of relating the clinical information to the formal legal question.

According to Morse's view of diminished capacity, R.R. would not have been a candidate since he was evaluated to be legally sane. However, it is likely that the clear documentary evidence of his past illness may have encouraged the plea bargaining process and the judge's willingness to accept such an agreement. Thus, indirectly and informally, the diminished capacity defense may have entered into the overall disposition of the case.

In summary, forensic mental evaluations should be carefully documented at the time the interviews occur. Quotations should be recorded carefully, and the clinical data should be fully explored. That the reports will often be presented in court and form the basis of cross-examination should always be kept in mind whenever a forensic case study is prepared. On the other hand, one is never in possession of all the potentially available facts in a case. Often, the undisclosed data are critical and may not appear until trial. Opinions must always be based on the available data. Therefore, if new facts are presented, revision of opinion may be necessary. The multidisciplinary approach facilitates thoroughness and minimizes this source of error. Invariably, clarity and precision of language are desirable. Evaluative reports are usually directed to lawyers, judges, and juries—all of whom will be confused, rather than assisted, by jargon. Finally, it is important to understand the legal questions and to answer appropriately. Thus, the evaluator must insist on clear questions from the legal community and adequate interpretations of its jargon.

Performing forensic mental evaluations of violent sexual offenders is demanding and at time terrifying work. The emotional stresses on the examiner in collecting the data, confronting and evaluating the accused, facing the tension of the courtroom, and working in forsaken dungeons are only rivaled by the strain of containing the extreme countertransference forces engendered. The offenses are sordid and repugnant; the defendants are often aggressive and hostile. One's own inner emotional forces become powerfully aroused and threatening. The clinician, trained to attempt to empathize with his patient, may experience self-revulsion. It is important, therefore, that those in the field work together, share their experience, and provide group support. The importance of some institutional setting, such as a hospital, court clinic, or university clinic, providing multidisciplinary resources cannot be overemphasized in this context. The work, while trying, absorbs clinicians of many backgrounds in its challenge. The boundaries of knowledge in the behavioral sciences are closely scrutinized and public policy is shaped as mental health workers explore this interface with the law.

REFERENCES

1. Ferriter, M.G. Report of Investigation. Prince George's County, Md., 1981, CCN 81-095-659.
2. Ferriter, M.G. Report of Investigation. Prince George's County, Md., 1981, CCN 81-102-021.
3. Frank, W. Admission Note (excerpt from Case Records of Clifton T. Perkins Hospital Center: #8449). Jessup, Md., 1981.
4. *Hill* v. *State*, 35 Md. App. 98, 369 A.2d 98 (1977).
5. *Raithel* v. *State*, 280 Md. 291, 372 A.2d 1069 (1977).
6. Cf. reference; see also: *Dusky* v. *United States*, 362 U.S. 402 (1960).
7. Thornton, L. Nursing Note (excerpt from Case Records of Clifton T. Perkins Hospital Center: #8449). Jessup, Md., 1981.
8. McGarry, L. et al. *Handbook, Competency to Stand Trial and Mental Illness.* Rockville, Md.: National Institute of Mental Health, 1973.
9. Silver, S.B. *Forensic psychiatry in Maryland–present and future.* Presented to the Maryland Community Mental Health Advisory Council, Catonsville, Md., 1980.
10. Slovenko, R. *Psychiatry and Law.* Boston: Little, Brown, 1973, p. 37.
11. Silver, S.B. Court Letter (excerpt from Case Records of the Clifton T. Perkins Hospital Center: #8449). Jessup, Md., 1981.
12. Loveless, E.A. Order. Circuit Court for Prince George's County, Md. 1981.
13. Szasz, T. *Law, Liberty, and Psychiatry.* New York: Collier, 1968.
14. Ray, I. *Treatise on the Medical Jurisprudence.* Boston: Little, Brown 1838, pp. 276-278.
15. Halpern, A.L. *The insanity defense: a judicial anachronism. Psych. Annals* 7(8):398–409 (1977).
16. Menninger, K. *The Crime of Punishment.* New York; Viking, 1968.
17. Spodak, M.K. et al. The hormonal treatment of paraphiliacs with Depo-Provera. *Criminal Justice and Behavior* 5(4):304-314 (1978).
18. Goldmeier, J. et al. A halfway house for mentally ill offenders. *American Journal of Psychiatry* 134(i):45-49 (1977).
19. Silver, S.B. Criminal responsibility: a psychiatric point of view. In Fields, J.R. et al. (Ed.) *Handbook of Violence and Prevention* (in press).
20. Daniel M'Naghten's Case. 10 Clark & Fin. 200, 8 Eng. Reprint 718 (1843).
21. American Law Institute, Model Penal Code, Proposed Official Draft Sec. 4.01 (1962).
22. Allen, R.C. Ferster, E.Z., & Rubin, J.G. *Readings in Law and Psychiatry.* Baltimore: Johns Hopkins Press, 1968, pp. 414-447.
23. Sauer, R.H. and Mullens, P. The insanity defense: M'Naghten vs. ALI. *Bull. Amer. Acad. Psychiatry Law* 4(1):73-75 (1976).

24. Fingarette, H. and Hasse, A.F. *Mental Disabilities and Criminal Responsibility*. Berkeley: University of California, 1979.
25. *Mental Disability Law Reporter*. Commission on the Mentally Disabled, American Bar Association, Washington, D.C.
26. Annotated Code of Maryland, Art. 59, Sec. 23.
27. *Diagnostic and Statistical Manual of the Mental Disorders*, 3rd. ed. Washington, D.C.: The American Psychiatric Association, 1980.
28. Rappeport, J. Personal communication.
29. *The Compact Edition of the Oxford English Dictionary*, New York: Oxford University Press, 1971.
30. Case Records of Clifton T. Perkins Hospital Center: #8449 Jessup, Md. 1981.
31. Slovenko, op. cit., pp. 143-156.
32. Wechsler, D. *The Measurement of Adult Intelligence,* 4th ed. Baltimore: Williams & Wilkins, 1958.
33. *Mental Disability Law Reporter* **4**(4):229-230 (1980).
34. Morse, S.J. Diminished capacity: a moral and legal conundrum. *Int. J. Law Psychiatry* **2**:271-298 (1979).

4
Program Considerations in the Treatment of Incest Offenders

Kee MacFarlane, M.S.W.

This chapter conceptualizes and describes some of the common themes and components of specialized intrafamily child sexual abuse treatment programs. The author points out that there is currently a lack of available evaluation data on the effects of intervention programs as well as on the validity of various types of treatment methods. This is a general critique of all such programs as well as a description of their major techniques and goals. The purpose is to provide a broad view of the major issues, and in relation to this, the author discusses the clinical, legal, and systematic problems which led to the development of such specialized programs for incest offenders.

INTRODUCTION

Sexual abuse of children is a problem that has received widespread media coverage and attention from the professional community only in the last few years. Despite ample documentation that children have been sexually exploited by adults throughout history (Rush, 1980), that childhood sexual experiences are so widespread as to be considered virtually universal by some researchers (Finkelhor, 1979), and that the problem has been reported and discussed in professional literature since the turn of the century (Finkelhor, 1979), society has been slow to respond with any systematic efforts to prevent or treat it. Although estimates of incidence range from several hundred thousand to several million cases annually, child sexual abuse has, until recently, retained the status of an isolated social problem, rather than what Finkelhor (1979) defines as a public issue — one that is recognized by a broad segment of society, intervention systems, and policy makers.

Its rapidly changing status from that of a hidden issue to the subject of daytime television talk shows has been accompanied by many promising developments in the fields of child protection and treatment. Despite the fact that sexual abuse is thought to be the most under-reported form of child abuse, the number of cases which are investigated and substantiated by public child protection agencies has nearly doubled each year since 1976, when data collection began on a national level (*Annual Summary of National Child Neglect and Abuse Reporting,*

1976-1980). This is generally thought to be a reflection of increased awareness and reporting, rather than an increase in actual incidence. Similarly, after decades of very sparse literature, consisting primarily of clinical observations reported in medical journals, more than a dozen books and scores of articles devoted to the subject of child sexual abuse have been published since 1978. As is often the case in a newly evolving field, most of these publications have focused on problem definition, describing the population, and speculation as to causes and effects of the problem, rather than on what to do about it once it has been discovered.

Despite the limited availability of historical data, evaluation research, and treatment theory, rapid progress in the area of program development has occurred throughout the country. As recently as 1976, in a survey of treatment programs for sex offenders in the United States, only one program* was identified that dealt exclusively with perpetrators of child sexual abuse (Brecher, 1978). Today there are more than 300 programs nationwide that either contain specialized components or were exclusively designed to deal with various aspects of this problem. Although there is wide variance with regard to the philosophies, treatment approaches, and level of services offered by these programs, the fact of their establishment in such a short period of time (most are less than three years old) speaks to the growing awareness of the need to systematically address this pervasive problem.

The purpose of this chapter is to provide a broad view of the major treatment issues and approaches that are currently being utilized, and to describe some of the clinical, legal, and systemic problems that led to the development of specialized treatment programs. More detailed information on the various types of treatment models, specific treatments methods, and legal approaches is available in some of the publications listed in the references at the end of this chapter.

The terms "incest" and "intrafamily child sexual abuse" have various definitions depending upon the purpose and context in which they are being used. For purposes of this chapter, they will be used interchangeably to mean sexual contacts or interactions (ranging from exhibitionism and inappropriate touching to forcible penetration) between a child and a family member when the child is being used as an object of sexual gratification for adult needs. To further clarify the scope of this discussion, the terms "family member" and "adult" are used to refer to a parent, legal guardian, permanent caretaker, parent figure (such as a live-in partner of a parent), or a relative in the home who is in a position of power or authority over a child (such as a grandparent or significantly older sibling). It is not the intention of this definition to minimize the nature of the abuse, but rather to emphasize the relationship between perpetrator and child since that is such a strong focus of the program issues to be discussed. Further, this chapter is limited to an examination of only those programs and services that provide treatment to entire families in

---

*The Child Sexual Abuse Treatment Program, Juvenile Probation Department, San Jose, California.

nonresidential, community settings. It does not attempt to address any forms of nonfamilial pedophilia; rather, its focus is on those unique aspects of intrafamily child sexual abuse which have been found to require specialized treatment considerations.

PROGRAM CONSIDERATIONS

The problem of intrafamily child sexual abuse falls into many categories and can be viewed from many perspectives. The fact that it may be regarded simultaneously as a crime, a form of child maltreatment, a mental illness, a type of sexual deviance, and a family problem or dysfunction that affects every member of a family gives rise to a wide range of different attitudes, as well as to the involvement of a variety of intervention systems. It is not uncommon for a case to fall within the purview of the police, district attorney's office, criminal court, juvenile court, mandated child protection agency, and any number of other public and private mental health and social service agencies. Aside from the confusion felt by families who must relate to these various systems, the professionals involved often find themselves in positions that involve overlapping mandates and conflicting objectives. In order to understand the rationale and goals of the specialized programs that were designed to address these and other issues associated with treating child sexual abuse, it is important to be aware of the major factors that led to their development. The following is a brief summary of some of the program considerations and treatment limitations of traditional legal and therapeutic approaches to this problem.

Incest as a Crime

Few would dispute the fact that our criminal justice system was not well designed to deal with the crime of child sexual abuse. In a system that relies heavily on physical and circumstantial evidence, reliability of testimony, and cooperation from witnesses for the prosecution, there is little room for the legal and interpersonal difficulties associated with these cases. Often, there is no physical or medical evidence of sexual contact, no corroborative witnesses, and little or no substantive grounds for establishing motive, opportunity, or even the fact that a crime has been committed. Expert testimony, psychological evaluations, and testing often amount to no more than educated guesswork. Establishing the credibility of child victims (especially in the increasing number of cases of children under the age of 5) is a major barrier to successful prosecution. Even so, the word of a young child may be the only thing the prosecution has on which to establish the basis for a criminal case. In addition, the cooperation of the victim and other family members is not something which can be assumed once they realize that their testimonies may contribute to the incarceration and ultimate loss of their major source of economic and emotional support. The ties that bind some incestuous families, regardless of how dysfunctional, are no less strong than those found in many other families. Many initial reports have later been retracted out of fear of family disintegration and a child's guilt at being asked to help convict his or her parent (Giarretto, 1976). Similarly, few accused perpetrators are motivated to plead guilty when alternatives to incarceration or loss of their children are few, and they perceive themselves as having little to gain and everything to lose.

Incest as an Illness

Traditional approaches to psychotherapy, like traditional forms of legal intervention, usually operate on the basis of certain broad assumptions or premises. Often these are related to concepts of client motivation, voluntariness, personal insight, and the desire to change attitudes or behavior. Not only are many of these factors initially absent in most incest cases (which usually come to public and professional atttention only after discovery and involuntary intervention by the system), but the very act of voluntarily seeking psychological counseling for this problem can put perpetrators in jeopardy of criminal prosecution and/or removal of their children. Indeed, therapists in virtually every state are required by law to breach confidentiality with regard to their suspicions or knowledge of child sexual abuse by reporting all cases to mandated authorities.

Even in cases where therapy is court ordered as a result of a criminal or juvenile court disposition, traditional once-a-week, individual modes of psychotherapy have not proven to be very effective with this population when offered in the absence of other types of intervention (Giarretto, 1976; MacFarlane and Bulkley, 1981). Without the therapeutic involvement of other family members, there is little opportunity to confront any family dynamics that may have resulted from, contributed to, or acted to prevent the abuse. In addition, there is no real feedback loop to provide the therapist with an ongoing barometer of how things are going in the home—a particularly critical issue if the whole family is still living under the same roof. Private, individual therapy may also serve to reinforce the secrecy and collusion associated with incestuous families, and reduce a sense of accountability in the therapist.

Finally, the stigma and shame that usually accompany this problem are so great, and the treatment issues are so painful to confront, that even when a client is not afraid of further retribution from the system, his denial and resistance to treatment are formidable obstacles for the most skilled therapists. Unfortunately, few psychotherapists, regardless of their educational credentials, have any real expertise in treating this problem due to lack of experience with these cases and limited, if any, specialized training.

Incest as Child Abuse

Child protection systems, including public child welfare agencies and juvenile or family courts, are oriented toward protecting children at risk and strengthening familes when that is in the best interests of children and other family members. As such, their objectives are presumed to be less threatening to families than those of the criminal court, and their procedures less rigorous and traumatic for children. However, they also have less control over perpetrators and other adults in the home, which leaves control over the placement and custody of children as their main source of leverage in bringing about needed changes. In some families that threat serves as a major motivating factor, but in others it is not enough to overcome the fear or resistance to the changes being asked. In such cases, it is usually the children who suffer the greatest consequences. Probably the most common example of this occurs when the court lacks the authority or the ability to order a perpetrator whom it considers to be a continuing risk to a child, out of a home in which that child might otherwise be able to remain with the rest of his or her family. Sometimes all of the siblings in a family are removed as well and placed in separate foster homes due to the shortage of residential placements. When this happens, the guilt that children often feel for the abuse, or for its discovery, is usually greatly increased, and they are left feeling abandoned and punished for their perceived part in it.

Additionally, although juvenile courts have the authority to order needed family supervision and supportive services, and child protection agencies have the mandate to provide them, rarely, if ever, do they receive the resources necessary to meet the demand. Even before the current budget cuts were applied to social service agencies throughout the country, child protection units were understaffed, underpaid, undertrained, and overworked. Today, as case loads continue to increase while resources rapidly dwindle, their ability to respond adequately to the long-term treatment needs of incestuous families is minimal at best.

Incest as an Avenue to System-induced Trauma

No discussion of the factors that led to the development of specialized treatment programs for intrafamily child sexual abuse would be complete without mentioning the concern on the part of many involved professionals that some children were as traumatized by the insensitive and duplicative efforts of our intervention systems as they had been by the original abuse. Multiple interviews by as many as 10 or 15 different professionals were (and still are) not uncommon. Insensitive interrogation by police, prosecutors, and social workers—both in and outside of courtrooms— and subjection to gynecological, psychological, and polygraph testing left many children feeling as though they were only valued as sources of evidence. It came as no surprise to many who worked in this system that as this process continued, many children became frightened and denied the abuse, were reluctant to cooperate, or began to exhibit new behavioral and emotional problems. Some of those professionals began to search for more coordinated and flexible systems for dealing with this problem—ones that could accommodate some of the vulnerabilities and needs of children that go beyond merely assuring their physical safety.

PROGRAM APPROACHES

The specific approaches or objectives of incest treatment programs are often related to such factors as the nature of the interface between their legal and therapeutic components, the auspices under which they operate, and the professional disciplines that had the most influence on their development. As a consequence, they are difficult to characterize as a group, and most generalizations can be punctuated by their exceptions. Nonetheless, at the risk of oversimplification, some observations on a few of the most common characteristics of these programs are offered for consideration.

Program Objectives

Although the diversity among treatment programs calls for program analysis on an individual basis in order to fully appreciate their goals and objectives, there are things to be learned about intrafamily child sexual abuse by examining some of the similar assumptions and objectives that exist across programs. The following are examples of overall program objectives which this author has found to be indicative of most specialized incest treatment programs.

Therapeutic Alternatives to Incarceration.   While there are some state prisons and psychiatric inpatient facilities that provide specialized treatment for incest offenders, most are quite limited in what they are able to offer, and few provide therapy that involves other family members. Some community-based treatment programs do provide therapy for parents who are confined in county correctional facilities through work-release type programs and special arrangements that allow perpetrators to attend weekly therapy sessions outside of jail. Most clients of specialized community treatment programs, however, do not serve time in any type of correctional facility, and few programs, as a general rule, advocate that they do so.

Since so few prisons offer specialized treatment for this problem, incarceration for sexually abusive parents is regarded by many as (1) nonproductive time during which there is little opportunity for perpetrators to receive help or gain insight into the underlying causes of the abuse; (2) a disincentive to obtaining treatment following incarceration due to the feeling that the debt to society has been paid; (3) more costly to society than outpatient treatment, while doing little or nothing to prevent the perpetrator and other family members from later establishing another dysfunctional family in which children will be exploited; and (4) an unnecessary financial and emotional hardship on the rest of the family, regardless of whether or not they choose to try to rehabilitate the family as a unit. Further, incarceration of incest offenders or their nonprotective spouses is thought by many to do little to deter potential abusers because of the complex nature and motives of the crime. It may even serve the opposite purpose, since so many children report that they remained silent because of their fear of causing a parent to go to prison.

Incarceration of child sex offenders can be seen to serve two other primary purposes in cases of incest. One is strictly as a punishment for a crime committed and proven in court. The other may be seen as a means of protecting society (in this case, its children) from persons who represent a continuing threat to health or safety. The first purpose is hardly debatable (aside from the previously mentioned costs and problems associated with obtaining convictions), but the second point is important in understanding the approaches and experiences of most of the specialized programs. In keeping with the conceptualizations formulated by Nicholas Groth (1978) in his differential theory concerning fixated versus regressed child sex offenders, incestuous child abuse is generally regarded as a different phenomenon from the type of pedophilia associated with child molestation or assault by a stranger. Unlike the fixated pedophile who, as a lifelong pattern, derives primary or exclusive sexual gratification from prepubertal children, the perpetrators of intrafamily child sexual abuse usually derive sexual gratification from adult heterosexual partners. They usually do not present histories as sexual predators of children; rather, they are more likely to have turned to a child close to them for sexual gratification at some conflictual point in their lives.

Although it is clear that there are cases which overlap these two categories (since fixated offenders are hardly immune from sexually abusing children in their own homes), Groth's differentiation of these two types of offenders has been met with general concurrence over the years from professionals working in this field. A significant consequence of this differentiation, in relation to treatment approaches, has to do with the question of a perpetrator's ongoing dangerousness to children once the sexual abuse has been detected. The detection and exposure of intrafamily child sexual abuse may themselves act as major deterrents to its continuance, since incest can usually only continue in homes where it is kept a secret between the victim and the perpetrator, or where its occurrence is consciously or unconsciously denied by others. This is not to imply that intervention is not warranted or that regressed, incestuous offenders do not require treatment, but rather that the focus of intervention and the risks of revictimization are usually different from cases of fixated pedophiles. The primary issue, in most cases of regressed intrafamily child sexual abuse, becomes one of protecting the child or children with whom the perpetrator has had sexual contact, rather than necessarily having to protect children in general. Since such protection can be obtained through several means which do not require imprisonment of the perpetrator, the use of incarceration in cases of incest, given the previously mentioned disadvantages, is often regarded as both unnecessary for the protection of society and undesirable with regard to the best interests of children and families.

This discussion represents an attempt to explain some of the reasons why incarceration is often seen as unnecessary and unhelpful to the treatment process in these cases. However, the objective of most programs in offering a therapeutic alternative to prison usually goes beyond even these factors. It goes back to the fundamental issue of serving the best interests of children by providing their abusers with incentives to cooperate with a system that seeks to protect children from the rigors and effects of criminal prosecution and from the guilt and self-blame that can accompany that process. When forced to choose between incarceration and even a slim chance of saving themselves and their families through an acquittal, parents and siblings will often sacrifice the identified child victim and fight the charges all the way. This can happen even in cases where perpetrators genuinely care about their children and know that they need and want help for themselves. The therapeutic alternatives to imprisonment offered by virtually every comprehensive incest program not only seek to avoid choices that leave children as the losers, but also contribute to the increased reporting of cases that otherwise would go unreported due to families' fear of consequences and assumption that real help is not available.

Reduction of Trauma to the Child.   It is clear that prevention or reduction of system-induced trauma to children is a major objective of specialized incest treatment programs, and there are many ways that this mandate is being addressed. As already mentioned, children are being spared lengthy interrogation, evidence gathering procedures, and exposure to criminal and juvenile court proceedings through programs which are having marked success in obtaining guilty pleas or acknowledgment by perpetrators of responsibility for the sexual abuse. Similarly, placement of children outside their homes is often unnecessary because a frequent program objective is getting the abuser out of the home. In some cases, this is accomplished by means of court orders; in other programs, it is an initial condition of acceptance into treatment; and in some instances, it is done on a more voluntary basis—as a part of a program's recommendations to a family concerning what will further the interests of the treatment process. In cases where placement is determined to be in the best interests of a child (usually during the initial crisis of discovery or when the nonabusing parent is unsupportive or blames the victim), efforts are made to keep placement as short-term as possible and to secure specialized homes where adults have been sensitized and trained to deal with this problem. Similarly, some programs have helped to arrange group living facilities for perpetrators where they can get needed emotional support from one another and reduce the additional financial burden of supporting two households.

Many techniques also have been developed to lessen the negative impact of the criminal justice process on children when it is necessary to take cases to trial. Coordinating the information needs of the various intervention systems into one or two interviews with skilled professionals using specialized toys and art materials has reduced the need for a child to repeat the story over and over. Videotaping such interviews not only aids in meeting that objective but may be able to substitute for live testimony in some cases. The types of modifications of legal and medical procedures that have been developed in the interests of childrens' needs are too numerous to mention, but they stand as clear evidence of a strong and common objective among programs.

Providing Treatment for the Entire Family.   In seeing incestuous abuse as a symptom of a perpetrator's and a family's problems, rather than as a cause or end product in itself, most programs advocate strongly that treatment efforts involve all members of a family. This is not to say that the goal of treatment is necessarily to reunify or "save" the family as a unit. Rather, the goals are more often focused on helping family members to gain insight into the dysfunctional patterns that may have existed among them, to understand how they have been affected by the problem, and to recognize the options that are available to them so that they can make responsible choices about their futures. Family treatment helps to develop channels of communication that are often missing, to reduce scapegoating of individual members, and to break open the secrets and distrust that fostered the environment in which incest could occur. Children need individual treatment to help them cope with what has happened to them or their siblings. They, like the nonabusive parent, usually benefit from the opportunity to work out some of those issues with the perpetrator in a structured, supportive setting. Few therapists can provide a child with the kind of absolution of guilt that an abuser can when he acknowledges to the child his full responsibility for the abuse. Family treatment in therapy does not necessarily mean seeing all family members together in therapy sessions—it can include a variety of treatment modalities—but it does involve engaging family members in examining those issues and events that have affected them all.

Legal and Therapeutic Coordination

The relationship between the legal and the therapeutic components of incest treatment systems obviously has had a major influence on how these systems operate and what they can provide for families. Few treatment programs operate independently of the mandated justice and child protective systems in their communities, although the nature and the degree of their involvement vary greatly. While some programs regard the applied coercion of the criminal justice system as antithetical to the goals of the treatment process (and, therefore, seek to avoid its involvement), many view the legal system as crucial in providing the authoritative incentive necessary to get perpetrators and their families to participate in treatment (Bulkley, 1981(b)). Some approaches have involved a major restructuring of traditional legal processes and dispositions in incest cases, and have resulted in considerable statutory and procedural changes in several jurisdictions. Detailed descriptions of some of the programs which exemplify these changes are currently available (Bulkley, 1981(a)). The following represents a brief overview of the three major types of coordinated approaches.

Postconviction, Therapeutic Sentencing.   One approach, sometimes referred to as "alternative sentencing," involves providing treatment for the perpetrator (and, hopefully, the rest of the family) as a condition of the criminal court disposition. It is usually characterized by innovative police or presecutor's techniques for securing confessions (thereby avoiding the involvement of children in trials) and the immediate engagement of families in treatment (giving additional validity to professional's recommendations with regard to "treatability," depending on the amount of time before the dispositional hearing and sentencing). The length of sentences or probation varies, and prison terms are infrequent in these programs. However, if incarcerated, perpetrators generally serve time in local county jails which often permit them to retain their jobs and attend treatment sessions. Like the model program in this category which was begun in San Jose, California, most systems utilizing this approach rely heavily on the participation of self-help groups, such as Parents United, to provide support to new parents and encourage their voluntary participation in the programs. It is usually the crisis intervention by families who have been through the experience that provides the validation and trust needed by new families.

Pretrial Diversion.   Another approach involves diverting an accused perpetrator from the criminal process prior to trial and sometime prior to the filing of formal charges. As with the sentencing arrangements in the previous approach, the diversion is usually offered in exchange for a perpetrator's acknowledgment of guilt and performance of carefully specified obligations—most notably, successful completion of a treatment program (though it may include such provisions as vacating the home, assuming financial responsibility for treatment, and maintaining no contact with his or other children except under supervision). Advocates of diversion point out the added motivation for a perpetrator to avoid the stigma of a criminal record, since charges are usually dropped or the case dismissed once he has been discharged from treatment. At the same time, he remains under the control of the criminal justice system during the entire period of treatment or supervision, fully subject to the instigation of charges, prosecution, and criminal sanctions if the terms of the diversion agreement are violated.

Coordinated Criminal and Juvenile Court Processing.   While most specialized treatment systems involve considerable coordination between criminal and juvenile courts, the primary focus of action and legal jurisdiction of those previously mentioned is clearly the criminal court. The approach being considered here, however, involves primary jurisdiction in the juvenile court where efforts are made to secure agreements from the perpetrator and family to obtain treatment or undertake other obligations in exchange for deferring criminal prosecution (Bulkley, 1981). This approach is similar to pretrial diversion in that prosecution is subsequently initiated if agreements are violated, but it utilizes the juvenile court to avoid the need for initiating separate proceedings.

Program Settings and Program Components

The settings for specialized incest treatment programs are as diverse as some of their philosophies. They include child protection agencies, probation departments and court services, hospitals, mental health centers, runaway youth programs, rape centers, university outpatient programs, a host of private service agencies, and even police departments. Program settings do not necessarily determine program approaches since so many factors that influence program direction are dependent upon the individuals, attitudes, and resources available in a community. It is interesting to note, however, that most programs grew out of the convictions and coordinated efforts of a very few people in each community, (usually with very limited funds), who were determined to improve the systems that existed to deal with this problem.

Some of the treatment components of specialized programs have already been mentioned or alluded to in this chapter. One of the most common components across programs consists of self-help groups. Some of these are formal organizations—notably the more than 80 chapters of Parents United, and Daughters and Sons United, that exist in many parts of the country; others are more loosely affiliated networks of family members associated with the various treatment programs. In keeping with the belief of many professionals that group intervention is one of, if not the, preferred mode of treatment for incestuous abuse, self-help organizations are regarded as crucial components for the successful operation of many programs.

The emphasis on group work has not minimized the need that many programs see for sustained individual treatment of family members. Not only does individual therapy permit the privacy and security that victims and perpetrators often need to deal with certain kinds of therapeutic material, but it also allows the therapist to operate in the role of advocate for individual family members who may be overwhelmed by the system or by other family and group members. In addition, many programs develop treatment teams made up of all the professionals working with individual members of a family, in order to gain perspectives on the various family dynamics and coordinate a consistent treatment plan.

Similarly, in most communities which have specialized programs to treat intrafamily child sexual abuse, there are very active multidisciplinary teams of professionals who work in the many agencies that must interact around this problem. Sometimes these teams participate in staffing conferences focused on individual cases. More often, the problems that occur with individual cases are used as examples and vehicles for examining the broader problems within the system. Such teams, like the treatment teams which are their counterparts, are usually very useful in maintaining systemic communication, identifying areas where the system is failing, and preventing one agency from working at cross-purposes to another.

GOALS AND METHODS OF TREATMENT

Despite the apparent replication of several major types of program models, very few—if any—treatment programs are exactly alike. Nonetheless, they appear to have many treatment goals and a number of treatment methods in common. Most of the prevalent features progressed independently because of the lack of published or even written information on the development of individual programs and the lack of specific coordination or opportunity for communication among them. The fact that despite variations in system models, there are strong common themes and techniques running through most of the programs, can be seen as supportive of their validity and of the common lessons that treatment providers are learning about the needs of incestuous families.

Treatment Goals

Regardless of the particular approach taken, an initial goal of most programs is to help reduce the crisis atmosphere that usually accompanies the public discovery of parent/child incest. This often involves confronting the disbelief of family members and helping to lessen their need to deny the situation and blame each other. Efforts are focused on reducing the guilt felt by the victim (both for the abuse and for its discovery) while attempting to minimize the additional stresses brought on by systemic intervention. Treatment issues include helping individuals to deal with their very real feelings of loss, separation, betrayal, and fear of upcoming consequences. Other crucial goals include providing victims and nonabusing family members with appropriate channels for their rage and hurt; recognizing suicidal, self-destructive, or aggressive wishes that often surface at the time; and offering a supportive, rational frame of reference which validates the fact that they are not crazy and can survive the changes that are taking place in their lives.

Many programs emphasize the early need to strengthen, rebuild, or create a mother/child bond that will help to reduce the sense of rivalry and enable the mother to assume a more protective, supportive role. One goal in working with mothers of victims is to help them develop a realistic understanding of their own roles in relation to the family situation, and deal with any issues of overdependence and victimization that may exist in their own lives.

A major goal in working with perpetrators is to lessen the need for denial so that they will be able to acknowledge responsibility for their actions, both to themselves and to the child who often needs the kind of reassurance that can only come from the abuser himself. Another major treatment issue for many incestuous fathers has to do with the use and abuse of power within the family. Often, there is a strong power imbalance between parents which may be played out in terms of autocracy or resentment on the part of the father. His negative attitudes toward women and his own sexual identity are also common treatment themes, especially in relation to early sexual trauma or physical violence in his childhood. Most perpetrators have developed strong rationalizations for their abusive behavior which generally allow them to minimize, in their own minds, the impact of the abuse on the victim. In many cases, there is a need to work on specific goals of developing basic empathy for the needs and feelings of the women and children who share his world.

Many professionals in this field have observed that while a major consequence of early childhood victimization of females appears to be the turning of destructive and conflicted feelings inward on themselves, vicitmized male children may react in the opposite extreme, that is, by identifying with their abusers and turning their reactions outward on those who are close to, or weaker than, they are. Whatever the causes, the issues of early trauma and negative self-esteem are central ones in the treatment of incestuous child abusers.

Issues in the treatment of victims often are initially focused on reducing their shame, guilt, and self-blame, on the one hand, and helping them to cope with their feelings of anger and betrayal (sometimes directed as vehemently toward the non-abusing parent), on the other. Incestuous family members usually struggle with strong feelings of ambivalence about each other. Therefore, another goal involves providing them with an environment in which it is safe to admit and express their rage, while being permitted to acknowledge their positive ties or feelings of support without having to condone the abuse.

One of the most immediate goals (and usual results) of involvement by incestuous families in a specialized treatment program is breaking the isolation that generally surrounds these families. This can offer an immediate sense of relief to family members by providing a supportive milieu in which peers and professionals reinforce the awareness that they can't and don't have to cope with the problem alone. It also helps treatment providers to develop feedback loops and internal safeguards by reinforcing the fact that the "family secret" is out and will not be tolerated again. The goal of fostering a greater sense of personal awareness and accountability for the behavior of individual family members is also enhanced by providing immediate support and reinforcement for clients' actions to get help.

Treatment Methods

As with treatment goals, there are far more treatment methods being undertaken than can be described here. However, it is interesting to note that despite the strong philosophical differences which separate some of the existing programs (such as the use of the criminal justice system to mandate participation in a treatment program or the question of who is qualified to provide services), many of them are utilizing the same or similar techniques and methods of treatment. In an attempt to summarize some of the methods most frequently found in specialized programs, they will be described under the categories of "talking therapies," "concrete therapies," "educational components," and "group methods."

The "talking therapies" are the most difficult to describe because they are often presented (as they are here) in terms of shorthand labels which have common meanings to mental health professionals, but which would require far more lengthy explanations if they were to be operationally defined. It must suffice to say that these include supportive therapy, humanistic psychology, ego-centered therapy, Gestalt psychology, confrontation approaches, transactional analysis, and others. Traditional insight-oriented therapy is being employed by many programs, although a number of treatment providers are beginning to question its overall utility for some types of families which appear to function on very concrete levels. Similarly, traditional psychoanalytic methods are not commonly used (except on a private basis, usually with adults who were victimized as children) because of the limitation of treatment time, expense, client receptivity, need for short-term results, and availability of trained treatment providers. Talking therapies in sexual abuse projects take many forms including individual, dyads (usually parent/child), couples, family, and a variety of groups.

What might be termed "concrete therapies," because they are more specifically targeted toward particular problems or results, include various types of behavior modification, sex therapy, body awareness techniques (including assertiveness training and self-defense methods), aversion therapy (including electric shock treatment and other methods), and drug therapies used in association with other therapeutic methods. As with the "talking therapies," many of these approaches are being tried on a demonstration or pilot basis over a period of time, and very few to date have been objectively evaluated or reported in the literature.

Many programs have developed educational components aimed both at their own client populations and at professionals, local groups, and the general public in their communities. Educational programs for individuals and families in treatment include sex education, parenthood education, teaching of social skills, and anger control. When educational efforts are geared toward the families being served by a program, they are usually aimed at increasing self-awareness, personal skills, and basic knowledge, which are frequently underdeveloped in these families. When they are focused on other populations such as school children or local professionals, their goals are likely to be prevention and public awareness of the problem.

As mentioned previously, one of the most common and frequently spoken of treatment methods, in terms of its positive effects, is group therapy. Groups help to meet some of the immediate needs for mutual support and to break the social and emotional isolation that so characterizes incestuous families. This seems to be especially true for victims, particularly adolescents, who may have had to keep the "family secret" for a long period of time and who respond well to the opportunity for peer support in a setting where others understand what they are feeling. Many treatment programs, which only served existing families when they began, now incude group therapy for adults molested as children. This is a population that appears to be especially enthusiastic about the positive effects of such a treatment method. There are a wide variety of specialized groups associated with some programs (some conduct more than a dozen), including groups for mothers, fathers, couples, separated parents, new clients in crisis, juvenile sex offenders, siblings, and even boyfriends or girlfriends of older victims or parents. Some of the groups are short-term and targeted toward specific, time-limited goals; others may continue with the same members for a year or more.

The duration of treatment for families in sexual abuse programs varies, but for most of them, it appears to involve at least a year to 18 months; for other families, treatment may continue for several years. As programs mature and gain experience, they are developing more sophisticated criteria for termination of treatment.

CONCLUSION

This chapter has attempted to conceptualize and describe some of the common themes and components of specialized intrafamily child sexual abuse treatment programs. It has focused on their similarities because in a specialty as new as this one, it is often the differences that are highlighted at the expense of those underlying elements which are common to all. Frustrating as it may be for those who seek to replicate the "best" or most effective approach to dealing with this problem, neither the state of our knowledge nor the available outcome data will support such absolute choices at this point in time. This is probably as it should be, given the relatively short life spans of most existing programs and the still rudimentary level of our understanding of the nature and causes of child sexual abuse. Many of the differences among programs reflect very real differences among community attitudes, resources, and state laws. Some also may be reflections of differences in treatment populations where programs are located. However, as mentioned earlier, it is not their differences but the surprising degree of similarity among so many programs that is remarkable, when one considers the independent ways in which they have developed throughout the country.

One of the greatest gaps in this field at the present time is the lack of available evaluation data on the effects of intervention and the outcomes of various types of treatment methods and approaches. This is due not only to the newness of so many programs but also to the fact that federal and state funding sources, like the programs themselves, focused their early efforts and limited resources on program development more than on follow-up. Some of the older comprehensive treatment programs throughout the country have been collecting data and conducting their own internal evaluation studies, and over the next few years, they will be able to produce more empirical evidence of program effectiveness than is currently available.

Some of the short-term evaluations of individual programs, such as the state-funded follow-up study of the Child Sexual Abuse Treatment Program in San Jose, California (Kroth, 1979), as well as the preliminary findings of federally funded treatment programs, show extremely promising results in terms of positive change among family members, prevention of negative outcomes for victims, and exceptionally low recidivism rates of 1–2%. Although many of these studies are not long-term (most represent case tracking of a year or two at best) and they lack the methodological rigor that might be possible with more sophisticated and much more costly evaluation studies, they represent the first steps toward being able to quantify and measure the results of the treatment methods described. Further, they reflect the optimism about, and confidence in, the effectiveness of these specialized programs that are being voiced almost universally by treatment providers who are currently working with incestuous families. This is not to imply that all families in treatment for child sexual abuse can be similarly rehabilitated or that all perpetrators in these programs can be pronounced "cured" and released with absolute confidence that the problem will never reoccur. There is an evolving sense, however, within specific limitations on intake criteria, that families being treated in specialized incest treatment programs represent a population particularly amenable to the treatment methods and approaches currently in use.

While there are some limited evaluation studies in progress in conjunction with a few of the federally funded treatment programs, most of the available public funds in the area of child sexual abuse have supported program development and the training of treatment providers. Unfortunately, the expectation that funding for evaluation and research would follow the establishment of treatment programs grows increasingly dim as federal and state fiscal priorities rapidly shift away from categorical programs and domestic priorities in general (MacFarlane and Bulkley, 1982). Similarly, as certain elements of the public react to the highly publicized

cases of child abductions, sex-related child murders, and arrests of recidivist pedophiles, public funding for the support or evaluation of treatment programs is
rapidly diminishing.

As programs in the treatment field become more sophisticated, there is an increasing need to be able to distinguish the types of intervention that are most
effective with various types of perpetrators and families that come into treatment. It
is doubtful that any single approach will ever be totally effective with all cases, and
the credibility of existing programs will be hurt if they are judged by such absolute
measures of effectiveness. As with the evolution of all systemic attempts to redress
any pervasive human problem, there must be a period of time for sorting out the
theoretical from the practical, and for assessing what works best and on whom.

Having gone through an initial period of case management by the "recipe"
approach (i.e., applying the same treatment plan or formula to every family accepted into a given program), treatment programs are beginning to develop better
typologies of the people and the problems they encounter. These focus on such
factors as the nature of the abuse itself, its duration, the victim's age at onset of the
abuse, the nature of the relationship between victim and perpetrator, the existence
of physical force or coercion, the relationships and strengths of family ties between
adult members of a household, and the personality characteristics of the perpetrator
and other family members. All of these variables play a role in determining which
approaches should be taken and what methods should be used to achieve particular
treatment goals.

Unfortunately for children, their families, and the programs undertaking these
tasks, such efforts require time and continuing resources to reach the level of
theoretical confidence and demonstrable outcome needed in this field. Even more
unfortunate is the fact that both the time and the financial resources required to
assure the existence of these programs are in considerable jeopardy due to increasing budget cuts in human services and to punitive or apathetic attitudes regarding
treatment of this problem.

It is ironic that these specialized programs, whose development was primarily
motivated by the desire to improve the plight of sexually victimized children and
by society's response to the discovery of their abuse, are under attack from some
who see themselves as champions of child victims. While it is certainly true that
accountability for intervention in this area must be very stringent, it seems equally
apparent that statutory reform and increased criminal sanctions are insufficient solutions to a problem as complex as intrafamily child sexual abuse. Several states
already carry the death penalty or sentences of life imprisonment for conviction of
this crime, but the problems described earlier still exist: families continue to be
traumatized by the intervention system, and the majority of child victims undoubtedly remain unidentified and untreated.

REFERENCES

Annual Summary of National Child Neglect and Abuse Reporting. Denver: American Humane, Annual Report, 1976–1980.

Berliner, L. and Stevens, D. Advocating for sexually abused children in the criminal justice system. In *Sexual Abuse of Children: Selected Readings*, National Center on Child Abuse and Neglect. Washington, D.C.: U.S. Government Printing Office, 1980.

Brecher, E. M. *Treatment Programs for Sex Offenders.* Washington, D.C.: National Institute of Law Enforcement and Criminal Justice, Law Enforcement Assistance Administration, U.S. Department of Justice, 1978.

Bulkley, J. (Ed.) *Child Sexual Abuse and the Law.* Washington, D.C.: National Legal Resource Center for Child Advocacy and Protection, Anerican Bar Association, 1981. (a)

Bulkley, J. (Ed.) *Innovations in the Prosecution of Child Sexual Abuse Cases.* Washington, D.C.: National Resource Center for Child Advocacy and Protection, American Bar Association, 1981. (b)

Finkelhor, D. *Sexually Victimized Children.* New York: The Free Press, 1979.

Giarretto, H. Humanistic treatment of father-daughter incest. In Helfer, R. and Kempe, H. (Eds.) *Child Abuse and Neglect: The Family and the Community.* Cambridge, Mass.: Ballinger Press, 1976.

Groth, A. Patterns of sexual assault against children and adolescents. In Burgess, A. W. et al. (Eds.) *Sexual Assault of Children and Adolescents.* Lexington, Mass.: Lexington Books, 1978.

Kroth, J. *Child Sexual Abuse: Analysis of a Family Therapy Approach.* Springfield, Ill.: Thomas, 1979.

MacFarlane, K. Sexual abuse of children. In Chapman, J. and Gates, M. (Eds.). *The Victimization of Women.* Beverly Hills: Sage, 1978.

MacFarlane, K. and Bulkley, J. Treating child sexual abuse: an overview of current program models. In Shore, D. and Conte, J. (Eds.) *Social Work Perspectives on Child Sexual Abuse.* Chicago: Haworth Press, 1982; also in *Journal of Human Sexuality and Social Work* **1**(1) (1982).

MacFarlane, K., Jones, B., and Jenstrom, L. (Eds.) *Sexual Abuse of Children: Selected Readings*, National Center on Child Abuse and Neglect. Washington, D.C.: U.S. Government Printing Office, 1980.

Rush, F. *The Best Kept Secret: Sexual Abuse of Children.* Englewood Cliffs, N.J.: Prentice-Hall, 1980.

Summit, R. and Kryso, J. Sexual abuse of children: a clinical spectrum. *American Journal of Orthopsychiatry* **48**(2): 237-50 (1978).

Part II

Biomedical Perspectives and Biomedical Treatment

5

Sex Offenders: A Biomedical Perspective and a Status Report on Biomedical Treatment*

Fred S. Berlin, M.D., Ph.D.

Individuals may be considered sex offenders if they behave in particular ways, for example, by becoming sexually intimate with a child. In general, behavior, whether sexual or nonsexual, is a reflection of one's state of mind, as persons tend to act in response to their thoughts and feelings. Some states of mind can be considered pathological, for example, when an individual loses the capacity to determine whether heard voices are coming from the environment or are imaginary. This type of psychological impairment can occur in a variety of psychiatric syndromes such as schizophrenia, dementia, delirium, or manic depressive illness—each of which requires a different form of treatment. Persons mentally ill in these ways sometimes commit sex offenses. On the other hand, some persons commit sex offenses in response to intense, unconventional sexual hungers (e.g., for children). Individuals with deviant or unconventional sexual orientations may also require psychiatric help. Properly diagnosing whether a sex offense is the manifestation of a specific psychiatric syndrome such as schizophrenia, dementia, mania, exhibitionism, or pedophilia can be important in trying to provide optimal care. The etiological determinants of conventional, as well as of unconventional, erotic interests are undoubtedly multiple, but there is evidence that biological factors such a hormone levels or chromosomal makeup sometimes play a major contributory role with respect to the nature of an individual's sexual desires. Biological treatments which alter the physical milieu of the brain, for example, by decreasing the amount of the "male sex hormone" testosterone that is present, may sometimes be able to facilitate better self-control of sexual behavior. This, might be the case, for instance, if treatment that lowers testosterone levels results in a pedophile experiencing a decrease in the subjective intensity of his unconventional sexual appetite. There may be implications regarding how society through its laws should view some sex offenders if (a) it is the case that biological factors, such as

---

*The author gratefully acknowledges the kind and invaluable assistance of Ms. Maggie Rider, Ms. Claudia Halko, Ms. Deborah Holifield, Ms. Nancy Mace, Mr. Timothy Rider, and Dr. Phillip Slavney in the preparation of this manuscript.

chromosomal abnormalities, contribute to the development of unconventional erotic desires that may tempt persons to want to commit sex offenses, and if (b) it is also the case that surgical or antiandrogenic medication treatments can result in biological and psychological changes that provide such individuals with an increased capacity for self-control not previously present.

PART I: SYNDROMES AND THE IMPORTANCE OF DIFFERENTIAL DIAGNOSIS

Introduction

The present chapter discusses the importance of making a proper differential diagnosis in assessing "sex offenders" for potential treatment. It also explores the relationship between biological factors, such as hormone levels or chromosomal anomalies, and sexual phenomenology (i.e., the mental experiences, thoughts, lusts, and fantasies that constitute states of erotic desire). Currently available treatments are briefly reviewed from a biomedical perspective, with a particular emphasis on the use of surgery and medications. The idea of using pharmacological agents to treat sex offenders is relatively modern, although surgical procedures such as castration which, like some medications, diminish androgen levels have been employed for this purpose for quite a while. The following is a brief case vignette which serves as an example of the type of patient for whom medication treatment may be appropriate, as well as a basis for the subsequent discussion of the various issues and considerations, diagnostic and otherwise, which must be reflected upon in trying to provide optimal understanding and care.

Case Presentation

Mr. A., a 40-year-old white male, was referred by his attorney for assessment as a consequence of the patient's sexual involvement with a 13-year-old boy. Having been charged five years earlier with a similar offense, at the time of his assessment the patient was on court-mandated probation. Though apprehended only once before, he had been sexually active almost exclusively with young males, most ranging between the ages of 14 and 17 (but some as young as age 8), since he himself was 7 years old.

Sexual activity, which included undressing, fondling, mutual masturbation, and oral-genital contact occurred frequently with a variety of partners, sometimes as often as several times per month. In almost all cases the children were persuaded rather than coerced, but in two instances, while intoxicated, Mr. A. threatened the victims with a paring knife. The patient indicated that he had begun to drink frequently "to get up the courage to approach potential partners."

After each incident the patient felt ashamed and guilty, vowing that he would try not to act similarly in the future. However, in time, as his sexual urges began once again to intensify, he would give in to temptation. The mere happenstance of watching young boys in television commercials would sometimes elicit a strong urge to focus his attention towards the child's genital area. In describing the mental experiences that led him to act in these ways, the patient, in an interview with Dr. John Money, made the following comments:

If I have seen an exceptionally nice looking boy I get aroused. I want to go over there, but then again I don't. I see him, and I want to get out of there because I know I am going to start fantasizing. I have noticed that the first thing is I drop my eyes to his genitals. It gets more intense, the fantasies, that is. I dream about a South Sea island, nothing but boys on the island. It is kind of like a fight between the good side and the bad side, like Dr. Jekyll and Mr. Hyde. Sometimes the way to cure it is to masturbate, and that takes care of it. There are other times when I get so aroused I just have to get it sexually together. It worries society. It worries me very much. I know it is wrong. I know what the legal issues are, but at the time I am not thinking of legal issues. All I can think about is getting the boy. I want to keep doing it, and doing it, and doing it. No matter how. Getting the boy. Sometimes I think, "Hey, what are you doing? I don't want to hurt anyone." I really do not want to hurt these children, but I am very afraid that I might.

In attempting to understand his condition, the patient made the following comments:

What starts a person like myself doing what I do? Why me? Why can't I be normal like everybody else? You know. Did God put this as a punishment or something towards me? I am ashamed. Why can't I just go out and have a good time with girls? I feel edgy when a female is present. An older "gay" person would turn me off. I have thought about suicide. I think after this long period of time I have actually seen where I have an illness. It is getting uncontrollable, to the point where I can't put up with it anymore. It is a sickness. I know it's a sickness, but as far as they [society] is concerned, you are a criminal and should be punished. Even if I go to jail for 12 or 15 years, or whenever, I am still going to be the same when I get out.

This last statement was not meant to be defiant.

Physical and laboratory examination of the patient revealed a number of biological pathologies (see Table 5-1). These findings suggest that the patient has Klinefelter's syndrome, the significance of which will be discussed subsequently.

Table 5-1.   Abnormal Physical and Laboratory Findings on Mr. A.

Physical Findings:
1. Scars on chest from previously performed bilateral mastectomies, done because of gynecomastia (enlarged breasts) which developed at puberty
2. Hypogonadism (small testicles)
3. Abnormally long arms and fingers

Laboratory Findings:
1. Low sperm count
2. Elevated luteinizing hormone (148 ng/ml); normal LH in adult males = 36–64 ng/ml
3. Elevated follicle stimulating hormone (618 ng/ml); normal FSH in adult males = 98–276 ng/ml
4. Low testosterone (153 ng/100 ml); normal (s.d. = 2) range in adult males = 275–875 ng/ml
5. 47 XXY chromosome pattern; normal male pattern = 46 XY

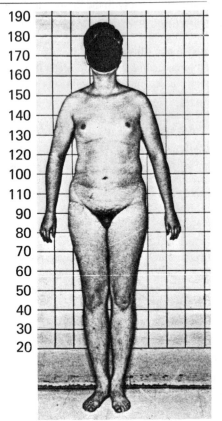

Typical patient with Klinefelter's syndrome. Note the gynecomastia and female distribution of adipose tissue. (Photo courtesy of Dr. John Money.)

Pedophilia as an Example of a Diagnosable Sexual Deviation Syndrome

The case just presented is an example of homosexual ephebophilia, which means that the patient is a man whose sexual orientation, interests, and preferences are directed predominantly towards postpubertal boys. Were he interested mostly in prepubertal boys, a diagnosis of pedophilia, rather than ephebophilia, would be more accurate. For purposes of the present discussion, the term pedophilia will be used when referring to persons sexually oriented towards children, regardless of whether the children are pre- or postpubertal.

According to the 3rd edition of the *Diagnostic and Statistical Manual of Mental Disorders* (DSM III), there are three criteria which must be satisfied in order to make such a diagnosis.[1] First, it is necessary to establish that the patient becomes erotically excited by the act or fantasy of engaging in sexual activities with children. Secondly, if the patient is an adult, rather than an adolescent, the children must be at least ten years his junior. Finally, it must be clear that any sexual acts engaged in with children are not either due to other mental disorders such as schizophrenia, dementia, or drug intoxication, or due to lack of an suitable age-appropriate partner, which occurs in some cases of incarceration or incest.

As is true of persons with conventional heterosexual interests, the onset of sexual behavior in persons with unconventional, or "deviant," erotic desires usually begins around the time of puberty. Related fantasies, however, may have been experienced much earlier. In the absence of appropriate treatment, the course of such syndromes tends to be chronic, which is not surprising because the sex drive is maintained over time.

In terms of reported cases, pedophilia appears to be almost exclusively a male problem, although its exact prevalence is unknown. The majority of cases in the literature have involved heterosexual pedophilia (men attracted towards little girls), but more recently some centers have reported a higher frequency of homosexual involvements.[2] In ancient Greece, homosexual pedophilic behavior was considered acceptable. Socrates, for example, wrote, "A valued company might be composed of boys and their lovers . . . for of all men they would be ashamed to desert one another."[3] Judeo-Christian beliefs, however, based in part upon the biblical story of Sodom and Gomorrah (hence, the term sodomy), clearly consider it to be immoral.[4-6] In some states, a possible legal sentence for engaging in sex with a minor is the death penalty.[7] Although in American society a child can clearly become quite distressed by involvement with a pedophile (hence the importance of applying effective interventions to stop such behavior), it is also the case that some children become even more upset by the reactions of well-intentioned adults who find out about their sexual involvements.[8] Tragically, sometimes children also feel guilty and responsible for any punishment imposed upon a former partner, a person (perhaps even a relative) whom they may actually like a great deal.

Sexual activity by pedophiles with children rarely involves physical assaultiveness and is usually the result of persuasion rather than coercion, although the series of brutal slayings in Atlanta, Georgia, during 1980 and 1981 represented an exception.[9] A study in Detroit, Michigan, of over 1252 sex offenses against children found that physical injury occurred in less than 9% of the cases.[10] When a pedophile craves sadistic sexual involvement with children, a second diagnosis of erotic sadism should also be made. Though most children are warned to be leery of strangers, the victims of pedophiles, unlike the victims of exhibitionists, usually know their partners well, and sexual activity (which is often mutual fondling and masturbation rather than intercourse) frequently occurs in the home of either the victim or the perpetrator.[1,8] Whereas some pedophiles merely lust after children, some seem to fall in love with them, which may make treatment more difficult.

Why persons differ from one another in sexual orientation and in the nature and intensity of their erotic desires is unknown. It is unclear why most men find women sexually appealing whereas some are erotically attracted towards young boys. Nor is it clear why still others experience recurring urges to expose themselves publicly or to rape repeatedly. In some instances, certain types of early childhood experiences seem to play a contributory factor in determining adult sexual interests. Many pedophiles, for example, were themselves sexually involved with adults as youngsters.[11] In other cases, biological pathologies such as structural brain damage, hormonal dysfunctions, genetic anomalies, or electrical disturbances of the brain seem to play a role.[2,12] Persons who meet the diagnostic criteria for a sexual deviation syndrome, of which pedophilia is an example, may be appropriate candidates for treatment with antiandrogenic medications.

Diagnosing a Sexual Deviation Syndrome

The term used in DSM III to categorize sexual deviation syndromes is paraphilia, which means attraction to deviance.[1] Diagnosis of a sexual deviation syndrome can be made by inquiring about a person's thoughts, feelings, and behaviors. Individuals with deviant sexual interests ordinarily experience repeated erotic fantasies about engaging in unconventional forms of sexual activity. Asking an individual about his masturbatory fantasies can be revealing in this respect because erotic arousal for the purpose of masturbation may be difficult in the absence of erotic mental imagery.[13,14] The homosexual pedophile frequently fantasizes about young boys, whereas the heterosexual exhibitionist has recurring thoughts about exposing himself to women. The male transvestite is preoccupied with the idea of cross-dressing in female clothing. Rather than depending solely upon introspective reports, Dr. Gene Abel of the New York State Psychiatric Institute suggests that the rate of change in the diameter of the pupil of the eye can also be used as a means of determining whether a particular stimulus, such as the picture of a nude child, is sexually arousing (see Figure 5-1). Measures of penile tumescence and other forms of polygraphic data have also been used to try to document unconventional sexual interests.[15]

Accompanying the unconventional sexual fantasies experienced by persons who can be diagnosed as having a sexual deviation syndrome are intense erotic cravings. These cravings are experienced as frustrating and discomforting when deviant fantasies cannot be enacted. Karl Jaspers, the emminent German phenomenologist (who was probably influenced in his thinking by Krafft-Ebing and Havelock Ellis), characterized deviant sexual cravings as intolerable states, similar to addictions, that demand action in order to be alleviated.[16] However, many persons with conventional heterosexual interests can also feel discomforted if sexually frustrated; such frustration may motivate a person to seek out a consensual sexual partner. The individual with a pedophilic sexual orientation, however,

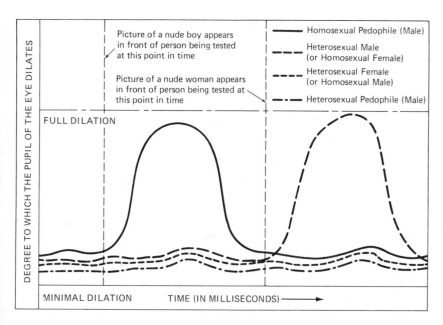

Figure 5-1 Schematic representation of the pupillary responses of four persons with different sexual orientations.

faces much greater difficulties in the sense that all those whom he may find naturally appealing (i.e., children) are forbidden as partners. Living in a world where all those who are sexually appealing are forbidden as partners must be difficult—a situation heterosexual adults can, perhaps, empathize with by imagining living in a world where one was expected to have sex only with children.

People do not decide voluntarily what will arouse them sexually. Rather, they discover within themselves what sorts of persons and activities are sexually appealing to them. Sexual behavior in general tends to be in part a response to one's erotic desires and fantasies. Thus a man with conventional heterosexual interests tends to seek out adult women, just as the homosexual pedophile (who may be impotent with women) seeks out boys. The heterosexual voyeur repeatedly seeks out situations where he can "peep" upon unsuspecting naked or partially clad females in response to his sexual cravings, whereas the male transvestite repeatedly cross-dresses.

DSM III lists nine major diagnostic subcategories of paraphilia (see Table 5-2).[1] In earlier, outdated classification schemes, sexual deviation syndromes were often considered to be a subdivision of the so-called sociopathic personality type. It is important to appreciate that sexual orientation can be assessed independently of character traits. Some men with unconventional sexual orientations show no other evidence of "sociopathic personality traits," such as disrespect for authority, other kinds of criminal behaviors, truancy, vocational irresponsibility, or lack of concern for others. On the contrary, men with unconventional sexual orientations such as pedophilia can manifest a range of character traits, just as is true of persons with conventional heterosexual orientations.[17] Thus, terms such as pedophilia refer to the nature of a person's sexual orientation or to the nature of his sexual desires, and not to his traits of character. A paraphiliac man who has been consistently non-violent in temperament would not ordinarily be expected to undergo a sudden change in personality so as to become a physical danger to others.

Table 5-2.   Major Diagnostic Subcategories of Paraphilia.

1. Pedophilia
2. Exhibitionism
3. Transvestism
4. Voyeurism
5. Zoophilia
6. Fetishism
7. Erotic sadism
8. Erotic masochism
9. Other (includes paraphiliac or compulsive rape)

Differential Diagnosis as a Basis for Determining Appropriate Psychiatric Treatment

Many persons are referred for psychiatric assessment and possible treatment by virtue of the fact that they have behaved in a particular way (e.g., by having sexual involvement with a child) and, thus, they carry the label "sex offender." Not all sex offenses (a legal term), however, are the reflection of a sexual deviation disorder or paraphilia (a medical term). In assessing a sex offender for possible treatment, the psychiatrist or evaluator must try to ascertain (1) the state of mind the individual was experiencing that led him to act in a particular way, and (2) whether the behavior in question was the manifestation of a diagnosable and potentially treatable psychiatric syndrome.

A sex offense could represent the expression of any of a number of psychiatric conditions. Schizophrenia, for example, is a syndrome comprised of (1) delusions, which are rigidly held, idiosyncratic, false beliefs that cannot be corrected by reason (e.g., the belief that one has a bomb inside one's head); (2) auditory hallucinations ("hearing" voices when no one is speaking); (3) disorganized thinking (in both logic and syntax); (4) insomnia; (5) agitation; (6) emotional apathy; (7) loss of initiative; and (8) bizarre behavior.[18] The term schizophrenia refers to the cluster of associated features comprising the syndrome and not to the person manifesting the condition.[19] Schizophrenia must be differentiated from other psychiatric syndromes such as dementia, delirium, and affective illness because delusions, hallucinations, and bizarre behavior may occur in these disorders as well. In dementia and delirium, however, delusions and hallucinations when present are accompanied by disorientation and intellectual decline, whereas in affective illness these symptoms occur within the setting of a sustained mood change. The age of initial onset of schizophrenia is almost always in the late teens or early twenties, and like a variety of other medical conditions (such as juvenile onset diabetes), its course is chronic. There is evidence that this form of mental illness, in which persons lose the capacity to perceive accurately whether heard voices are real or imaginary, may be associated with a genetic predisposition.[18] Thus, schizophrenia seems to occur most frequently within certain families. An associated biological pathology may be the presence of heightened levels of various chemical neurotransmitter substances (such as dopamine) in the brain.[20]

Mr. B. was a patient who developed the delusion that he needed to drink the blood of women in order to remain alive. Initially, in response both to this rigid false belief and to "voices telling him to do so," he sacrificed several animals and drank their blood. Subsequently, he physically assaulted several women in an effort to obtain blood from them, which resulted in his being charged with a second degree sex offense. In this case, the offense in question was clearly a behavioral manifestation of his schizophrenic condition, and his sexual orientation and erotic desires were apparently quite conventional. Appropriate treatment for the symptoms of schizophrenia includes the use of phenothiazine medications or other sorts of neuroleptic drugs.[21] However, just as is the case when insulin is employed to treat diabetes, present-day pharmacological therapy does not represent a complete cure for this illness.

Sex offenses can also be a reflection of other psychiatric conditions such as manic-depressive illness.[22] In addition to delusions of grandeur (e.g., the belief that one is Christ) and elated mood, one of the other symptoms of the manic syndrome is often an increase in sexual appetite. Mr. C. is a 54-year-old man who would repeatedly expose himself to middle-aged women only when in the midst of such an episode. At other times, when his mood was stable and his capacity to perceive reality intact, he would never act in such a fashion. The appropriate treatment in his case, as a prophylaxis against future recurrences of this psychiatric illness (whose natural course, like asthma, is episodic rather than chronic), is lithium carbonate. When well, this patient experienced perfectly conventional erotic interests and, thus, would not satisfy the diagnostic criteria of a sexual deviation syndrome.

Sex offenses can be perpetrated by persons with conventional sexual desires and orientations while intoxicated with drugs or alcohol. Here psychological counseling (plus, perhaps, Antabuse—a medication that makes a person feel physically ill if he consumes alcohol while taking it) would likely be the treatment of choice. A mentally retarded person with conventional erotic interests who "didn't know any better" might also commit a sex offense and possibly require counseling plus sex education. Mr. D. is an intelligent man with conventional sexual interests who began an incestuous relationship with his sister before either of them was old enough to appreciate the implications of such behavior. Here, counseling to help them deal with their guilt and family concerns was the treatment employed. Finally, a self-centered, self-indulgent person with conventional sexual desires, but with no concern for the well-being of others, might also commit a sex offense. An example would be the criminal who rapes a woman in the midst of a robbery because he feels he can get away with it. Such a person might well have no diagnosable psychiatric illness, and a proper disposition might include quarantine in the form of incarceration.

Rationale for Treatment When a Sex Offense Is the Manifestation of a Sexual Deviation Syndrome

Based upon the preceding discussion it should be clear that some sex offenses are committed by men who are not simply self-indulgent individuals with conventional erotic interests misbehaving. Unlike the homosexual pedophile, most men (including homosexual men) experience absolutely no desire to engage repeatedly in sexual involvements with young boys.[23] Rather, the average man would be repulsed by such an idea. Whereas the exhibitionist lusts for the opportunity to repeatedly expose himself publicly, most men would be embarrassed or humiliated at the prospect of behaving in such a fashion. Though many men might indeed turn their gaze towards a partially clad woman visible through a nearby window, few experience recurrent urges to "peep" repeatedly at the risk of job, reputation, family, and incarceration as does the voyeur.[24,25] The average man would feel foolish dressed in woman's clothing, whereas the male transvestite finds this erotically arousing. Although many men find themselves capable of being sexually stimulated by descriptions or scenes of coercive sexual acts, the average man certainly does not experience repeated ruminations and cravings to rape. Nor, as is the case with the paraphiliac (or compulsive) rapist, does he repeatedly have to resist the temptation to rape in order to remain out of trouble.[2] Thus, the assumption that paraphiliac behavior is little more than misbehavior is a conceptually invalid oversimplification. This kind of oversimplification leads to interventions that are rehabilitatively ineffectual. The recidivism rate is extremely high when punishment is the "treatment" of choice, as punishment does virtually nothing to make it any easier for a man to resist deviant sexual cravings. One hears of numerous instances in which a paraphiliac rapist, recently freed from prison on work release, has already raped again repeatedly. Quarantine, as opposed to punishment, may indeed be necessary so long as an individual poses a threat to others (as is sometimes true of some persons with contagious diseases), but if effective treatment that assures public safety can be applied, the need for isolation from the community may be obviated.

PART II: BIOLOGICAL PATHOLOGIES AND ETIOLOGIES

Klinefelter's Syndrome as an Example of a Biological Condition Possibly Predisposing towards Sexual Deviation

Mr. A., whose case was discussed earlier, was found to have Klinefelter's syndrome. Dr. Harry Klinefelter and his colleagues described this condition for the first time in 1942 in the *Journal of Clinical Endocrinology.*[26] Klinefelter's syndrome is a condition characterized by (1) the development of gynecomastia (enlarged breasts) at the time of puberty, (2) aspermatogenesis (low sperm production), and (3) an increased excretion of follicle stimulating hormone (FSH) by the pituitary gland in the brain.

Normally a person without Klinefelter's syndrome has 23 pairs, or a total of 46, chromosomes—each of which contains millions of genes. One-half of each chromosome pair is obtained from the mother, and the other half from the father, at the moment of conception. Twenty-two of the 23 chromosome pairs are termed autosomes, and as far as is known they are not directly related to the determination of the body's gender appearance.

In most cases, every cell in a person's body contains a replica of all 46 chromosomes. Any cell can be obtained from an individual, prepared in a special way, and then looked at under a microscope, to actually visualize them. When this is done, ordinarily by looking at a white blood cell, the chromosomes can be lined up and numbered as shown in Figure 5-2. Usually these chromosomes look the same in every cell. When this is not so, as when some cells contain 46 chromosomes but others 45, this is known as a mosaic pattern. The top part of each chromosome pair is called the p-section, and the lower part the q-section. If a chromosome abnor-

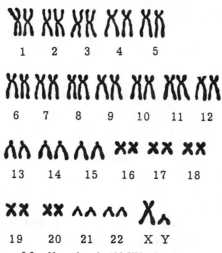

Figure 5-2.   Normal male (46 XY) chromosome pattern.

mality were to consist of extra genetic material being present on the top part of chromosome pair number 9, this would be indicated by the notation 9 (p+).

If one of the 23 pairs of chromosomes looks like a small X matched with another small X, a person will look like a female at birth (barring certain medical complications).[27] On the other hand, if that chromosome pair looks like a small X matched with a small Y, the person will usually look like a male because the presence of a Y-shaped chromosome ordinarily instructs the body to take on a male appearance. On rare occasions, a woman may be found to have an XY rather than an XX chromosome pattern, if chemical receptors in the cells in her body lack the capacity to respond to genetic messages sent out via hormones from the Y chromosome.[28]

In Klinefelter's syndrome, instead of having 23 pairs of chromosomes for a total of 46, 47 chromosomes are present, one of which is an extra X. Thus, although due to the presence of a Y chromosome, the Klinefelter's child ordinarily appears to be a boy at birth; genetically speaking, the child can be thought of either as a male (XY) with an extra X chromosome or as a female (XX) with an extra Y chromosome. Although most Klinefelter's patients have only one extra X chromosome and are therefore said to have a 47 XXY karyotype pattern, some have even greater numbers of additional X chromosomes present.

Besides the XX or XY pattern, other physical indices have been used to try to ascertain biological gender. Although most women have two X chromosomes in every cell, one of these two is ordinarily partially inactivated.[29,30] As a result, if a cell is taken from a woman, by gently scraping the buccal surface of her tongue, and it is then properly prepared and looked at under a microscope, a clump of stained chromatin will be seen within this cell's nucleus. Lyon was the first to suggest that this "chromatin positive material," also known as a Barr body, is actually a partially inactivated and clumped up extra X chromosome.[31] Since the "normal" (XY) male has only one rather than two X chromosomes, he has no extra one present to clump, and thus he will test chromatin negative. The Klinefelter's male, however, because he does have two X chromosomes will stain chromatin positive and thus, on the basis of this test, appear to be a female.

Another test sometimes used to identify biological gender involves looking at neutrophils, a type of white blood cell, under a microscope. Ordinarily the nucleus inside a neutrophil obtained from a woman contains a drumstick-like appendage (see Figure 5-3).[31] This "drumstick" is not seen in neutrophils obtained from "normal" (46XY) males, but it is seen in Klinefelter's patients.

As early as 1957, Money and Hampson suggested that sex differences can be looked at in a variety of ways besides physical appearance (see Table 5-3).[32] When this is done using Klinefelter's patients as an example, it becomes clear that questions as to whether an individual is a man or a woman, and questions about what sexual orientation and gender identity should be, become much more difficult to answer than is ordinarily appreciated. Because Klinefelter's patients are born looking like males, their parents naturally enough routinely assign them a male sex role, and they are raised as boys. However, in terms of gender identity, some of

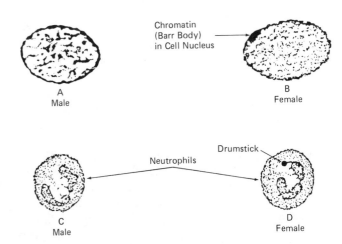

Figure 5-3. (A) Cell nucleus from buccal smear of "normal" male. (B) Cell nucleus from buccal smear of "normal" female. (C) Neutrophil from "normal" male. (D) Neutrophil from "normal" female.

Table 5-3. Male versus Female Sexual Characteristics in Klinefelter's Patients.

	IN KLINEFELTER'S SYNDROME (K.F.)
1. Sex of assignment and rearing	*Male*
2. Feelings of gender identity	May be *male* or *female*
3. (a) Sexual orientation (b) Sexual behavior	May be towards members of the same or opposite sex (which sex is the opposite sex in K. F. syndrome?)
4. External anatomical sex (phenotype)	*Male* at birth; then becomes both *male* and *female* (e.g., enlarged breasts) at puberty
5. Hormonal sex	Hormonal profile (of testosterone, FSH, and LH) is similar to postmenopausal *females*
6. Gonadal (and internal anatomical) sex	Male, but *hypogonadal*
7. Chromosomal sex (genotype)	*Male/female* — karyotype (XXY) *Female* — Barr body *Female* — neutrophilic drumstick

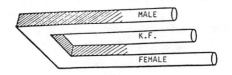

them, as early as age 7, have felt themselves psychologically to be girls.[33] Dr. John Money described the case of an otherwise normal 8-year-old boy brought for psychiatric assessment by his frustrated parents because he insisted he felt more comfortable dressed in girls' clothing. Chromosomal analysis revealed that he had Klinefelter's syndrome. As demonstrated by the case of Mr. A. discussed earlier, a number of Klinefelter's patients are sexually attracted to little boys rather than to members of the opposite sex, but in some ways it is unclear which sex is the opposite sex when it comes to Klinefelter's syndrome. Why some Klinefelter's patients find children rather than adults appealing is unclear. It is clear, however, that the sight of an infant usually elicits some feeling (albeit asexual) in most people. The possibility that feelings towards children (including the so-called maternal instinct) may be at least partially influenced by genetic factors cannot be excluded.[34] Although body phenotype is masculine during childhood, 80% of Klinefelter's patients grow large breasts and develop a "female distribution of adipose tissue" at the time of puberty (see Table 5-1).[35,36] The "hormonal sex" of these patients as measured by levels of FSH, LH, and testosterone is somewhat similar to that of a postmenopausal woman. Although Klinefelter's patients have testes rather than ovaries, their testes are very small, and produce little testosterone and virtually no sperm. As noted earlier, in terms of (1) chromosomal karyotyping, (2) Barr body testing, and (3) assessment of neutrophils for the presence of "drumsticks, "Klinefelter's males produce the same test results as females. Thus, perhaps it should come as no surprise when one discovers that a patient like Mr. A. who has Klinefelter's syndrome also has problems in terms of sexual orientation and in terms of the nature of his erotic desires.

Although Klinefelter's patients have been well studied medically, little epidemiological data surveying the prevalence of sex-related disturbances in the Klinefelter's population as a whole are available.[37] In many studies, pertinent questions regarding sexual phenomenology and experience were never asked.[38] Furthermore, the prevalence of sexual deviation, gender dysphoria, and related phenomena amongst the general public has not been well documented and therefore is unavailable for comparison purposes. For these reasons, in spite of the case of Mr. A. presented earlier, conclusions regarding the relationship between Klinefelter's syndrome and sexual deviation must be evaluated cautiously. Nevertheless, review of the literature (despite some disagreements[35,39,40]) suggests that the prevalence of sexual deviation syndromes in Klinefelter's patients may indeed be higher than it is amongst non-Klinefelter's men.[41–50] Baker and Stoller, for example, reviewed over 100 pertinent articles and arrived at such a conclusion.[33] Since most Klinefelter's patients appear to be essentially normal boys until puberty, it is difficult to account for this apparently high prevalence of sexual deviation on the basis of child rearing practices or other types of early life experiences.

Not all patients with Klinefelter's syndrome show evidence of sexual deviation; rather some are hyposexual instead. In such cases, testosterone has sometimes been administered to increase rather than decrease sexual capacity. When this has been done, these patients have reported a heightening of erotic desire, which again demonstrates the apparent relationship between testosterone levels and sexual phenomenology.[51-53]

Although most Klinefelter's patients have low testosterone levels, often the levels are not so low as to obliterate sexual desire significantly. Therefore, when sexual desires are deviant, as is the case with pedophilia, attempts to further reduce sexual appetite may still be warranted. This highlights the fact that the rationale for utilizing testosterone-depleting methods to treat paraphiliacs is based upon appreciation of the nature and intensity of the individual's erotic cravings, and not upon documentation of a biological abnormality. However, just as lung cancer is more likely to occur if a person smokes than if he does not, the likelihood of sexually deviant urges may be greater in the presence of certain kinds of biological abnormalities than in their absence.

Etiology of Conventional and Unconventional Sexual Desires— Associated Biological Pathologies

Mr. A., whose case of homosexual pedophilia was discussed earlier, was also diagnosed as having Klinefelter's syndrome. This, coupled with the fact that medications may sometimes be used in treatment, raises the question of whether one should routinely look for possible biological contributors to sexual behavior. In animal species other than man, biological factors clearly contribute significantly to such behavior. Female dogs, for example, become sexually responsive to male dogs only while in heat (estrus). At such times, in response to the odor of chemical substances emitted from the females, the males themselves become sexually much more assertive. In many species of birds, only the male sings. If a female zebra finch is given estradiol as an embryo, plus androgen hormones as an adult, she will sing a male courtship song without having heard it previously.[54] In addition, she will display typically male mating behavior and, like normal males (but unlike normal females), will have an increased number of cells in the nucleus robustus archistratialis and other brain regions (see Figure 5-4a).

In most species of rat, normally only males mount. "Mounting" is a behavior that involves placing the forepaws on the back of another animal while posturing the body in a fashion conducive to intercourse. Adult female rats given testosterone at a specific time in utero will also show this behavior which normally predominates in males.[55] Male rats do not normally build nests or care for their young, but they will build nests and show other kinds of "maternal behavior" if electrical stimulation is applied to certain brain areas.[56] Male Siamese fighting fish are preprogrammed genetically to respond aggressively to the sight of another male. Tinbergen described in great detail how specific configurations of visual stimuli can elicit (or "release") specific sexual behaviors in stickleback fish.[57] The same is true of spiders and blowflies[58] (see Figure 5-4b). In some cases, animals are pre-

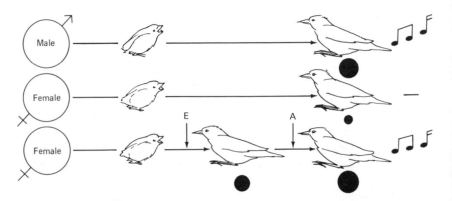

Figure 5-4a.   Sex differences in male and female finches. Male birds sing; females do not. However, females treated with estradiol (E) just after hatching, and with androgen (A) at adulthood, do sing and exhibit other male behavior. Shaded disks represent the relative size of one brain region involved in song production. (From reference 54.)

Figure 5-4b.   Visual specificity of the sexual responsiveness of spiders. Male spiders with no prior sexual experience may attempt to mate (or attack) moving colored objects shaped like those on the left, but they will not do so with those on the right. (From reference 58.)

programmed genetically to respond sexually to sounds rather than vision. The sound of the wing beat of the female is the stimulus which attracts male crickets and mosquitos.[58] Some animals have an innate predisposition to follow, and become psychologically attached to, the first large object they see moving during a "critical time period" in early life. Attractions acquired in this fashion are said to be "imprinted."[59] Lorenz described young ducks who became so imprinted towards him that they tried to feed him live worms—a drive apparently so strong that they would try to force them into his ears if he closed his mouth.[60] Early life imprinting can influence the nature of an adult animal's sexual attractions.

In 1978, researchers reported a study in the *New England Journal of Medicine* documenting the observation that some women initiate sexual behavior most frequently during the ovulatory period (days 12 through 17) of their menstrual cycles.[61] This is a time in the cycle when the androgenic hormone androstenedione is ordinarily at its peak.[62] When estrogen and progesterone hormones were given to these women in the form of birth control pills, the result was a suppression of the ovulatory peak of female-initiated sexual behavior. Since regular menstrual cycling, including monthly menstruation, continued normally, this decrease in the frequency of female-initiated sexual behavior around the time of ovulation was apparently attributable, either directly or indirectly, to the altered hormonal status of the women in question.

Human males do not have to be taught how to obtain an erection. Instead, at some time in their lives, presumably because they are genetically preprogrammed to do so, they begin to have erections in response to specific kinds of tactile, mental, olfactory, or visual stimuli (such as the sight of a shapely female) Even human infants seem to respond instinctively in specific ways to certain stimuli such as a loud sound (which causes a startled reaction), the visual perception of height (which causes hesitation), or the sight of a familiar face (which causes smiling).[58] Goy and McEwen at a symposium at the Massachusetts Institute of Technology in 1977 suggested that biological factors may contribute more than previously appreciated to human social and sexual experience.[63] Recently, Pillard and co-workers summarized data suggesting that there may be a genetic predisposition towards male homosexuality.[64]

In humans (as well as in animals), structural and functional differences in the brain between males and females seem to depend upon exposure to various "sex hormones" during particular phases of embryonic development.[65–70] Females exposed prenatally to high doses of androgens tend, as adults, to show patterns of psychosexual development more typically seen in males.[71,72] Prenatal exposure to progesterone may have a "feminizing effect."[73,74] Exposing a male human fetus to medications containing estrogen may lead to a pattern of adult psychosexual behavior more frequently seen in women.[75,76] Oral administration of 10 mg per day of testosterone to adult women can increase sexual responsiveness and libido without causing masculinizing bodily changes.[77]

Because it seemed possible that biological factors might contribute significantly to human sexual behavior, a variety of laboratory tests were performed on a group of paraphiliac patients.[2] These data, which have recently been updated, are presented in Table 5-4. Although it will be important to perform similar tests on an appropriately matched group of persons with conventional sexual desires, for comparison purposes, there does appear to be a very high frequency of biological pathologies in these patients. These pathologies include structural brain damage, hormonal abnormalities, electroencephalographic dysfunctions, and chromosomal anomalies (such as Klinefelter's syndrome).

Thus far, the possible role of biology as an etiological contributor to sexuality has been discussed. However, Stoller hypothesized that whereas biological factors may become a compelling determinant of sexual experience and function in the presence of significant organic anomalies (Stoller's "biological force" hypothesis), sometimes environmental influences such as early life experiences may play a more dominant role.[33] In this connection, Dr. John Money has discussed the case of a pair of genetically identical twins, one of whom required a total penectomy (surgical removal of the penis) a few days after birth, due to trauma suffered during circumcision. Subsequent to that penectomy, plus additional reconstructive surgery (and hormone supplementation at puberty), the child in question was reared as a girl. Although perhaps somewhat "tomboyish" in interests and play during childhood, this 46 XY female, now a teenager, feels herself psychologically to be a woman. Her sexual orientation and interests are directed towards age-appropriate males, and someday she hopes to marry and adopt children. Her genetically identical twin feels himself to be masculine, and he finds females appealing. Thus, it is clear that both biological and environmental factors can influence sexual phenomenology and behavior.

PART III: THERAPIES

Psychotherapy and Behavior Therapy as Treatments—Biological and Syndromal Considerations

Four major types of treatment have been proposed to try to help sex offenders. They are psychotherapy, behavior therapy, medication, and surgery. Unfortunately, recognition that optimal treatment may depend upon proper differential diagnosis has often been unappreciated. Sometimes the goals of therapy are stated explicitly, for example, to help a person gain greater capacity for self-control, but this is not always the case.

Most psychodynamic theories make the assumption that conventional heterosexuality alone is natural, and that other orientations and preferences are pathological variants which only occur when proper development goes awry. These theories see sexual deviation as a reflection of "unconscious" psychological conflicts and postulate that such conflicts come about as a result of unsatisfactory early life experi-

Table 5-4. Associated Findings in a Group of Male Patients with Sexual Disorders.

PATIENT DIAGNOSIS	ASSOCIATED FINDINGS
1. Erotic sadism	Oculomotor abnormality suggestive of basal ganglion dysfunction. Unexplained gait disturbance.
2. Homosexual pedophilia	Dyslexia; childhood lisp requiring speech therapy.
3. Homosexual pedophilia	Cortical atrophy; grand mal seizures; recurrent slow delta waves and sharp activity over frontal brain regions on EEG.
4. Hypersexuality	Elevated testosterone; family history of adrenogenital syndrome.
5. Homosexual pedophilia	Klinefelter's syndrome, mosaic (90% 47 XXY, 10% 46 XY). Elevated FSH and LH. Low testosterone.
6. Homosexual pedophilia	Strabismus; childhood learning disorder.
7. Heterosexual pedophilia	Schizophrenia.
8. Exhibitionism	Elevated testosterone; prior history of coma several months following head trauma; grand mal seizures.
9. Heterosexual pedophilia	Cortical atrophy ($2°$ to trauma); right-sided partial hemiparesis; visual spatial deficits.
10. Homosexual pedophilia	Elevated testosterone.
11. Heterosexual pedophilia	Near total blindness due to brain damage.
12. Heterosexual pedophilia	Elevated testosterone; mild ventriculomegaly and cortical atrophy most pronounced in area of right sylvian fissure (by CAT scan); elevated 24-hour urine pregnanctriol (3.1 mg — normal is less than 2.5 mg).
13. Homosexual pedophilia	Elevated LH. Generalized muscular hypotonia.
14. Paraphiliac rape	Elevated testosterone; grand mal seizures.
15. Homosexual pedophilia	Elevated testosterone.
16. Hypersexuality	Cortical atrophy; cortical blindness; mild mental retardation.
17. Voyeurism	Elevated LH.
18. Homosexual pedophilia	Dyslexia.
19. Homosexual pedophilia	Mosaic chromosomal pattern (97.5% XY, 2.5% XX); large heterochromatic region at centromere of autosome number 19 (polymorphic variant); low LH.
20. Homosexual pedophilia	46 XY, inversion 9(p+ q−) chromosome pattern. High LH.
21. Homosexual pedophilia	47 XYY chromosome pattern. Elevated testosterone, FSH, and LH.
22. Paraphiliac rape	Elevated FSH.
23. Exhibitionism	Elevated LH.
24. Homosexual pedophilia	Low LH.
25. Heterosexual pedophilia	Elevated testosterone, FSH, and LH.
26. Homosexual pedophilia	Klinefelter's syndrome; elevated FSH and LH. Low testosterone.
27. Heterosexual pedophilia	Elevated testosterone.
28. Homosexual pedophilia	Elevated testosterone.
29. Voyeurism	Elevated testosterone and LH.
30. Hypersexuality	Elevated testosterone; structural brain damage.
31. Homosexual pedophilia	Elevated testosterone, FSH, and LH. EEG abnormality.
32. Transexualism	Klinefelter's syndrome. Low testosterone.
33. Homosexual pedophilia	Elevated testosterone.
34. Homosexual pedophilia	Klinefelter's syndrome. Elevated FSH and LH. Low testosterone.

NOTE: Normal (s.d. = 2) testosterone range in men = 275–875 ng/100 ml. Normal FSH in males = 98–276 ng/ml. Normal LH in males = 36–64 ng/ml. No associated abnormalities were detected in seven other patients with sexual disorders who were also assessed.

ences. However, in the author's opinion, they rarely explain adequately why such experiences should be expected to result in specific problems such as exhibitionism, rather than pedophilia or juvenile delinquency. Usually the intent of therapy is to try to "uncover" conflicts so that an individual can rework his developmental problems. In point of fact, there is reason to doubt whether sex offenders come to fully understand or change their sexuality by such means.

In an investigation published in *Lancet* in 1979, Eicher studied a group of transsexuals (persons who feel themselves to be psychologically "trapped in the body of the wrong sex").[78] He examined the white blood cells of these persons, looking for the presence or absence of a cell surface substance known as H-Y antigen.[28] Ordinarily (as depicted schematically in Figure 5-5), H-Y antigen is present on the surface of cells taken from men, but absent in women. In some transsexuals, Eicher found that the gender the individual felt himself (or herself) to be corresponded with the presence or absence of H-Y antigen, rather than with that individual's bodily appearance. If Eicher's observations can be replicated, this suggests that "sex change operations," which have been performed on some transsexuals, may actually serve to correct body phenotype (external appearance) to conform with H-Y antigen genotype.[79,80] Such knowledge is clearly not accessible via introspective methods alone. Even if a person could come to such an understanding, this would not necessarily make it any easier for him to change his behavior. There is little solid evidence that traditional psychotherapies, when used alone, are consistently effective in treating paraphiliac syndromes.

Behavior therapists tend to be less concerned with the historical antecedents of unconventional sexual behavior than with the question of what can be done about it. The feature common to most behavior therapies is that the therapist prescribes a course of action for the patient to follow which is intended to help decrease his attraction towards previously erotic deviant stimuli, such as children. Often a simultaneous attempt is made either to teach the patient more appropriate ways of achieving sexual satisfaction or to condition him to become sexually arousable by an age-appropriate consensual partner. This is clearly a formidable task.

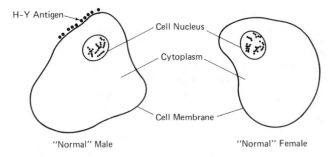

Figure 5-5. H-Y antigen is ordinarily present on the surface of cells taken from men but absent in women, as shown schematically in this figure.

Much of the literature regarding the behavioral treatment of sex offenders is anecdotal. However, Isaac Marks at the Maudsley Insitute in England documented good therapeutic results at two-year follow-up in treating transvestites (men who become erotically aroused by dressing in women's clothing), but the very same behavioral approach failed with transsexuals (men who feel themselves to be women).[81,82] Blair and Lanyon obtained good results in using behavior therapy to treat some exhibitionists.[83] Behavior therapy has not proven consistently effective in treating pedophilia. This suggests that some sexual deviation syndromes may be responsive to behavioral therapy treatments, whereas others may not. Perhaps more attention needs to be paid to differences amongst these syndromes, in addition to studying their common features.

Medication to Treat Sexual Deviation Syndromes

The purpose of utilizing medication to treat sexual deviation syndromes is to try to decrease sexual libido. The rationale for doing this is based upon the assumption that if one experiences sexual hungers of the sort that might cause problems, for example, a hunger for children, one is better off being less hungry. Because the various medications used for this purpose are not intended to make a man impotent and incapable of sexual activity, they may be most helpful in facilitating self-control in cooperative persons whose "offending behavior" is an expression of unconventional sexual tastes. They may be less helpful when the "offending behavior" is a manifestation of diminished intellect, psychosis, personality problems, or drug-induced intoxication—though such as hypothesis requires validation.

In utilizing drugs as a possible treatment method, one can address the issue of the relationship between biological factors, such as testosterone levels, and states of mind, such as those related to sexual desire. It is important to recognize, however, that the use of biological methods to successfully treat a condition does not prove that the condition and the treatment are directly and simply related. Aspirin can be used to treat a fever, but fever is not due to, or precipitated by, aspirin deficiency.

Amongst the drugs that have been used investigatively to try to treat sexual deviation syndromes are certain of the major tranquilizers such as benperidol.[84-86] Initially, use of these drugs for this purpose was based upon the observation that patients taking them for other reasons sometimes reported diminished libido. However, there is little substantive evidence to support the notion that these drugs can be used successfully in the treatment of paraphiliacs.

A class of drugs not yet utilized which may play a future role in treating these conditions are the gonadotropin releasing hormone (Gn-RH) agonists.[87] Again, rationale for their use is based upon the theory that the hormone testosterone "fuels" the sex drive in men. It is the increased production of testosterone by the testes around the time of puberty which correlates with (a) masculinizing bodily changes such as deepening of the voice and growth of facial hair and (b) an increased psychological interest in sex. Prolonged (as opposed to brief) administration of Gn-RH agonists, for reasons that are poorly understood, paradoxically inhibits the release of follicle stimulating hormone (FSH) and luteinizing hormone (LH) from the anterior pituitary gland in the brain (see Figure 5-6). This, in turn, results in decreased testosterone output by the testes, which require stimulation from FSH and LH in order to produce testosterone. The adrenal gland, which also

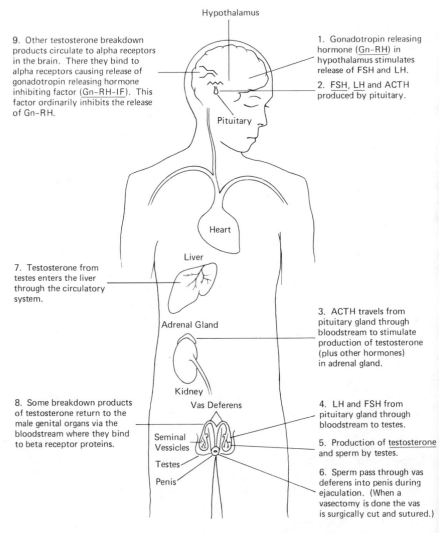

9. Other testosterone breakdown products circulate to alpha receptors in the brain. There they bind to alpha receptors causing release of gonadotropin releasing hormone inhibiting factor (Gn-RH-IF). This factor ordinarily inhibits the release of Gn-RH.

1. Gonadotropin releasing hormone (Gn-RH) in hypothalamus stimulates release of FSH and LH.

2. FSH, LH and ACTH produced by pituitary.

7. Testosterone from testes enters the liver through the circulatory system.

3. ACTH travels from pituitary gland through bloodstream to stimulate production of testosterone (plus other hormones) in adrenal gland.

8. Some breakdown products of testosterone return to the male genital organs via the bloodstream where they bind to beta receptor proteins.

4. LH and FSH from pituitary gland through bloodstream to testes.

5. Production of testosterone and sperm by testes.

6. Sperm pass through vas deferens into penis during ejaculation. (When a vasectomy is done the vas is surgically cut and sutured.)

Hypothalamus
Pituitary
Heart
Liver
Adrenal Gland
Kidney
Vas Deferens
Seminal Vessicles
Testes
Penis

Figure 5-6.   Relationships among various "male sex hormones."

produces testosterone in very small amounts, does not depend upon FSH and LH stimulation for this purpose. ACTH, another hormone produced by the pituitary gland, on the other hand, can influence adrenal testosterone output. A recently identified substance, Gn-RH inhibiting factor (see Figure 5-6), which may some-day be useful in decreasing sex drive, has not yet been synthesized and therefore is unavailable for therapeutic purposes at present.[88]

Two other drugs that reduce testosterone levels which have been used in an attempt to treat sexual deviation syndromes are cyproterone acetate (CPA) and medroxyprogesterone acetate (MPA). Cyproterone acetate, which must be taken daily in pill form, is currently unavailable in the United States. A controlled dou-ble-blind clinical trial performed in Canada concluded that this medication could successfully reduce sexual interest and libido in a group of paraphiliac patients.[89] This investigation did not use a pharmacologically active substance with similar side effects for comparison purposes, however, thereby leaving doubt about whether study participants were indeed "blind" as to when CPA was or was not actually being administered. This raises the possibility that patients may have re-ported reduced libido as a psychological reaction to feeling "drugged" and that their feelings of diminished sexual interest may not have been attributable entirely to a pharmacologically induced decrease in testosterone levels.

When cyproterone acetate is administered, the pituitary gland does not increase production of FSH in response to decreased testosterone levels as occurs when an individual is castrated. This suggests that the drug has an effect not only upon the testes but upon the brain as well, presumably in areas relevant to sexual phe-nomenology and function. The same is true of medroxyprogesterone acetate.

None of the drugs used in the treatment of sexual deviation syndromes acts specifically to decrease deviant sexual desires while leaving conventional sexual interests intact. Thus, currently available medications do nothing to change sexual orientation; rather, if successful, they simply suppress sexual appetite in general.

Two major options are possible as a means of trying to reduce the presumed sex drive stimulating effects of testosterone. One is to try to interfere with testosterone production, whereas the other is to try to block the effects of testosterone (or more accurately, of its breakdown products) upon the brain. In the future, it may be possible to block the central effect of testosterone breakdown products upon the brain without interfering with levels of circulating testosterone peripherally. How-ever, this cannot yet be done safely in humans.

The theoretical rationale for using testosterone-depleting medications to treat paraphiliacs would be strengthened if it could be shown empirically that intensity of sexual desire is indeed correlated with testosterone level. Davidson and col-leagues showed that administration of testosterone to men whose plasma levels were below 150 ng per 100 ml led to a prompt increase in sexual appetite and activity.[90] However, Brown and others, in a study involving 101 men, demon-strated that variations in testosterone level within the intermediate range (275 to

875 ng per 100 ml in many laboratories) did not necessarily correlate with self-reports of sexual interest.[91] In animal studies, moderate decreases in testosterone level due to CPA administration failed to decrease sexual activity as significantly as had been expected.[92] Thus, in order to achieve therapeutic sex drive reduction, a significant decrease in testosterone level may be essential.

According to Laschet and Laschet, 80% of the men involved in a nonblind clinical trial reported significant reductions in sex drive in response to a daily oral dose of 100 mg of cyproterone acetate.[93] Twenty percent of the men required 200 mg per day orally, or 300 to 600 mg intramuscularly every week to ten days, in order to achieve a comparable effect. Follow-up of over 300 men for periods as long as eight years revealed few serious side effects when these dosages were employed.[94]

Stern and Eisenfeld showed that administration of radioactive-labeled testosterone to castrated rats pretreated with CPA did not result in its being bound to peripheral target tissues such as the seminal vesicles.[95] Thus, CPA appears to prevent the binding of testosterone to peripheral target organs. However, CPA does not block testosterone uptake in central hypothalamic brain regions thought to mediate sexual behavior.[96] In contrast, medroxyprogesterone acetate does, but it does not prevent testosterone binding peripherally. MPA inhibits FSH more than LH, whereas CPA inhibits only LH (see Figure 5-6). Thus, these two antiandrogenic drugs appear to exert an effect in slightly different ways. Both, however, reduce production of testosterone from its chemical precursors.[97,98] Antiandrogens may also exert an effect by preventing the rise in testosterone which ordinarily occurs as a consequence of sexual stimulation.[99]

Medroxyprogesterone Acetate (Depo-Provera).   In the United States, medroxyprogesterone acetate is the drug that has been used most frequently to treat paraphiliac patients.[2] This medication is available in depot form, which means that it is prepared in such a fashion that it can bind to muscle, from where it is gradually released into the bloodstream. Injecting a depot drug into muscle accomplishes the same purpose as taking pills daily, in that both keep medication constantly present within the bloodstream so that it can act on appropriate tissue and organ receptors (see Figure 5-7). Some of the medication travels through the circulation bound to carrier proteins, whereas the remainder circulates in an unbound (or free) form. The customary starting dosage of MPA has been 500 mg per week of the 100 mg per ml solution. No more than 250 mg is given into a single injection site. The 100 mg per ml solution has greater bioavailability (i.e., it produces higher blood levels at a given dosage) and is less painful than the 400 mg per ml concentration. Periodic blood tests can be performed to document decreases in serum testosterone levels, and the medication is not feminizing (e.g., it does not cause breast enlargement). Dosage can be titrated so as not to cause total impotence, but studies to determine optimal dosage levels have yet to be performed.

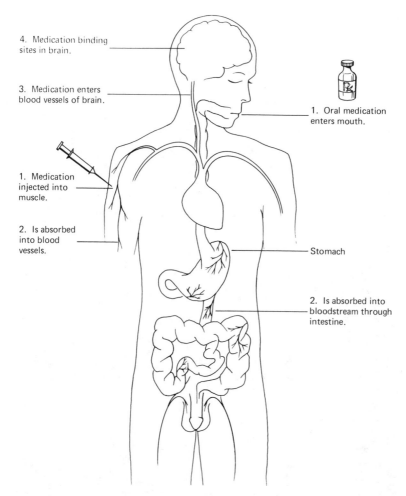

4. Medication binding sites in brain.

3. Medication enters blood vessels of brain.

1. Oral medication enters mouth.

1. Medication injected into muscle.

2. Is absorbed into blood vessels.

Stomach

2. Is absorbed into bloodstream through intestine.

Figure 5-7. Comparability of oral and intramuscularly injected medication treatment.

The major side effects of MPA include weight gain, mild lethargy, cold sweats, nightmares, and hot flashes. Hypertension is common. Elevated blood glucose, dyspnea (shortness of breath), hypogonadism (shrunken testicle size), and malignant breast tumors (in female beagle dogs) have also been reported. The drug causes a decreased sperm count which makes impregnation unlikely, but the remaining sperm can be atypical which suggests that the fetus might be deformed were a man to father a child while taking the drug. It is believed that these major side effects are reversible if medication is stopped.

Table 5-5 shows changes in sexually deviant behavior in a group of 20 chronic paraphiliac patients treated with medroxyprogesterone acetate.[2] Of these patients,

Table 5-5. Changes in Sexually Deviant Behaviors in 20 Chronic Paraphiliac Male Patients Treated with Medroxyprogesterone Acetate.*

PATIENT	AGE (YEARS)	DIAGNOSIS	AVERAGE FREQUENCY OF SEXUALLY DEVIANT BEHAVIORS BEFORE TREATMENT†	DRUG TREATMENT‡ LENGTH	DRUG TREATMENT‡ MAXIMUM DOSAGE	OCCURRENCE OF SEXUALLY DEVIANT BEHAVIORS DURING TREATMENT	OCCURRENCE OF SEXUALLY DEVIANT BEHAVIORS AFTER TREATMENT
1	34	Homosexual pedophilia	Once/week	5 years, 9 months	500 mg/week	None	Treatment dropout; no relapse less than 1 year after treatment
2	31	Homosexual pedophilia	Twice/month; 1 known arrest	1 year	300 mg/week	None	Treatment dropout; relapsed less than 1 year after treatment
3	30	Heterosexual exhibitionism	Twice/week	10 months	250–300 mg/ week	None	Treatment dropout; relapsed more than 1 year after treatment
4	34	Homosexual masochism	4 times/week	3 months	200 mg/week	None	Treatment dropout; relapsed less than 1 year after treatment
5	27	Bisexual pedophilia	Twice/week	3 months	400 mg/week	None	Treatment dropout; relapsed more than 1 year after treatment
6	43	Transvestism; homosexual incest	7 times/week; 2 incidents	1 year, 4 months, intermittently	150 mg every other week	None	Relapsed less than 1 year after treatment
7	52	Heterosexual sadism	Once every 2 weeks for 25 years	3 years, 5 months	600 mg/week	None	Treatment continues; no relapses
8	29	Homosexual pedophilia	Twice/week; 6 arrests in 6 years	10 months	500 mg/week	None	Treatment dropout; relapsed less than 1 year after treatment
9	36	Homosexual pedophilia	Once every 2 months; 4 arrests in 6 years	2 years	500 mg/week	None	Treatment continues; no relapses
10	56	Homosexual pedophilia	Once/week; 14 arrests in 29 years	3 years, 9 months	300 mg/week	Relapsed	Treatment continues
11	40	Homosexual pedophilia	Twice/week; 7 known arrests	4 years, 2 months	400 mg/week	None	Treatment continues; no relapses

	Age	Diagnosis	History	Duration	Dose	Relapse	Outcome
12	45	Voyeurism; heterosexual pedophilia	Twice/week; 5–8 arrests; numerous institutionalizations	5 years, 3 months	300 mg/week	None	Relapsed less than 1 year after treatment; treatment now resumed
13	27	Homosexual pedophilia	Twice/week since age 10	5 years, 9 months	200 mg/week	None	Treatment completed; no relapse more than 1 year after treatment
14	41	Homosexual pedophilia	Once/month; numerous arrests; 4 convictions; 4 reported parole violations	3 years, 8 months	500 mg/week	Relapsed	Treatment continues
15	37	Homosexual pedophilia; exhibitionism	Record unclear; probably several incidents/year	3 years, 9 months	350 mg/week	None	Treatment completed; no relapse less than 1 year after treatment
16	26	Homosexual pedophilia	Once/week	1 year, 1 month	200 mg/week	None	Treatment dropout; relapsed more than 1 year after treatment
17	24	Heterosexual voyeurism	Once/month	1 year	400 mg/week	Relapsed after alcohol consumption	Treatment continues; in prison
18	40	Heterosexual exhibitionism	Five times/day since age 11; first arrest at age 21; numerous others	2 years, 2 months	200 mg/week	None	Treatment dropout; relapsed less than 1 year after treatment
19	29	Heterosexual exhibitionism	Twice/week	2 years, 1 month	250 mg/week	None	Treatment dropout; relapsed less than 1 year after treatment
20	46	Heterosexual exhibitionism	Four times/week; binges of 20/day	2 years, 3 months	300 mg/week	None	Treatment continues; no relapses

*Sexually deviant behavior was considered to have occurred if the patient was accused of having or admitted having a deviant sexual contact (e.g., an episode of public genital exposure). Any occurrence of such behavior was scored as a relapse once treatment had been initiated, even if it did not come to the attention of the law as an official complaint.

†Based on institutional records and patients' statements.

‡Study participants who stopped taking medroxyprogesterone acetate did so against medical advice, except in the cases of patients 13 and 15. Some patients were irregularly compliant with medication even during the period when it was being prescribed.

15% (3 of the 20) showed recurrences of deviant activity while taking the medication, indicating that it is not 100% effective. On the other hand, 85% of these men were without further legal involvements while receiving medication, sometimes for periods as long as several years. The number of patients reported upon was small, and additional studies with larger numbers of patients need to be conducted. Some of the patients were self-referred and had no legal charges against them.

Most of the patients reported upon in Table 5-5 were not hospitalized to initiate treatment and were not required to take medication as a condition of probation. In time, many became noncompliant, sometimes because they believed themselves cured. Currently, most patients are briefly hospitalized for three or four weeks at the beginning of treatment, and subsequent outpatient compliance has improved dramatically.

The data presented in Table 5-5 show clearly that in most cases, when paraphiliac patients discontinue medications they relapse. This supports the hypothesis that this form of treatment is not a cure or a temporary catalyst to be used until psychotherapy can become effective. Rather, for the majority of patients, the medication appears to act as a sexual appetite suppressant. If deviant hungers are allowed to return, most patients seem again to be at risk of giving into temptation by satisfying those hungers. In a few cases, patients have reported that MPA fails to significantly decrease their sexual drive. Why this should be so is not known.

In the future, it will be important to conduct a controlled double-blind study in which neither the patient nor the evaluator is aware of whether MPA or a placebo with similar side effects has been administered. Fluphenazine, a drug with a similar intramuscular route of administration and similar side effects, which does not lower testosterone could be utilized for this purpose. Such a study could help document that any reduction in the frequency of sexual fantasies and in the intensity of erotic cravings experienced while receiving MPA was indeed related to lowered testosterone levels, rather than to psychological expectation or other factors independent of testosterone level. Such a study is now being planned. If it can be shown conclusively in this way that MPA does indeed decrease sexual appetite, changes in long-term recidivism rates could then also be ascertained amongst sex offenders treated with MPA, whose offending behavior either was, or was not, thought to be the manifestation of a sexual deviation syndrome.

Ancillary Care. Treating patients with antiandrogenic medications involves considerably more than simply providing injections. Although psychological counseling has not been shown to be a method capable of reducing sexual desire, such counseling may well be beneficial in other ways to the person who has been experiencing such desires. Although medication may decrease the lust a homosexual pedophilic man experiences for little boys, it cannot replace feelings of companionship, intimacy, affection, devotion, or love that may previously have been provided by children. Thus, once deviant erotic urges have been diminished by medication, an individual may also find counseling helpful in his effort to adopt a new life-style. For those who fail to respond to medication, supportive therapy and guidance to encourage efforts to resist temptation should be tried.

In initiating medication treatment, a brief period of psychiatric hospitalization lasting three to four weeks may be useful for three reasons, in addition to affording an opportunity for more comprehensive assessment. First, it removes the patient from unsupervised situations in which he might succumb to temptation before medication can begin exerting its anticipated effect. Secondly, many patients seem to develop a stronger alliance with potential help givers when living in hospital than when treatment is initiated on an outpatient basis. It is perhaps for this reason that brief hospitalization has sometimes been found to significantly increase subsequent outpatient compliance. Finally, while hospitalized, patients can speak with a group of other men having similar difficulties, which often brings a sense of relief and of being accepted as a person, thereby opening up the opportunity for greater candor. Many of these men have never before had a chance to talk openly with others without fearing that they would be perceived, and dealt with, in a demeaning way. Although the hospital staff in no way condones their behavior—quite the contrary—they do attempt to appreciate the basis for it, and they treat patients respectfully and kindly. The families of these patients can also be seen at this time, which can be important given the nature of their problems. How does a wife tell the neighbors that her husband has been arrested for exhibitionism or for sexually fondling the child next door? Patient confidentiality is maintained, but noncompliance is reported to the courts when appropriate. Rehospitalization may be required if outpatient treatment, which can include group therapy, is proceeding poorly. It is made clear to patients that a goal of therapy is to try to help them discontinue sexual behavior that violates the rights of others—not to make them feel better or less guilty about continuing it.

Surgery as Treatment for Sexual Deviation

The use of surgery to treat paraphiliac patients is well summarized in an article entitled "Therapeutic Sex Drive Reduction" written in 1980 by Dr. Kurt Freund of the Clark Institute of Psychiatry in Toronto.[100] The two major types of surgical procedures which have been used are (1) orchidectomy (castration) and (2) stereotactic neurosurgery. Stereotactic neurosurgery is performed with the aid of microscopic-sized surgical instruments capable of producing minimal-sized brain lesions. The effects of surgery (and of electrical and chemical stimulation or ablation of potential surgical sites) have been studied in both animals and men. Obviously, surgery should be considered as a therapeutic option for sex offenders only under extraordinary circumstances.

Castration.   There are few well-controlled studies assessing the effects of castration upon an animal's tendency to approach a potentially available sexual partner.[100] Nevertheless, there appears to be little doubt that removal of the gonads eventually decreases sexual interest significantly in most animals. In comparison to the rate of testosterone depletion, however, the corresponding postsurgical fading out of sexual behavior in castrated animals can be very slow. Furthermore, sexual interest may wane more slowly than sexual capacity as evidenced by the observations that (1) ejaculatory capacity often disappears before the animal loses the ability to sustain an erection and (2) the animal may continue attempting to mount receptive females even after erections have become rare.[101]

Individual differences amongst castrated animals are frequent. Pheonix and colleagues observed a substantial overall decline in virtually all aspects of sexual behavior in ten castrated monkeys.[102] However, while some of the animals ceased ejaculations immediately following surgery, others did not do so until over a year later. These postsurgical differences could not be attributed to presurgical differences in frequency of sexual behavior. The causes of individual variations in the rapidity with which various animals cease sexual behavior following orchidectomy are not clear, just as it is unclear why some humans continue to have apparently high libidos even after treatment with testosterone-depleting agents.

A number of studies have looked at the recidivism rate of sex offenses following castration in humans. Sturup and others conducted over 4000 follow-up examinations of 900 castrated sex offenders in Denmark over a 30-year period between 1929 and 1959.[103,104] There was definite recidivism of only 1.1% after castration, and if unclear cases were included, the recidivism rate was 2.2%. Wiffels reported comparable findings.[105] Ficher Van Rossum reported a 1.3% recidivism rate amongst 237 Dutch cases, and Kinmark (and Oster) reported similarly low rates on 307 Swedish patients.[103] Bremer found a 7.3% recidivism rate after five years in a group of 41 castrated sex offenders who, prior to treatment, had a recidivism rate of 58%.[106] Reported recidivism rates of castrated German sex offenders were also low.[107] This study also reported on normal German men forcibly castrated under Hitler.

Cornu, in Switzerland, compared 121 castrated sex offenders with 50 offenders who had refused recommended castration.[108] Follow-up ranged between 5 and 30 years. The recidivism rate of castrated offenders was 5.8%, indicating that castration does not make further sexual offenses impossible. However, the recidivism rate of the 50 offenders who had refused castration was 52% (15 committed one additional offense, while 11 others committed between two and seven additional offenses each). Presumably, these differences in recidivism rate were a reflection of whether or not castration had been performed, although the possibility that the voluntarily castrated group contained more patients genuinely motivated to stop offending behavior cannot be entirely excluded. Prior to castration, both groups had a comparable frequency of offending behavior.

Freund pointed out that the degree to which sexual drive decreases after castration appears to depend upon the length of time of testosterone depletion.[100] Thus, if it is the case that some repeat sex offenses occur a short time after surgery, even further lowering of the recidivism rates might be possible by keeping patients in the hospital longer following castration.

Besides documenting changes in recidivism rate, a number of investigators obtained self-reports from sex offenders regarding potency. In many cases following castration, some degree of erotic desire and the capacity to perform sexually remained.[107-109] Hackfield pointed out that this does not present a problem in terms of treatment since the surgery fulfills its intent if it decreases sex drive sufficiently to enable the patient to refrain from acting upon unacceptable erotic urges.[110] Sturup described several cases in which pleasurable intercourse was successfully practiced for many years following castration in response to advances from consensual female partners.[104] Although a castrated man could reverse his condition by undergoing testosterone treatment, few cases have been detected in which this has occurred without medical approval.

Testosterone appears to be a prehormone which is broken down in the liver to form other metabolically active substances. Some of these bind to receptor sites in the brain, presumably stimulating areas related to erotic desire. Other testosterone breakdown products bind to receptors on peripheral tissues likely related to physical capacity to obtain erection and to ejaculate (see Figure 5-6). Freund suggests that someday it may be possible to administer active breakdown products of testosterone to castrated sex offenders, which will enhance their sexual capacity by affecting peripheral receptors without increasing sexual desire (via central brain stimulation) to a level where it becomes difficult to resist temptation.[100]

Neurosurgery.   The second type of surgical procedure used in the treatment of sex offenders is stereotactic neurosurgery. In order to try to determine whether such surgery might be feasible in humans, a great deal of animal experimentation has been performed. That work has attempted to identify structures in the brain (1) that accumulate relatively large amounts of sexual hormones, (2) that lead to changes in the output of sexual hormones in response to either stimulation or ablation, or (3) that lead to changes in sexual behavior in response to either stimulation or ablation. Some researchers have also studied "experiments of nature" by looking at alterations in sexual behavior that correlate with human brain pathology.[111]

It is clear from studies done upon animals that lesions in some brain regions can readily decrease the frequency of sexual behavior without affecting either perceptual-motor capacity or circulating testosterone levels.[112,113] The area preoptica in the hypothalamus is one such region.[113] It seems to be particularly rich in sex hormone receptors. Other areas of the brain such as the limbic system accumulate sexual hormones to a lesser degree or not at all.

Exposing various areas of the brains of live animals to sex hormones to see whether sexual behavior will occur is another method used in an attempt to identify potential neurosurgical sites. This has produced some intriguing observations. Estrogen applied locally to specific hypothalamic sites in male rats leads to a lordotic response—a backward elevation of the pelvis that facilitates intercourse in females.[112] Testosterone implants in certain hypothalamic sites can reactivate mating behavior in castrated male animals, but similar implants in other brain sites cannot.[114] Electrical stimulation in the dorsal part of the lateral area preoptica causes almost uninterrupted mounting and frequent ejaculations in male rats.[115]

In 1939, Kluver and Bucy described a syndrome in cats, produced by bilateral temporal lobectomy, that included intensified indiscriminate sexual behavior.[116] In 1954, Schreiner and Kling showed that this hypersexual activity could be abolished by castration but reinstituted with testosterone replacement therapy—which suggests that the behavior in question was sex hormone related.[117] They demonstrated that lesions to specific sites in the ventromedial nucleus of the hypothalamus could also abolish this hypersexual activity.

In 1966 a team of neurosurgeons performed stereotactic brain surgery on a homosexual pedophile, making a lesion in the ventromedial nucleus of the hypothalamus in the same area that had seemed to decrease hypersexuality when it had been ablated in Kluver-Bucy cats.[118] The patient subsequently indicated that his erotic fantasy life was virtually abolished and that he had lost his pedophilic urges. In 1979, Orthner (and others) reported that substantial therapeutic sex drive reduction had been achieved in 34 sex offenders treated neurosurgically in a similar way.[111,112,119] Although no formal instruments were used to confirm the validity of the patients' self-reports, in many cases follow-up extended over several years with no known rearrests. Major side effects were increased appetite, weight gain, and reported absence of dreaming. Freund feels that this surgical team may have obtained genuine success and that if it can be more conclusively established that neurosurgery appreciably lowers the recidivism rate of sex offenders, none of the reported side effects appeared disproportionate.

Schmidt and Schorsch cautioned that psychosurgery of this sort has sometimes been performed without proper safeguards with poor results.[120] They cited a study by Muller involving ten paraphiliac patients. Three years after surgery, four of the ten patients were lost to follow-up, three were said to be significantly improved, and two unimproved. Of the two unimproved patients, both subsequently underwent castration. The tenth patient in this series, a pedophile with sadomasochistic fantasies, was relased from prison after neurosurgery and was administered antiandrogenic medication until he complained of impotence with an age-appropriate girlfriend, at which time medication was stopped. Several weeks later he was accused of murdering a 10-year-old child.

A recent governmental task force appointed to consider the topic of psychosurgery in the United States concluded that it does hold therapeutic promise but recommended that its use be confined to designated research centers to try to assure proper safeguards.[121,122] Some authorities feel that brain surgery to attempt to decrease troublesome sexual appetites should for the time being be discontinued until further data from animal experimentation become available.[123]

Future Research

Figure 5-8 shows pictures obtained by means of a CAT scan and a PET scan. The term CAT scan is an abbreviation for computer assisted tomography. The equipment involved in producing these X-rays is manufactured by the EMI Corporation; thus, EMI scan is also sometimes employed.

When first marketed, the CAT scan represented a significant improvement over previously available X-ray procedures because not only could it show the presence of hard structures such as bones or tumors, but it was also capable of depicting the details of softer tissues such as kidney, lung, or brain. Furthermore, with the aid of computer analysis it could safely produce pictures of these structures corresponding to various depths within the tissue being X-rayed. X-rays of the brain taken by CAT scan depict structure but not function.

The term PET scan is an abbreviation for positron emission tomography. This test, like thyroid scanning, requires that the patient be administered a small amount of radioactive material—in this case glucose—which emits positrons. A computer attached to Geiger counter type sensors placed around the patient's head then produces a series of cross-sectional pictures of the brain at various depths. These pictures vary in color according to the amount of glucose being utilized as a source of energy at a given anatomical site. In this manner, the PET scanner can provide a picture showing which areas of the brain are most active metabolically at a given time—for example, during sexual arousal. Because the half-life (decay time) of radioactive glucose labeled in this fashion is short, the test is believed to be safe; it is no more dangerous than conventional thyroid scanning procedures which have been used medically for many years.

The PET scanner may help provide answers to the following questions. What areas of the brain are metabolically active during sexual arousal? Do these areas differ in persons with unconventional sexual orientations or interests? Do these areas differ in persons with organic anomalies such as Klinefelter's syndrome? What are the effects of testosterone-diminishing medications, which given in low or higher dosage forms, upon brain activity during sexual arousal?

PART IV: MEDICOLEGAL ISSUES AND SUMMARY

Medicolegal Issues

In considering the treatment of sex offenders with surgery or with antiandrogenic medications, a number of ethical and medicolegal issues must be addressed. Recently, in an editorial in the *American Journal of Psychiatry*, Dr. Seymor Halleck called for the establishment of guidelines regarding the use of antiandrogenic medications.[124] Two issues of concern to him related to (1) maintaining the constitutional rights of citizens, even those convicted of sex offenses and (2) the question

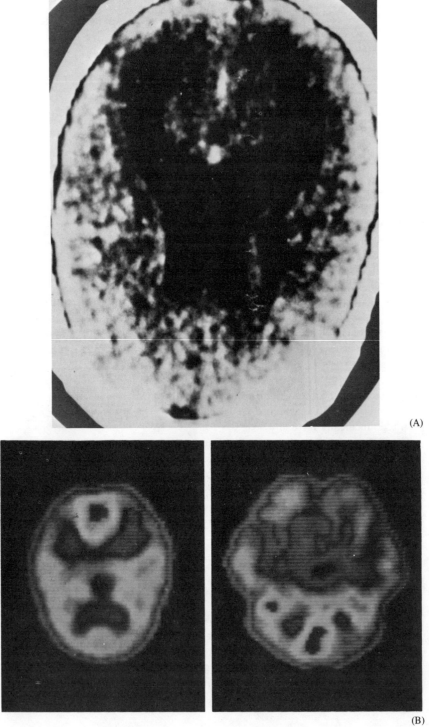

Figure 5-8. (A) CAT scan. (B) PET scan.

of whether persons facing prolonged incarceration are capable of giving informed consent regarding the use of this form of treatment.

In most democratic societies, individuals are generally free to do whatever they choose, as long as in doing so they do not interfere with the rights and well-being of others. When a person's behavior does pose a threat to the well-being of others, as clearly occurs when an individual rapes, for example, his freedom and rights are diminished for the common good. Thus, a convicted sex offender does not possess all the rights of a person who has not violated the law.

When an individual represents a threat to the safety of others, there is legal precedent for requiring him to take medication (e.g., measles vaccine). In this sense, then, requiring a convicted sex offender either to take antiandrogenic medications as a condition of probation or to go to prison may not be an unconstitutional violation of his rights.[125] Admittedly, making such a decision can be difficult, but just because the consequences of a decision may be difficult does not mean that one loses the capacity to choose. Cancer patients often have to choose between taking medication and dying.

Paraphiliac patients should not be denied access to antiandrogenic medications they wish to take which might be helpful in their treatment. Recently, a prisoner in Maryland successfully petitioned the court for the right to receive such treatment. Administering a properly informed, convicted person medication that may directly benefit him is very different from using him to study the effects of a drug, such as rabies vaccine, unrelated to his personal well-being. Paraphiliacs taking antiandrogenic medications can benefit if (1) they gain greater capacity for self-control, (2) they obtain relief from intrusive erotic obsessional fantasies, or (3) they avoid the necessity for quarantine from the community.

The medical profession needs to make clear the nature of the effects of psychiatric medications in general. They are not administered to control attitudes or behaviors such as those relating to political affiliations. They are not "mind controlling." Rather, they are usually given with the intent of increasing the capacity for self-control and restoring function (such as the ability to determine whether "heard" voices are real or imaginary).[126] Antiandrogenic medications are given in an attempt to increase rather than decrease self-control.[126]

Summary

Sexual deviation syndromes (paraphilias) are diagnosable psychiatric conditions manifested by (1) recurrent deviant fantasies, (2) intense erotic cravings, and (3) relatively stereotyped behaviors as a response to those cravings. The behaviors are stereotyped in the sense that exhibitionists expose themselves, whereas pedophiles seek out children and transvestites cross-dress. Paraphiliac syndromes are not necessarily mutually exclusive, but like conventional heterosexuality, their course is chronic. They may respond to biological treatments and may have associated organic pathologies (such as Klinefelter's syndrome), but their etiologies are poorly understood.

Sexual offenses, as defined legally, may or may not be perpetrated by persons with one of these syndromes. When offending behavior is related to such a syndrome, (1) intramuscularly administered medroxyprogesterone acetate, (2) orchidectomy to diminish testosterone, or (3) cyproterone acetate may be helpful. However, antiandrogenic medication can only help if the patient is compliant. Orally administered medroxyprogesterone (at a daily dosage of 150 mg) has not been shown to be helpful.[128] It is not known whether antiandrogenic medication can help when offending behavior is unrelated to deviant sexual cravings, as when rape is committed opportunistically or in response to anger and hostility. Stereotactic psychosurgery is still a somewhat controversial procedure that is not yet widely enough available to be considered a practical treatment option for sexual deviation syndromes at this time. Behavior therapy may help some patients learn how to better resist their urges, but it may work less well with some paraphiliac syndromes than with others. When a sex offense is the reflection of a psychiatric illness such as schizophrenia or manic-depressive syndrome, medication treatment appropriate to that condition should be instituted. Legal demands for justice and safety as well as medical concerns for understanding care must both be considered, because each is important. When a person seeks help, his difficulties should be appreciated rather than scorned as perversions.

REFERENCES

1. *Diagnostic and Statistical Manual of Mental Disorders*, 3rd ed. Task Force on Nomenclature and Statistics of the American Psychiatric Association, LI-L33, 1978.
2. Berlin, F.S. and Meinecke, C.F. Treatment of sex offenders with antiandrogenic medication: conceptualization, review of treatment modalities, and preliminary findings. *American Journal of Psychiatry* **138**:601-607 (1981).
3. Abramson, H.A. The historical and cultural spectra of homosexuality and their relationship to fear of being a lesbian. *Journal of Asthma Research* **17**(4):117 (1980).
4. Gilbert, A.N. Buggery and the British Navy 1700–1761. *Journal of Social History* **10**:72 (1976).
5. Ford, C.S. and Beach, F.A. *Patterns of Sexual Behavior*. New York: Harper and Row, 1951.
6. Gadpaille, W.J. Cross species and cross cultural contributions to understanding homosexual activity. *Archives of General Psychiatry* **37**:349-356 (1980).
7. Koan, L. and Bulkley, J. Analysis of criminal child sex offense statutes. In Bulkley, J. (Ed.) *Child Sexual Abuse and the Law*. Washington, D.C.: American Bar Association, pp. 6-12, 1981.
8. Bulkley, J. and Davidson, H.A. *Child Sexual Abuse: Legal Issues and Approaches*. Washington, D.C.: National Legal Resource Center for Child Advocacy and Protection, American Bar Association, 1981, p. 9.
9. Fear stalks the streets. *U.S. News and World Report* (October 30, 1980).
10. Tobias, J.L. and Gordon, T. Special projects: operation victimization. *Oakland County Homicide Task Force* 3 (1977).
11. Groth, A.N. Sexual trauma in the life histories of rapists and child molesters. *Victimology: An International Journal* **4**(1):10-16 (1979).

12. Regestein, R.R. and Reich, P. Pedophilia occurring after onset of cognitive impairment. *Journal of Nervous and Mental Disorders* **166**:794-798 (1978).

13. Crepault, C. and Conture, M. Men's erotic fantasies. *Archives of Sexual Behavior* **9**(6):565-581 (1980).

14. Evans, D.R. Masturbatory fantasy and sexual deviation. *Behavioural Research and Therapy* **6**:17-19 (1968).

15. Quincy, U.L., Chaplin, T.C., and Varney, G. A comparison of rapist's and non–sex offender's sexual preferences for mutually consenting sex, rape, and physical abuse of women. *Behavioral Assessment* **3**:127-135 (1981).

16. Jaspers, K. *General Psychopathology*. Chicago: University of Chicago Press, 1972, pp. 323, 631.

17. Mohr, J.W., Turner, R.E., and Jerry, M.B. *Pedophilia and Exhibitionism*. Toronto: Toronto University Press, 1964.

18. Woodruff, R.A., Goodwin, D.W., and Guze, S.B. *Psychiatric Diagnosis*. New York: Oxford University Press, 1974, pp. 25-44.

19. Berlin, F.S. In defense of the disease model in psychiatry. *Psychiatric Annals* **11**:39-45 (1981).

20. Snyder, S.H., Banerjee, S.D., Yamammura, H.I., and Grunberg, D. Drugs, neurotransmitters, and schizophrenia. *Science* **184**:1243-1253 (1974).

21. Hollister, L.E. *Clinical Use of Psychotherapeutic Drugs*. Springfield, Ill.: Thomas, 1975, pp. 13-55.

22. Ward, N.G. Successful lithium treatment of transvestism associated with manic depression. *Journal of Nervous and Mental Disease* **161**(3):204-206 (1975).

23. Newton, D.E. Homosexual behavior and child molestation: a review of the evidence. *Adolescence* **13**(19):29-43 (1978).

24. Berlin, F.S. and Coyle, G.S. Sexual deviation syndromes. *Johns Hopkins Medical Journal* **149**:119-125 (1981).

25. Smith, S. Voyeurism: a review of the literature. *Archives of Sexual Behavior* **5**(5):585-607 (1976).

26. Klinefelter, H.F., Reifenstein, E.C., Jr., and Albright, F. Syndrome characterized by gynecomastia, aspermatogenesis without A-Leydigism, and increased excretion of FSH. *Journal of Clinical Endocrinology* **2**(2):615 (1942).

27. Sorensen, K., Nielsen, J., Froland, A., and Johnsen, S.G. Psychiatric examination of all eight adult males with the karyotype 46 XX diagnosed in Denmark until 1976. *Acta Psychiatrica Scandinavica* **59**:153-163 (1979).

28. Ohno, S. The role of H-Y antigen in primary sex determination. *Journal of the American Medical Association* **239**(3):217-220 (1978).

29. Gordon, J.W. and Ruddle, F.H. Mammalian gonadal determination and gametogenesis. *Science* **211**(20):1265-1271 (1981).

30. Haseltine, F.P. and Ohno, S. Mechanisms of gonadal differentiation. *Science* **211**(20):1272-1278 (1981).

31. Kosek, M.S. Medical genetics. In Krupp, M.A. and Chatton, M.J. (Eds.) *Current Diagnosis and Treatment*. Los Altos, Calif.: Lange Medical Publications, 1972, pp. 883-884.

32. Money, J., Hampson, J.G., and Hampson, J.L. Imprinting and the establishment of gender role. *Archives of Neurology and Psychiatry* **77**:333-336 (1957).

33. Baker, H.J. and Stoller, J. Can a biological force contribute to gender identity? *American Journal of Psychiatry* **124**(12):1653-1658 (1968).

34. Fisher, A.E. Maternal and sexual behavior induced by intracranial chemical stimulation. *Science* **124**:228-229 (1956).

35. Becker, K.L. Cultural and therapeutic experience with Klinefelter's syndrome. *Fertility and Sterility* **23**(8):568-578 (1972).

36. Hardin, J.A., Cocker, A., and Scott, C.W. Medical Grand Rounds for the University of Alabama Medical Center. *Southern Medical Journal* **62**:1211-1219 (1969).

37. Nielsen, J., Tsuboi, T., Turner, B., Jensen, J.T., and Sachs, J. Prevalence and incidence of the XYY syndrome and Klinefelter's syndrome in an institution for criminal psychopaths. *Acta Psychiatrica Scandinavica* **45**(4):402-424 (1969).

38. Raboch, J., Mellan, J., and Starka, L. Klinefelter's syndrome: sexual development and activity. *Archives of Sexual Behavior* **8**(4):333-339 (1979).

39. Orwin, A., James, S.R.N., and Turner, R.K. Sex chromosome abnormalities, homosexuality, and psychological treatment. *British Journal of Psychiatry* **124**:293-295 (1974).

40. Slater, E. and Cowie, V. Sex chromosome anomalies. In *The Genetics of Mental Disorders*. London: Oxford University Press, 1971, pp. 317-319.

41. Nielsen, J. Gender role identity and sexual behavior in persons with sex chromosome aberrations. *Danish Medical Bulletin* **17**(8):269-275 (1972).

42. Hunter, H. A controlled study of the psychopathology and physical measurements of Klinefelter's syndrome. *British Journal of Psychiatry* **115**:443-448 (1969).

43. Schroder, J., De La Chapelle, A., Hakola, P., and Virkkurnen, M. The frequency of XYY and XXY men among criminal offenders. *Acta Psychiatrica Scandinavica* **63**:272-276 (1981).

44. Money, J., Annecello, C., Van Orman, B., and Borgaonkar, D.S. Cytogenetics, hormones, and behavior disability: comparison of XYY and XXY syndromes. *Clinical Genetics* **6**:370-382 (1974).

45. Baker, P., Telfer, M.A., Richardson, C.E., and Clark, G.R. Chromosome errors in men with antisocial behavior. *Journal of the American Medical Association* **214**(5):869-878 (1970).

46. Nielsen, J. Criminality among patients with Klinefelter's syndrome and the XYY syndrome. *British Journal of Psychiatry* **117**:365-369 (1970).

47. Tsuboi, T. Crimino-biologic study of patients with the XYY syndrome and Klinefelter's syndrome. *Humangenetik* **10**:68-84 (1970).

48. Wakeling, A. Comparison study of psychiatric patients with Klinefelter's syndrome and hypogonadism. *Psychological Medicine* **2**:139-154 (1972).

49. Crowley, J.T. Klinefelter's syndrome and abnormal behavior: a case report. *International Journal of Neuropsychiatry* **5**:359-363 (1964).

50. Pasqualine, R.Q., Vidal, G., and Bur, G.E. Psychopathology of Klinefelter's syndrome: review of thirty-one cases. *Lancet* **2**:164-167 (1957).

51. Beumont, P.J.V., Bancroft, J.H.J., Beardwood, C.J., and Russel, G.F.M. Behavioral changes after treatment with testosterone: case report. *Psychological Medicine* **2**:70-72 (1972).

52. Huffer, V., Scott, W.H., Connor, T.B., and Lovice, H. Psychological studies of adult male patients with social infantilism before and after androgen therapy. *Annals of Internal Medicine* **61**:255-268 (1964).

53. Myhre, S.A., Ruvalcaba, R.H.A., Johnson, H.R., Thuline, H.C., and Kelley, V.C. The effects of testosterone treatment in Klinefelter's syndrome. *Journal of Pediatrics* **76**:267-276 (1970).

54. Miller, J.A. A song for the female finch. *Science News* **117**:58-59 (1980).

55. Money, J. Clinical aspects of prenatal steroidal action on sexually dimorphic behavior. In Sawyer, C.H. and Gorski, R.A. (Eds.) *Steroid Hormones and Brain Function*. Berkeley: University of California Press, 1971, pp. 325-338.

56. Fisher, A.E. Behavior as a function of certain neurobiochemical events. *Current Trends in Psychobiological Theory*. Pittsburgh, Pa.: University of Pittsburgh Press, 1960, pp. 70-86.

57. Tinbergen, N. The curious behavior of the stickleback. In McGaugh, J.L., Weisberger, N.M., and Whalen, R.E. (Eds.) *Psychobiology: The Biological Basis of Behavior* San Francisco: Freeman, 1966, pp. 5-9.

58. Foss, B.M. *New Horizons in Psychology*. Baltimore: Penguin Books, 1966, pp. 185-208.

59. Hess, E.H. Imprinting in animals. In McGaugh, J.L., Weinberger, N.M., and Whalen, R.E.

(Eds.) *Psychobiology: The Biological Basis of Behavior.* San Francisco: Freeman, 1966, pp. 107-111.

60. Lorenz, K.Z. *King Solomon's Ring: New Light on Animal Ways.* Thomas Y. Chromwell, 1952.

61. Adams, D.B., Gold, A.R., and Burt, A.D. Rise in female initiated sexual activity at ovulation and its suppression by oral contraceptives. *New England Journal of Medicine* 299:1145-1150 (1978).

62. Murad, F. and Gilman, A.G. Androgens and anabolic steroids. In Goodman, L.S. and Gilman, A. (Eds.) *The Pharmacological Basis of Therapeutics.* New York: Macmillan, 1975.

63. Goy, R. and McEwen, B.S. *Sexual Differentiation of the Brain.* Cambridge, Mass.: MIT Press, 1977.

64. Pillard, R.C., Poumadere, J., and Carretta, R.A. Is homosexuality familial? A review, some data, and a suggestion. *Archives of Sexual Behavior* 10(5):465-475 (1981).

65. Levine, S. Sex difference in the brain. In McGaugh, J.L., Weinberger, N.M., and Whalen, R.E. (Eds.) *Psychobiology: The Biological Basis of Behavior.* San Francisco: Freeman, 1966, pp. 76-81.

66. Adkins, E.K. Hormonal basis of sexual differentiation in the Japanese quail. *Journal of Comparative and Physiological Psychology* 89(1):61-71 (1973).

67. Prenatal determination of adult sexual behavior. *Lancet* 11(81):1149-1150 (1981).

68. McEwen, B.S. Neural gonadal steroid actions. *Science* 211:1303-1311 (1981).

69. MacLusky, N.J. and Naftolin, F. Sexual differentiations of the central nervous system. *Science* 211:1294-1303 (1981).

70. Witson, J.D., George, F.W., and Griffin, J.E. The hormonal control of sexual development. *Science* 211:1278-1284 (1981).

71. Ehrhardt, A.A., Epstein, R., and Money, J. Fetal androgens and female gender identity in the early treated adreno-genital syndrome. *Johns Hopkins Medical Journal* 122:160-167 (1980).

72. Ehrhardt, A.A. and Baker, S.W. Prenatal androgen exposure and adolescent behavior. In Porter, R. and Wheelan, J. (Eds.) *Sex, Hormones, and Behavior.* Amsterdam: Excerpta Medica, 1979, pp. 41-50.

73. Ehrhardt, A.A. and Money, J. Progesterone induced hermaphrodism: IQ and psychosexual identity in a study of ten girls. *Journal of Sexual Research* 3:83-100 (1967).

74. Ehrhardt, A.A., Grisanti, G.C., and Meyer-Bahlburg, H.F.L. Prenatal exposure to medroxyprogesterone acetate (MPA) in girls. *Psychoneuroendocrinology* 2:391-398 (1977).

75. Yalom, J.P., Green, R., and Fisk, N. Prenatal exposure to female hormones. Effect on psychosexual development in boys. *Archives of General Psychiatry* 28:554-561 (1973).

76. Meyer-Bahlburg, H.F.L., Grisanti, G.C., and Ehrhardt, A.A. Prenatal effects of sex hormones on human male behavior: medroxyprogesterone acetate (MPA). *Psychoneuroendocrinology* 2:383-390 (1977).

77. Carney, A., Bancroft, J., and Mathews, A. A combination of hormonal and psychological treatment for female sexual unresponsiveness: a comparative study. *British Journal of Psychiatry* 132:339-346 (1978).

78. Eicher, W., Spolijar, M., Cleve, H., et al. H-Y antigen in transsexuality. *Lancet* 2:1137-1138 (1979).

79. Money, J. and Gaskin, R.J. Sex reassignment. *International Journal of Psychiatry* 9:249-282 (1970-71).

80. Sex change: good for some. *Science News* 117(17):262-263 (1980).

81. Marks, I., Gelder, M., and Bancroft, J. Sexual deviants two years after electric aversion. *British Journal of Psychiatry* 117:173-185 (1970).

82. Marks, I.M. Review of behavioral psychotherapy. II: Sexual disorders. *American Journal of Psychiatry* 138(6):750-756 (1981).

83. Blair, C.D. and Lanyon, R.I. Exhibitionism: etiology and treatment. *Psychological Bulletin* 89:439-463 (1981).

84. Tennet, T.G., Bancroft, J.H.J., and Cass, J. The control of deviant sexual behavior by drugs: a double blind coltrolled study of benperidol, chlorpromazine, and placebo. *Archives of Sexual Behavior* **3**:261-271 (1974).

85. Bancroft, J.H.J., Tennent, T.G., Loncas, K., and Cass, J. Control of deviant sexual behavior by drugs: behavioral effects of estrogens and antiandrogens. *British Journal of Psychiatry* **125**:310-315 (1974).

86. Murray, M.A.F., Bancroft, J.H.J., Anderson, D.C., Tennent, T.G., and Carr, P.J. Endocrine changes in male sexual deviants after treatment with antiandrogens, oestrogens, or tranquilizers. *Journal of Endocrinology* **67**:179-188 (1975).

87. Crowley, W.F. Development of a male contraceptive—a beginning. *New England Journal of Medicine* **305**(12):695-696 (1981).

88. Schally, A.V., Arimura, A., and Kastin, A.J. Hypothalamic regulatory hormones: at least nine substances from the hypothalamus control the secretion of pituitary hormones. *Science* **179**:341-350 (1973).

89. Cooper, A.J. A placebo-controlled trial of the antiandrogen cyproterone acetate in deviant hypersexuality. *Comprehensive Psychiatry* **22**(5):458-465 (1981).

90. Davidson, J.M., Canargo, C.M., and Smith, E.R. Effects of androgen on sexual behavior in hypogonadal men. *Journal of Clinical and Endocrinological Metabolism* **48**:955-958 (1979).

91. Brown, W.A., Monti, P.M., and Carrivean, D.P. Serum Testosterone and sexual activity and interest in men. *Archives of Sexual Behavior* **7**(7):97-103 (1978).

92. Michael, R.P., Plant, T.M., and Wilson, M.I. Preliminary studies on the effects of cyproterone acetate on sexual activity and testicular function in adult male rhesus monkeys (*Macaca mulatta*). *Adv. Biosci.* **10**:197-208 (1972).

93. Laschet, V. and Laschet, L. Three years' clinical results with cyproterone-acetate in the inhibiting regulation of male sexuality. *Acta Endocrinologica Suppl. 138* 103 (1969).

94. Laschet, V. and Laschet, L. Antiandrogens in the treatment of sexual deviations in men. *Journal of Steroid Biochemistry* **6**:821-826 (1975).

95. Stern, J.M. and Eisenfeld, A.J. Androgen accumulation and binding to macromolecules in seminal vesicles: inhibition by cyproterone. *Science* **166**:233-235 (1969).

96. Whalen, R.E. and Luttage, W.G. Effects of the anti-androgen cyproterone acetate on the uptake of 1,2H-testosterone in neural and peripheral tissues of the castrated male rat. *Endocrinology* **84**:217-222 (1969).

97. Gordon, G.G., Southern, A.L., Tochimoto, S., Olivo, J., Altman, K., Rand, J., and Lemberger, L. Effect of medroxyprogesterone acetate (Provera) on the metabolism and biological activity of testosterone. *Journal of Clinical Endocrinology* **30**:449-456 (1970).

98. Brotherton, J. and Bernard, G. Some aspects of the effect of cyproterone acetate on levels of other steroid hormones in man. *Journal of Reproduction and Fertility* **36**:373-385 (1974).

99. Fox, C.A., Ismail, A.A., Love, D.N., Kirkham, K.E., and Loraine, J.A. Studies on the relationship between plasma testosterone levels and human sexual activity. *Journal of Endocrinology* **52**:51-58 (1972).

100. Freund, K. Therapeutic sex drive reduction. *Acta Psychiatrica Scandinavica Suppl. 287* **62**:1-39 (1980).

101. Beach, F.A. Coital behavior in dogs. VI. Long-term effects of castration upon mating in the male. *Journal of Comparative and Physiological Psychology* **70**(2):1-32 (1970).

102. Pheonix, C.H., Slof, A.K., and Goy, R.W. Effects of castration and replacement therapy on sexual behavior of male rhesuses. *Journal of Comparative and Physiological Psychology* **84**:472-481 (1973).

103. Sturup, G.K. *Treating the "Untreatable" Chronic Criminals at Herstedvester*. Baltimore: Johns Hopkins Press, 1968.

104. Sturup, G.K. Castration: the total treatment. In Resnik, H.P.L. and Wolfgang, M.E. (Eds.) *Sexual Behaviors: Social, Clinical and Legal Aspects*. Boston: Little, Brown, 1972, pp. 361-382.

105. Wiffels, A.J.A.M. Het castratie Vraagstuk. *Nach der englischen zusammenfassung (The Problem of Castration)*. Leyden: Holland, 1954.
106. Bremer, J. *Asexualization: A Follow-up Study of 244 Cases*. New York: Macmillan, 1959.
107. Lasngeluddeke, A. Die Entmannung von Sittlichkeitsverbrechern in Deutschland. In *Die Entmannung von Sittlichkeitsverbrechern*. Berlin: De Gruyter, 1963.
108. Cornu, F. Katamnesin bei Kastrierten sittlichkeitsdelinquenten aus farensischpsychiatrischer sicht. *Bib. Psychiat.* **149**:1-132 (1973).
109. Lange, J. Die Folgen der Entmannung Erwachsener an Hand der Kriegserfahrungen dargestellt. *Arb. Gesundh.* **24**:1-178 (1934).
110. Hackfield, A.W. Uber die Kastration bei Vierzig Sexuall Abnormen. *Monatsschrift Psychiatry and Neurology* **87**:1-31 (1933).
111. Orthner, H. Sexual disorders. In *Textbook of Stereotaxy of the Human Brain*. Albuquerque: University of New Mexico Press, 1979.
112. Whalen, R.E. Brain mechanisms controlling sexual behavior. In Beach, F.A. (Ed.) *Human Sexuality in Four Perspectives*. Baltimore: Johns Hopkins University Press, 1976.
113. Hutchison, J.B. *Biological Determination of Sexual Behaviors*. Toronto: John Wiley and Sons, 1978.
114. Kierniesky, N.C. and Gerall, A.A. Effects of testosterone propionate in the brain on the sexual behavior and peripheral tissue of the male rat. *Psychological Behavior* **11**:633-640 (1973).
115. Malsbury, C.W. Facilitation of male rat copulatory behavior by electrical stimulation of the medial preoptic area. *Psychobiological Behavior* **7**:797-805 (1971).
116. Kluver, H. and Bucy, P.C. Preliminary analysis of functions of the temporal lobes in monkeys. *Archives of Neurology and Psychiatry* **42**:979-1000 (1939).
117. Schreiver, L. and Kling, A. Behavioral changes following paleocortical injury in rodents, carnivores, and primates. *Federation Proceedings* **12**:128 (1953).
118. Roeder, F.D., Muller, D., and Orthner, H. The sterotaxic treatment of pedophilic homosexuality and other sexual deviations. In Hitchcock, E., Laitinen, L., and Vaernet, K. (Eds.) *Psychosurgery*. Springfield, Ill.: Thomas, 1972.
119. Sweet, W.H., Obrader, S., and Martin-Rodriguez, J.G. *Neurosurgical Treatment in Psychiatry, Pain, and Epilepsy*. Baltimore: University Park Press, 1977.
120. Schmidt, G. and Schorsch, E. Psychosurgery of sexually deviant patients: review and analysis of new empirical findings. *Archives of Sexual Behavior* **10**(3):301-323 (1981).
121. Cullington, G.J. Psychosurgery: national commission issues surprisingly favorable report. *Science* **194**:299-301 (1976).
122. Bridges, P.K. and Bartlett, J.R. Psychosurgery: yesterday and today. *British Journal of Psychiatry* **131**:249-260 (1977).
123. Rieber, I. and Sigusch, V. Psychosurgery on sex offenders and sexual "deviants" in West Germany. *Archives of Sexual Behavior* **8**(6):523-527 (1979).
124. Halleck, S.L. The ethics of anti-androgen therapy. *American Journal of Psychiatry* **138**:642-643 (1981).
125. Berlin, F.S. Ethical use of antiandrogenic medications. *American Journal of Psychiatry* **138**(11):1516-1517 (1981).
126. Berlin, F.S., Bergey, G.K., and Money, J. Periodic psychosis of puberty: a case report. *American Journal of Psychiatry* (in press).
127. Berlin, F.S. Determinism versus predeterminism. *American Journal of Psychiatry* (in review).
128. Langerin, R., Paitich, D., Hucker, S., Newman, S., Ramsay, G., Pope, S., and Anderson, C. The effect of assertiveness training, Provera, and sex of therapist in the treatment of genital exhibitionism. *Journal of Behavior Therapy and Experimental Psychiatry* **10**:275-282 (1979).

Part III

Treatment, Evaluation, and Research

6

A Treatment Program for Intrafamily Juvenile Sexual Offenders*

Joyce N. Thomas, R.N., M.P.H.
Carl M. Rogers, Ph.D.

This chapter explores the increasing recognition that intrafamily sexual abuse cases involving nonparental offenders are just as serious and in need of treatment as father/daughter incest cases. Situations in which the abuser is an adolescent who resides with the victim pose special problems, and require special techniques in case management and therapeutic interventions. A pilot intervention and treatment program designed to cope with cases involving adolescent offenders is described. Sample case histories are presented as illustrative of the problems facing the staff. Examples of the consent form for treatment and the medical evaluation forms currently in use at this agency are included.

INTRODUCTION

Of all the childhood experiences that impact upon later emotional adjustment, intrafamily sexual abuse or sexual assault of a child must rank among the most potentially damaging. In recent years there has been a great deal written about this problem in terms of its etiology and treatment, with the primary emphasis being upon enhanced understanding of father/daughter incest and its remediation. To date, little systematic attention has been given to what is perhaps the most common form of child sexual abuse: sexual victimization of a child by a teenager or adolescent. In the course of this chapter we will briefly explore the magnitude of this problem and the common characteristics of cases encountered; we will also describe a pilot intervention and treatment program designed to cope with cases involving the adolescent offender. Our particular emphasis is upon the larger group of adolescent offenders, the juvenile intrafamily sexual abuser.

Estimates regarding the frequency either of sexual victimization of children in general or of intrafamily sexual abuse in particular are difficult to come by and susceptible to the distorting effects of local reporting requirements, definitional

*This chapter was written based on a special service improvement grant No. 90-CA-825 funded by the National Center on Child Abuse and Neglect, OHDS, DHHS, ACYF. The authors wish to acknowledge input from program staff: Paul Mitchell, M.Ed., M.S.W.; David W. Lloyd, J.D.; Nancy Horstmann, Ph.D.; and Stanley Ridley, Ph.D.

criteria, and site of data collection (Makstein et al., 1979). The best available estimates suggest that perhaps 50,000 to 60,000 children are victims of intrafamily sexual abuse every year (Giarretto, 1976; National Center on Child Abuse and Neglect, 1981). Other studies suggest that approximately 80% of all children sexually victimized knew the abuser prior to the abusive incident (e.g., Burgess, 1975; Finkelhor, 1979; Peters, 1976). Growing evidence would strongly support the view that intrafamily sexual abuse occurs most frequently among persons of roughly the same generation (e.g., brothers and sisters, step-siblings, cousins, etc.; Finkelhor, 1979; Gebhard, 1965; Henderson, 1972; Rogers, 1979; Weeks, 1976; Weiner, 1964; etc.), yet research and theory about father/daughter incest continue to dominate the field (e.g., Burgess et al., 1978; Justice and Justice, 1979; Meiselman, 1978). Finkelhor (1979) speculates that sibling incest receives less attention because the social taboo against this form of sexual abuse is less strong than against cross-generational incest. This speculation in turn is based upon the view that these cases pose less likelihood of disclosure and, if disclosed, less likelihood of outside intervention or family disruption.

Regardless of the relative frequencies of different forms of intrafamily sexual abuse, practitioners in the field have slowly come to identify intrafamily child sexual abuse cases involving nonparental offenders to be just as serious and just as in need of intervention and treatment as father/daughter incest cases. Situations in which the abuser is an adolescent who resides with the victim pose a special problem for both mental health professionals and law enforcement personnel in terms of case management and specific therapeutic interventions (Rogers, 1980). Our experience has been that disclosure of child sexual abuse involving an adolescent family member as the abuser usually results in substantial family disruption and negative psychological consequences for the victim, other family members, and the adolescent involved. Family loyalties are often in conflict with strong ambivalent parental feelings toward either the offending juvenile or the child victim. The adolescent offender may be characterized by varying degrees of psychosocial maladjustment with evidence of limited impulse control, low self-image, poor family relationships, social isolation from peers, and so forth. Common child victim reactions encountered include somatic complaints, disturbed sleep and eating patterns, depression, feelings of guilt and/or shame, and similar problems.

When these cases are referred for treatment, the entire family is usually in a state of crisis. Often the abusing juvenile has been, or is about to be, expelled from the family, or the child victim has been removed from the home to prevent further victimization. In either case, there is substantial family turmoil and at least temporary dissolution of the pre-disclosure family structure. The counselor or mental health professional attempting to manage the case is understandably under great pressure to bring clarity to an extremely chaotic situation.

Regrettably, very little research data or other information is currently available, either about juvenile sexual offenders themselves or about appropriate intervention approaches, to provide guidance to the practitioner encountering such cases. Although it is proposed by some (e.g., Groth, 1978; Wenet et al., 1981) that there is a relationship between engaging in adolescent sexual offenses and later adult sexual misconduct, there is little empirical evidence to support or refute this contention. Retrospective projections based upon interviewing adult offenders are even less specific regarding the psychodynamic factors related to sexually abusing behavior while an adolescent. Still less is known about how professionals do or should intervene when such incidents come to their attention. Services planning and therapeutic intervention are fraught with legal complications and problems posed by a lack of sufficient understanding of the underlying etiology and dynamics of the situation.

In the ensuing sections we will attempt to shed some light upon these issues by sharing our experience to date regarding the design and implementation of a specialized treatment program for intrafamily juvenile sexual abusers. The findings, approaches, and theoretical underpinnings of the program must be considered tentative at this time: our program is new and in an ongoing process of refinement and elaboration as our understanding of the problem grows.

PROGRAM RATIONALE

The Juvenile Abuser Treatment Program (JATP) at Children's Hospital National Medical Center in Washington, D.C., was launched in 1980 through the efforts of the staff of the Child Protection Center/Special Unit (CPC/SU). During the preceding two years of operations, CPC/SU staff had become increasingly concerned about the problems of juvenile abusers in general and intrafamily juvenile abusers in particular. Of all child sexual abuse cases known to CPC/SU at that time, 54% involved a juvenile offender, with over 40% of these involving a family member. The primary goal of the program was, and is, to provide an alternative to the traditional approaches of removing the offender from the home, removing the victim from the home, or placing the offender on unsupervised probation. Given the relatively young ages of the abusers themselves—from 8 to 17 years of age, with an average age of 14 years—in most cases strong punitive measures such as commitment to a juvenile detention facility seem to be inadvisable. One-third of these young men (91% of juvenile abusers are males) are siblings or step-siblings of the victimized child; the remainder are almost evenly divided between juvenile uncles and cousins on the one hand, and live-in babysitters (usually a nonrelated juvenile being raised by the victim's family) on the other. The lack of formal treatment resources often resulted, however, in either incarceration of the abuser or removal of the child victim from the home, essentially forcing parents to choose between children. JATP attempts to avoid such long-term disruption of the family unit through provision of social, mental health, and case management services for the juvenile abuser and other family members.

JATP functions as an integral subcomponent of CPC/SU, with JATP staff providing all services to the juvenile abuser and CPC/SU staff providing all corollary services to the child victim and other family members. The program is an expansion of CPC/SU services provided routinely to child sexual abuse victims and their families, and is currently supported in part by a federal grant from the National Center on Child Abuse and Neglect (OHDS, DHHS).

In addition to its primary goal of enhancing family structural stability through provision of a comprehensive treatment program, JATP attempts to achieve the goals of reducing further sexual abuse, ensuring that child victims receive supportive mental health services, improving public and private sector coordination of intervention services, and finally, increasing public and professional awareness of the problem and its remediation. Avoidance of further abuse is a central aim of the treatment process; this includes offender therapy which addresses psychodynamic causative factors, as well as family-based therapy which addresses family dynamics that may either support or tolerate the abusive behavior. As will be discussed later, parental denial in these cases is common and often leads to a rejection of supportive mental health services for the child victims. Provision of a comprehensive treatment approach which does not require dissolution of the family structure encourages parents to ensure that the abused child's mental health needs are met. JATP also attempts to ensure overall improved service delivery in these cases by assuming responsibility for the coordination of existing services being provided, or to be provided, by elements of the legal, mental health, and social services systems. Finally, JATP is committed to increasing public and professional awareness through a variety of strategies including advocacy through various media sources, professional publications and presentations, and ultimately, development, evaluation, and dissemination of a comprehensive intervention and treatment model for these cases.

ELIGIBILITY CRITERIA

Cases enter JATP from a variety of different sources. One primary source consists of cases which come to the attention of CPC/SU directly within the context of providing emergency crisis intake services to child victims and their families. When the CPC/SU intake worker ascertains that a particular case involves an intrafamily juvenile abuser, an immediate referral is made to JATP for consideration of the adolescent for inclusion in the program. In addition to cases initially identified by CPC/SU, JATP routinely receives case referrals from elements of the juvenile justice system, from protective services agencies, and from other social services and mental health agencies. The program accepts referrals for evaluation provided that the juvenile is 12 years of age or older and not yet 18 years of age. Additional eligibility requirements, which will be discussed in more detail, include acceptability of the case in terms of JATP's operational definition of sexual abuse, factors related to the criminal or juvenile justice system processing of the case, consent of the juvenile both to treatment and to appropriate disclosure of treatment information, and mental health screening criteria.

Operationally defining what constitutes intrafamily sexual abuse when both parties involved are juveniles poses somewhat of a dilemma. Legal definitions, at least in the jurisdiction within which JATP operates, provide little help. Legally, all sexual contact between juveniles in the District of Columbia is proscribed, with the potential for imposition of legal sanctions. This includes both consensual and nonconsensual contacts between same-age children over the age of 8 years. Operationally, a treatment program must be able to discriminate between inherently abusive contacts and contacts that can be considered either normal peer sexual play and exploration, or socially unacceptable—but not inherently abusive—consensual peer sexual contacts.

Mrs. B. brought her 12-year-old daughter Susan to Children's Hospital with her primary concern being that she believed that 13-year-old James, her nephew who lives with them, was "messing around with Susan." Investigation by CPC/SU staff revealed that James and Susan had been intermittently engaging in sexual intercourse for the last three to four months. Careful examination of the situation indicated that both James and Susan found this behavior intrinsically satisfying and that neither was participating because of threats or other undue pressures.

Although the behavior described in the preceding example may be socially unacceptable and is in fact illegal in the District of Columbia, such a situation would not be considered abusive under JATP's operational definition. A case is considered to be abusive when one child (usually an adolescent) is engaging in sexual contacts with another child through the use of force, physical or nonphysical threats, bribery, misuse of authority, or similar types of coercive behavior. Situations involving an age span of greater than three years between the participants are also considered to be abusive—the assumption being that the older participant's greater social and intellectual maturity allows manipulation of the younger child into a compromising position without true consent. In the preceding example, the case would not be referred to JATP, although CPC/SU staff would continue to work with the family to attempt to resolve the problem.

William, a 15 year old, was referred to JATP for assessment and treatment by the local protective services agency. It was reported that he was engaging in sexual activities with his 6-year-old sister. He would entice her to an isolated setting, then he would persuade her to perform fellatio. The enticements included purchasing toys for her, giving her money, playing special games with her, and similar activities. When he was not able to provide her with special rewards or she was not willing to participate, he would threaten her with physical harm (spanking). The sister developed a sore throat which was subsequently diagnosed as positive for gonorrhea. Disclosure of the sexually abusive situation occurred during the venereal disease contact investigation, and protective services were notified.

In this case, referral to JATP was appropriate both because of the use of bribery and threats to gain the sister's compliance, and because of the age differential between the participants. Had bribery and threats not been present, the case nonetheless would have been considered to be one involving abuse.

How a particular case is handled within the law enforcement and legal systems also determines eligibility for inclusion in JATP. As a general rule, JATP will accept cases in which no petition is to be brought against the juvenile abuser as well as cases in which treatment of the juvenile is proposed as either a diversionary or a dispositional alternative. In the diversionary situation, charges are pending against the juvenile but processing of the case will stop in return for a commitment by the juvenile to complete a treatment program. In the dispositional situation, the juvenile has already been adjudicated delinquent and treatment is being offered in lieu of alternative dispositions available to the juvenile court. As a matter of policy, JATP will not accept cases in which the juvenile's special status has been waived and the juvenile will be treated as an adult within the criminal justice system. Usually these cases, few in number, involve older juveniles with extensive prior offense records or involve cases of an unusually serious nature (e.g., rape/murder; particularly violent, forcible assault; etc.).

In those situations involving diversion of the juvenile into treatment prior to adjudication, JATP requires that certain conditions must be met. These include the following:

- The juvenile must reside outside of the home of the victim until an evaluation has been completed.
- A comprehensive psychological or psychiatric evaluation of the juvenile must be completed prior to acceptance into the program for treatment. This evaluation may be conducted by an outside professional or by JATP staff. If JATP conducts the evaluation, juvenile authorities must allow at least 30 days for completion. Arrangements for the evaluation remain the responsibility of the probation officer assigned to the case.
- JATP must be provided with a court order which specifies the conditions of participation including the juvenile's return home, the period of court supervision, any special treatment compliance or behavioral restrictions, and an agreement by the juvenile and his/her parent to allow JATP to provide periodic reports on treatment progress to the court.

In those cases in which treatment is contemplated as a dispositional alternative following adjudication of delinquency, the following conditions apply:

- The juvenile must reside outside of the home until an evaluation has been completed.
- At least 30 days must be allowed for JATP evaluation of the juvenile, and the evaluation must be conducted at program facilities and not in a receiving home or juvenile detention facility.

- At the disposition hearing, the juvenile must be placed on supervised probation or suspended commitment.
- Specific conditions of probation and treatment must be provided in writing to JATP by the probation department, and there must be agreement by the juvenile and his/her parents to allow JATP to provide the probation officer with periodic reports of treatment progress.

Although not an eligibility requirement per se, formal criminal or juvenile justice involvement in the case is seen as directly affecting parental and juvenile willingness to participate in treatment. Some families are so distraught by the emotional explosion that occurs upon disclosure that they deny that sexual abuse has occurred. The families seem willing to disbelieve the child victim even in the face of supporting evidence and to believe the alleged abuser, thus denying both children needed mental health services. The decision to involve the law enforcement systems often reduces this denial, although parents may continue to discount the seriousness of the situation. However, involvement of the law enforcement system at least temporarily increases, rather than decreases, family instability. This is true first because the systemic expectation and pressures are for the parents to align themselves with the victimized child throughout the legal process. At the same time, the juvenile abuser's attorney is exercising his/her professional obligation to evaluate the strength of the legal case against the juvenile and to make recommendations regarding whether to plea bargain, plead guilty as charged, or stand trial. This attorney-client relationship reinforces the juvenile's psychological distance from the family, particularly his sense of freedom to ignore parental wishes and his disassociation from the child victim.

If it is clear that the legal authorities can and will prove the case at trial, diversion is likely. The coercive power of the legal system to secure participation in treatment as a condition of future dismissal of the charges can equal that of the court to order treatment as a condition of probation. Thus, the family and the juvenile can save face by agreeing to participate without the stigma of an adjudication of delinquency or neglect. Unfortunately, the strength of the case is primarily based upon evidentiary considerations. Hence, motivation to agree to treatment and to continue with the treatment regimen often must be considered in light of the strength of the legal case against the alleged juvenile offender. Eligibility for inclusion in the program, therefore, is indirectly influenced by the ability of the law enforcement systems to make their case persuasively. In general, our experience has been that juveniles and their families who enter treatment under diversion are motivated to accept treatment, but that the degree of motivation is closely tied to the strength of the government's case.

Consent of the juvenile and his/her parents to evaluation, treatment, and disclosure of treatment information is an additional prerequisite for acceptance into the program. In all situations, the program attempts to balance the interests of client confidentiality with the need for information about treatment compliance and progress, evaluation findings, and ongoing treatment prognosis on the part of the probation officer, the attorneys, and other involved parties. The consent form currently being used by JATP is reproduced in Figure 6-1.

CHILD PROTECTION—SPECIAL UNIT
Intrafamily Child Sexual Abuse/Juvenile Abuser Treatment Project

PERMISSION FOR EVALUATION AND TREATMENT

I hereby give consent to the Children's Hospital National Medical Center and its employees to evaluate _____ for acceptance in treatment and to provide such treatment
              Name of Client
and counseling as deemed advisable and necessary in the Intrafamily Child Sexual Abuse/Juvenile Abuser Treatment Project.

I am aware that the practice of counseling and mental health treatment is not an exact science and I acknowledge that no guarantees have been made to me as to the results of the evaluation, treatment, and counseling.

In the event that _____ has been referred by court order, I understand
                    Name of Client
that Children's Hospital National Medical Center and its employees will furnish that court with a report of the results of the evaluation and, if he/she is accepted for treatment, with periodic reports of his/her progress in treatment. Such reports will be disclosed only as permitted by the District of Columbia Mental Health Information Act of 1978.

Signed _____   Signed _____
              Client   Parent or Guardian

Age _____   Relationship _____

Date _____   Date _____

              Witness _____

Figure 6-1. Sample consent form.

Finally, eligibility for the program is dependent upon the results of the psychological evaluation conducted on the juvenile abuser. Potential clients presented as psychotic, suffering from organicity, or with serious substance abuse problems may be excluded from treatment. Psychological assessment tools will be discussed in more detail in subsequent sections, but it should be noted that clients judged to have an extremely poor prognosis for treatment based upon testing results and assessment findings may also be excluded from the program.

PROGRAM STRUCTURAL COMPONENTS

Treatment Rationale

Based upon our own experience with many of these cases, as well as perusal of the available literature, we conceptualize the overall problem of intrafamily child sexual abuse with a juvenile perpetrator as being multifaceted and complex, reflecting idiosyncratic, interpersonal, and familial levels of disrupted functioning. Intervention and treatment must be targeted on all three levels to be successful.

The treatment orientation assumes that idiosyncratic factors either contributing to, or resulting from, the occurrence of abuse must be identified and addressed. This is true not only for the juvenile abuser but also for the victim and other family members, particularly parents. While a small percentage of cases involve an adolescent abuser who is either psychotic or a sexual sociopath, the vast majority of abusers present less serious psychological and behavioral problems. These include low self-concept, social isolation from peers, aggression and hostility, poor impulse control, poor reality testing, and similar factors. Frequently, the abuser has a prior history of sexual abuse as a victim. Regardless of the underlying dynamic, we believe that it is essential for the abuser ultimately to assume personal responsibility for the abuse.

Intrapsychic factors or issues which need to be addressed with the child victim, although somewhat dependent upon the victim's age, include reactions to the abuse or disclosure of the abuse, as well as possible contributing factors including low self-esteem, poor body image, guilt or shame, anxiety, fear, and a host of somatic and behavioral complaints (e.g., headaches and stomachaches, disturbed sleep patterns, phobias, problems in school, etc.). Specific attention must be given to those victim idiosyncratic factors which may make the child more vulnerable to sexual victimization, such as dependency or nurturance needs which have gone unmet, a passive coping style, and so forth.

Personal characteristics of the parents or other close family members also need to be addressed as part of the treatment process. Denial processes, psychosocial immaturity, and similar factors may be present that serve to establish and support an environment in which abuse is likely to occur. In addition, the abuse and its disclosure generate individual reactions which must be dealt with and ultimately overcome. These reactions frequently include anger directed at the abuser, the abused child, or outside intervenors, shame, guilt, and depression.

The approach of JATP also sees the problem as having an interpersonal dimension which requires intervention. In addition to the obvious maladaptive or dysfunctional relationships between the abuser and the victim, there often exist dysfunctional or disrupted patterns of interaction either contributing to, or resulting from, the abuse and its disclosure. These problems occur most frequently between the abuser and other family members, but not infrequently also exist between the abused child and other family members. Particular interpersonal relationships within the family must be carefully explored and addressed within the therapeutic process; of primary importance are the identification and resolution of such issues as anger, hostility, mistrust, and feelings of emotional abandonment arising among family members.

Sexual abuse is viewed as being a family problem above and beyond the particular disrupted or dysfunctional relationships between family members. As social units, many of these families are perceived as fostering, maintaining, and occasionally condoning deviant patterns of the respective family members. Family norms, interpersonal boundaries, role definitions, and similar characteristics of the family structure often contribute to the development and maintenance of the sexual abuse.

The treatment model adopted by JATP is designed to impact on these cases of child sexual abuse at all three of the conceptual levels discussed above. The model follows the experience and findings from existing father/daughter incest treatment programs, more generic juvenile offender treatment programs, and CPC/SU's own experience with these cases. As will be seen later, the model provides individual therapy for all family members, as well as family therapy to address both the interpersonal and the familial factors contributing to the abusive environment.

Screening and Evaluation

Clients must be screened for program appropriateness prior to acceptance into the specialized treatment program. In addition to the eligibility requirements discussed earlier, acceptance into the program is contingent upon careful evaluation of the abuser and overall prognosis for treatment. As already noted, abusers routinely receive a complete psychological evaluation, as well as a detailed clinical interview with program staff prior to acceptance. Evidence of psychosis, organicity, sexual sociopathy, or severe substance abuse are grounds for exclusion with recommendation of the abuser to other more controlled programs.

Psychological evaluation of the abuser relies heavily upon standard psychological batteries and inventories routinely used in assessment including the Wechsler Intelligence Scale for Children—Revised (WISC—R; Wechsler, 1974) or the Wechsler Adult Intelligence Test (WAIS; Wechsler, 1955), the Bender-Gestalt Test (Bender, 1938), the Rorschach Ink Blot Test (Rorschach, 1942), the Thematic Apperception Test (Murray, 1943), and the Minnesota Multiphasic Personality Inventory (MMPI; Hathaway and McKinley, 1940). Less well-known instruments and techniques are also employed, including the Family Adaptability and Cohesion Evaluation Scale (F.A.C.E.S.; Olson et al., 1979) which is used to assess structure and cohesion within the family, and assorted projective drawing tasks.

Assessment interviews focus heavily upon the abuser's explanation of the event, collection of a detailed social and sexual history, and psychosocial adjustment factors. Assessment interviews with the abuser usually take three to four hours to complete, and are usually conducted over two or three separate sessions.

Psychological testing information, information provided by the courts, information provided by other family members, and information gleaned during the assessment interviews are synthesized and summarized to obtain an overall prognosis for treatment. Preliminary steps have been taken toward development of a standardized approach to recording treatment prognosis, and the current forms in use may be seen in Figure 6-2. Major areas of presumed predictive utility for prognosis include intellectual functioning, school functioning, family factors, peer relationships, substance abuse and juvenile offense histories, and specific subareas of psychological functioning. Items on the evaluation summary are not evenly weighted in terms of a decision to accept or reject a particular referral. Poor prognosis factors in intellectual functioning, functioning within society, and psychological functioning are considered to be more serious contraindicators for acceptance into the program. So far, we have not attempted to devise a standard format to govern decision making regarding treatment prognosis, nor have we attempted to devise a quantitative approach to be used with the summary. Such efforts must wait until we have had sufficiently broad experience with large numbers of juvenile offenders.

In addition to the rather extensive abuser evaluation, the child victim and other family members are also screened for inclusion in the treatment program through personal interviews. Formal psychological evaluations of these family members are only conducted when specifically indicated. As with the adolescent abuser, organicity, psychosis, or a severe substance abuse problem are grounds for rejection of a given family member from the treatment program. Elimination of a particular family member has no bearing, however, on the juvenile abuser's acceptability for treatment.

Treatment Modalities

Given the limited experience and information available on working specifically with juvenile sex offenders, the clinical services regimen is in a continual process of revision and refinement. Since the start of the program, there have been substantial changes both in the structuring of services and in the treatment model itself. The original approach of the program was heavily influenced by the experience and findings of father/daughter incest treatment programs and of more generic juvenile offender treatment programs. Original expectations were unduly optimistic regarding accessibility of the clients to treatment and the rate of treatment progress. We have found that treatment takes longer than originally anticipated, that moving from one modality of treatment to another in these cases (i.e., from individual to family therapy) takes longer than routinely expected when dealing with other types of problems, and that most of these juvenile offenders have multiple problems each of which requires substantive intervention if overall treatment progress is to be achieved.

The structural components of the current treatment model may be summarized as follows:

- *Individual victim counseling/therapy.* Almost all child victims receive counseling and therapy, with the exception of those children under the age of 3 and others electing (or whose parents elect) not to participate. Therapy approaches are eclectic, reflecting both the age range of victims and the particu-

Name: _____

Results: Accepted _____ Rejected _____

Completed by: _____

Reasons: _____

FACTOR	PROGNOSIS FOR TREATMENT				
	POOR 1	2	3	4	EXCELLENT 5
Intellectual Functioning: 1 < 60; 2 = 60–70; 3 = 70–80; 4 = 80–90; 5 = 90 or +					
School Adjustment: Academic 1 = 3 or more yrs behind; 3 = 1 yr below; 5 = on or above	-----	-----	-----	-----	-----

Behavioral
  1 = frequent suspensions; 3 = minor behavior problems;
  5 = no problems reported
	-----	-----	-----	-----	-----

Attendance
  1 = frequent truancy; 3 = occasional truancy;
  5 = no problem reported					

Family Characteristics: Support shown for offender 1 = none; 3 = some; 5 = great deal	-----	-----	-----	-----	-----
Willingness to participate in treatment 1 = none; 3 = some; 5 = great deal	-----	-----	-----	-----	-----
Family structure 1 = chaotic, few controls; 3 = some; 5 = good structure and controls					
Relationships with Peers: 1 = no friendships; 3 = few friends; 5 = several close friends					

Functioning within Society:

Hx of substance abuse

  1 = hard drug use or chronic alcohol abuse; 3 = moderate use of milder drugs or alcohol; 5 = no problem reported

Prior juvenile record (sexual)*

  1 = many charges; 3 = 1 prior charge; 5 = no prior charges

Prior juvenile record (nonsexual)

  1 = many; 3 = one prior; 5 = none

Force used in assault*

  1 = use of weapon or threat of physical harm; 3 = verbal threats

  5 = no force used

Psychological Functioning:

Impulse control

  1 = explosive person, few controls; 3 = some controls;

  5 = good impulse control

Responsibility for act

  1 = complete denial; 3 = some ability; 5 = responsible

Level of empathy for victim

  1 = no concern shown (i.e., did not stop despite protests);

  3 = some concern; 5 = good (i.e., stopped when asked to)

Willingness to participate in program

  1 = none; 3 = some; 5 = great deal

Able to discuss sexuality

  1 = unable; 3 = some ability; 5 = great deal

Presence of thought disorder

  1 = evidence of significant thought disorder; 3 = some questions about possible disorder; 5 = no evidence

Suicidal thoughts

  1 = serious threat of suicide; 3 = some threats, but not considered serious; 5 = no suicidal thoughts

*Especially significant indicators.

Figure 6-2.   Clinical staffing evaluation summary.

lar issues that need to be addressed. Approaches commonly used include play therapy, art therapy, behavioral modification, and more traditional psychodynamic approaches. Major goals of the therapy generally include crisis resolution for the victim, identification and exploration of feelings toward the abusing juvenile and other family members, dealing with psychological and behavioral reactions to the incident and its disclosure (e.g., guilt, shame, anger, somatic complaints, etc.), and preparation for entrance into family therapy.

- *Parental counseling/therapy.* Depending upon the family configuration, either individual (single-parent family) or conjoint (two-parent family) therapy is provided. Major goals of this treatment component include identification and resolution of parental feelings about the incident, the abuser, the victim, and other family members; exploration of what elements, if any, of their own parenting styles may have contributed to the development of the abusive situation; and preparation for family therapy.

- *Individual juvenile abuser counseling/therapy.* Clearly the most important single component of the treatment model, therapy with the juvenile abuser, is also the most complex. In addition to the more general psychological assessment of the offender, a specific focus of therapy is to ascertain the underlying dynamics of his behavior and to develop and implement remedial strategies aimed at substantially affecting both the dynamics and the behavior. By necessity, the approach undertaken is offender-specific, tailored to the particular case and to offender characteristics. Major themes which are, however, common across many of these cases include an inability to empathize with the victim, social and sexual immaturity, and varying degrees of social isolation, particularly from peers. In addition, offender therapy focuses on exploration of offender feelings and attitudes in terms of the victim, other family members, the abuse circumstances, and the disclosure of abuse. Finally, individual abuser therapy is used as a mechanism for preparing the juvenile for family therapy.

- *Family therapy.* When appropriate, family therapy incorporating all family members—or appropriate subconfigurations including the child victim, the abuser, the parent or parents, and other siblings or family members residing in the home—is initiated. Family therapy is considered inappropriate only when there is a clear decision on the part of the family not to attempt to reunite the family. Major objectives of the family therapy component include the identification of underlying needs of family members and more appropriate means of addressing those needs; identification, ventilation, and resolution of negative feelings between family members engendered by the abuse and its disclosure; and fostering more positive and adaptive patterns of family interaction.

The treatment components described above are seen as being in some instances consecutive and in others concomitant. In general, abuser, victim, and parental therapy components begin as soon as possible and continue at least four to six months. Family therapy usually begins at about the fourth month of treatment, with individual therapy and family therapy components overlapping for about two months. Parents and child victims are generally seen at either one- or two-week intervals. The juvenile abuser is seen at least weekly and often twice a week. Once initiated, family therapy generally occurs biweekly for a period from six months to one year. Depending upon the individual case circumstances, individual juvenile abuser therapy may continue throughout the treatment period (i.e., continuing indefinitely while family therapy is also in place). The overall time in treatment is long, ranging anywhere from ten months to two years.

The original JATP treatment model envisioned a shift from individual abuser treatment to group treatment at about the four-month point in therapy. It became clear, however, that preparation of the individual juvenile for group therapy would require substantially more time than originally anticipated, given the slow rate of progress in individual therapy. We are just beginning our first adolescent treatment group at this time. A group treatment modality is seen as a major and necessary addition to the treatment model. These groups are envisioned as providing a favorable setting for exploration of the dynamics and underlying causes of the abuse by offering a climate of peer social sanctions for abusive behavior as well as mutual support and reinforcement of positive behavioral change. It is also expected that these groups will provide a corrective emotional experience for participants, particularly in terms of social isolation from peers and the self-abasement frequently encountered in these adolescents.

DISCUSSION

As of March 1982, JATP staff had evaluated over 60 juvenile abusers for possible inclusion in the program. Of these, slightly more than half were accepted into the program, with the most common reasons for not accepting a case for treatment being lack of eligibility (i.e., refusal to consent, too young or too old, etc.) or extremely poor prognosis for treatment (e.g., multiple prior offenses, extremely low mental functioning, and so forth). Only four cases had completed treatment as of March 1982, with an additional three juveniles terminating treatment against caseworker advice.

Cases referred to JATP and screened for inclusion in the program reflect the diversity and complexity of the problem. Juveniles as young as 10 years of age have been referred to the program. Offenses perpetrated range from single incidents of fondling to violent forcible rape or ongoing incestuous contact with extremely young children. Many of the juveniles referred to JATP need, in the opinion of program staff, a more controlled setting in which treatment should be pursued, rather than outpatient treatment. The lack of formal focused treatment programs for juvenile sexual offenders within the juvenile corrections system, however, often places the courts and JATP staff in the position of having to choose between incarceration for the juvenile without treatment or freedom for the juvenile with appropriate treatment. Slowly but surely there is increasing pressure for JATP to accept into treatment increasingly serious offenders or offenders who are poor prospects for outpatient treatment. Ultimately, for rational placement planning to be feasible, specialized treatment programs for juvenile abusers must be available to all juvenile abusers regardless of the dispositional option considered most appropriate for a particular offender. The decision to incarcerate a juvenile offender would then ideally be made without consideration of whether treatment would be available.

Ultimately, JATP efforts are seen as preventative in nature. Although the evidence is only anecdotal, there appears to be a growing concern that the juvenile abusers of today, if not effectively treated, may be the fixated pedophiles and incestuous fathers of tomorrow. Certainly we see such propensities in our own clients. Carefully planned and executed treatment programs for the juvenile abuser may be instrumental in interrupting this logical progression from juvenile to adult sexual offender.

REFERENCES

Bender, L. A visual motor Gestalt test and its clinical use. *American Orthopsychiatric Association Research Monograph* 3 (1938).

Burgess, Holmstrom, and McCausland, Divided loyalty in incest cases. *Sexual Assault of Children and Adolescents.* Lexington, Mass.: Lexington Books, p. 115.

Child Sexual Abuse: Incest, Assault and Sexual Exploitation—OHDS—CYF—Children's Bureau, NCCAN—1981.

Finkelhor, D. *Sexually Victimized Children.* New York: Macmillan, 1979.

Gebhard, P., Gagnon, J., Pomeroy, W., and Christenson, C. *Sex Offenders: An Analysis of Types.* New York: Harper and Row, 1965.

Giarretto, H. Humanistic treatment of father-daughter incest. In Helfer, R.E. and Kemp, C.H. (Eds.), *Child Abuse and Neglect: The Family and the Community.* Cambridge, Mass.: Ballinger, 1976.

Groth, A.N. The adolescent sexual offender and his prey. *International Journal of Offender Therapy and Comparative Criminology* 21(3) (1977).

Groth, A.N. Guidelines for assessment and management of the offender. In Burgess et al. (Eds.) *Sexual Assault of Children and Adolescents.* Lexington, Mass.: Lexington Books, 1978.

Groth, A.N. Sexual trauma in the life histories of rapists and child molesters. *Victimology: An International Journal* 4 (1979).

Groth, A.N. and Birnbaum, H.J. *Men who Rape: The Psychology of the Offender.* New York: Plenum Press, 1979.

Groth, A.N. and Loredo, C. Juvenile sexual offenders: guidelines for assessment. *International Journal of Offender Therapy and Comparative Criminology* 25(1) (1981).

Hathaway, S.R. and McKinley, J.C. *The Minnesota Multiphasic Personality Inventory Manual.* New York: Psychological Corporation, 1951.

Henderson, J. Incest: a synthesis of data. *Canadian Psychiatric Association Journal* **17**: 299-313 (1972).

Loredo, C. Sibling incest. *Handbook of Clinical Intervention in Child Sexual Abuse*. In Sgroi, S. (Ed.) Lexington, Mass.: Lexington Books, 1982, p. 177.

Makstein, McLaughlin, and Rogers, *Sexual abuse and the pediatric setting: treatment and research implications*. Paper presented at the Annual Convention of the American Psychological Association, New York, September 1979.

Murray, H.A. *Thematic Apperception Test*. Boston: Harvard University Press, 1943.

Olson, D.H., Sprenkle, D.H., and Russell, C.S. Circumplex model of marital and family systems: cohesions and adaptability dimensions, family types, and clinical applications. *Family Process* **16**(1): 3-28 (1979).

Peters, J. Children who are victims of sexual assault and the psychology of offenders. *American Journal of Psychotherapy* **30**(3): 7-76.

Rogers, C.M. *Intrafamily child sexual abuse/juvenile abuser treatment program*. Proposal submitted and funded by Department of Health and Human Services, Office of Human Development Service, National Center on Child Abuse and Neglect, 1980.

Rorschach, H. *Psychodiagnostics: A Diagnostic Test Based on Perception*, 4th ed. New York: Grune and Stratton, 1942.

Seabloom, W. *Beyond pathology: the economy of early intervention and enrichment treatment modalities for adolescent sexual behavior disorders*. Paper presented at the 5th World Congress of Sexology, Israel, 1981.

Wechsler, D. *WISC-R Manual Wechsler Intelligence Scale for Children–Revised*. New York: Psychological Corporation, 1974.

Weimer, I. Father-daughter incest: a clinical report. *Psychiatric Quarterly* **36**:607 (1962).

Wenet, C. et al. Adolescent sexual offense behavior. Submitted to *Journal of Adolescent Health Care* (June 1981).

7
Tension-reduction Training in the Treatment of Compulsive Sex Offenders

Raymond C. Rosen, Ph.D.
Jeffrey C. Fracher, Ph.D.

Negative arousal states of anxiety or anger are commonly, but not universally, experienced as precursory to sexual acting out by offenders. For aggressive offenders anger appears to be the major antecedent, while nonviolent offenders (e.g., child fondlers) frequently experience anxiety. By contrast, sociopathic offenders appear to experience little or no affect prior to sexual crimes, but may engage in such behavior in order to experience affective arousal. For offenders who usually experience affective precursors, tension-reduction techniques constitute a limited but valuable component of their treatment program. By utilizing three case studies, this chapter illustrates the process of selecting from the many tension-reduction techniques available those which are suitable for an individual client and points out the specific contribution of tension reduction to overall treatment outcome. The reader is cautioned that tension-reduction training cannot be regarded as an adequate treatment regimen by itself and is not effective with the sociopath or the unmotivated client.

Among the first reports of behavioral treatment for sexual deviance was a series of three case studies by Stevenson and Wolpe (1960). These authors described the use of reciprocal inhibition and assertiveness training as a means for overcoming the social inhibitions that appeared to underlie deviant sexual behavior in these cases. Similarly, Bond and Hutchinson (1960) reported on the use of anxiety reduction by means of systematic desensitization in the behavioral treatment of a chronic exhibitionist. This patient appeared to experience predictable anxiety states as a precursor to acts of exposure, and treatment was aimed at eliminating his antecedent anxiety by means of systematic desensitization. Treatment was not wholly effective, however, as two subsequent relapses were reported.

In the early 1970s, a trend began to develop towards a more broad-spectrum or multifaceted behavioral approach to treatment. Bancroft (1974), for example, stressed the importance of social skills training and orgasmic reconditioning as components of therapy for sexual deviance. Furthermore, Barlow (1974) has proposed the need for a comprehensive behavioral treatment program to be focused on the following major areas of intervention: (1) gender identity and role, (2) heterosocial skills, (3) heterosexual relationship(s), and (4) deviant arousal patterns. Other authors (e.g., Lazarus and Rosen, 1976) similarly have emphasized the use of a more flexible and individualistic approach to the behavioral treatment of sex offenders.

In this chapter, we will discuss the use of tension-reduction training as one specific component of our multifaceted treatment program. While we have become convinced that these methods have considerable clinical value in certain cases, it is essential that tension-reduction training be viewed in the context of a *comprehensive* treatment approach. Thus, we have found that it is most often necessary to include other modalities of treatment, many of which are described in other chapters. In this sense, we tend to view tension control as a limited, albeit useful, component in our overall treatment package and would rarely, if ever, recommend it as the sole therapy intervention. However, as the present chapter will attempt to make clear, there is much to be said for including a systematic assessement and treatment focus in this largely overlooked area.

The term "tension," as we will will be using it here, is broadly construed to include a variety of negative arousal states, ranging from anger to anxiety. Specifically, we consider tension to include significant cognitive, somatic, and behavioral manifestations, which may vary widely from one offender to another. Similarly, our notion of "tension reduction" includes methods for dealing with specific stresses, chronic anxieties, and inappropriate anger states in many of our clients. In this chapter, we will discuss the role of various stress and negative arousal states (tension) as key antecedents to compulsive sexual misconduct, and the kinds of coping strategies we have found to be valuable in this regard. Finally, we will address the key issues of outcome and maintenance of treatment gains.

THE ROLE OF TENSION AND NEGATIVE AROUSAL STATES IN COMPULSIVE SEXUAL DEVIANCE

The relationship between negative arousal states and antisocial (aggressive) behavior has recently been addressed in depth from a cognitive-behavioral perspective by Novaco (1975, 1977). Specifically, aggressive behavior in general is considered by this author (Novaco, 1976) to be mediated by a chain of affective antecedents and cognitive mediation in the following way:

Anger is an affective stress reaction to aversive events that are called provocations. Anger, as a subject affect, consists of a combination of arousal, identifiable by autonomic nervous system and central nervous system indices, and a cognitive labeling of that arousal as anger. Consistent with psychological views of stress, anger is determined by one's cognitive structuring of the situation. To put it simply, anger can be examined in terms of aversive events, how these events are appraised or interpreted, and the behaviors that are enacted in response to these events.

Among the various forms of aggressive or antisocial behavior that are enacted in this way in response to anger are acts of *sexual aggression*. As emphasized by Novaco, however, it is not only the experience of anger *per se* but also the all-important cognitive appraisal by the individual that mediates such antisocial behavior. In some instances it appears that a low threshold for arousal results in an immediate perception of provocation and a rapid escalation of uncontrollable affect. Depending on the learning history of the individual and the extent of environmental constraints, such arousal may or may not facilitate sexual aggression. When acting-out does occur, it typically results in temporary reduction of anger arousal. In this sense, the chain of compulsive behavior involved may be viewed as intrinsically "self-reinforcing."

The external events leading to anger as described above may precipitate other negative affective states, such as anxiety or depression, typically resulting from a sense of loss of control. Despite the apparent differences in the kind of affective arousal involved, we have observed marked similarities in the underlying mediational processes. For example, interpersonal conflict may precipitate either anxiety or anger, depending upon the cognitive appraisal and conditioning history of the individual, which, in turn, may mediate a sequence of events culminating in sexual aggression. Meichenbaum (1977) has also characterized the effects of negative arousal states as follows: "The client perceived a treat to his self-worth, he wanted to be in control of a situation, and he engaged in acts of antagonism, which escalated his anger [or anxiety]" (p. 164).

We have also found that anxiety or anger states vary in importance depending upon the type of offender involved. For example, we tend to distinguish between the aggressive offender, for whom *anger* appears to be a major antecedent, and the seductive offender, for whom *anxiety* tends to be more problematic. A third type, the sociopathic offender, appears to experience little or no affect prior to sexual aggression, but may engage in such behavior in order to elicit or experience some form of affective arousal. In view of the fact that tension-reduction treatment interventions are generally inappropriate for the latter group, further discussion of this group will not be included here.

Similar typologies emphasizing motivational antecedents have recently been developed by other authors. For instance, Groth (1979) has developed a typology of rapists, distinguishing between the *anger* rape, in which sexuality "becomes a hostile act"; the *power* rape, in which sexuality becomes an expression of domination; and the *sadistic* rape, in which, "anger and power become eroticized."

Regarding the relationship between negative arousal and sexual aggression, Groth (1979) notes the following:

> Rape is always and foremost an aggressive act. In some offenses, the assault appears to constitute a discharge of anger; it becomes evident that the rape is the way the offender expresses and discharges a mood of intense anger, frustration, resentment, and rage.

Especially in the case of the "anger" rapist, the link between tension states and sexual aggression is very clear. As Groth (1979, p. 16) also notes, "The offense itself is typically preceded by some upsetting event, often, but not invariably, involving some significant women in the assailant's life. *The assault is in response to some identifiable precipitating stress*" (italics added).

An additional, albeit more speculative function of such high arousal states, is in regard to the possible alterations produced in the consciousness of the offender. Money and Bennett (1981) have recently commented that "paraphilic behavior [sic] takes place during an altered state of consciousness." Numerous authors have also described various types of dissociative phenomena experienced by some offenders (Rosen, Fracher, and Perold, 1979). It is our impression in this regard that certain negative arousal or tension states may greatly facilitate the occurrence of a trance-like state of consciousness in which sexual impulses and fantasies are (more) easily acted upon. Research is currently being conducted in our laboratory to further clarify this relationship.

Example

> William S., a 26-year-old married truck driver was referred for evaluation following arrest for multiple counts of forcible rape. Clinical assessment revealed a history of major marital conflict, characterized by frequent verbal humiliation and rejection of sexual intimacy by his wife. These interactions resulted in feelings of powerlessness and loss of control, associated with high levels of anxiety or anger, bordering at times on rage. In turn, his feelings of anger or anxiety led increasingly to fantasies of female domination and rape. On several occasions, following particularly negative interactions with his wife, he left home in an escalating state of agitation and anger which culminated in several actual and attempted rapes. Following these instances, he reported a temporary reduction in his feelings of anger and anxiety.

This case typifies the way in which negative arousal states can serve as precursors to acts of sexual agression. While this individual's inability to cope with significant interpersonal conflicts was clearly important as an etiological determinant in this case, his choice of rape as a particular behavioral response would need to be understood in the context of his total psychosexual history. In this regard, we are proposing that negative arousal states be viewed as a necessary, but not a sufficient, explanation of certain instances of sexual aggression.

CLINICAL ASSESSMENT OF NEGATIVE AROUSAL PATTERNS

Because of the variety of motivational factors that may mediate sexual aggression, a detailed individual assessment of each client is always necessary at the outset. As noted above, tension states such as anxiety or anger typically contain certain key cognitive, somatic, and behavorial components, each of which needs to be individually addressed. For example, assessment of the *cognitive* dimension may include the client's perception and appraisal of the situation, his expectations for self or others, and his self-statements in this regard.

On the other hand, *somatic* manifestations of tension can include a variety of physiological responses such as increased respiration, muscle tension, and elevated cardiovascular functions. For example, one recent offender, J.P., a 32-year-old aggressive pedophile, reported severe tension headaches immediately preceding most acts of child molestation. Additionally, the *behavioral* response component needs to be independently addressed. Patterns of avoidance or escape are commonly associated with an inability to cope with stressful situations and may exacerbate existing interpersonal conflicts, as in the case of William S. described above. Clearly, deficits in social skills or assertiveness are important here.

The relationship of these mediating responses to the ultimate behavior of sexual aggression, as well as the potential interrelationship between components, is illustrated in Figure 7-1. As indicated in this figure, the chain of events usually begins with some external situation which is viewed as leading to frustration or conflict. While these situations most often involve interpersonal or occupational stresses, any event which poses a potential threat to self-esteem or masculinity can serve as an initial antecedent. Next to be considered in the chain of events is the cognitive style of the individual. We have observed many instances in which distorted perceptions, unrealistic or irrational expectations, and a tendency for self-defeating self-statements mediate the effect of external events. Assessment must delineate the specific problematic perceptions and cognitions of the client, and determine their possible role in the mediation of arousal states and subsequent aggressive behavior.

Regarding the specific manner in which such an assessment is typically conducted in our clinic, we have made use of several different levels of assessment. Based on the intake interview and a life-history questionnaire, an initial assessment is usually made of the offender typology and the role of negative arousal patterns. A more in-depth assessment might then consist of questionnaires and daily behavioral recording of significant stress events and consequent arousal states. In cases where the client's self-report is questionable, we have also made use of corroborative observations by spouses or significant others.

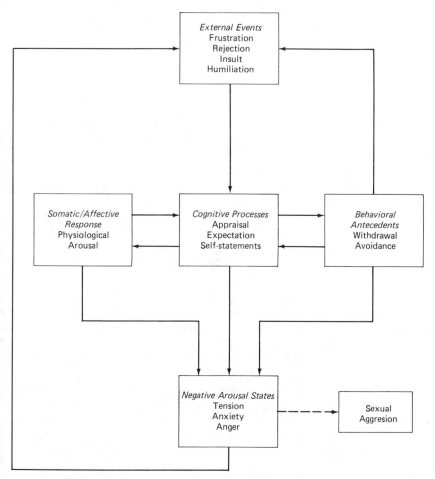

Figure 7-1. Negative arousal states in the mediation of sexual aggression. (Adapted from Novaco, 1977.)

In recent years we have come to rely increasingly on the use of psychophysiological assessment methods in addition to a variety of self-report measures. While much attention has been focused in the sex offender literature on the use of laboratory methods for the assessment of sexual arousal patterns (see Part IV), relatively little attention has been paid to the use of psychophysiological methods in the assessment of antecedent tension states. As noted by Davidson and Schwartz (1976) and others, however, there appear to be marked individual differences in physiological response patterns to various forms of stress. Some individuals, for example, manifest strong patterns of autonomic arousal, while others tend to show more pronounced somatic muscle tension responses to stress. In addition to delineating the specific response patterns involved, we have also found the laboratory assessment can be of value in determining the range of external cues by which the individual is likely to become aroused. Finally, such assessment information can serve as a guide to the choice of the optimal tension-reduction training method to be used in subsequent treatment.

THE USE OF TENSION-REDUCTION TRAINING METHODS IN THE CONTEXT OF A COMPREHENSIVE TREATMENT PROGRAM

Before discussing the specific use of tension-reduction training methods in particular, it is necessary for us to emphasize again our belief in the importance of a *comprehensive* treatment approach as outlined by Barlow and Abel (1976). The compulsive sex offender has been found to exhibit significant behavioral deficits or excesses in a number of areas, some of which we will only briefly touch upon here. Techniques for the reduction of deviant arousal, for example, are obviously of major importance and currently utilized in most cases. Similarly, deficits in social adjustment are of major concern to most clinicians (Bancroft, 1974).

While thus recognizing the need for therapeutic interventions at several levels, we have also noted certain major benefits from the inclusion of a tension-reduction training component in the context of our overall treatment package. The primary goal of treatment interventions in this area is to disrupt the chain of antecedents that characteristically precede the problem behavior. By providing the offender with behavioral alternatives and new coping skills, we aim to diminish the likelihood of his acting-out again in response to uncontrollable negative affect. In addition, tension-reduction training tends to promote a general sense of self-mastery and enhanced self-esteem, both of which appear to be positively correlated with outcome. Finally, because most offenders appear to readily recognize the practical benefits of tension-reduction training, we have also noted nonspecific positive effects in terms of compliance and motivation for change.

Regarding the desired matching of specific training methods of clients in treatment, we have preferred to use only well-established behavioral techniques (see Lehrer and Woolfolk, in press, for a recent review) and to base our interventions on the assessment findings in each individual case. In particular, physiological, cognitive, and behavioral manifestations of tension are independently addressed by means of specific techniques. In those cases in which physiological stress responses are to be treated, for example, we have made extensive use of progressive muscle relaxation (Jacobson, 1938), autogenic training (Lehrer, 1979), and training in various biofeedback modalities. Interventions at the cognitive level consist primarily of confronting the client's negative perceptions of self and others, as well as training in positive imagery rehearsal (Lazarus, 1977). Finally, we have found it necessary in several cases to deal with social inhibitions and sexual performance anxiety through a combination of assertiveness training and sex education/therapy techniques.

While tension-reduction training can be conducted on either an inpatient or an outpatient basis, our experience in this regard is limited to an outpatient setting. Inpatient treatment, however, offers a possible advantage in permitting a more intensive training program under closer supervision. On the other hand, outpatient training could lead to stronger generalization of treatment effects. The following two cases reports are provided to illustrate our present treatment format in depth.

Case Study — J.M.

J.M. is a 32-year-old, single factory worker currently living in a common-law relationship with a 46-year-old divorced female. Mr. M. has a 14-year history of deviant sexual behavior including voyeurism, aggressive pedophilia, and exhibitionism. He was referred for treatment following a recent arrest for exposure to adolescent females in a crowded shopping mall. Although he had committed hundreds of previous offenses, he had never before been apprehended.

J. is the product of a markedly disturbed family background. Though from an intact family, he perceived his mother as weak and ineffectual, whereas his father was described as an "abusive drunken tyrant" who frequently and unpredictably beat the five children, of which J. was the oldest. J. reported that beginning in adolescence he would escape from the tension and anxiety created by his father's outbursts by remaining in the shower for long periods of time and masturbating, an activity which he found very relaxing. This pattern of using masturbation to avoid conflict and to reduce feelings of anxiety and tension continued throughout adolescence. He developed an elaborate fantasy life to accompany masturbation, with the predominant theme being one of women finding him irresistible as a sexual partner. Assessment indicated that masturbation functioned as a means of tension reduction, as well as sexual satisfaction, for J.

On one occasion at age 17, after a particularly stressful interaction with his father, J. left home feeling very tense and angry. He encountered a group of adolescent girls while walking in a park and became obsessed with the idea that if they saw his penis they would be unable to resist him sexually. He became very aroused by his fantasy and exposed himself, which resulted in subsequent feelings of satisfaction and relief. This led gradually to a pattern of exhibitionism on a regular basis at a frequency of about two to three times per week.

During his 20s he described himself as a "loner" who, though holding a steady job, did not date or participate in social activities. His primary form of recreation involved either masturbation as an escape from his feelings of anxiety and inadequacy, or exhibitionism to enhance his feelings of self-esteem. On several occasions, while intending to expose himself to a single victim, he used threats of force to require the victim to touch his penis. He also began looking into windows at his apartment complex when returning home after dark. Subsequent to the episodes of voyeurism, he would return home and masturbate to fantasies of being sexually desired by the women he had been viewing.

Upon entering treatment, the client described himself as chronically tense and anxious, with few meaningful relationships. His primary coping strategy appeared to be either masturbation with deviant fantasies or some form of aggressive sexual behavior. He had recently begun living with an older female co-worker whom he perceived as critical and controlling. He described the quality of the sexual relationship with his mate as infrequent and unsatisfying.

Progessive muscle relaxation (PMR) training (Jacobson, 1938) was begun early in treatment using a cassette recording of the therapist's instructions. The reasons for introducing this intervention in treatment were threefold: (1) to provide J. with a sense of self-control and self-mastery as a means of enhancing his self-esteem; (2) to improve his commitment to therapy; and (3) to provide him with a new coping skill designed to address his antecedent symptoms (tension/anxiety) more adaptively and effectively. PMR was one of several interventions introduced in order to disrupt the chain of J.'s deviant behavior. Other interventions focused on his inappropriate cognitions by relabeling negative self-statements, and his characteristic avoidance of interpersonal stress was treated with role playing of assertive and more appropriate interpersonal behaviors.

Finally, the compulsive urge to engage in sexually aggressive behavior was treated directly by means of masturbatory satiation. At the termination of treatment, the client reported being free of urges to expose himself or commit other deviant acts, as well as feeling considerable improvement in his ability to cope with tension and anxiety. He also reported an overall sense of confidence and control due to improved interpersonal effectiveness.

Case Discussion.   This case is typical of our use of a multifaceted behavioral treatment approach which focuses on both the control of deviant arousal (Barlow and Abel, 1976) and the development of positive coping skills, in addition to tension-reduction training. This client's pattern of deviant sexual response can be formulated in terms of the model presented in Figure 7-1. Following this model, the external antecedents of tension consisted primarily of interpersonal conflicts with significant others (e.g., father, girlfriend). In response to various conflict situations, J. usually experienced a high level of physiological arousal along with negative self-statements involving tension, anxiety, and feeling generally "uptight and panicky." This negative arousal state in response to interpersonal stress had also typically been accompanied by a behavioral pattern of avoidance and escape. The final component of the chain consisted of his feeling the need to discharge accumulated tension by means of ejaculation in the context of either deviant fantasies or overt acts of sexual aggression.

The treatment program was aimed at developing a number of alternative coping responses to substitute for various critical links in the chain. Specifically, we chose to use training in progressive muscle relaxation as a means of identifying internal cues associated with tension and, further, of controlling the physiological components of tension. Positive self-statements (e.g., "I can handle this") were used to replace previously self-defeating cognitions. Also, the client was strongly encouraged to deal directly with the immediate interpersonal conflict rather than engage in inappropriate escape and avoidance behavior. All of these interventions appeared to result in an enhanced sense of mastery or self-control and a greater ability to effectively manage tension in the face of conflict.

As we have emphasized before, there is also a need to intervene directly in the reduction of deviant arousal in cases such as this. As noted above, masturbatory satiation appeared to be the intervention of choice for this purpose and seemed to work well for this client. Finally, while we often find it necessary to address problems in the area of heterosexual functioning, this client spontaneously reported a marked increase in sexual activity and satisfaction with his partner after about six weeks of treatment. Perhaps the combination of improved self-esteem and control of deviant arousal was sufficient in this instance to stimulate a renewed interest and desire for normal heterosexual contact.

While this case illustrates our general treatment format and approach, variations in this approach are often indicated in the course of assessment. In some instances a more in-depth intervention is needed for certain areas of response (i.e., cognitive, physiological, or behavioral). The following case report illustrates a somewhat different treatment emphasis as well as the use of tension-reduction training with a highly educated and motivated offender.

Case Report — L.R.

L.R. is a 37-year-old chaplain in the U.S. Air Force. He has been married for the past 12 years and has three children. At the time of referral, he complained of a long-standing and compulsive urge to expose himself to young female victims and, more recently, to engage in voyeuristic and sadistic fantasies. Despite numerous past incidents of exhibitionism, usually accompanied by masturbation, he has been arrested only once and was released without sentence.

L. was an only child in a New England Quaker family. His childhood was marked by a series of unhappy events at home and generally poor peer relationships. He remembers himself as a tense and introverted child. His father is portrayed as weak-willed and ineffectual, and his mother as having an overbearing and dominating personality. Due to a long period of illness during adolescence, he seems to have felt out of place and shy in the company of his age peers. His college years were uneventful, and after graduating as an average student from college, he decided to enter the ministry. About this time he also met M., his wife, and they were soon engaged to be married.

Although the first few months of marriage were relatively harmonious, L. soon began to feel dominated and controlled by his wife — similar feelings to those he had experienced towards his mother. Their sexual relationship was frustrated by a rapid ejaculation problem, which resulted in dissatisfaction for both and a declining frequency of intercourse as the years progressed. His inability to satisfy his wife in intercourse added to L.'s general sense of inadequacy, as well as to his feelings of hostility towards women in general.

Three years after they had been married, and a few months after the birth of their first daughter, he accepted the position of chaplain in the air force. At first, this new position offered a sense of security and financial stability. Soon, however, it became apparent that the demands of military life and the responsibilities of his post were a source of increasing stress and tension. In the client's own words,

> Stress came from my being task oriented and working in a total institution which is so work-oriented and perfectionistic. The feeling of stress came by [my] pressuring myself to try to meet all the demands that were being placed on me by job and family life.

Additional tensions were added by his difficulties in dealing with authority in the military hierarchy and a number of postings to bases in remote areas:

> Being away from home for extended duty created more stress. The feeling of loneliness was predominant. On other occasions I felt distressed by tension with a supervisor. Plus my wife's being unhappy in dealing with a toddler created additional stresses for me.

Faced with increasing pressures from both his work and his family responsibilities, he began to use sexual fantasies and masturbation as a primary means of escape. Although he recalls having had occasional exhibitionistic fantasies since adolescence, these fantasies increased greatly in frequency and intensity at about this time. The first actual incident of exposure occurred following a reprimand from his superior at an overseas posting. The incident was apparently not reported but nevertheless caused L. to experience powerful feelings of anxiety and remorse.

Returning home from overseas assignment, he attempted to make some efforts to improve his marital relationship and work adjustment. However, the continuing sexual and interpersonal conflicts with his wife, as well as his ongoing difficulties in dealing assertively with his superiors, led to periods of depression and occasional suicidal thoughts. Exhibitionistic fantasies again became more frequent and increasingly difficult to resist. He remembers driving around alone for hours at a time, preoccupied with his fantasies, and searching the streets for possible young female victims. Occasionally, he would offer rides to young female hitchhikers and expose himself to those who accepted. On other occasions he would park the car on a side street and expose himself to passing female pedestrians. He recalls being especially aroused if the victims appeared to be intimidated or embarrassed by his exposure.

It is interesting to note that L. was able to continue in this vein for almost two years before the inevitable report and arrest for indecent exposure occurred. His wife, who had been unaware of his behavior until this time, recalls being shocked and outraged at the time of his arrest. He, in turn, expressed great remorse and offered to seek help immediately for his problem. In view of the patient's military record and position in the ministry, prosecution was waived on condition that he enter counseling immediately.

Perhaps motivated by an increasing fear of being caught again, his fantasies and activity had become more clandestine and voyeuristic in nature in recent years. These activities included surreptitious tape recordings of the sexual activities of other officers at the base. At the beach or swimming pool, he would often attempt to observe women undressing and would occasionally expose himself when the occasion presented itself. During this period, his relationship with his wife continued to deteriorate, and he described himself as always feeling lonely, tense, and depressed. With a growing sense of fear and desperation he entered treatment a year ago.

Initial assessment suggested a highly motivated, anxious, and intelligent individual with major behavioral excesses and deficits in several areas. While not lacking in social skills, his chronic anxiety and lack of self-esteem greatly inhibited his ability to deal with any form of interpersonal stress. His deviant sexual fantasies and behavior appeared to provide some degree of short-term relief from tension, as well as a form of inappropriate assertion of power and masculinity. He also appeared to suffer from long-standing performance anxieties in his sexual relationship with his wife, which contributed to an emasculating premature ejaculation problem.

Further assessment of his response to stress indicated a characteristic pattern of somatic, autonomic, and cognitive component responses. Specifically, chronic muscle tension in the face and head area appeared to result in frequent tension headaches, and L. reported a tendency to shallow breathing and rapid heart rate in stressful situations. This pattern was frequently accompanied by feelings of helplessness and an inability to engage in rational problem solving.

In view of the apparent importance of L.'s stress pattern as an antecedent of his compulsive deviant behavior, the first phase of treatment was focused on a series of tension-reduction training sessions. In order to gain control over the somatic component of the stress pattern, four weeks of combined electromyography (EMG) biofeedback training and PMR were conducted. EMG training was primarily focused on the frontalis muscle, and after approximately seven sessions of training, L. was able to reduce his EMG to a criterion level of less than 5 mV over the course of a 20-minute training session. Progressive muscle relaxation training also appeared to be of some value in training L. to become more aware of the differential effects of muscle tension and relaxation.

Relaxation *imagery* was also found to have a marked positive effect on both the somatic and the cognitive aspects of stress. Using a recent manual of imagery techniques (Lazarus, 1977), the client and therapist were able to construct a number of positive images for systematic desensitization training. When these positive images were systematically rehearsed along with biofeedback training, the optimal conditions for desensitization appear to have been established. As a result of acquiring these various new coping skills, L. reported being more able to cope with conflict situations, and better able to handle criticism from his wife, as well as experiencing a steady decline in the frequency of urges to expose himself.

Despite the apparent success of the first phase of treatment, it was felt necessary to include an additional treatment component aimed at directly reducing the salience or reinforcement value of the deviant sexual fantasies. The masturbatory satiation technique described above was again used for this purpose. The technique involved daily sessions of extended masturbation, during the course of which the patient was required to verbalize into a tape recorder detailed account of all deviant fantasies and images. This procedure was found to be increasingly aversive and drastically reduced deviant arousal after only five weeks of practice.

A third important area of treatment focused on L.'s heterosexual inadequacies, and specifically his performance anxiety and rapid ejaculation problem with his wife. Much of the treatment intervention here involved dealing with his self-defeating notions and unrealistic expectations regarding sex. Several conjoint sex therapy sessions with his wife were also helpful in this regard. By the end of treatment, the couple reported a striking improvement in the frequency and satisfaction of intercourse.

The entire course of treatment was conducted over five months and included 19 therapy sessions in all. Such a relatively brief treatment duration was apparently due to the high motivation and intelligence level of this client, and particularly to the compliant manner in which all assignments were carried out. A very positive and trusting relationship with the therapist was also a key factor.

As is our standard procedure in such cases, L. was given a detailed set of instructions for maintenance and follow-up. These included a daily record-keeping assignment for the first three months following termination and scheduled follow-up visits at regular intervals. A tension-reduction maintenance program was outlined, and continued marital therapy was recommended in view of the number of ongoing conflicts that had not been resolved at the time of termination.

Discussion

Clearly it is difficult, if not impossible, to isolate the effective elements in such complex and multifaceted treatment programs as those described here. While it was our clinical impression that L.'s chronic inability to cope with interpersonal stress and negative affect was an important antecedent to his deviant sexual behavior, we felt it unwise to restrict our therapy to interventions in this area. For this reason, the decision was made to include techniques for directly reducing deviant arousal, as well as conjoint marital sessions for dealing with marital/sexual difficulties.

A basic question raised by a comparison of the two case studies described above is the choice of which method of intervention to use for dealing with the client's negative arousal states. The first case involved a relatively unsophisticated client who appreared to respond well to a more global and generalized self-control approach. On the other hand, the second case illustrates the potential value of more structured and specific interventions such as biofeedback training and imagery rehearsal. In still other instances, we have had notable success with the use of hypnosis-assisted relaxation, autogenic training, clinically standardized meditation, and a variety of other tension-reduction methods (Lehrer and Woolfolk, 1982). In general, we feel it is important to maintain a flexible approach to treatment, and to match clients and interventions as far as possible in an individual fashion (Lazarus and Rosen, 1976).

IMPLEMENTING MAINTENANCE AND FOLLOW-UP PROCEDURES

The comprehensive behavioral treatment approach described in this chapter requires the inclusion of a systematic maintenance and follow-up component. Regular follow-up visits, at the very least, need to be scheduled at clearly defined intervals following termination. We have previously reported on the unfortunate results of an overreliance on self-report in this regard (Rosen and Kopel, 1977), and we now recommend the inclusion of physiological assessment, where possible, as part of the follow-up assessment procedures. In addition, the corroborative reports of spouses and significant others can be of major significance to the clinician in this regard. Unfortunately, however, ethical considerations often limit the extent of information available from potential corroborative sources.

Tension-reduction training offers certain important advantages with regard to the assessment of treatment generalization. Laboratory methods are available, for example, for the objective assessment of physiological components of the client's stress response. In fact, a comprehensive maintenance program ideally includes most, if not all, of the following components: (1) regular self-monitoring of stress levels and the client's rehearsal of coping responses; (2) immediate reporting of relapse incidents to the treatment staff; (3) repeated laboratory assessments and booster training sessions; and (4) follow-up interviews with spouses, employers, etc., where possible.

Of the tension-reduction techniques described above, biofeedback appears to offer certain unique advantages with regard to the implementation of maintenance and follow-up. Several of our clients have recently opted to purchase portable biofeedback units for home use following the termination of treatment. These units make it possible for clients to systematically monitor tension levels at home on a daily or weekly basis, and also facilitate regular practice sessions throughout the follow-up period. Although we do not have sufficient data at present to evaluate the long-term effectiveness of such maintenance procedures, it is our clinical impression that outcome has been significantly improved by their use.

SUMMARY AND CONCLUSION

In this chapter we have outlined the role of negative arousal states in the mediation of compulsive sexual behavior and the clinical application of tension-reduction training as one component of a broad-spectrum behavior therapy approach to treatment. We have particularly emphasized the importance of individual assessment, as well as the need for a comprehensive intervention approach. The case studies described provide some indication of the usefulness of this approach, as well as some idea of the practical issues involved in application. In addition, we have also emphasized the need for follow-up assessment and planned maintenance strategies in dealing with chronic offenders.

Despite the obvious clinical advantages of the comprehensive behavioral approach advocated in this chapter, it is nevertheless advisable to conclude with a cautionary note. There is unfortunately a dearth of well-controlled, long-term outcome studies on treatment effectiveness generally. Our own experience suggests that unless treatment is continued over several months, perhaps even years, the possibility of relapse remains high (Rosen and Kopel, 1977). In addition, behavioral treatment methods might be more appropriate for some offenders than for others. These methods generally require the active participation of the offender, and the treatment is unlikely to succeed with unmotivated, mentally retarded, or psychotic offenders. As Bancroft (1974, p. 225) has aptly observed, "Modifying deviant sexual behavior involves considerable commitment for both subject and therapist and should not be undertaken lightly by either."

REFERENCES

Bancroft, J. *Deviant Sexual Behavior: Modification and Assessment*. London: Oxford University Press, 1974.

Barlow, D. The treatment of sexual deviation: toward a comprehensive behavioral approach. In Calhoun, K.S., Adams, H.E., and Mitchell, K.M. (Eds.) *Innovative Treatment Methods in Psychopathology*. New York: Wiley, 1974

Barlow, D.H. and Abel, G.G. Sexual deviation. In Craighead, W., Kazdin, A., and Mahoney, M. (Eds.) *Behavior Modification*. New York: Houghton Mifflin, 1976, pp. 341-360.

Bond, I.K. and Hutchinson, H.E. Application of reciprocal inhibition therapy to exhibitionism. *Journal of the Canadian Medical Association* **83**:23-25 (1960).

Davidson, R.J. and Schwartz, G.E. The psychobiology of relaxation and related states: A MULTI/ process theory. In Mostofsky, D. (Ed.) *Behavior Control and Modification of Physiological Activity*. New York: Prentice-Hall, 1976.

Groth, N. *Men Who Rape*. New York: Plenum Press, 1979.

Jacobson, E. *Progressive Relaxation*. Chicago: University of Chicago Press, 1938.

Lazarus, A. *In the Mind's Eye*. New York: Rawson Associates, 1977.

Lazarus, A. and Rosen, R.C. Behavior therapy techniques in the treatment of sexual disorders. In Meyers, J.K. (Ed.) *Clinical Management of Sexual Disorders*. Baltimore: Williams and Wilkins, 1976.

Lehrer, P. Anxiety and cultivated relaxation. In McGingam, F.J. (Rd.) *Tension Control: Proceedings of the Association for the Advancement of Tension Control*. Louisville, Kentucky, 1979.

Lehrer, P. and Woolfolk, R. *Stress and Treatment*. New York: Guilford Press, in press.

Meichenbaum, D. *Cognitive-Behavior Modification*. New York: Plenum Press, 1977.

Money, J. and Bennett, R.G. Postadolescent paraphilic sex offenders: anti-androgenic and counseling therapy follow-up. *International Journal of Mental Health* **10:**122-133 (1981).

Novaco, R.W. The functions and regulation of the arousal of anger. *American Journal of Psychiatry* **133:** 1124-1128 (1976).

Novaco, R.W. Stress inoculation: a cognitive therapy for anger and its application to a case of depression. *Journal of Consulting and Clinical Psychology* **45:**600-608 (1977).

Rosen, R.C., Fracher, J.C., and Perold, E. *Psychophysiological correlates of compulsive sexual misconduct. EEG laterality results on 3 case studies*. Paper presented at the American Society for Sex Therapy and Research, Philadelphia, March 1979.

Rosen, R.C. and Kopel, S. The use of penile plethysmography and biofeedback in the treatment of a transvestite-exhibitionist. *Journal of Consulting and Clinical Psychology* **45:**908-916 (1977).

Stevenson, I. and Wolpe, J. Recovery from sexual deviations through overcoming non-sexual neurotic responses. *American Journal of Psychiatry* **116:**737-741 (1960).

8
Treatment of the Sexual Offender in a Correctional Institution

A. Nicholas Groth, Ph.D.

This chapter focuses on practical experiences derived from providing clinical services to sex offenders confined to a correctional institution. It identifies common problem areas characteristic of such clients and suggests approaches to address these issues while examining the obstacles and limitations imposed by the restrictive setting. It specifically describes differences in the personalities and belief structures of child molesters and rapists, and details the requisite treatment techniques and goals for both. In addition, there is a description and discussion of the treatment components utilized in the nine specific groups constituting the sex offender program at a correctional institution. The emphasis throughout is upon practical applications of successful procedures developed as a result of experiences within such a setting.

Sexual assault is complex and multidetermined. To combat it requires a multidisciplinary approach and interagency cooperation. It is an interpersonal offense and, therefore, to deal effectively with this problem the needs of both parties—the victim and the offender—must be addressed. There has been much significant progress over the past decade in regard to developing and providing victim services. Unfortunately, there has been relatively little attention paid to the perpetrator, and personnel in the human services and criminal justice systems have been caught off guard and unprepared to deal effectively with identified offenders.

Characteristically, persons who commit sexual assaults do not self-refer to mental health or social service agencies for a number of reasons. (1) They do not appreciate the seriousness of their behavior and do not recognize that they have a problem. (2) They do not know where to turn to receive dependable help. (3) They fear the adverse social and legal consequences of disclosure. (4) At times of stress they act out, rather than work out, their problems. (5) They perceive other persons, especially those in some position of authority, as obstacles, opponents, or objects in their lives rather than as sources of help and assistance. Consequently, human services providers have had little or no opportunity to work with such clients. The behavioral sciences have not thoroughly researched or studied this form of sexual

160

pathology, and criminal justice personnel lack the specialized knowledge required for effective disposition, management, supervision, and treatment of such cases. The serious consequence resulting from this state of affairs is that dangerous sex-offenders such as rapists and child molesters are recycled back into the community with no reduction in, or safeguards against, the risk they pose of repeating their sexual crimes.

A comprehensive approach to combating sexual assault and reducing sexual violence requires a component which focuses on the assessment, management, and treatment of the perpetrator. It is insufficient to limit services to persons who have already been sexually assaulted. It is necessary to work to prevent individuals from being sexually victimized, and a necessary and crucial factor in such a protection plan is the effective management and treatment of the offender.

Identified sex offenders will be found in all settings: in correctional institutions, in mental hospitals, in residential programs for the retarded, in outpatient programs and agencies, and in the community. Services, therefore, need to be available in all these settings. To provide such services requires a dependable understanding of the psychology of the offender and the dynamics of his behavior, as well as an adaptation of traditional clinical intervention techniques and treatment procedures to address the specific needs of this client population.

Rape itself is not a diagnostic category. It is a behavioral act and, as such, cuts across all conventional diagnostic categories and psychiatric conditions. Like other behavioral acts such as suicide, homicide, or alcohol abuse, it is something anyone is capable of doing. Most people, fortunately, will never exhibit such behavior. Some may attempt to commit the act once, appreciate its inappropriateness, and self-correct. A few may resort to such behavior under unexpected and extraordinary but transient life stresses or crises. Then there are others for whom sexual assault is characteristic behavior: there is high risk that these individuals will repeat such acts since they find life demands and adult responsibilities overwhelmingly stressful. To a large extent, it is this latter group—for whom sexual assault is a chronic behavioral pattern—that is most likely to come to the attention of the clinician. By virtue of the repetitive nature of their offenses, their chances for detection and apprehension are enhanced. In an ideal situation, where treatment services are available in a variety of settings, placement would be determined by the offender's primary condition. The sex offender who is mentally ill (psychotic) would be treated in a mental hospital. The individual who is a habitual criminal and whose sex offenses form one of many types of antisocial and criminal behavior would be treated in a correctional institution. An individual whose serious sexual offenses constitute a departure from an otherwise law-abiding life would be treated in a security treatment center specifically designed for sex offenders. Finally, that individual who is being released from an institutional program back into the community or whose situation determines that an alternative to incarceration is warranted as a disposition in his case would be treated in an outpatient program by a community agency. Too often, however, having failed to develop alternative programs and treatment services for rapists and child molesters, the majority of such convicted offenders, by default, are incarcerated. What ought to be apparent, but is too often ignored, is the fact that it is not how long the offender is confined, but rather what opportunities exist for evaluation and treatment while he is confined, that will determine whether or not it is safe for him to return to the community upon expiration of his sentence.

This chapter will focus on the provision of clinical services to sex offenders who are incarcerated in a correctional institution. It will identify some of the common problem areas characteristic of such clients, suggest some approaches to address these issues, and examine some of the obstacles and limitations imposed by such a setting. The observations and ideas presented in this chapter have been derived from our experience in operating a sex offender treatment program at the Connecticut Correctional Institution at Somers.

INMATE CLIENTS

The Sex Offender Program at CCI-Somers operates within the confines of a maximum security prison for adult male felons. It provides diagnostic and treatment services for convicted rapists and child molesters, consultation and training in regard to working with such clients, and research and publication to enhance and expand existing knowledge in regard to this form of sexual pathology. Currently CCI-Somers houses 1200 inmates, 250 of whom are serving time for a sexual offense. There are approximately another 100 inmates whose crime is sex related but whose offense of record is not specifically a sex offense. Instead, they may have been convicted of such crimes as homicide, breaking and entering, kidnapping, and the like, but examination of their pre-sentence investigation reports reveals that their offenses also involved an attempted or completed sexual assault. In addition, there are another 25 to 30 inmates who have prior convictions for sexual assault on their records even though they are currently doing time for a nonsexual offense. Approximately 30%, or almost one out of every three, of the inmates at this facility have been identified as having committed a sexual assault. From our experience in Connecticut (which has been verified by other correctional facilities in Florida, Kansas, North Dakota, and Vermont), we would estimate that between 25 and 30% of the inmates incarcerated in prison are sex offenders. If one out of three inmates in prison were serving time for an alcohol-related crime, the administration and the community would recognize the need for operating an alcohol recovery program for them. If the incidence of sex-related crimes was as apparent, the need for services to address this problem would be similarly evident. Unfortunately, for a variety of reasons, sexual abuse is not as visible as alcohol abuse, and the majority of such incarcerated offenders are neglected with respect to services in regard to their sexual assaultiveness.

The Sex Offender Program at CCI-Somers has been in operation since 1978. Its staff is comprised of one full-time and one part-time paid employee, four clinical

trainees, and ten volunteers. Approximately 125 inmates (or 30% of the sex offender population) participate in the treatment program, which is voluntary, on a
weekly basis. These clients are housed in the general population and come to the
hospital wing of the prison at the time of their treatment sessions.

The sex offenders seen by us for treatment at CCI-Somers are adult males over
the age of 18. On the average they are repetitive offenders who have committed
more offenses than they have been convicted of—the majority having attempted or
committed their first sex offense prior to the age of 16. All were found competent to
stand trial, were convicted, and are serving prison sentences. For the most part
they have led marginal lives in regard to school, work, military, marital, and social
achievements. Few exhibit any evidence of serious mental illness (psychosis) or
intellectual deficit (retardation), but most reflect few conflict-free areas of psychological functioning. Their offenses appear to be the product more of internal, psychological determinants than of external, situational factors.

PERSONALITY DEFICITS

In the development and operation of the Sex Offender Program, we have proceeded from the premise that sexual assault is the product of defects in
development and deficits in life management skills. It is the long-term consequence
of trauma and maltreatment (abuse, neglect, exploitation, and/or abandonment)
during the formative years which have interfered with the psychological maturation
of the individual. We are dealing with clients who physically are adults but emo-
tionally remain battered children. At the risk of overgeneralizing, the rapist appears
to be the angry child and the child molester appears to be the frightened child—
both tend to exhibit pronounced personality deficits in regard to the following:

1. *A sense of worthlessness and low self-esteem.* The sexual offender tends to
possess little sense of self-worth or personal value. His early abuse, neglect, or
other maltreatment communicated to him that he is deserving of mistreatment and
instilled in him a negative self-image.

2. *A sense of vulnerability and helplessness.* As a consequence of not receiving
reasonable discipline and support during his formative years, the offender comes to
experience himself as unprotected and at risk in a hostile world. His deep-seated
feelings of personal insecurity and inadequacy result in experiencing his control
over himself and his life as very tenuous. He tends to experience himself more as
the victim than as the creator of the problems, difficulties, and hardships he finds in
dealing with adult life demands and responsibilities.

3. *Impaired social relationships.* Early adversities and mistreatment lead the
offender to keep others at a distance. Social, emotional, and even physical intimacy is threatening since it poses the risk of exposing his inadequacy as a person.
This, combined with his perception of others as adversaries, precludes interpersonal relationships based on warmth, trust, and reciprocity. Psychologically the
offender is a loner. A quality of detachment, isolation, and unrelatedness coupled

with a self-centered orientation and a wariness of others, prevails in his social interactions. Relationships tend to be superficial and transitory.

4. *Dysphoric mood state.* The offender's sense of personal inadequacy and interpersonal ineffectiveness results in an underlying mood state of anger, fear, and depression (resentment and resignation). The responsibilities of adult life management are experienced as exceeding his skills and resources to cope with them, and fill him with anxiety. His unmet needs for acceptance, validation, affection, approval, and intimacy result in feelings of depression. His perception of others as depriving, rejecting, or exploiting results in feelings of anger and hostility. His sense of isolation from others produces a feeling of emptiness. Consequently, the offender tends to find little joy, pleasure, or long-lasting satisfaction and contentment in his life. Warmth, humor, happiness, and affection are noticeably absent, and his characteristic mood state is more one of distress, discomfort, frustration, emptiness, disappointment, and resentment.

5. *Mismanagement of aggression.* The offender's feelings of personal inadequacy and betrayal by others prompt him to mismanage his aggression. The rapist characteristically deploys his aggression into compensatory and retaliatory behaviors in order to deny his vulnerability or helplessness, assert his power and mastery, and get even for the mistreatment accorded him in his life. More self- than other-oriented, lacking much self-respect, and feeling outside of and apart from community life, he finds no way to neutralize, modulate, or redirect his aggression into more socially appropriate channels. Having been the target of abuse, he comes to identify with the aggressor and to regard aggression in the form of domination, intimidation, manipulation, exploitation, and physical force as necessary for psychological survival and a means of achieving control and/or exacting revenge.

The child molester, in contrast to the rapist, adopts a more passive, submissive posture. Rather than use aggression as a form of counterattack, he retreats from adult relationships and turns to children who are psychologically less threatening to him, easier to control and manipulate, and easier to dominate. The child molester abandons any constructive expression of aggression (i.e., assertiveness, perseverance, etc.) and resigns himself to a role of passivity and dependency. A quality of learned helplessness undermines his coping with adult life responsibilities in an effective and adaptive fashion.

Both, then, mismanage aggression—the rapist by using force to achieve his ends and the child molester by avoiding aggression to the point of ineffectual passivity. Neither employs aggression in an adaptive fashion to assert himself without transgressing against others.

6. *Tenuous masculine identity.* A sense of failure in regard to most sources of personal identity such as educational achievement, work success, meaningful relationships, and the like produces disturbing doubts in the offender about his manhood. Such insecurities may be reflected in exaggerated and stereotyped masculine behavior (on the part of the rapist) or through the abandonment of any masculine strivings (on the part of the child molester). Having developed few nonsexual and

nonaggressive sources of personal identity, the offender tends to place a premium on sexuality and aggression as an expression of his masculinity. Both become overemphasized in his psychological functioning. Sexuality is experienced as especially threatening or conflictual since it becomes the focus of expression of the unresolved issues in the offender's psychological development; sexuality thus becomes the means of trying to fulfill nonsexual needs and resolve nonsexual issues. Attitudes and values surrounding sexuality and aggression are especially maladaptive; when either drive or impulse is activated or aroused, the offender's ability to accurately perceive, comprehend, and respond to reality situations or demands becomes impaired or undependable.

In understanding sexual assault, then, we see the sex offender as a person whose personality resources to negotiate life demands are tenuous or deficient and who consequently experiences the world as one filled with overwhelming stresses. Early abuse, neglect, and trauma have predisposed him to perceive others as adversaries, and himself as worthless, and to anticipate further rejection. Consequently, he experiences considerable anxiety in regard to interpersonal intimacy, which becomes especially intense in the area of sexuality and escalates into anger, hatred, and fear of others. His attempt to cope with this situation is either to adopt aggression as a defense and counterattack, or to withdraw from adults sexually. Such maladaptive coping efforts result in increased frustration and tension, and the offense constitutes a desperate attempt to escape from the mounting inner turmoil. Since we are dealing with personality defects, our treatment approach is one of reeducation, resocialization, and counseling.

TREATMENT ASSUMPTIONS

The goal of treatment is to reduce the risk of the sex offender's repeating his offense. The assumptions underlying our treatment approach are as follows:

1. Sexual assault is a complex, multidetermined act which is the product of an interaction between internal psychological determinants (such as needs, attitudes, defenses, etc.) and external factors (such as precipitating stresses, victim availability, disinhibitors, etc.). Rape and child molestation are not, in and of themselves, psychiatric conditions or diagnostic entities—they are behaviors which cut across all conventional psychiatric classifications and diagnostic categories.

2. Sexual assaultiveness is the product of defects in human development, defects which result from adversities in early life and a failure to receive consistent love and support and reasonable discipline. It is the long-term consequence of early neglect, maltreatment, and sexual abuse.

3. Sexual assault is equivalent to symptom formation. The sex offense is an acting out or living out of some unresolved developmental issue—an attempted resolution to some early life crisis—either a persistent, ongoing concern or a dormant issue which has been reactivated by a current life situation or event. As a symptom, it is, therefore, repetitive behavior—self-defeating and self-perpetuating—and an in-

dicator of psychological distress. It serves to defend against anxiety, to express a conflict, and to gratify an impulse.

4. By definition, sexual assault is an interpersonal act involving both sexuality and aggression. It is the sexual abuse of power and the sexual expression of needs, motives, and issues that are predominantly nonsexual. It is the sexual expression of aggression rather than the aggressive expression of sexuality.

5. There need to be changes in the offender's internal psychological state and/or his external environment in order to reduce the risk of repetition. Some change must occur in his capability, intent, and/or opportunity to commit a sexual assault if the risk of recidivism is to decrease.

TREATMENT GOALS

We see the task of treatment as assisting the sex offender to achieve the following goals.

1. *To recognize and acknowledge that he does have a problem, through an understanding of his symptoms.* However insight alone, although necessary, is insufficient. It is not enough that the offender realize he has a problem, he must also do something about it.

2. *To accept responsibility for his actions.* Explanations are not excuses. The offender must do more than admit his guilt; he must develop better ways of dealing with his problems and coping with life demands, and must make amends for his transgressions.

3. *To reevaluate his attitudes and values towards sexuality and aggression.* The offender must come to appreciate the inappropriateness of sexual coercion and assault, and the serious consequences of sexual aggression both to others (especially its impact on the victim) and to himself. Attitudinal change is a precursor to behavioral change.

4. *To realize that sexual assaultiveness is repetitive or compulsive behavior over which he must gain control.* The offender must accept the fact that he has a chronic problem, one he must face and work on indefinitely—perhaps for the rest of his life. His problem cannot be cured, but it can be treated; it cannot be eliminated, but it can be controlled.

Essentially the task for the offender is to reduce the risk of his repeating a sexual offense by developing better control over his behavior, through becoming more in touch with the motives prompting his offenses and finding more adaptive ways of expressing such needs and feelings; by identifying the stresses impacting on him that activate his assaults and either avoiding them or developing better defenses to withstand them; by being on guard against disinhibitors which serve to release his sexual assaultiveness; by recognizing early indicators or warning signals in his characteristic behavior patterns which, if ignored, will evolve into a sexual offense and taking action to interrupt this cycle. The offender must appreciate that this is an ongoing task, one he must face each and every day of his life.

ENGAGEMENT STRATEGIES

In working with sex offenders we are dealing, to a large extent, with involuntary clients; that is, for the most part, these are not individuals who recognize or readily acknowledge that they have problems or are interested in treatment as it is traditionally offered. Realizing the adverse social and legal consequences of disclosure, few sought help while on the street. Now, finding themselves in prison, they feel they have much to lose if they admit to being a sex offender since such inmates occupy a low social status in the prison hierarchy. How then does one go about engaging an unmotivated client in the enterprise of psychological treatment? A combination of the following strategies will be required to accomplish this.

1. *Outreach.* Rather than expecting such inmates to self-refer, the clinician must establish a system whereby individuals convicted of sex offenses are identified upon admission. The institutional reception-classification unit that processes the inmate upon arrival, should inform him of the existence of a sex offender treatment program, identify the services available to him through this program, and instruct him as to how he can participate in it. In turn, the reception-classification unit should inform the program of the inmate's admission to the institution, and a program staff member should then follow up this referral by contacting the inmate and screening him for involvement in the treatment program. If the inmate is not receptive to treatment, he should be followed up at regular intervals and given the message that "we won't go away and we won't give up on you." What we have found particularly useful in this regard is to have a printed description of treatment services available in the form of an application which is given, upon admission, to each inmate referred to our program and which is sent out on a regular (yearly) basis (or whenever a new group or treatment service is being offered) to all inmates serving time for a sex-related offense. Persistent outreach is necessary in order to engage unmotivated clients.

2. *Leverage.* The clinician must identify leverage points and utilize them in order to get the client to participate in treatment. Some inmates arrive in a state of personal crisis, or some such distress develops during their course of incarceration which may serve to make them more receptive to outreach efforts. More commonly, preferred housing or work assignments and the prospects of parole, family (conjugal) visits, community access, transfer to a minimum security prison, and the like can be used to induce inmates to participate in the program. Family and even peer pressure from fellow inmates can be used to this end. Benefits such as "good time" credit which will serve to reduce the amount of time spent in prison would prove a major incentive. In so far as prison visibility constitutes an obstacle to client participation, treatment groups can be identified with "face-saving," yet accurate, titles such as a "management of aggression" group or a "relating to women" group, rather than labeling the sessions as sex offender groups. Working with involuntary clients, then, requires a "carrot-and-stick" intervention: there need to be real benefits for engaging in treatment and real (and, preferably, imme-

diate) adverse consequences for failure to participate in the program if involuntary clients are to be expected to take part in treatment.

3. *Confrontation.* Working with involuntary clients requires intervenors who are confronting, that is, who can demand responsible behavior from their clients by identifying their maladaptive attitudes, erroneous thinking (reasoning and judgment), and inappropriate behaviors, and by imposing and enforcing limits. The clinician must be able to exercise his authority in a responsible fashion. He must be open, direct, truthful, and consistent in working with the involuntary client. He must not be hostile, punitive, or deprecating. He should carefully communicate that it is the offense which is reprehensible, not the offender himself. Not only must the clinician tell the client he has a problem, he must also offer him help and insist that the client work to improve himself in a responsible fashion. He must recognize the client's sense of personal injury, that is, his hurt, loneliness, anger, guilt, etc., and validate his worth as a person. To effectively accomplish the task of acknowledging the offender's own maltreatment and personal victimization, and at the same time hold him accountable for his abusive behavior towards others, we have found that a knowledge of victimology is essential for clinicians who are working with offenders. This is necessary in part so that the ultimate goal—to protect others from sexual abuse—is not lost sight of, and in part because the offense is, in itself, one of the long-term consequences of the offender's unaddressed early victimization. Again, at the risk of oversimplification, the role of the therapist is comparable to that of an effective parent who, through the proper use of authority, instruction, example, assistance, and caring, facilitates the psychological maturation of the client into a responsible adult.

4. *Concrete help.* Outreach, leverage, and confrontation may encourage an unmotivated client to participate in a treatment program, but for him to really engage in the enterprise of treatment he must be offered something that feels like help. He must experience the treatment as useful and helpful to him. Obviously this will require an intervenor who has specialized knowledge of the dynamics of sexual assault—in regard to both the offender and the victim—which will permit him through his questions and responses to instill in the client a sense of being understood and of being helped. There may be a number of immediate practical problems or concerns the incarcerated offender is facing in regard both to his separation from his family and community, and to his adjustment to prison life. Orientation, advice, direct intervention, or appropriate referral can provide crisis intervention for the client and assistance in handling these concerns. Anticipatory guidance, in which the clinician identifies both the concrete event and the client's feelings and expectations in regard to it, outlines alternative strategies for dealing with it, and points out what result a given course of action is likely to have, is an effective communication of concrete help. Initially, goals must be identified which can realistically be attained within a reasonably short period of time in order for the client to experience a sense of accomplishment. As Sgroi (1981) points out, a subtle but

important corollary to providing concrete help "is the therapist's conscious use of self to convey to the client by providing some concrete service that the benevolent use of power is possible, that authority need not be fearful, that isolation and denial are ineffective coping mechanisms because they cut the client off from much that is positive, that encounters with the outside world can be affiliative and that magical expectations can be replaced by realistic and appropriate ones." Treatment services then must address the felt needs of the client. With common problem areas in regard to men who commit sexual assaults having already been identified, the treatment sessions attempt to target these issues through the design of the groups.

TREATMENT COMPONENTS

The treatment program we provide to help the offender to address his sexual assaultiveness involves reeducation, resocialization, and counseling. The primary intervention modality is group treatment which operates on a guided self-help and mutual aid concept. Not only is group treatment a practical approach for providing services to a large number of clients when there are limited staff resources, but also it is the treatment of choice when working with involuntary clients whose major problem behaviors are in the area of interpersonal peer relationships. The aim of treatment is to help the client control his abusive sexual behavior, and one of the most successful approaches to behavior control—whether it be alcohol abuse, spouse abuse, child abuse, drug abuse, compulsive eating, compulsive gambling, or the like—has been the self-help, group treatment model. The nine specific groups which constitute the core of the Sex Offender Program at CCI-Somers will be discussed in the remainder of this section.

Reeducation

1. *Sex education.* We have found that by and large, sex offenders are uninformed or misinformed about human sexuality. In addition, their attitudes and values in regard to sexual behavior tend to be very conservative even if their sexual experiences have been wider or more adventurous. Adult sexuality for both rapists and child molesters appears to be psychologically threatening. At the same time, such offenders seem to have few inhibitions in regard to transgression. For example, in response to a query as to what he considered better behavior, consenting sexual activity between two men or the rape of a woman, one offender responded, "Raping a woman is better [behavior]—at least that's normal." His criterion thus was not one of consent versus coercion, but of opposite-sex versus same-sex contact. The sex education group, then, provides a basic introduction to human sexuality. Discussion focuses on myths and misconceptions about human sexuality, the anatomy and physiology of sex, sexual roles, gender and identity issues, reproduction, variations in sexual behavior, fantasies, values, attitudes, and common questions

and concerns. The sex education group is aimed at enhancing the offender's knowledge of human sexuality and improving his attitudes and values in regard to this area of human behavior.

2. *Understanding sexual assault.* Many sex offenders have stereotyped notions of what constitutes a sexual offender and, therefore, do not regard themselves as falling within such a client population. One offender who entered an Alford plea to a charge of first degree sexual assault (his second offense of record) alleged false accusations in both instances and denied having "a sex problem" since he was "married and had plenty of girlfriends." Other offenders commonly believe that their sexual offenses were the result of alcohol abuse and that they only need to address their drinking problems in their recovery program. The understanding sexual assault group focuses on the dynamics of rape and child molestation, patterns of assault, the psychology of the offender, characteristic traits and behavior patterns, and the state of clinical knowledge in regard to this form of pathological sexual behavior. It is aimed at dispelling the self-deceptions, rationalizations, and projections of responsibility that sex offenders use to avoid recognizing their problems and to diminish their responsibility for their offenses.

3. *Victim personalization.* The majority of sex offenders have little realization of the consequences of their offenses in regard to the victim. For the rapist, the victim is often depersonalized into an impersonal object and no thought is given to her or him following the assault. For the child molester, the victim becomes a fantasy object, and he maintains the illusion that the child welcomed, appreciated, enjoyed, and may even have benefited from the sexual activity. Neither fully appreciates the harm he did or the risk he posed to his victims. The victim personalization group focuses on the impact of various types of sexual offenses on the victim. Attention is given to the immediate and long-term aftereffects of sexual assault on victims, both female and male, adult and child. This group is aimed at helping the offender to more fully realize and understand why victims behave as they do and how their lives are affected by being victimized.

The reeducation groups serve to provide information to the offender in three primary areas related to his crime: the offense, the offender, and the victim. Knowledge is legitimate power, and enhancing cognitive understanding in these areas can help the offender to identify and address the tasks of recovery.

Resocialization (Skills Development)

Personality deficits develop as a result of the adversities encountered by the offender during his formative years, which impair his ability to negotiate adult life demands in an effective and responsible fashion. The following treatment groups aim to help him develop or improve his social skills:

1. *Interpersonal relationships.* Sexual assault is, by definition, an interpersonal act, and it is in their interpersonal relationships that the social deficits of sexual offenders are most pronounced. In this group, attention focuses on concerns and

problems experienced in relating to others, both male and female. Attitudes in regard to role expectations are explored; problems in communications are analyzed; and issues pertaining to forming and maintaining relationships based on trust, intimacy, and reciprocity are addressed. The interpersonal relationships group is aimed at helping the offender to feel more comfortable with others, to diminish his sense of social isolation, and to improve his negotiation of interpersonal relationships.

2. *Management of aggression.* Sexual assault is more the sexual expression of aggression than the aggressive expression of sexuality. Characteristically, the offender has problems in regard to the appropriate management of aggression. Under chronic stress, and encountering frustration in coping with adult life responsibilities, he has problems channeling his aggression into useful and constructive outlets. This group focuses on the mismanagement of aggression—such as having a problem with one's temper; getting involved in high-risk activities for excitement; or trying to deal with others through manipulation, exploitation, intimidation, or physical force—and offers alternative ways of handling such situations. It aims at helping the offender to be assertive without transgressing against someone else, to deal with adversity in ways other than through retaliation or withdrawal, and to appreciate the long-term adverse consequences of the misuse of aggression even though it may prove temporarily effective in regard to an immediate goal.

3. *Parents Anonymous.* Since the majority of sex offenders experienced something that fell short of an adequate upbringing, they in turn have poor skills in regard to the upbringing of their own children. A chapter of Parents Anonymous was organized—only the second in the country to be established inside a prison, and the first to address predominantly the sex offender—to improve the care-taking skills of these men. Operating on the self-help model, members of this group set their meeting agendas, and focus on better recognizing and responding to the needs of children in a responsible and caring fashion.

The resocialization group aids the offender in developing improved social skills to deal with adult life demands and responsibilities. As he learns how to better cope with such demands, he comes to feel less vulnerable, less threatened, and more in control of himself. As self-control increases, there is less need to attempt to control others in an abusive and exploitative fashion.

Counseling

1. *Group therapy.* Group therapy is used to address the problems of the offender's sexual assaultiveness in order to help him better control and avoid such behavior. Attention is focused on the offense itself and the psychological components of the crime: precipitating stresses, disinhibitors, accompanying fantasies, subjective reactions, mood states, and the like. The aim is to help the offender discover the dynamics of his offense, to identify what are contributory factors that increase the risk of such behavior, to recognize early warning signals that are

precursors of his offense behavior, and to find alternative ways of managing the unresolved life issues underlying his sexual assaultiveness. Since one of the offender's major problem areas is his sense of isolation from peers, group therapy is seen as a particularly appropriate modality for addressing his interpersonal offense behavior.

2. *Personal victimization.* Since the majority of sexual offenders experienced significant maltreatment during their developmental years in the form of abuse, neglect, exploitation, and abandonment, this group focuses on the impact such victimization has had on their lives. Particular attention is given to the sexual victimization and trauma experienced during their formative years which are prominent in the life histories of both rapists and child molesters. The questions, feelings, attitudes, concerns, and problems experienced in regard to having been a victim of sexual and/or physical abuse are dealt with. The aim is to help the offender come to grips with such unresolved life issues.

3. *Combating sexual assault.* An important component in treating sex offenders is restitution for their transgressions. Regular meetings with persons from the community who deal with sexual assault, such as law enforcement officers, parole and probation officers, victim counselors, child protection workers, and the like offer sex offenders the opportunity to provide valuable input, based on their own knowledge and experience, in the effort to combat sexual assault and make the community safer for everyone. Such participation serves to enhance their own self-esteem and sense of worth. Being able to be of help in the very area in which they offended constitutes some reparation for the harm they have done others.

ADDITIONAL TREATMENT COMPONENTS

Although group treatment is regarded as the treatment of choice, other interventions are also employed. The offender is encouraged to engage in self-help enterprises such as biofeedback to learn how to reduce stress through practicing relaxation exercises. One such self-help enterprise that we have found to be especially therapeutic is to have the offender write an autobiography. This encourages him to be reflective and self-observant. It instills the message that treatment is something he must work at every day, not only on the days of assigned sessions. It helps him to get an overview of his life and to see relationships between life events and courses of action on his part. It helps him to identify problem areas in his life, especially in discovering what life events or times he has little or no information about, and it also serves to help him retrieve information that he has tended to shut out or block out of his mind, and to reassess and process it.

Individual treatment sessions are necessary for crisis intervention or in those situations where the offender is too intimidated by the prison experience to begin treatment in a group setting. The assignment task is to differentiate between those situations in which the offender is attempting to use individual treatment to avoid group treatment and when it is in fact an appropriate intervention. Given the variety of treatment groups, we find in most cases that the client should be able to accept some group assignment in addition to individual sessions.

Since offenders characteristically tend to expect immediate need satisfaction and, when left to their own devices, tend not to persist with long-range, goal-directed behaviors, we have found it advantageous to identify specific goals in treatment and establish timetables in regard to addressing these issues. Both individual and group sessions are time limited. Such task-oriented sessions provide the client with a sense of accomplishment and the experience of treatment as something that feels like help.

Given that the inmate-clients tend to function more on a concrete, behavioral rather than an abstract, intellectual level—they are more prone to act out rather than talk out their problems—we have found treatment sessions which employ role playing and video playback more productive and useful to them than those which are confined exclusively to verbal exchange. In so far as such clients tend towards concretized thinking, the use of sociodrama, a combination of role play, demonstration, instruction, and video feedback, is an especially appropriate treatment procedure.

DISADVANTAGES IN WORKING WITH SEX OFFENDERS IN A CORRECTIONAL SETTING

Although it has been our experience that a great deal can be accomplished with minimal resources in treating the sex offenders in a prison population, there are a number of disadvantages inherent in working in such a setting. First, the sex offender by virtue of his crime occupies a low social status in the inmate hierarchy and is exposed to considerable verbal or physical (and sometimes sexual) harassment and abuse from other prisoners. This state of affairs encourages some sex offenders to maintain that they were innocently convicted and/or to avoid treatment in an effort to diminish their visibility. This is especially true for the child molester who finds adults psychologically intimidating. Such maltreatment only serves to enhance his fear of adults and reinforce his attraction to children whom he sees as physically and psychologically safer and more accepting of him. A second major disadvantage is the sex offender's exposure to a subculture of violence and a value system that emphasizes aggression as a way of managing one's life—aggression in the form of deception, manipulation, threat, intimidation, coercion, force, and assault. Character traits such as warmth, trust, reciprocity, sharing, and affection are equated with weakness and vulnerability, and prove maladaptive in regard to prison survival where exaggerated masculine behavior in the form of toughness prevails. In prison, admitting to a problem and seeking or accepting help are regarded as signs of personal weakness.

In addition to these obstacles to engaging in treatment, a prison setting poses other difficulties with regard to the treatment of the sex offender. The close supervision and structuring of the offender's day-to-day activities in a maximum security prison remove him from the responsibility of structuring and managing his own life. Although prison life is not pleasant, it does protect the offender from life responsibilities which he had difficulty managing on the street, such as earning a living, supporting a family, relating to women, etc. Alcohol, weapons, victims, and the like are not readily available. Even when stressed, the offender is locked in his cell or under the scrutiny of a guard. The result of this state of affairs is that the sex offender often comes to feel he has changed or improved when, in fact, much of this improvement may be due to the change in his external environment and his response to a structured environment in which many things are provided for him (work, recreation, treatment, etc.), rather than to his internal maturation and growth. For this reason, it is difficult to assess the client's improvement and readiness for release based on his behavior in prison. Once an inmate has been released from prison, this usually terminates contact with his treatment group since reentering the prison for outpatient treatment would raise a number of security issues. Thus, an offender is cut off from the support of the group he has learned to turn to for help at the very time he is most in need of their help, when he is reentering the life situations that he had previously been unable to manage adequately.

Finally, although there may be a number of other limitations to treatment which are unique to specific institutions, one major problem commonly encountered is the perception, on the part of the inmate, of the treatment staff as having some power or control in regard to his eventual release and the concern he has as to how personal disclosure may adversely affect his release. We have addressed this issue in the following fashion. First, we inform the inmate that nothing he discloses in treatment is confidential, with regard either to the treatment staff or to the administration. There is no confidentiality or secrecy. His participation in treatment, or refusal of such, will be documented in his records. If asked by the parole board for an evaluation of an inmate, our report will attempt to document the problem areas the offender has exhibited in his life, the treatment efforts he has made to address these problems, and the stipulations we would recommend as conditions of parole if he were to be released at this time. We will neither advocate for nor oppose his parole. The inmate may see the report and ask for an explanation of what is said therein.

COST EFFECTIVENESS OF SEX OFFENDER TREATMENT

As things stand now in most correctional institutions there are no treatment services available for sex offenders. In part this is due to a lack of awareness of the number of such offenders serving time for sex-related offenses, and in part it is due to a shortage of resources to staff and fund such programs. We have found that much can be accomplished with very little. Trainees and volunteers can be recruited from the community, schools, colleges, and volunteer organizations, who have basic skills and expertise in their own fields and who are willing to invest some time and energy in return for an opportunity to enhance their knowledge about the special needs of sex offenders as well as to improve their skills in working with such clients. The services of persons who have a vested interest in understanding sexual assault, such as police, parole and probation officers, sexual abuse crisis counselors, clergy, and the like, can be recruited. Although one would appreciate a reasonable budget for supplies and equipment, all that is really required to begin a program is a minimum of two staff members and a space for group meetings. If different groups are not feasible, one group can be structured to cover, at different stages, the various tasks of reeducation, resocialization, and counseling. For a couple of dollars a week per inmate, some basic treatment can be provided which can serve to protect someone someday in the community from the trauma of sexual victimization.

However, we find that before anyone wants to spend money on sex offenders, the question is posed, How effective is your treatment? This question can never be satisfactorily answered for a variety of reasons. Most sexual assault goes unreported, and therefore, it is impossible to prove that such behavior is not happening on the part of a released client. Then, too, treatment may begin in prison but it must continue on the street, and when an offender reoffends this may not reflect as much on what was available to him in prison as on what was not available to him in the community. Finally, even when it can be demonstrated that sex offenders who participate in treatment have a lower recidivism rate than sex offenders who do not, this may merely reflect better judgment and a wish to change and improve themselves on the part of the former group, rather than the effectiveness of treatment per se.

In any case, it is only by establishing treatment services for sex offenders that we will learn how to treat them. It is through such programs that we will improve our knowledge and skill to address this problem. Failure to do this means that the offender and the danger he poses will eventually be recycled back into the community, and that the number of sex offenses and victims of such crimes will continue to increase. Our program has been in operation for a little less than four years (1979–82), and although outcome data are sparse, they are encouraging.

Program Evaluation

In assessing the outcome of the Sex Offender Program, four basic areas should be considered. To what extent has the program been successful in (1) engaging offenders in treatment, (2) reducing their risk of recidivism, (3) enhancing the state of knowledge about the sexual offender, and (4) improving the skills of human service providers to better address the needs of this client population?

1. *Direct services.* Every inmate who is serving time for a sex-related crime or has a prior history of a sex offense is identified upon admission to the institution, and efforts are made to engage him in the Sex Offender Program. At the onset of the program, 47 inmates (14% of the sex offender population) were initially involved in treatment. During its first year of operation, 60 inmates (17% of the sex

offender population) participated in the program. During the second year of operation, 79 inmates (20% of the sex offender population) took part in treatment; currently, there are 116 inmates (28% of the sex offender population) actively involved in the treatment program. These figures would indicate that the program is increasingly successful in recruiting inmate participants from the prison's sex offender population.

2. *Recidivism.* Since its inception, 72 of the inmates who participated to some extent in the Sex Offender Program have been released to the community. Of these, 14 (19%) have either violated parole or been rearrested: 6 for a sex-related offense, 6 for a nonsexual offense, and 2 for a parole violation. During this same period of time (1979–82), 122 inmates who were serving time for a sex-related offense but who refused to become involved in the program were released to the community. Of these, 44 (36%) have either violated parole or been rearrested: 19 for a sex-related offense, 16 for a nonsexual offense, and 9 for a parole violation. These follow-up data would indicate that sex offenders who participate in the program pose a significantly lower risk of recidivism following release than those who do not take part in this program.

3. *Research.* As part of the Sex Offender Program, a number of studies have been conducted which have served to enhance the state of knowledge about sexual offenders, specifically rapists and child molesters. To date, two books, ten book chapters, and ten journal articles have been published documenting what knowledge has been derived from our work.

4. *Training.* Since the inception of our program, 7 interns and 18 volunteers from different professional backgrounds (law enforcement, psychology, social work, etc.) have trained with us in order to improve their skills in working with sex offender clients. In each successive year, more individuals either volunteered their services or requested the Sex Offender Program as their intern placement than the previous year, which indicates that we are increasingly successful in attracting human service providers and interesting them in this work.

Given that our program has been in operation for only a few years and that it operates with no budget and only two paid staff, we regard its accomplishments to date as promising and hope it will encourage others likewise to begin to develop treatment services for incarcerated sex offenders in order to combat this serious social problem.

REFERENCES

Burgess, A.W., Groth, A.N., Holmstrom, L.L., and Sgroi, S.M. *Sexual Assault of Children and Adolescents.* Lexington, Mass.: Lexington Books, 1978.

Groth, A.N. *Men Who Rape: The Psychology of the Offender.* New York: Plenum Press, 1979.

Groth, A.N. *State police participate in Connecticut program. TSA News* **4**(3) (1981).

Rada, R.T. *Clinical Aspects of the Rapist.* New York: Grune and Stratton, 1978.

Sgroi, S.M. *Handbook of Clinical Intervention in Child Sexual Abuse.* Lexington, Mass.: Lexington Books, 1981.

West, D.J., Roy, C., and Nichols, F.L. *Understanding Sexual Attacks.* London: Heinemann, 1978.

9

Administering a Comprehensive Sexual Aggressive Treatment Program in a Maximum Security Setting

Robert E. Longo, M.R.C.

Because the field of offender treatment is so new, there is still a need to share very practical information about the administration of an ongoing program, particularly in a secure setting (prison or state hospital). This chapter addresses the practical issues that a new administrator may be faced with: housing arrangements, resources, staff, relationships to higher administrative levels. The framework within which treatment takes place is important to the success of the treatment. It is also important in gaining program acceptance by the community, and in attracting and retaining competent staff.

This chapter will cover some basic issues in developing and administering a treatment program for sexually aggressive offenders. Seven primary areas will be addressed: physical setting, clientele, program staff, use of resources, staff training, treatment issues and program planning, and special considerations for the adolescent offender.

PHYSICAL SETTING

Generally, one will find the sexual offender being treated in one of three settings: community-based programs, mental health hospitals, and prisons. For purposes of this chapter, two main settings will be discussed: the prison setting and the state hospital or forensic facility, both of which are secure settings. Differences in terms of program development are few, but worthy of note.

In a forensic facility or state hospital, one may find the offender who suffers from another problem that might have been a primary causation of the sexual offense such as psychosis, retardation, organicity, and the like; in prison, the offender may have a lengthy history of criminal offenses of which the sex offense may be just one part of an antisocial, criminal history. In both settings, however, one will also find the sexual offender whose sexual offense is the primary area of conflict and a departure from an otherwise law-abiding life. In setting up a sexual aggressive treatment program, the nature of the offense and the offender's attitude may play an important role in determining his disposition. The offender who acknowledges his crime and is seeking help may be better suited for a program housed in a mental health institution, while the offender who denies or minimizes his crime may be more appropriately placed in the prison setting. Because of funding and limited resources, however, individual states may not have the option of developing programs in several locations. Whatever the setting, differences will exist in terms of the primary mission.

In a forensic state hospital, the program and staff may be required to observe specific patient rights as set forth by the institution and/or its governing agency. Such concerns for these mental health patients might include special housing conditions, patient abuse issues, freedom of movement, and the like. Security standards which are in existence may be considered secondary to the primary mission of treatment and therapy where documented patient care must be constantly maintained. If the hospital has a medical records department, certain standardized forms may need to be filed and institutional procedures observed (i.e., clinical summaries written every six months; treatment guidelines followed according to standards set down by the Joint Commission on the Administration of Hospitals; progress notes written daily; etc.). On the other hand, if the program is housed in a prison setting, standard policy and procedure protocol will have to be adhered to unless the program is autonomous in nature. Since the primary mission of most prisons is security and custody, there may be more restrictive security measures which have to be followed, and therapeutic activities may have to be scheduled around required work detail.

In either setting, security must be taken into consideration. The individual with a history of repetitive violent crimes will need to be housed, at the very least, in a minimum security setting and preferably in a medium to maximum security setting. Yet, what a mental health facility might consider to be a maximum security setting, a prison or correctional institution may view as minimum security. In either instance, it is recommended that at least minimum security be considered for any involuntary or inpatient treatment setting. In general, most programs in existence today are located on a locked ward of a hospital with hospital security or in a correctional facility with correctional officers performing routine security procedures. Very few sexual offenders can be treated in a community setting initially. Less than 10% of sexual offenders fall into the low-risk criteria for first time offenses by taking responsibility for their crime, exhibiting a high level of motivation for treatment and an adequate support group, etc., and can therefore be considered for outpatient treatment.

CLIENTELE

Whether a program is located in a forensic facility, a mental health hospital, or a correctional facility, chances are that the population of a particular institution will consist of the full spectrum of offenders or mental health clients. Thus, insofar as it is possible, it seems to be an advantage to separate the sexual offender from the general institutional population. In prison, for example, there are several things which work against the individual identifying himself as a sexual offender, and thus reinforce his minimization and denial of the problem or his avoidance of therapy. In the mental health hospital, the sexual offender may take advantage of or victimize other patients. Mixing other patients or offenders not involved in the sexual offender program may have several effects: (1) it has the potential for infiltration of others who may consequently be disruptive to treatment procedures, may introduce contraband to the program, or may destroy property; (2) the potential for breach of confidentiality is greatly increased; and (3) the potential for a self-help atmosphere among offenders in the program during free or leisure time is greatly reduced. The separation has several advantages and no apparent disadvantages. This may best be accomplished through housing the program and offenders on a separate wing or ward.

Even though sexual offenders may be housed in a secluded ward, diversified feelings amongst the offenders towards treatment are present. Integrating sexual offenders with varying levels of motivation, therefore, is another area of concern when starting a program as well as maintaining one. Some offenders initially show a voluntary attitude towards treatment by taking responsibility for their behavior and recognizing the need to help themselves. Others tend to minimize the crime and the severity of the act, rationalize about their behavior, or simply deny having had any part in what occurred and claim to be totally innocent. The question then is, Does one treat these groups separately or mix them? If the program is a new one, it is best to avoid putting all deniers or minimizers into the same group sessions. This just tends to reinforce minimization or denial of their offense. Generally, if the group consists of offenders who acknowledge their crime and are self-motivators, the gradual introduction of offenders who deny or qualify their offense tends to help these less motivated offenders become comfortable in talking about their offenses and eventually taking responsibility for their actions. The motivated offenders, through a combination of peer pressure and the slow building of trust in the denier, can identify and help draw out feelings the new offender is experiencing: "I was where you are, I was denying it too, but I've learned . . . ." Therefore, if one is just starting up a new program it may be advantageous to initially hand select those offenders who are motivated and willing to talk about their problems in creating therapy groups. This will give the program a solid foundation upon which to build before introducing the more difficult clientele.

Housing a homogeneous population on a separate wing or ward facilitates peer interaction, develops a cohesive program, and enhances one's ability to effectively supervise the clinical aspects as well as the overall management of the program. The offenders and staff have more time and opportunity to maintain contact with each other, and therapy sessions can develop in a more spontaneous fashion. Homogeneous housing also provides for continuous peer interaction and peer pressure—two important elements in treating sexual offenders. This is especially true when the offenders are interacting in group therapy sessions on a daily basis.

The number of sexual offenders in a particular program is a relative issue. Whether one has enough offenders to fill a group or to fill an entire institution is secondary to the fact that offering some type of treatment, regardless of numbers, is better than offering none at all. Naturally, large numbers of offenders may place limits on the type or amount of treatment offered, depending upon the number of staff working with the program and the available resources. Each program will differ in the number of offenders involved, number of staff, and so forth. Thus, it is advisable to assess one's resources and develop the program accordingly, working the best way possible with available resources. Many have become discouraged because they have developed a program and philosophy first, and found that what they hoped for and what they realistically had to work with were quite different.

Another concern is the length of time an offender should be in treatment. Simply put, there is no specific length of time that it takes to treat an offender. Whether the program is housed in a state hospital or a prison should not make a difference, although one may be faced with time constraints if the program is housed in a state hospital, due to limited bed space and higher costs of operation. Sexual aggression is not something that has a 100% cure. Like the alcoholic, the offender will be faced with this problem the rest of his life and, through treatment, will hopefully learn to cope with stress and develop the necessary internal controls to prevent himself from acting out on impulse or under stressful conditions. Thus treatment is an ongoing process through which the offender will continuously work to improve himself the rest of his life. Any type of intervention, be it for only several months or a year, is better than no treatment at all.

If the program is housed in prison, however, the length of sentence will vary from one offender to the next. Thus one may only be in the program for 1 or 2 years, and another may be in the program for 25 years. The point to be made is that treatment is not something the offender does for two years or five years, but rather a problem he will work on for the rest of his life. The question often arises as to when one should engage the offender in treatment. Should it be during the first part of his sentence, during the last part, or during his entire incarceration? Once again, it is advisable to assimilate the offender into treatment from the day he arrives for the duration of the time he is incarcerated. If one is forced to make a determination as to when the offender should be treated because there are time constraints, then the most desirable alternative is to administer treatment prior to his release into the community. Another option may be to put the offender in the program initially to enable him to learn basic skills and acquire basic insights so that he will be able to work with himself in some fashion while he is incarcerated. Treatment can then be completed during the last part of his sentence. For the offender who may spend the rest of his life in prison, the issue may be one of deciding at what the treatment is aimed: improvement or release.

Adequate physical space is also important. Overcrowding in such a setting may be a catalyst for increased tension and frustration for both the offenders in the program and the staff working with it. While peer interaction is essential to successful treatment programming, the offender may also occasionally require time free from therapy, staff, and peers. Ideally there should be adequate space to conduct program meetings, group therapy sessions, and the like. Personal living quarters for offenders are not a major concern—private or semiprivate rooms have no advantage over ward or dormitory housing. Once again, the particular setting in which the program is housed will determine what resources are available.

Therapy sessions should be held in a place that offers the least amount of disruption and maximum confidentiality from other patients or offenders not directly involved in the treatment program. The length of time the offender is in treatment may determine whether therapy sessions are held weekly or daily, as will the number of staff working with the program. The bottom line is that limited treatment or infrequent sessions are still better than nothing at all.

RESOURCES

Resources of various types are important to the operation of any inpatient program, as staff will generally have ample work to keep themselves busy outside of the hours spent in contact with the offenders in treatment. Having resources available to assist in working with the offenders can greatly enhance any program. Volunteers from the community can be used to develop and maintain recreational programs and occupational therapies, or to assist in teaching arts, crafts, and hobbies. A local member from an Alcoholics Anonymous program or a drug rehabilitation program may be willing to donate time to work in this specialized area. If a university or community college is in the area, volunteers may be recruited to teach various courses that may benefit the offenders and their treatment, such as marriage and family, communication skills, life skills, parent effectiveness training, and so forth. In addition, such resources serve as a direct source for hiring personnel and graduate students who need practicum or internship sites and can be incorporated into the program to assist staff in treatment. Also, universities constitute a readily available source for outside consultation and program evaluation.

Community resources, such as the ones mentioned above, can help reduce the overall costs of operating a program and, with proper supervision, can greatly enhance the quality of the program. Such community interaction also serves the field of public relations and solicits support for the program.

STAFFING A PROGRAM

Outside of the offenders in the program, the locus of success of the program lies in the degree of staff cohesion. The team approach is the preferred method in any setting as it affords the opportunity to review cases, participate in clinical staffings, and become involved in treatment planning, etc. Since treating the sexual offender often requires a lengthy period of time, proper staff training, staff morale, and program continuity are three important ingredients in program effectiveness. The staff/offender ratio will determine the intensity and frequency, as well as the amount, of adjunctive services the program can afford the offenders. Unfortunately, budget guidelines will determine the number of paid staff a given program can employ. In terms of professional staff, a simple formula is the higher the ratio, the better. Don't let a low ratio discourage the development or continuance of a program, however, since many programs in existence treat over 100 offenders with just a handful of staff. The largest concern is that if the work load is too great, the negative effects will be visible in the amount and quality of services delivered, and burnout will be more prevalent. Increase in staff turnover will directly affect program continuity, treatment, and the overall program philosophy.

Many programs in existence today believe in attempting to balance the number of male and female employees. Sexual offenders generally do not interact well with either men or women for various reasons. In many cases they do not relate well with peers regardless of age or sex, as they are nontrusting of people in general, have poor social and communication skills, and are generally loners. Thus, having male and female staff in itself helps the offenders develop proper social skills and learn to interact in a mature, responsible fashion with people in general.

Most programs will require around-the-clock staffing patterns for security as well as general maintenance of the program. Often, paraprofessionals can best be utilized in this capacity. If the shift workers are security personnel, they should receive training in communication skills as well as human relations/services. Often-times, shift workers, especially those who work evening, late night, and weekend shifts, will have to deal with program problems or crises that occur when the professional staff are not present (i.e., offenders that become depressed, have suicidal thoughts, or display inappropriate behavior). Paraprofessional staff or properly trained security officers should not have any major problems handling such situations when they arise and can be an asset to this type of program. Common duties and responsibilities which such personnel may perform would be assisting in group sessions, charting observation and progress notes, giving general input to clinical staffings, and co-leading other adjunctive therapies such as social skills training, stress management, etc.

If budget restraints are such that the program cannot hire the number of staff it needs or desires, then as mentioned earlier, the use of volunteers and graduate students can help supplement staff needs and reduce work loads. If the program has OPS (other personal services) funds or a similar budget item, such funds might be used to offer paid internships or practicum experiences for graduate students.

Finally, in respect to staff, it is important to incorporate periodic in-service training for all staff involved in the treatment program. In-service training is an opportunity for staff to be updated on the latest research in the area of sexual aggression, to acquire specific clinical training, and to discuss and develop ideas for program development and research. These sessions are extremely important, especially if the program does not have a budget for staff travel and training from outside sources. In-service training tends to keep staff involved in the program, and enhances staff morale and effectiveness, while reducing staff burnout and turnover. These sessions can also be used to generate staff discussion about program and treatment issues, to air concerns, and to reach potential solutions to problems. In addition, this is an opportune time to train staff in victimology, an important area requiring the professional's attention when working with sexual aggression.

Since the study and treatment of sexual aggression constitute a relatively new area, one may find that staff members often become frustrated, discouraged, and concerned about their effectiveness in working with the offender. In-service training is one avenue to help overcome the feelings of inadequacy that often lead to staff burnout. Therefore, the addition of research is beneficial to several aspects of program operation. First and most important is the acquisition of data to enhance the knowledge regarding the offender. Naturally, this in turn will make the treatment program more effective. Staff will benefit from this activity whether they are directly involved or just observers. Staff involvement in research can not only act as a built-in training and learning experience, but also aid in developing staff cohesion and often reduce potential staff burnout. Staff can derive many personal rewards from the discovery of new data or the verification of existing data, from publishing data collected through research, and from speaking to concerned groups about treatment, research findings, and the implications of acquired data as a public service.

EVALUATION AND TREATMENT

In any type of program, be it inpatient or outpatient, there are two major tasks: evaluation and treatment of the offender. Thus, there are several issues to consider when developing a treatment plan and program philosophy for sexual offenders. Should the tasks of evaluation, treatment, and determination of release be separated or combined as program responsibilities? In some states, initial assessment is ordered by the courts, prior to conviction and sentencing, to determine if the offender is suffering from a psychosexual disorder or is a sexually dangerous person. The offender may be evaluated by an outside professional or agency, or transferred to the treatment program for evaluation before sentencing occurs. In other states, the person is convicted and sentenced by the courts, and it is the job of the program to evaluate his amenability to treatment.

There are pros and cons in either case. If the courts take care of the initial assessment, then the program's task is clear in that a more extensive evaluation will occur during the offender's treatment. If the program is required to perform the initial assessment, then a conflict of interest may arise. The program will ask this offender to be open and honest and to reveal everything about himself for the purposes of evaluation. The offender who may be looking to "beat the charge" is asked to trust the very same people who may end up influencing the courts to commit him to treatment for an indefinite amount of time. Then, when the offender returns to the program, he will be asked to trust that program again in terms of his being treated. Certainly this is one method of selecting clients who will work best in the program and will have the motivation to help themselves, although the chances of receiving clients who are sexual psychopaths (or whatever legal/clinical label is applied), but totally unmotivated, are also present.

On the other hand, if the offender is committed to the program with or without prior assessment, the potential conflict of interest is no longer an issue. However, the program is bound to receive offenders who continue to deny the offense, are not motivated for treatment, and may be a constant source of disruption. One possible solution is to make treatment voluntary, but two problems then arise. First, one will find a certain percentage of offenders who want nothing to do with any type of treatment. Many programs find that initially 65–75% of the offenders deny the crime and will not talk about it. With adequate time and exposure to other offenders working well in the program, many offenders will slowly begin to drop their defenses, become more open in discussing their offense, and begin to participate in treatment.

The other problem involves what to do with those offenders who continue to deny their crime and will not participate in treatment. The options here are limited. Either the offender is continued in treatment in the hope that he will eventually get involved, or he is placed in the prison setting to serve his sentence. If the treatment program is in prison, then another option is available. One may decide to have a major program in one facility and develop small, satellite programs in other institutions. These satellite programs can offer varying levels of treatment with a range of intensities. Group sessions, adjunctive courses, or other therapeutic activities can be held as frequently or infrequently as the program chooses. The point in this type of arrangement is that at least some form of treatment or therapy does occur, even for uncooperative offenders. This type of approach is especially useful if state law mandates treatment for the sexual offender.

Another point worth mentioning is the eventual discharge of the offender from prison or a state hospital back into the community. Once again, this may be the responsibility of the program, the courts, or the probation and parole department. If the program and its recommendations are directly responsible for the disposition of the offender, one may expect the offender to be more manipulative, persuasive, and into "playing the therapy game" to convince the program and staff that he is "cured" or "rehabilitated." The task becomes more difficult if the program was the agent that performed the initial assessment to have the offender committed to treatment and now must decide whether or not he is ready for the streets. Again, the program and staff may be faced with a conflict of interest or with a task that is undesirable. This is not to say that the program should not play a role in the offender's release. Determining what type of follow-up services the offender will need and various parole or probation guidelines can best be developed by the offender and the program that has treated him. Simply stated, both the committing and the release agencies should be separate and distinct from the treatment program if at all possible. If one must be involved in these areas in addition to treating the offender, then one must be open to the possibility that this may have an effect on the treatment of the offender.

In treating the offender, especially if the program is new or to be developed, several areas need to be addressed. First and foremost is to take into consideration that this particular population is extremely manipulative and often very resistant to treatment during the initial stages. Therefore, it is important to recognize program continuity as a key ingredient to success. If program design and philosophy are continuously changing, and staff are inconsistent in treatment planning, the offenders may use this to their benefit by blaming their lack of progress on the changes that are occurring. Once your program is developed and on paper, stick with it. Introduce changes slowly after they have been well planned and thought out.

Once the offender has entered the program, the first step is evaluation. As mentioned earlier, approximately 25–30% of the offenders will initially appear amenable to treatment. Evaluation should include what modalities of treatment these individuals may respond to. Treatment and therapy are not synonymous. Group and individual counseling are the two modalities of therapy most commonly used in treating sexual offenders. These therapeutic approaches are supplemented by other adjunctive therapies and course work. Yet some programs using only these approaches report difficulty or total lack of success in treating the rapist who has murdered his victim(s), pedophiles with chronic histories of child molestation, and those offenders who appear to be chronic, habitual criminals or who continuously deny their offenses. If one form of treatment does not work with certain offenders, consider other treatment modalities such as behavioral therapies, drug therapies, and so forth. In some programs, treatment consists of course work such as sex education, assertiveness training, social skills training, and limited amounts of group or individual counseling.

During the evaluation phase, a detailed assessment of the offender's sexual behavior should be performed using all possible resources such as police reports, victim(s) statements, pre-sentence investigation reports, FBI rap sheets, and the like. Naturally, a complete social and psychosexual history needs to be completed. Since many sexual offenders will not offer the "complete story" upon initial intake interviews, it is recommended that these histories be retaken after the offender has begun to participate in treatment and has dropped his defenses to some degree. In addition, such information offered by the offender should be verified if at all possible by contact with family members, friends, employers, and school records.

Within the evaluation phase, a complete medical workup should also be performed including substance addiction, physical traumas, and somatic complaints.

Most sexual offenders will require a period of time to adjust to treatment, whether it be inpatient or outpatient, for few typical sex offenders are self-referred mental health treatment patients. Initially, the clinical staff should expect to see some denial and rationalization on the part of the offender concerning the crime he has committed. It is, therefore, suggested that a minimum of six months be allotted for offenders to become seriously involved in treatment, if the program has the option to treat him or dispose of him somewhere else in the system.

While in the evaluation phase, the offender's progress should be noted in several areas. One key area is his willingness and ability to disclose meaningful and spontaneous information about himself, which relates directly to his motivation and amenability to treatment. As previously mentioned, the clinician can expect the offender to use several defenses when he first enters treatment. However, this behavior should begin to dissipate as the offender becomes more comfortable with his peers, staff, and the program, while observing other offenders doing what is expected of him. In addition, the offender should be open to feedback about himself, his problems, and treatment goals from both the staff and his peers. Self-disclosure and openness to critical feedback are two of the most difficult tasks the offender faces because they reaffirm many of the negative thoughts which he has had about himself most of his life and has been afraid to face.

Sexual offenders are generally able to demonstrate reasonable behavioral control. While major behavioral problems, in terms of displaying highly aggressive and inappropriate behavior, are generally absent, staff should be aware of the offender's disposition in controlling outbursts of anger and his willingness to comply with program rules and regulations. One needs to be careful, however, about how one interprets behavior. If the offender's behavior is good, does this mean that he is in control of his behavior, or does it mean that his behavior is being controlled by institutional policy and program rules?

Satisfactory behavior on the part of the offender does not necessarily mean that he is growing and maturing. In an institutional setting, there is no dependable measure of growth and maturity. Responsible, mature behavior may mean nothing more than that the offender has settled down to institutional living and has become accustomed to his daily routine. In this environment, he is not burdened with typical adult responsibilities. His retiring at eleven in the evening does not necessarily mean that, given the freedom to do so, he would not be down at the local tavern.

If the offender demonstrates the desire and motivation to be treated, then he should be able to assist in the development of his problem list and treatment goals. This basic insight into his problems and needs is a good indicator that his prognosis for completing the treatment program is favorable. Many offenders are resistant to realizing these insights initially because of the emotional pain that accompanies them.

Psychological testing is an important part of any evaluation, although some offenders will show up relatively normal on some psychometrics. A standard battery of tests should include measures for personality, intelligence, presence of stress, sexual knowledge, values, and social well-being. For more difficult cases, projective testing may be necessary in order to perform a more comprehensive assessment. Tests incorporated into evaluation should also be routinely administered during the course of treatment and prior to discharge. It is not uncommon to see a sexual offender "fake sick" upon initial testing and then "fake well" prior to release.

A final area of consideration during evaluation is the offender's comprehension of the effect his crime had upon the victim's life. Initially, the offender will express superficial remorse and empathy for the victim. Some programs periodically show the offenders films about victims of sexual assault and their reactions to being assaulted, or they have actual victims come to the program and talk to the offenders about what happened to them and their lives after the assault took place. This is an excellent method of empathy training for the offender. If the offender continues to deny responsibility for his crime and his actions while minimizing the harm he has caused the victim, he should continue to be considered highly dangerous.

CLINICAL STAFFINGS

Sexual offenders, like any other mental health patients, should be clinically staffed by the treatment team on a regular basis to determine their responsiveness to treatment. The first such staffing should occur either at midpoint or upon completion of the evaluation phase. This initial staffing will determine whether the offender (1) has made satisfactory progress during the evaluation phase, and demonstrates the necessary motivation and ability to be formally admitted into treatment; (2) needs to continue in the evaluation phase to better determine his motivation and amenability to treatment; or (3) does not have the necessary motivation or ability to be treated, is not amenable, and should therefore be discharged from the program and a new disposition of his case considered.

Routine staffings should be conducted a minimum of once each year and preferably once every six months from the day of admission until the offender has completed the program. These clinical staffings should be attended by the program director, the professional staff members who compose the treatment team, and any other individuals who play a role in the offender's therapy (i.e., the person who supervises the offender's work assignment; teachers, if he is working on his education; recreation therapists; and the like). It is also helpful to have one or two offenders from his therapy group offer their input as peers. Often the observations of other offenders in treatment are extremely relevant to a particular offender's treatment planning. Staffings should be scheduled to allow sufficient time to cover all aspects of the offender's treatment. The same criteria used during the evaluation phase should be discussed in each clinical staffing, that is, the offender's motivation, peer interaction, development of his problems list, his personal insight into his problems, and his overall progress in the treatment program. The following list of criteria is offered to develop a basic checklist for progress:

1. Responsibility	8. Social maturity
2. Behavioral control	9. Empathy
3. Accepts feedback	10. Self-esteem/concept
4. Self-disclosure	11. Impulse control
5. Stress management	12. Self-expression
6. Use of leisure time	13. Self-awareness
7. Insight into offense	14. Participation in program

It may be helpful to develop standardized forms and checklists for the program in order to document what progress the offender has made up to the time of his staffing, to insure that key areas have been addressed, and to note proceedings in the staffing and what recommendations were made for further treatment. Depending upon departmental regulations or program requirements, it is suggested that if clinical summaries are required to be written about the offenders, they coincide with clinical staffings.

The nature and format of staffings should be ones that the program staff agree to and are comfortable with. For instance, a typical staffing may last for 90 minutes during which time the offender's progress in treatment is discussed among the staff themselves. After case presentation, the offender may be brought into the staffing for questioning about key issues arising from the staff discussion. The staffing may then wind up with another discussion, after the offender leaves, to determine what progress he has made and what specific treatment issues need to be addressed for his individual case. At the end of that discussion, the offender may be brought back into the staffing and given feedback about his progress to date and what he needs to focus on during the next phase of his treatment.

TREATMENT MODALITIES

The types and administration of treatment to be used in the program are decisions best made by the program director and the professional staff based upon available resources, including time. Many programs use group therapy as a primary mode of treatment as well as individual sessions and other adjunctive therapies. In working with sexual offenders, there are some general assumptions which are helpful in programming.

First, one can assume that the offender's commission of a sexual crime only provided him with a temporary source of relief from the stress in his life and that if pleasure was an outcome of committing such a crime, it was short-lived. Most sexual offenders do not enjoy the crimes they commit. Some understand that the harm which comes to the victim may affect her or him for life. The compulsion to commit such a crime, however, is so strong that it overrides any other concerns at the time of the offense. Thus, treatment based upon stress management may need to be a part of individual or group sessions, or to be conducted as a separate adjunctive therapy.

Anything of importance to the offender should be brought out and dealt with in group therapy sessions. Sexual offenders are "pros" at manipulating others. They offer a wide variety of excuses for not talking about problems in group while simultaneously seeking individual help for the same problems. Withholding information is a common pattern among most sexual offenders and a part of their pathology. Generally, from a very early age most were abused, and learned to keep their thoughts and feelings to themselves. Others have experienced repeated rejection. Consequently, sexual offenders are poor communicators and loners who end up holding back their feelings, socially withdrawing, and maintaining poor social and intimate relations. Withdrawal and superficial relations are defenses for them—to protect them from further emotional pain or rejection by others. Withholding information in therapy often becomes a device by which the offender tries to manipulate others so as to receive the attention he desires or to avoid dealing with painful emotional issues or problems.

The sexual offender can be an important part of the treatment team and has significant influence on his peers. Sex offender treatment and therapy groups have the same influence and effect on individual group members as the Alcoholics Anonymous meeting does on a new member. The offenders have had similar abuse, problems, and experiences in their lives, and can offer support to other offenders in the group as well as confront those offenders who lie or are resistant to becoming involved in the treatment process. Sharing similar concerns and problems serves as an "icebreaker" for newer members, and helps develop trust between all members. No one knows a sex offender better than another sex offender! Often program members are much more aware of an individual offender's behavior and attitudes than are staff members.

In order to change behavior, the individual must have a clear understanding of what behavioral changes he needs to make. Therefore, it is important to have the offender involved in his treatment planning and in the development of his problems list. To aid the offender, it may be helpful to pose the following seven basic questions about behavior to him.

1. What is the behavior?
2. What is inappropriate about the behavior?
3. What needs do you have that this behavior supplies?
4. How is this behavior harmful?

5. How have you modified this behavior?
6. What will you do to control this behavior in the future?
7. What are the early warning signals that the behavior is going to occur?

As the offender comes to understand himself and his behavior, he should come to the realization that behavior is not separate from attitude. If he is going to change his behaviors, he will need to change the attitudes that influence his behaviors too.

Finally, when working with this type of offender in a therapeutic community setting, it is important to teach the offender a sense of responsibility and to realize that one learns to be responsible by being given responsibility. The offender should be held accountable for his behavior and actions. In the treatment setting, offenders are initially willing to let the staff make all their decisions, while placing responsibility for their actions on others, on an uncontrollable series of events, on the environment, or on other circumstances "beyond their control." Placing the offender in a position of responsibility, be it a simple task such as keeping his room clean or a major one such as participating in his treatment planning, enables him to begin to realize that he has control over his life and destiny.

Since many sexual offenders have similar problems and deficiencies, some treatment time might best be utilized in the development of adjunctive therapies or course work which addresses key treatment issues. While any of the issues covered in specialized adjuncts are also topics that come up frequently in group therapy sessions, the following areas appear to be common among most sexual offenders and may be better addressed in groups or course work outside of the main group therapy sessions.

Research and clinical histories of hundreds of offenders reveal that a large number of offenders have themselves been sexually abused or experienced a sexual trauma during their childhood. My experience reveals that as many as 70% or more of sexual offenders report such experiences. This type of life trauma is believed to be a major factor in the development of a psychosexual disorder among sexually aggressive offenders. Therefore, one such specialized treatment group a program might want to institute would be a victimization group in which offenders can discuss their own sexual abuse. Their willingness and ability to deal with and resolve this conflict in their lives are significant in terms of the progress they make while in treatment.

Many sexual offenders have very little knowledge concerning the sexual functioning of both adult males and adult females. In addition, they may have a poor body image, feel inadequate sexually around women, or fear intimate contact. These offenders will benefit from a sex education or human sexuality course, where they will learn about male and female anatomy, human sexual functioning, birth control, VD, and other related topics. While a part of their lack of sex education may surface in group therapy sessions, one might choose to administer a sex knowledge inventory to determine which offenders in the program need a specialized course or training in this area.

Most sexual offenders have extremely poor social skills, and some are totally unable to negotiate peer relations with either sex, but especially with women. They generally fear and mistrust women as well as often feeling inferior to them. In some instances they are overtly hostile to women as they have felt abused or controlled by women for a good portion of their lives. To help offenders overcome these difficulties and learn to negotiate relationships, social skills training is often required. In social skills training, the program may choose to utilize female volunteers in mock social settings as part of the course work. The use of videotaping in practicing such skills gives the offender and the staff a clear understanding of what areas the offender is lacking in, and enables both to see progress as it occurs during the course of training. Such skills are maintained when the program has made a practice of employing female staff so that the offenders have continuous access to talking with women.

Many sexual offenders have histories of alcohol and substance abuse, and have turned to drug abuse when they experienced stress in their lives. Many report the use of drugs and/or alcohol during the commission of their crimes. Those offenders with a history of substance abuse can be enrolled in a substance abuse course or an AA program where they can learn about substance use and abuse, the effect it has on the human body, and how various drugs interact with each other. In addition, they can learn how to cope with stress without the use of, or dependence upon, such substances.

Since stress was a factor in the lives of most offenders and most of their crimes occurred during stressful periods, a course in stress management should be available or combined with the substance abuse course. In such courses, offenders learn appropriate coping methods and will have a chance to test what they have learned during the course of treatment. It is helpful to offer this type of training during the early part of treatment as staff will have ample time to observe how the offender reacts to stressful situations while he is in treatment.

Sexual offenders tend to be either aggressive or passive-aggressive individuals. They are generally unable to express the way they feel towards others and tend to either suppress those feelings or release them in an inappropriate fashion. Assertiveness training will afford the offender the opportunity to learn the skills and knowledge he requires to appropriately and effectively express his needs and rights.

The ability to communicate is an extremely important treatment issue for all sexual offenders, especially if they are being treated in a program based around communicating to others. Most offenders do not possess adequate communication skills and have had a problem communicating with others for most of their lives. Special courses in communication skills are an asset to any program for two basic reasons: (1) they help the offender to work through a problem he has had most of his life, and (2) they help the offender in terms of his participation in group therapy and other program activities.

If the treatment program is going to incorporate group therapy sessions as a major part of treatment and utilize other group sessions such as the adjuncts mentioned above, it is helpful to offer a basic course in group skills to all offenders. This type of course teaches the offenders in the program how to listen to others and respond to their feelings in an appropriate manner; how to self-disclose, confront, and trust; and the importance of confidentiality in the therapeutic setting.

Almost any activity the offender engages in during the course of his treatment can be considered therapeutic or can be designed in such a fashion that he will receive therapeutic benefit from participation in it. In some settings, the offender will be required to work at some job during his incarceration, while in others, working in a job will be optional or on a voluntary basis. In all settings, the offender will have the opportunity to participate in recreational programs. Both of these activities can be of therapeutic value to the offender while offering the staff additional data on his progress in the treatment program.

Whether the offender is required to work or volunteers to do so, almost any work assignment can be paired with therapeutic need. For example, if the offender has tended to be shy and withdrawn for most of his life and has held jobs where he worked by himself or had little contact with other workers, one might consider job placement in a position that brings him into contact with others, such as serving in a cafeteria or working in a canteen. Isolated jobs should be reserved for those offenders who do not have difficulty socializing. If job placement occurs, the supervisor should be willing to fill out periodic reports to the program describing the offender's work, attitude, ability to work with others, and so forth. In addition, it is helpful if the supervisor is willing either to come to clinical staffings to give input on the offender's job performance or to write periodic progress notes in the offender's chart or records. This type of input is important because it is not unusual to notice differences in the offender's behavior in groups and around the living quarters versus his behavior on the job. Often, many dynamics involved in the commission of his crime will come forth in various activities while he is in treatment. If such dynamics begin to surface, they may occur outside of the immediate program area with persons who are not familiar with his pathology.

Recreation is another area that is excellent for observing the offender and his behavior. Often pent-up aggression comes out on the playing field, especially against other offenders that a particular offender does not get along with. Alternatively, if the offender is in the position of referee or team captain, he may use such a position of authority to dominate and control others. Sometimes this type of aggression comes out against staff. One offender in our program deliberately selected a new female employee to play racquetball with. She had never played the game before and he offered to teach her. Once out on the court, he became highly aggressive and played as if he were competing for a medal. When she made mistakes, he put her down, and before long she ran off the court almost in tears. When he was confronted about the episode, he denied that his actions were deliberate and could see no similarity between his aggressive behavior on the court and his crime (rape).

Naturally, there are therapeutic benefits in recreation. It has the potential to teach the offender leadership qualities, healthy competitiveness, sportsmanship, and how to interact with others. For the younger offender, it is a means of burning up excess energy and experiencing what little time he has left in adolescence in a normal fashion. Leisure time is an opportune time to see the offender as he really is. Programming should be such that offenders have free time to interact or do whatever they choose. The activities they engage in may be of clinical importance and should be noted in their records or charts. Social histories on sexual offenders often reveal that they did not use leisure time productively. Few engaged in sports, hobbies, or other productive activities. Most report using this time to drink, use drugs, or watch television. As the offender begins to progress in the program, one should take note of the changes, if any, in his activity during leisure time. Does he use this time to talk with staff persons or interact with his peers in a productive fashion? Has he taken up any hobbies or is he attending classes? When he interacts with peers, whom does he choose to interact with—those making progress in the program or those who are ready to be discharged as untreatable? How much television does he watch and what type of shows? What type of material, if any, does he read?

While some of these activities appear to be insignificant, they can be real indicators of where the offender is headed. For example, one offender in our program spent every Saturday morning glued to the TV set. A good amount of his viewing material was cartoons and children's shows. Since this fellow was a child molester with a lengthy record, it was obvious after we detected the regularity of his viewing that he was still very much attracted to children who were just at the age of puberty. While visiting the living quarters of another offender, I noticed that he had what appeared to be pictures of young girls up on his wall. On further examination, I discovered that the pictures obviously came out of a clothing catalogue for children and the print read "age 7–10." I inquired about this particular offender and found out that he was a child molester and that his victims were around 8 years old.

THE ADOLESCENT OFFENDER

Depending upon the program, the governing agency, and state laws governing juvenile offenders, the adolescent sexual offender may be part of a program. If one is going to treat adolescent sexual offenders, there are several issues worth taking into consideration. While it may be advantageous to have a separate program for adolescent offenders, it is often a luxury that government and institutions feel they cannot afford with existing budgets.

Probably the most important issue is assessment of the adolescent offender. All too often, the adolescent is misdiagnosed as adolescent adjustment reaction, or his behavior is viewed as normal, adolescent sexual experimentation. The chances are that if he has been referred to your program for evaluation or has been committed, this was not the first time he exhibited inappropriate sexual behavior. As with the adult offender, one should perform a thorough evaluation, taking note of behaviors observed by his family and teachers, and reviewing reports and victim statements. It is important to determine if his behavior was normative behavior common among his age group, as well as the relationship between the offender and the victim (e.g., was the victim much younger or much older than the offender?).

The next concern is housing. Should the adolescent be housed with older offenders or separately with peers? If the adolescent is to be housed with older offenders, there are several points worth noting. The older offender may serve as a role model for the adolescent if he is progressing in treatment and often is helpful in stabilizing some of the acting out behavior seen among adolescents. The older offender may also be able to offer the adolescent some of the attention he will seek and assist him in the treatment process. On the other hand, there are some negative points in housing the two age groups together. The older offender may not be a good role model for the adolescent and may encourage the adolescent's inappropriate behavior. If the adolescent has a difficult time establishing friendships with his own peers, then he may have a more difficult time with adults. The adolescent will tend to spend more time and energy proving his manhood around adults than he will around his own peers. Naturally, he will be at a greater risk of being sexually exploited among adults than among his own peers, or he may become involved sexually with the older offender as a means of gaining acceptance and attention. In addition, the adolescent may feel more uncomfortable discussing adolescent issues around the older offender than he would around his own peers. Because of their background and upbringing, most adolescent offenders have tended to skip adolescence in an attempt to gain acceptance in the adult world. Many are streetwise and resistant to authority. Separate housing allows them the opportunity to experience adolescence with their peers. If they are going to learn to negotiate friendships and relationships, they have to begin with persons their own age. The problems and frustrations they experience and the needs they have are often quite different from those of the adult. Adolescents need to be reassured that it is OK to be an adolescent and that the difficulties they experience are not unique to them.

Many adolescents coming into such programs show evidence of learning disabilities and may require some form of special education. In addition, they tend to have more problems than the older offenders in controlling their behavior. Thus, it is important to allow more time for the adolescent to adjust and progress through the treatment program. It is not unusual to find that it takes several months before the adolescent's behavior stabilizes, allowing him to take treatment seriously. This usually begins to occur once the adolescent starts trusting the therapist, other offenders, and the program.

In regard to treating the adolescent, a few points are worthy of mention. First, is the issue of bonding. As the adolescent comes to trust the program and the therapist, a bonding may take place between the adolescent and his therapist. It is suggested that, when possible, only one therapist work with the adolescent rather than moving him from one staff person to another. This bonding is healthy and will benefit the adolescent, since he will feel there is a person he can trust and count on.

Many adolescents become frustrated if they are required to sit in a therapy group or session two or three hours a day, five days a week. They often do not have the patience or attention span that the adult offender does. Therefore, the therapist in charge may want to use group sessions for various activities other than therapy. For example, getting the group involved in an exercise based upon trust or values can be fun as well as therapeutic. Such exercises help build character as well as assisting the adolescent in developing a closeness with his peers. From time to time, concerns may arise with one member that are centered around being an adolescent and growing up. In these instances, it may be beneficial to stop the group from acting as a therapy group and to pick up with a rap session where all members can participate in sharing their experiences and feelings about the issue at hand. For example, most adolescents are concerned with dating and their own sexuality. Others may express concerns about being, or becoming, homosexual if they have engaged in homosexual activity.

Most, if not all, adolescent offenders will need to be involved in both social skills training and assertiveness training. Adolescents tend to report that they have felt uncomfortable around females and have a difficult time negotiating friendships and relationships. In addition, they have often felt put down or ignored when it came to expressing themselves, and consequently, they tend to be either aggressive or totally passive when faced with expressing their own needs or desires.

Treatment of the adolescent sexual offender is an issue that has attracted much concern and attention in recent years. While statistics tend to vary from one source to the next, the reality is that an increasing number of adolescents are being arrested for sex-related crimes. Resources for treating the adolescent sexual offender are scarce at this time and should not be overlooked if one intends to develop or expand a sexual aggression program.

ADMINISTRATION AND BUREAUCRACY

One final, but major, area of concern in developing a treatment program for sexual offenders and in program planning is working with the state bureaucracy. Most programs operate under a state agency such as corrections or mental health. There are bound to be supporters of such programs as well as those totally opposed to them. Both groups are generally uninformed on the total scope of sexual aggressiveness, and developing programs and maintaining their existence usually involve a continuous battle. Arguments will cover the entire spectrum from security and cost to effectiveness and why the sex offender is singled out for treatment.

Generally, the first concern is where to house such a program: in a correctional facility, in a mental health facility, or in the community. The costs of operation will differ between corrections and mental health agencies. Many mental health hospitals tend to follow the medical model for running such a facility. This may include following various standards such as those set down by the Joint Commission on the Accreditation of Hospitals (JCAH). Such standards often require minimum staffing patterns, tight regulations with respect to medical records and patient charts, confidentiality regulations, quality control reviews, and the like. In addition, the offenders may be considered "patients" and entitled to various patient rights. Such an operation is bound to require more staff to carry out all the related tasks, and the costs of doing so may be two to four times higher than operating a similar program in a correctional facility. Security is another concern in a mental health facility, although the issue may be secondary to treatment. The prison setting may offer more in terms of vocational training, work release, and educational opportunities. In prisons, treatment tends to be secondary to security, and it may initially be a difficult task to get personnel to adjust to issues based on treatment and therapy. In both settings, one may be faced with the task of convincing the administration that separation of the sexual offender from the rest of the population is more advantageous than not.

Relating to the administration in such programs is no different from working with any other program in a similar setting, but some areas are worthy of note. Given the nature of the work, the relative youth of such programs, and the attention paid to sexual assault in the media, the program is bound to be the subject of media scrutiny and various forms of public relations (i.e., visitors to the program, public lectures, etc.). Many administrators are reluctant to participate in such activities and put restrictions on the programs' doing so because they are controversial. Such restrictions may ultimately be more harmful than helpful to maintaining programs as the public and legislators need to be kept informed.

Generally, it is the state agency and/or administration which sets policy and procedure for the operation of the institution in which the program is housed. Plan your program with administration officials and take time to explain, with examples, how certain policies may hinder the success of the program while others may enhance it. Often this can be accomplished by having the program director or a staff member become involved in committees that develop policy and procedure or periodically review such policies. If at all possible, try to develop specific policy and procedure for the sexual aggression program, for this aids staff in their duties and benefits the offender from a therapeutic standpoint.

Staff recruitment and supervision may or may not be a concern, depending upon the individual structure of the institution. Often the typical state job descriptions have minimal requirements and are vague in terms of qualifications and experience required. One very helpful method of obtaining good staff for a program is to send job announcements to other sexual aggression programs, state hospitals, and correctional facilities where there is a greater chance of finding applicants who have had some work experience with sexual offenders. Another method of recruiting staff is to take positions that are vacant and offer paid internships to graduate students, with the understanding that they will commit themselves to the program for a period of time after graduation.

Supervision of staff is no different in this type of program than in any other. Basic areas of supervision such as program management, clinical supervision over offender treatment, and so forth are necessary in any therapeutic or treatment setting. Once again, the team approach is suggested as the best way to operate such a program as it offers staff more well-rounded clinical experience and is an easier method for staff supervision and overall program management.

There is no magic involved in working with a sexual aggression program that makes it any different from other inpatient treatment programs. Yet, because this area is relatively new and somewhat controversial, one must be prepared to face harder battles for longer periods of time. To bring such programs into existence often requires changes in laws and a new way of thinking.

In summary, it is important to plan one's program well in advance of starting and to look into all areas that will affect its operation, treatment, the offenders, and the staff working with the program. Even if the program is already in existence, continuous evaluation of the program and its operation should be incorporated into its overall design. Because the treatment of sexual aggressiveness is relatively new in this country and elsewhere, one needs to remain flexible and open to change. It is necessary for the department or agency in which such a program is run and the administration of the institution in which it is housed to have an understanding of the offender, his pathology, and the most effective treatment methods in order to work with the program and its development in a positive fashion.

REFERENCES

Becker, Judith V. Treatment for sex offenders in Florida. *TSA News* **2**(2):1-2 (1978).
Groth, A.N. *Men Who Rape: The Psychology of the Offender*. New York: Plenum Press, 1979.

10

Program Evaluation: Recidivism Research Involving Sex Offenders

Frank Tracy, Henry Donnelly,
Leonard Morgenbesser, and Donald Macdonald

*This chapter discusses currently available recidivism research involving sex of-
fenders with a special focus on the repeat sex offender. A brief overview of the
methodological issues in this type of research is initially presented for the practitioner's use in formulating an evaluation plan or in critically reviewing research
reports. The major section of this chapter analyzes the research findings in the field
concerning variables related to recidivism among sex offenders. This section includes a summary of a recent study by the authors regarding the characteristics of
repeat sex offenders among those released from the New York State prison system.*

INTRODUCTION

What types of sex offenders are most likely to come into subsequent contact with
the criminal justice system? Variations of this basic question are frequently faced
by treatment staff and criminal justice officials in developing specialized programs
for sex offenders or in evaluating the effectiveness of operational programs.

Among the questions that must be considered in the development of sex offender
treatment programs are, What types of sex offenders are most likely to commit
additional crimes? Can certain variables be identified that serve to distinguish repeat sex offenders?

Treatment staff can expect to be repeatedly asked the questions, Does your
program work? Does it actually reduce recidivism? This chapter is designed to
assist program staff and other concerned individuals in addressing these research
questions.

A. OVERVIEW OF SELECTED METHODOLOGICAL ISSUES IN
RECIDIVISM RESEARCH INVOLVING SEX OFFENDERS

In order to critically review research findings or to design a program evaluation, an
appreciation of certain basic methodological issues is essential. To assist program
staff and other concerned individuals who do not have extensive research back-

grounds to undertake tasks, this section presents a brief checklist that covers certain of the major methodological issues in recidivism research involving sex offenders. This checklist is not envisioned as an exhaustive listing of all relevant methodological considerations in this field. The reader is provided with selected references that can be used to pursue these issues in greater detail. The sole purpose of this checklist is to highlight certain basic methodological issues by a series of brief questions regarding (1) the study population, (2) criteria for recidivism, and (3) the follow-up period.

1. Study Population

a. What is the nature of the population being studied in terms of relevant variables?
b. Is there any utilization of a comparison or control relative to the study population?

The initial task in reviewing any research report (or in preparing a follow-up study) is defining the study population.

Characteristics of the Study Population.   The basic objective of this review is to clearly define the characteristics of the study population, especially those factors that may be related to recidivism. Among the variables that should be reviewed are the point in the criminal justice system from which the sample was selected, the crimes involved, prior criminal record, alcohol abuse, and personality disorders. Research findings on the relation of various factors to recidivism are discussed in the second section of this chapter.

Control or Comparison Group.   The second major concern in this area focuses on the use of a control or comparison group relative to the study population. This issue is particularly important in program evaluations which are designed to assess the possible impact of a program on involved sex offenders.

An excellent overview of this issue and the differences between control and comparison groups is provided by Daniel Glaser in the study of sex offender projects edited by Brecher.[1] Glaser notes that there is a clear risk in utilizing comparison groups as opposed to classical experimental control groups which are selected by randomly assigning cases to treatment and to control groups. Comparison groups, which are selected by other procedures, may differ from the treatment group on variables that might affect the outcome more than the treatment itself.

General Use of Comparison Groups.   Despite the undisputed research advantages of the classical control group approach, comparison groups are generally utilized for a variety of reasons. Program managers are often reluctant to randomly assign individuals to treatment and control groups due to ethical, legal, or operational concerns. The reader is referred to Latzer and Kirby for a discussion of the legal issues involved in random assignment.[2]

The use of comparison groups obviously places the responsibility on the researcher to ensure the comparability of the groups in all possible ways and to conscientiously note any significant areas of difference.

Use of Control Groups.   Because of the limited use of classical control groups in recidivism research involving sex offenders, the reader should consult the study recently released by the Joseph Peters Institute.[3] The purpose of this research was to examine the effects of group therapy on probationed sex offenders. The sex offenders involved were randomly assigned to either the control or the treatment group as they were placed on probation in Philadelphia. This research is one of the very few studies in the field using random assignment procedures to develop a control group.

2. Criteria for Recidivism

    a. What is the criterion used for recidivism—subsequent arrest, reconviction, or recommitment?

    b. Does the criterion focus exclusively on subsequent criminal justice system contacts for sex crimes or does the recidivism rate also include subsequent contacts for other crimes?

Frequently, one reads a newspaper account or press release which states that a sex offender treatment program (or other offender program) has a "recidivism rate" of a certain percent. The reader is left to wonder what is specifically meant by the term "recidivism rate."

Needless to say, recidivism rate is a rather non-descriptive, generic term which may have a variety of meanings depending on the criterion used to define it specifically in the given study. Identifying the criterion used to define this pivotal phrase is often the critical task in determining the comparability of different sets of research findings.

Common Criteria for Defining Recidivism.   Three criteria are generally used to define recidivism: subsequent arrest, conviction, or commitment. A review of the literature in this field does not identify a widely followed policy in the choice of recidivism criteria. A number of studies match the recidivism criteria to the point in the criminal justice system from which the sample was selected. For example, a group of individuals convicted of sex crimes in a given year will be tracked to ascertain subsequent convictions. However, other studies involving incarcerated sex offenders utilize subsequent arrests as the measure of recidivism.

Subsequent Contact for Sex Crimes or Any Crime. The subsequent contacts of sex offenders with the criminal justice system do not necessarily involve sex offenses. Frequently, subsequent contacts of the sex offenders may involve other crimes. The failure to make this fundamental distinction, however, can lead to deceptively high statistics of recidivism rates among sex offenders. This observation is illustrated by numerous studies.[4]

Official Crime versus Actual Offense. In the area of recidivism research, it is also important to distinguish between the official crime and the actual offense. For example, persons who were convicted of sexual abuse may actually have committed rape or sodomy. The difference between the actual and the official crime may be largely attributed to plea bargaining. As such, the reader is advised to distinguish between categories of sex offenders by official crime and categories based on descriptions of the actual offense.

Recidivism Criteria as Accurate Measures of Subsequent Sex Crimes. In closing, the criticism of criminal justice system contacts as appropriate measures of subsequent sex crimes must be considered.

A review of criminal justice system statistics supports this argument. Yet it is generally accepted that a significant percentage of all sex crimes go unreported. A relatively high percentage of reported sex crimes do not result in arrests.[5] As such, it is suggested that criminal justice system contacts be considered as a *conservative* measure of the recidivism of sex offenders.

3. The Follow-up Period

a. What is the length of the follow-up period?
b. What is the rationale for the choice of this follow-up period?

It may be argued that an adequate follow-up reduces the degree to which criminal justice system contacts tend to underestimate the criminal activity of sex offenders.

How Long Should the Follow-up Period Be? The obvious question then is, How long a follow-up period should be used in recidivism research involving sex offenders? A review of the literature finds that follow-up periods of widely varying lengths are employed. In view of the need to generate program evaluation data as soon as possible, program evaluations often use follow-up periods as short as one year. On the other hand, certain European researchers (Soothill in England and Christiansen in Denmark) have utilized follow-up periods of over 20 years.[6]

Recommended Minimum Length of Five Years. Numerous corrections agencies utilize a five-year period for follow-up studies for released offenders including sex offenders.[7] The previously cited research by the Joseph Peters Institute stresses that five years should be the minimum length of an effective follow-up period for sex offenders. The authors of this chapter concur with this recommendation that recidivism research concerning sex offenders should utilize follow-up periods of at least five years, whenever possible. It is further suggested that program evaluation data based on shorter follow-up periods be characterized as preliminary.

B. REVIEW OF MAJOR FINDINGS OF RESEARCH INVOLVING SEX OFFENDERS

As noted above, program staff are often asked if certain variables are related to recidivism among sex offenders. To assist practitioners in responding to such questions, this section provides an overview of the findings of research in the field, concerning the relation of the certain major factors to recidivism among sex offenders.

1. Prior Record of Sex Crimes

Research has consistently found that a prior criminal record, especially for sex crimes, is one of the best predictors of future criminal behavior.

Extent of Prior Criminal Record among Sex Offenders.   The recently published study of Wolfe and Baker regarding forcible rapists committed to the California Corrections Department found that 86% of the 90 cases sampled had at least one prior felony conviction.[8] Of these 90 committed rapists, 53% had prior convictions for a violent crime while 31% had been previously convicted of rape. With respect to criminal record, Amir in his well-known study of rape arrests in Philadelphia from 1958 to 1960 found that 49% of the 1292 rape cases sampled had a prior arrest record.[9]

Prior Record as Related to Recidivism.   With respect to the relationship of prior record to recidivism, the findings of the Danish researcher Christiansen are noteworthy. Christiansen's research was a 12- to 24-year follow-up study involving 2934 male sex offenders who were registered with the Central Police Agency from 1929 to 1939.[10] A major conclusion of this research was that "a past career in crime is a decisive factor in recidivism." Christiansen found that the percentage of recidivism was higher among previously registered persons than among first offenders. Of the individuals with prior records, the recidivism rate was 38.6% as contrasted to the 18.6% rate among first offenders.

Prior Record of Sex Crimes as Related to Recidivism.   The ten-year follow-up study of the Joseph Peters Institute in Philadelphia found that the variable most strongly associated with subsequent arrest for a sex crime was the offender's prior sex arrest rate per year.[11]

Specifically, offenders with a low adult sex crime arrest rate (0.0 to 0.3 per year at risk) had a subsequent sex crime arrest rate of only 7.9%. In contrast, those offenders with a prior adult sex crime arrest rate of .31 to 1.39 per year had a substantially higher recidivism rate of 26.2%.

2. Alcohol Abuse

A major issue within sex offender recidivism research is the role of alcohol abuse. Studies have consistently found that alcohol abuse is prevalent among sex offenders. The research has generally concluded that alcohol abuse varies in importance among different categories of sex offenders and should be considered as a contributing, but not a causal, factor.

Extent of Alcohol Abuse among Sex Offenders.   Dr. Richard Rada has conducted a number of studies, including a recent survey of 382 persons incarcerated in California's Atascadero State Hospital as mentally disordered sex offenders. The methodology for this study included a questionnaire on the possible use of alcohol at the time of the crime, as well as completion of the Michigan Alcoholism Screening Test (MAST).[12]

In this study, Rada found that 53% of these sex offenders reported drinking prior to the offense. Based on the MAST data, 50% might be classified as alcoholics. Of those sex offenders categorized as alcoholic by means of the MAST data, the vast majority (81%) had been drinking prior to the crime as contrasted to 25% of the nonalcoholic sex offenders.[12]

Similar findings are reported by Groth based on offender samples from various sources, including Connecticut's Somers Prison and the Massachusetts Treatment Center (a mental health facility to which sex offenders adjudicated as "dangerous" are sent).[13] Groth reports that over 40% of the rapists and nearly one-third of the child molesters had histories of chronic alcohol abuse.

Role of Alcohol Abuse in Sex Crimes.   Although researchers such as Rada and Groth conclude that drinking, alcoholism, and sex offenses are related, it is generally pointed out that there is an absence of proof that alcohol plays a causative role in sex crimes.

Groth[13] points out that "the amount of drinking and/or drug use engaged in by the offender (rapist) at the time of his offense did not constitute a significant departure from his customary drinking or drug habits." He proceeds to note that "the use of alcohol, in and of itself, is insufficient to account for the offense." Alcohol was seen to play an important role when the individual "had reached a frame of mind in which he is prone to rape."

Rada also concludes that the data do not prove that alcohol plays a causative role in sex crimes. In his research, alcohol is seen to play a more causal role in child molestation cases than in rape cases. As he succinctly states, "Although alcohol may be an important factor in the commission of sex offenses, these data do not prove a cause and effect relationship. Many other factors are apparently more important such as the personality of the offender and the time and setting of the offense."[12]

3. Personality Disorders and Psychosis

Numerous researchers conclude that mental disorders play a key role in the commission of many sex crimes. However, a relatively small percentage of offenders are seen to be psychotic.

Psychotic Sex Offenders.   In his anthology of typologies of rapists, Rada states that less than 10% of rapists are generally viewed as psychotic.[14]

Sociopathic Sex Offenders.   Sociopathic rapists constitute the largest single category, comprising 30–40% of the total.

Rada[14] indicates that "rape is frequently one of . . . [the] antisocial aggressive and sexual acts" of the sociopathic rapist. Because of the pervasive personality disorder of this type of offender, "it is more difficult to determine any specific interpersonal or intra-personal conflict that lead to the rape event." Due to his extensive criminal experience, this type of rapist may be more cunning in the commission of the crime and less likely to be apprehended.

Other Personality Disorders.   The relationship of other personality disorders to the commission of sex crimes is reviewed by Rada. Since a full discussion of the psychology of the sex offender is beyond the scope of this chapter, the interested reader is referred to Rada's work as a concise summary of typologies in this area.[14]

4. Relationship between Victim and Offender

The victim's role in the commission of the crime has been the subject of increasing attention in criminological research since Wolfgang's famous 1958 study of homicide.[15] The findings of research on the relationship of the victim to the offender in sex crimes, however, have varied significantly.

Research Findings.   Amir, a student of Wolfgang, devotes a considerable portion of his study of rape arrests in Philadelphia to the relationship between the victim and the offender.[16]

The major finding of Amir was that there was a "primary contact relationship." This includes acquaintances, close neighbors, family friends, and relatives in 48% of the cases. Amir proceeds to classify 19% of the cases as "victim precipitated." The term "victim precipitated" is used to describe rape situations in which the victim is alleged by the offender to have initially agreed to, or appeared to agree to, intercourse.[16]

Similarly, a study by Groth of child molesters referred to a diagnostic program in Massachusetts which found that 71% of surveyed cases involved at least a casual relationship between the offender and the victim. In only 29% of the cases was the victim a complete stranger to the offender.[17]

On the other hand, a recent study of incarcerated rapists in California by Wolfe and Baker found that in 73% of the 90 cases of rape surveyed, the victim was a stranger and "completely unknown" to the rapist. The remaining 27% of the cases involved some prior knowledge of the victim by the offender.[18]

These varying findings suggest that the observed relationship between the victim and the offender may differ depending on the point in the criminal justice system at which the study population is selected, the offenses involved, and other factors.

C. THE REPEAT SEX OFFENDER

Relatively Low Rate of Recidivism among Sex Offenders.   Contrary to widespread public belief, sex offenders are generally found to have a relatively low rate of recidivism when compared to other types of offenders. For example, Clinard cited state correctional data from both California and Illinois with respect to the comparatively low parole violation rate of sex offenders when compared to other groups of institutional releases.[19] Similar statistics were reported by various state correctional agencies, including those in New York.[20]

It might be argued the significant number of unreported and uncleared sex crimes tends to cause official statistics to underrepresent the subsequent criminal activity of sex offenders. On the other hand, it might also be noted that only a percentage of the cases in which sex offenders come into subsequent contact with the criminal justice system involve sex crimes.

The above statistics on the relatively low recidivism rate among sex offenders have especially significant policy implications at this time due to current focus on career criminals in the overall criminal justice system.

Focus on Career or Repeat Offenders.   In recent years, a growing number of researchers and criminal justice officials have argued that a relatively small percentage of the offender population accounts for a disproportionately large percentage of the crimes.[21]

Based on this argument, there has been an increasing emphasis in the overall criminal justice system on targeting programs on these so-called career or repeat offenders. In line with this general focus on career criminals, public and legislative priority is frequently placed on establishing specialized programs for repeat sex offenders who are viewed as representing the greatest continuing danger to the community.

Need for Research on Repeat Sex Offenders. In view of the comparatively low rate of recorded recidivism among sex offenders, particularly for sex crimes, there exists a current need for research on repeat sex offenders to inform policy and program efforts. At this time, there are few comparative studies of characteristics of repeat and nonrepeat sex offenders.

The following section presents a summary of a recent exploratory survey conducted by the New York State Department of Correctional Services, which sought to distinguish between repeat and nonrepeat sex offenders with respect to the variables discussed in the preceding section.

The New York Experience

Previous research by the N.Y. State Department of Correctional Services had found that 23% of released sex offenders (defined as persons committed for rape and other sex offenses) were returned to department custody within five years.[22] This finding was based upon a study of 5593 inmates released from department facilities in 1972 by parole, conditional release, and maximum expiration of sentence. Each of these study cases was followed for a period of five years to determine how many were returned to custody either by the courts under sentences imposed for new crimes or by the Board of Parole for rule violations.

In 1972, 141 persons who had been committed for sex crimes were released. Of these 141 offenders, 23.4% were returned to department custody during the follow-up period.

	TOTAL 1972 RELEASES	RETURNED TO CUSTODY		NOT RETURNED TO CUSTODY	
		NUMBER	PERCENT	NUMBER	PERCENT
Rape	68	13	19.1%	55	80.9%
Other sex offenses	73	20	27.4%	53	72.6%
	141	33	23.4%	108	76.6%

Study Population. This survey reviewed the case folders of all 33 sex offenders returned to department custody: 13 rape cases and 20 other sex offense cases. These cases constituted the population of this exploratory study.

For comparison purposes, a sample of 50 of the total 108 nonreturned sex offenders was selected, and their case folders were also reviewed.

Returned Sex Offenders: Reason for Return. When a person reads that 23% of the sex offenders released during a given year were returned to the custody of the N.Y. State Department of Correctional Services, he generally assumes that all or most of these returns were the result of subsequent sex offenses. This report investigates the accuracy of this assumption with respect to the surveyed cohort of 1972 releases.

As such, the threshold question examined by this study is, How many of the 33 surveyed sex offenders were in fact returned for a subsequent sex offense? Of the 33 returned sex offenders, 18 were returned for a subsequent sex offense:

Returned for sex offense		18
New commitment for sex offense	13	
Parole violation involving arrest for new sex offense	5	
Returned for non–sex offense		15
New commitment for non–sex crime	8	
Parole violation not involving an arrest for a sex crime	7	
TOTAL	33	33

Definition of Repeat Sex Offender: Sex Offender Returned for Subsequent Sex Offense. In view of the above finding that only a percentage of the returned sex offenders were returned for sex crimes, this survey defines a "repeat sex offender" as one of the 18 sex offenders returned either with a new commitment for a sex offense or for a parole violation involving a sex offense.

Factors Distinguishing Repeat Sex Offenders. In an effort to identify any factors that distinguish the repeat sex offenders, the following sections of this chapter will compare these repeat sex offenders with sex offenders returned for non–sex crimes and with the sample of 50 nonreturned sex offenders.

Since complete file information was unavailable on one of these 18 repeat sex offenders, the following analysis is based on 17 cases.

Sex Offenders without Prior Criminal Records. All 32 of the returned offenders had an arrest record prior to the commitment which preceded their 1972 release. Of the 50 nonreturned sex offenders, 11 had no prior adult arrests.

	PRIOR ARREST RECORD		NO PRIOR ARREST RECORD		TOTAL	
Returned sex offenders	32		0		32	
Repeat sex offenders		(17)		(0)		(17)
Sex offenders returned for other crimes		(15)		(0)		(15)
Nonreturned sex offenders	39		11		50	
TOTAL	71		11		82	

Most Sex Offenders Have Arrests for Non–Sex Crimes. In view of the finding that 71 of the 82 surveyed cases had prior adult arrest records, the next logical question concerned the offenses involved in these prior arrests. Specifically, how many of these sex offenders might be labeled "generalized offenders" with arrests for a variety of crimes?

Of the 82 surveyed cases, the majority (77%, or 63 cases) had prior arrests for non–sex crimes. An illustrative case of an offender with arrests for various crimes is given below.

Case 1: This "repeat sex offender" was initially committed for attempted rape. Following his release in 1972, he was recommitted for robbery/rape. His previous record included other sex crimes as well as robbery, assault, burglary, and larceny.

Few Sex Offenders with Only Arrests for Sex Crimes.   Only 8 of the 82 cases had arrest records that exclusively involved sex crimes. These eight cases included two repeat sex offenders, two sex offenders returned for other crimes, and four nonreturned sex offenders.

Prior Arrests for Sex Crimes: Most Prevalent among Repeat Sex Offenders.   While most of the sex offenders reviewed in this report had prior arrest records, a notable difference between the "repeat sex offenders" and the other sex offenders was the *prevalence* of prior sex crime arrests among the repeat sex offenders (see Figure 10-1).

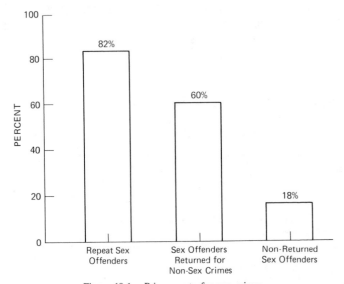

Figure 10-1.   Prior arrests for sex crimes.

Of the 17 repeat sex offenders, 82% (14) had prior sex offenses. In contrast, only 18% (9) of the 50 nonreturned sex offenders had prior sex crime arrests. Nine (60%) of the 15 sex offenders returned for other offenses had prior sex offense arrests.

Summary: Prior Arrest Record. In general terms, the findings of this survey concur with the literature in this area. A prior arrest record for sex crimes was found to be considerably more prevalent among the surveyed repeat sex offenders than among the other surveyed sex offenders.

Prevalence of Alcohol Abuse among Surveyed Sex Offenders.
Based on available case folder data, 46% (38) of the 82 surveyed cases contain evidence that alcohol abuse was a factor in the involved sex crimes.

While alcohol abuse was involved in a number of cases in the three groups, the importance of this factor seemed to vary considerably among the individual cases. It is noteworthy that in some cases, the offender's primary problem appeared to be alcohol abuse, such as in the following case.

Case 2: This individual has been sentenced to the department on three occasions. In 1959, he was committed for stealing a pickup truck while intoxicated. In 1966, he was sentenced for the rape of a young girl while he was reported drunk. After his release in 1972, he was returned in 1974 for the assault of a peace

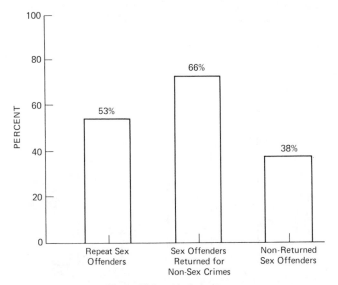

Figure 10-2. Alcohol abuse.

officer who was arresting him for driving while intoxicated. Both his parents were alcoholics, and he reports drinking since age 10.

Summary: Alcohol and Sex Crimes.   In broad terms, this survey's findings are consistent with the general findings of the literature in this area. It concludes that alcohol abuse plays a role in numerous sex offenses but should not be considered a causal factor.

Mental Disorders and Sex Offenses.   Another factor that is frequently cited with respect to violent sex offenses is the presence of mental disorders in sex offenders.

Prevalence of Personality Disorders among Repeat Sex Offenders.   This survey has found that mental disorders are particularly prevalent among repeat sex offenders (see Figure 10-3). Of the 17 repeat sex offenders, 71% (12) have been diagnosed as suffering from various personality disorders. Frequently, these individuals are labeled "sociopathic." On the other hand, diagnosed personality disorders were much less frequent among nonreturned sex offenders and among sex offenders returned for other crimes.

General Absence of Psychosis.   It should be emphasized that these repeat sex offenders are not generally diagnosed as psychotic. Occasionally, one reads an account of a sex offender who commits heinous crimes after reportedly receiving

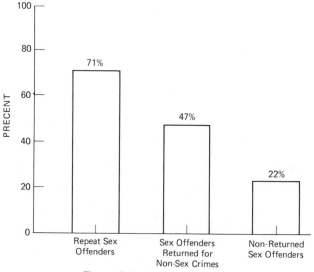

Figure 10-3.   Personality disorders.

directions from God, the devil, or some imaginary creature. There were no such extreme cases among the repeat sex offenders surveyed as part of this study. These individuals do not generally suffer from any auditory or visual hallucinations.

Typical of these repeat sex offenders with diagnosed personality disorders is the following case.

Case 3: This 38-year-old repeat sex offender has been committed to the department on three occasions for sex crimes. He has been diagnosed at various times as sociopathic but not psychotic. He exhibited little remorse or guilt over his offenses.

Relation of Offender to Victim.   In recent years, there has been an increasing emphasis in criminal justice literature on the relationship of the victim to the offender.

Prevalence of Incestuous Behavior Among Nonreturned Sex Offenders.   This survey found that a considerable percentage of the nonreturned sex offenders (30%) and sex offenders returned for non–sex offenses (27%) were originally committed for incestuous behavior; in contrast, none of the repeat sex offenders were sentenced for such crimes (see Figure 10-4).

With respect to this survey, incestuous relationship is broadly defined as one involving a natural child, stepchild, sibling, or collateral relative as well as the children of common-law spouses and paramours.

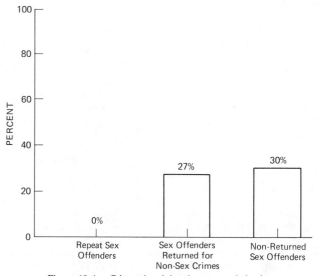

Figure 10-4.   Crimes involving incestuous behavior.

Typically, these cases involved the adolescent or preadolescent daughter or step-daughter of the offender. The actual crimes committed varied, and included incest, rape, sex abuse, and sodomy. An illustrative case is presented here.

Case 4: This 38-year-old father of eight children was committed to the department from a rural county for incest involving his 17-year-old daughter, who had borne two children by this relationship. He also admitted sexual contacts with another daughter. This man claimed long-standing marital problems with wife. Psychological examinations did not locate any evidence of mental illness. According to the case file material, the offenses were primarily attributed to "convenience" rather than to personality disorder.

This survey found a notable difference between the repeat sex offenders and the nonreturned sex offenders with respect to the relation of the offender to the victim. In a considerable percentage of the crimes of nonreturned sex offenders, incestuous behavior was involved or the victim was acquainted with the offender to some degree. In contrast, the victims of the repeat sex offender were rarely known to the offender.

Conclusion: Repeat Sex Offender. The findings of this explanatory study suggest that a core group of repeat sex offenders can be identified by using certain major variables for policy planning purposes. While this research must be considered as exploratory because of the sample size, it is felt that the findings of this study indicate worthwhile areas for future applied research on the characteristics of repeat sex offenders.

REFERENCE NOTES

1. Glaser, D. 'Evaluation of sex offender treatment programs', in Brecher, E. (Ed.) *Treatment Programs for Sex Offenders*. U.S. Department of Justice, 1978.
2. Latzer, B. and Kirby, M. Is experimental design constitutional? In Price, B. and Baunach, P. (Eds.) *Criminal Justice Research: New Models and Findings*. Sage, 1980.
3. Meyer, L. and Romero, J. *A Ten-Year Follow-Up of Sex Offender Recidivism*. Philadelphia: Joseph J. Peters Institute, 1980.
4. Ibid.
5. Groth, A.N. *Men Who Rape: The Psychology of the Offender*. New York: Plenum Press, 1979.
6. Christiansen, K., Elers-Nielsen, M., le-Maire, L., and Sturup, G. Recidivism among sexual offenders. In Christiansen, K. (Ed.) *Scandinavian Studies in Criminology*, Vol. 1. Oslo, Norway, 1965.
7. Soothill, K. and Gibbens, T. Recidivism of sexual offenders: a reappraisal. *British Journal of Criminology* **18** (1978). Soothill, K., Jack, A., and Gibbens, T. Rape: a 22-year cohort study. *Medical Science and the Law* **16**(1) (1976).
7. For example, see the recently released *Rates of Recidivism: A Five Year Follow-Up*, by Daniel P. LeClair, Massachusetts Department of Correction, October 1981.

8. Wolfe, J. and Baker, V. Characteristics of imprisoned rapists and circumstances of the rape. In Warner, C.G. (Ed.) *Rape and Sexual Assault: Management and Intervention*. Aspen Systems Corporation, 1980.

9. Amir, M. *Patterns in Forcible Rape*. Chicago, Ill.: University of Chicago Press, 1971.

10. Christiansen et al., op. cit.

11. Meyer and Romero, op. cit.

12. Rada, R., Kellner, R., Laws, D., and Winslow, W. Drinking, alcoholism, and the mentally disordered sex offender. *Bulletin of the American Academy of Psychiatry and the Law.* 6(3) (1979).

13. Groth, op. cit.

14. Rada, R. Classification of the rapist. In Rada, R. (Ed.) *Clinical Aspects of the Rapist*. Grune and Stratton, 1978. Also 10% of a rapist sample studied by Groth after referral to the Massachusetts Treatment Center "showed clinical evidence of some psychotic process operating at the time of the offense"—see Groth, A.N. and Burgess, A. Rape: a sexual deviation. *American Journal of Orthopsychiatry* 47(3) (July 1977).

15. Wolfgang, M. *Patterns in Criminal Homicide*. Philadelphia: University of Pennsylvania Press, 1958.

16. Amir, op. cit.

17. Groth, note 5.

18. Wolfe and Baker, op. cit.

19. Clinard, M.B. *Sociology of Deviant Behavior*. New York: Holt, Rinehart, and Winston, 1968.

20. Bala, G. and Donnelly, H. *1972 Releases: Five Year Post-Release Follow-Up*. New York State Department of Correctional Services—Division of Program Planning, Research and Evaluation, 1979.

21. For example, this trend has lead to formation of career criminal prosecution programs. A recent New York State report on this area is *Career Criminal Prosecution Program: Final Report*, prepared by K. Schoenberg.

22. Bala and Donnelly, op. cit.

11

Relapse Prevention with Sexual Aggressives: A Self-control Model of Treatment and Maintenance of Change*

William D. Pithers, Ph.D., Janice K. Marques, Ph.D.,
Cynthia C. Gibat, B.A., and G. Alan Marlatt, Ph.D.

Relapse prevention (RP) is a cognitive-behavioral program of assessment and treatment which is designed to enhance the maintenance of changes induced by other therapies for sexual aggressives. The model proposes that a major source of relapses, or repeat offenses, is the client's (and sometimes the therapist's) mistaken preconception that treatment will eliminate all of the client's fantasies of sexual aggression. Failure to counteract this belief sets the stage for a sequence of changes in functioning which ultimately ends in a relapse. The first goal of relapse prevention is to dispel this misconception and develop more reasonable expectations of treatment. Equally as important, this treatment program assesses the client's past behavior in order to detect situations which pose a high risk of relapse. The sequence of apparently irrelevant decisions (AIDs) made by the client, which eventually led to the client's final decision to commit a sexually aggressive act, is delineated. Finally, a systematic treatment program is conducted. Treatment under the relapse prevention model is designed to provide the sexually aggressive client with cognitive and behavioral skills which will better enable him to control his decision-making process and behavior, and reduce the probability of relapse.

INTRODUCTION

Empirical evidence has shown that many treatment modalities are effective in inducing beneficial modifications of cognition and behavior, including those in the sexual arena. Unfortunately, these short-term benefits often fail to become long-term changes. Failure to maintain change instilled by treatment is frustrating to both the distressed client and the disappointed therapist. However, when the presenting problem involves sexually aggressive behaviors rather than less socially

*The first author was supported by NIMH Grant #5-T32-GM007098 and the Margo Cleveland Biological Fund. Appreciation is expressed to the staff, administration, and clients at Atascadero State Hospital (California) for their assistance during development of this material.

troublesome symptoms (e.g., depression), the failure to maintain treatment-induced change presents more dire consequences. Clearly, increased attention must be focused on methods of maintaining treatment-induced behavioral change.

Although traditional models of therapy often neglect to consider the issue of maintenance, the behavioral models designed for treatment of indulgent behaviors (e.g., alcoholism, compulsive gambling, opium addiction) have emphasized the development of maintenance programs. *Relapse prevention* is a maintenance model that has demonstrated efficacy in providing individuals with the tools required to sustain changes that have been achieved in therapy. Relapse prevention begins by conducting a thorough assessment of the antecedents to performance of an indulgent behavior. By observing the precursors to relapse, information which is gleaned from the assessment can be turned around and used to maintain the preferred behavior. A combination of behavioral skill training procedures and cognitive restructuring techniques are then employed to remediate identified deficits in decision-making processes and coping skills that may predispose a return to the problem behavior.

Although a first impression suggests that the problem areas of sexual aggression and addictive behaviors are quite disparate, closer inspection reveals striking commonalities. Pithers, Marques, Gibat, and Marlatt determined that the precursors of relapse for sexual aggressives, or the events that precipitated a return to the forbidden behavior pattern, are highly similar to those that Marlatt found with the traditional indulgent behaviors.[2] In both cases, a negative emotional state was the most commonly found antecedent of relapse. Other similar characteristics of indulgent behaviors and sexual aggression include: (1) the immediate acquisition of short-term satisfaction at the expense of delayed negative consequences; (2) high personal and social costs; (3) an absence of any treatment model with proven superior effectiveness; (4) the lack of a single, empirically validated model of etiology; and (5) the difficulty in transferring initial behavioral changes occurring during treatment into enduring behavioral changes after treatment.[3]

Since indulgent and sexually aggressive behaviors are defined by common characteristics and precursors of relapse, programs designed to enhance maintenance of change of indulgent behaviors may logically be applied to individuals who have performed sexually aggressive acts. We begin this chapter by presenting a description of the sequence of behavioral changes which ultimately culminates in relapse (i.e., the performance of a sexually aggressive act). Next, we provide an outline of the basic concepts and terms of relapse prevention. We conclude with a thorough description of the behavioral assessment and treatment components of the relapse prevention treatment model for sexual aggressives.

Overview of the Relapse Prevention Model

Relapse prevention (RP) is a therapeutic approach specifically designed for the maintenance phase of behavior change programs. It is geared not toward producing cessation of a problem behavior, but toward helping the client maintain control of the behavior over time and across situations. For the sex offender, successful maintenance would be the achievement of long-term abstinence in regard to the performance of unlawful and offensive sexual acts. Conversely, a maintenance failure would be relapse, or a resumption of the pattern of sexually aggressive acts which preceded his treatment or incarceration.

What determines whether an individual will successfully avoid relapse? The RP model proposes that the determinants of relapse are embedded in the following process (see Figure 11-1). First, we assume that the individual experiences a sense of perceived control while maintaining abstinence and that this perception of self-control continues and grows until the person encounters a high-risk situation. Broadly speaking, a high-risk situation is one which threatens the individual's sense of control and thus increases the risk of potential relapse.

As mentioned previously, analyses of the relapse episodes reported by sexually aggressive clients have revealed common patterns of high-risk situations. A recent study reported that 75% of the relapses of sexual aggressives were precipitated by situations which had evoked a negative emotional state, mood, or feeling (e.g., frustration, anger, anxiety, or depression).[2] Another 20% of the sample relapsed in situations involving interpersonal conflict.

Many of these individuals experienced a similar sequence of changes in behavior which eventually culminated in relapse. The initial stage was characterized by a predominant mood of anger or depression. Fantasies of performing a sexually aggressive act then began to increase in frequency. As the negative emotion and fantasies continued, a conscious plan was devised to perform the act. After using a substance which may have impeded cognitive controls, the plan was acted out. The sequence of alterations in behavior was thus: affect → fantasy → conscious plan → behavior.

If an individual in a high-risk, stressful situation is able to perform a successful coping response (e.g., resisting an urge to perform a sexually aggressive act or resolving an argument), the probability of relapse decreases. Successful coping also bolsters the person's sense of control and feelings of confidence about facing the next challenging event. This "I know I can handle it" expectation increases as one copes effectively with more and more high-risk situations without relapsing.

What happens if an individual fails to cope successfully with a high-risk situation? A likely result is a decrease in his or her sense of control and a helpless feeling of "it's no use, I can't handle it." At the same time, one's expectations for coping successfully with future high-risk situations begin to fade. If these reactions occur in a situation containing cues associated with the indulgent behavior (such as the availability of alcohol or a potential victim), the stage is set for a probable relapse. This is particularly the case if the person also holds positive expectancies about the effects of performing the prohibited behavior. A problem drinker, for example, may anticipate the immediate positive effects of alcohol while forgetting

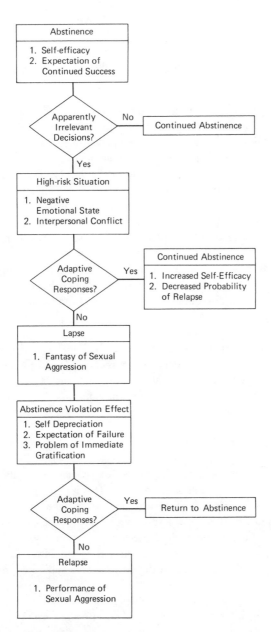

Figure 11-1.   Cognitive-behavioral model of relapse.

about the delayed consequences of drinking. Similarly, a rapist might focus on the immediate effects of performing a sexual assault, such as feelings of power and release of hostile feelings, rather than keeping in mind the full ramifications of the act.

The combination of being unable to cope with a high-risk situation and having a positive expectancy about the effects of indulging in the prohibited behavior greatly increases the individual's likelihood of crossing over the border from abstinence to relapse. At this point, the traditional RP model makes an important distinction between the initial occurrence of the prohibited behavior (a "lapse") and a complete return to a previous pattern of habitually performing the behavior (a "relapse"). An ex-smoker, for example, who takes one cigarette to help cope with a high-risk situation, may or may not continue down the road to total relapse (a return to two packs a day). If an abstaining smoker has been prepared to cope with the initial performance of the prohibited behavior (i.e., smoking a cigarette), the negative consequences of the lapse may be insignificant. However, since even the first performance of the prohibited behavior by a rapist or child molester is totally unacceptable, the traditional RP model must be revised for use with sexual aggressives.

In the orderly sequence of determinants which was found to precede sexual aggression (i.e., affect → fantasy → conscious plan → behavior),[2] it is apparent that the first stage that discriminates sex offenders from normal individuals is the predominance of fantasies involving sexual aggresion. Therefore, the modification of relapse prevention for sex offenders identifies the first occurrence of a *fantasy* about performing a sexually aggressive act as the initial *lapse*. A recurrence of a sexually aggressive *behavior* is defined as a *relapse*. Treatment under the relapse prevention model attempts to teach skills which will enable the client to interrupt the progression of the affect → fantasy → conscious plan → behavior sequence at the earliest possible point in order to reduce the likelihood that a sexual offense will recur.

Whether or not a lapse becomes a relapse depends on a number of factors, one of which is called the abstinence violation effect (AVE). A major source of the AVE is a conflict between the individual's previous self-image as an abstainer and his recent performance of the prohibited behavior. That is, "If I'm an *ex*-smoker, why did I just light that cigarette?" One way of resolving the conflict is to continue smoking, admitting that "I'm still a smoker after all." A second source of the AVE is the individual's attribution of the lapse to personal weakness or failure. To the extent that the person views a lapse as a personal failure, his or her expectancy for continued failure will increase, and the chances of a full-blown relapse also increase.

Another cognitive factor which may determine whether a lapse will snowball into a relapse is the subjective expectancy of the effect of performing the prohibited activity. If, for example, an alcoholic selectively recalls how the first drink gives one a sense of power which counters feelings of helplessness in a high-risk situation, then drinking is strongly reinforced as a coping response.

In the above discussion, the relapse process is depicted from the point at which a person encounters a high-risk situation. It is important to note, however, that the RP model also examines the events which precede the high-risk situation. Although individuals often relapse in situations which would have been difficult to avoid or anticipate, others appear to set the scene for their own relapse by putting themselves into high-risk situations. This can be done with or without awareness on the part of the individual involved. In some cases, a "craving" or "urge" is experienced and used to directly justify an indulgence. In other cases, however, individuals engineer their own relapses with little or no awareness. For example, an abstinent drinker who buys a bottle to take home "in case guests drop by during the holidays" is making a choice which we call an "apparently irrelevant decision" (AID).

Through the well-known cognitive processes of rationalization and denial, one can covertly plan a relapse by making a series of AIDs, each of which represents another step toward a tempting, high-risk situation. A case study illustrates this process.[1] On vacation in California, a compulsive gambler (currently abstinent) decided to see the "amazingly blue waters" of Lake Tahoe on his way home to Seattle. Unfortunately, this AID led him across the California-Nevada border into a high-risk situation. By the time he "found himself" in downtown Reno needing change for a quarter, his relapse was almost inevitable. By putting himself in an extremely tempting situation, the gambler could indulge, claiming he was overwhelmed by external circumstances which made resistance impossible.

The preceding analysis of the relapse process leads directly into the RP approach to treatment. While there is very little a gambler can do to avoid relapse in a "downtown Reno" situation, he can accept responsibility for initiating the chain of events which got him there in the first place. He can also learn to recognize the conditions which precede a relapse and be prepared to intervene before it is "too late."

RP begins by dispelling misconceptions that the client may have regarding the outcome of treatment and describing more realistic goals. RP continues with an assessment of the client's high-risk situations, which are the conditions under which relapse has occurred or is likely to occur in the future. Also included in the initial assessment is an evaluation of the client's coping skills, since any given situation can be considered high-risk only to the extent that the person has difficulty coping in it. After the high-risk situations have been identified, an intervention program is designed to train the client in how to avoid a first lapse and how to keep one lapse from snowballing into a full-blown relapse. In the following sections, specific procedures for attaining these treatment goals will be illustrated.

DISPELLING MISCONCEPTIONS AND DEVELOPING REALISTIC EXPECTATIONS

Misconceptions about Consequences of Treatment

Although recidivism rates of sex offenders are lower than those of the more general criminal population, the repetition of sexually aggressive acts is a discouragingly frequent occurrence.[4] Noting that the long-term efficacy of treatment for sexual aggression has not yet been demonstrated, the Group for the Advancement of Psychiatry has advocated incarceration, rather than treatment, of sex offenders.[5]

Rather than attributing sexual reoffending to ineffective treatments, the implicit assumptions and goals of therapy with sex offenders require revision. Treatment may successfully induce cognitive and behavioral changes in the sex offender, but the client's expectations about the long-term consequences of treatment for sexual aggression may actually increase the likelihood of relapse. Perhaps the anticipated consequent of treatment which is most likely to lead to another offense is that successful therapy should *eliminate* the preference for a socially unacceptable sex act or object.

In the client's past, successful treatment for a physical illness (e.g., influenza) has led to its elimination. Thus, the sex offender enters therapy with the mistaken preconception that his desire for deviant sexual stimuli (i.e., his "illness") will be eradicated. This erroneous belief is reinforced if the client receives treatment which either purports to "extinguish" the problem behavior or proposes to cure the illness pharmacologically without concomitant psychotherapy. The patient may believe that he need only remain a passive recipient of a potent treatment which will permanently terminate both his sexually aggressive behavior and his fantasies about those acts.

Imagine the case of a heterosexual pedophile who has been released recently from "successful" treatment. Reentering society and behaving responsibly increase his self-esteem. He takes great pride in noting the dramatic changes in his behavior from his days as a sex offender until, after a particularly vehement argument with his wife, he begins to question his self-control. Shortly after his wife storms out of their home, swearing never to return to him and their 9-year-old daughter, he senses a peculiarly familiar feeling of depression and rejection creeping into his thoughts. As he sinks more deeply into depression, his young daughter notices her father's sadness and reacts to it by approaching him, folding her hands on his knee, and resting her chin there. He notices the affectionate glimmer in his daughter's upturned, bright eyes, a look that he sadly recalls seldom having seen in his wife's, and imagines just how deeply the daughter cares for him. He returns her affectionate gesture by caressing her soft hair since he believes that any good father would do so.

For most individuals, the scene would remain an innocent and affectionate one. For the pedophile, this expression of affection may lead to an event with irreversible consequences. The father has entered a high-risk situation for which he may not have an immediate coping response available. As the situation unfolds, he begins to recall selectively the satisfaction derived from his previous sexual experiences with children, neglecting the negative aftereffects. A fleeting fantasy of sexual involvement with his daughter may flash through his mind. In an individual who has not been treated for a sexually aggressive act, the fantasy may be dismissed easily as a "silly thought." For the sex offender, the fantasy has far greater significance. He interprets the fantasy as an indication that treatment was not successful, signifying that he is now, and will be forever, a sex offender and nothing else.

The erroneous conclusion that he will always be a sex offender evokes the sense of helplessness and loss of self-control that typifies the abstinence violation effect (AVE). As a result of the changed cognitions, he passively yields to the temptation of the risk situation. Thus, the effects of several years of intensive treatment have been undone by a momentary fantasy, largely because the client believed that his successful treatment should have eliminated such desires. The client had not been prepared by his previous treatment to deal with the recurrence of a fantasy about sexually aggressive acts. Rather, he interpreted the single lapse into a sexually aggressive fantasy as proof that treatment was actually unsuccessful, that his desires have not been extinguished, and that he remains a sex offender. As this man enters a full-blown relapse, he may adopt the role of a sex offender as the core concept of his personality. Other roles filled by the client (e.g., husband, father, hard worker) are superseded by his role as a sex offender. He then behaves in accordance with this role.

It is interesting to speculate what this man might say during his first treatment session after having been incarcerated for the sexual involvement with his daughter. In response to the therapist's asking, "Why did you accost your daughter?" the client might well reply, "I did it because I was mad at my wife." Many therapists probably would label this response as scapegoating and possibly castigate the client for failing to accept responsibility for his behavior. Although initiating treatment with such a confrontation may be rationalized as an attempt to break through the client's denial system, the only accomplishment of an aggressive confrontation during the initial hours of therapy is a dramatic increase in the client's resistance to treatment.

However, the client actually may regard the disagreement with his wife as the cause of his act since it was the event that initiated the sequence of affective and cognitive changes which ultimately led to the offense. The offender maintains this view because he is unaware that the argument with his spouse was the first of several events that progressively brought him closer to an offense. Additionally, since the disagreement was the only externally observable event, with the remaining changes being less perceptible alterations in affect and cognition, the argument would be the most vividly recalled precursor of relapse from the client's perspective. As the client proceeds through treatment under the relapse prevention model, he will recognize that the interpersonal conflict was only the first in a sequence of events that ultimately led to the offense. He will also realize that he made a series of apparently irrelevant decisions (AIDs) which brought him closer to performing the act. Eventually, the client will acknowledge that he was actively involved in creating the situations which determined that sexual aggression would take place. At this point in treatment, the client will understand the sequence of changes that led up to the relapse. When the client comprehends his role in the events that preceded the offense and recognizes his failure to cope with these events, he can begin to accept responsibility for his socially, and often personally, unacceptable sexual behavior.

Developing Realistic Expectations

The first phase of intervention under the relapse prevention treatment model is designed to break down the assumption that treatment will ablate desire for atypical sexual preferences. The following introduction to the model, presented in a frank but nonconfrontational manner, may suffice. Although this introduction was devised for a child molester, it can be adapted easily for other sexually aggressive individuals.

> You have probably heard, and you may believe, that as a result of your treatment here your attraction to female children will decrease and you'll never need to be concerned about reoffending. I want you to know that your treatment here is not going to change your attraction to female children.
>
> Hearing this may make you feel hopeless about what you can accomplish in your treatment program, but I want you to know that even though you will not be able to eliminate your attraction to female children, the treatment program that you are entering today is designed to allow you to learn a series of behavioral skills and thinking patterns which you may learn to use to keep from acting out your desire for young children.
>
> Compare your attraction to children to an addict's craving for heroin. In each case, the addicting substance does not disappear magically as a result of treatment for substance abuse. In both instances, desire for the substance or the experience may recur after successful treatment ceases. So the most important part of treatment is to learn what to do when you feel the need to use a socially unacceptable substance, which in your case is female children.
>
> That's what this treatment program is all about. You'll discover, on your own, a variety of situations in which you make seemingly unimportant decisions that actually either lead you closer to performing an unacceptable sex act or take you away from the danger. You'll come to recognize these situations and the behavioral alternatives that reduce the likelihood that you will act out your unacceptable sexual desires. You'll also find that some situations are particularly dangerous for you (and others) because they present temptations that increase the

risk of you repeating a sexually aggressive act. You and I will work to specify these risk situations, find ways of avoiding them, and develop behavioral skills that you can use to cope with these risk situations when they arise unexpectedly.

This nonconfrontational introduction to the relapse prevention treatment model has several goals. By relating to the client as a colleague or co-therapist, we foster a sense of objectivity and detachment in the client's consideration of his own behavior. An atmosphere of openness and cooperation is established in which the client feels free to discuss threatening thoughts and behaviors. By adopting this objective and detached approach, the client and the therapist mutually may begin to explore the problem behavior without the defensiveness that otherwise might be encountered. The absence of a punitive confrontation and the focus upon a client's behaviors enable the client to see that we view sexually aggressive behavior as an unacceptable act that he has performed, rather than as an indication of something that he *is* (e.g., a sex offender).

The introduction to the relapse prevention treatment program asserts that the client was not a passive victim of the environmental and physiological circumstances preceding his aggression. Similarly, we declare to the client that he cannot view himself as a passive recipient of treatment. Rather, we try to facilitate the client's active participation in treatment. We encourage him to accept personal responsibility for learning the skills that he will need to reduce the likelihood of another act of sexual aggression.

ASSESSMENT

The initial phase of assessment should attempt to determine whether or not the client is appropriate for treatment under the relapse prevention model. Since the overall goals of relapse prevention are to increase the client's awareness about choices he makes which affect his behavior, to develop coping skills, and to enhance self-control abilities, it is obvious that not all sexual aggressives are good candidates for treatment under this model. Guidelines for selection of appropriate clients must be employed.

We believe that individuals who have demonstrated a history of prosocial behaviors, with the exception of their sexually aggressive acts, represent acceptable candidates for treatment. The client must be willing to make a voluntary commitment to treatment since his active participation in the program is necessary. Our experience suggests that even some clients who were originally confined involuntarily may later make a voluntary commitment to treatment if they believe it might be effective. The client must also have a manageable number of high-risk situations. If too many risk situations are apparent, treatment cannot possibly prepare the client to deal with all of them. Only those offenders who sincerely accept responsibility for their act and acknowledge the harm inflicted by it should be considered. Individuals who have a lifelong history of antisocial acts, the most recent of which happens to have involved sexual aggression, may not be considered appropriate candidates for treatment. Clients impaired by psychosis, whose thought processes bear little relationship to consensual reality, also must be regarded as poor candidates. When uncertain about the client's appropriateness, we provisionally accept the offender for the behavioral assessment given to all of our clients. The assessment and the client's willingness to engage in the evaluation process may be used to filter out most individuals who are not amenable to treatment.

A careful behavioral assessment is crucial to adequate treatment since it provides the basis for selecting intervention techniques for application from those offered within the relapse prevention approach. Carefully selecting appropriate interventions and focusing attention on one procedure at a time may enhance the client's compliance with treatment. Presenting each new assignment one at a time increases the likelihood that the client will experience small but incremental successes as the program continues, thereby enhancing his feelings of self-efficacy. In contrast, imposing a plethora of procedures simultaneously may overwhelm the client and demolish any hope he held of changing.

High-risk Situations

As described earlier, high-risk situations are defined as a set of circumstances which pose a threat to the individual's sense of self-control and increase the likelihood of relapse. The ability to perform an immediate coping response in a risk situation decreases the probability of the problem behavior emerging. If an adaptive coping response is not immediately emitted, the likelihood of relapse escalates.

The first phase of assessment involves a delineation of situations which pose a high risk of relapse. By identifying communalities in the circumstances that pose risk, various coping responses may be designed to enable the client to escape quickly from the risk and thereby lessen the chance of a relapse. Three procedures are employed to detect risk situations: self-monitoring, direct observation, and a structured interview.

Self-monitoring.   We require clients to maintain a self-monitoring record for three changes in functioning which we have found to precede relapse. Changes in affect present the first target of self-monitoring, since our research suggests the failure to handle anger or depression is a frequent precursor of relapse.[2] Fantasies of sexually agressive acts (or an urge to achieve gratification by performing such an act) are the second target for self-monitoring. Our clients are also requested to record occasions when they discover themselves drifting into a conscious plan about performing an act. With the more benign spectrum of sexual offenses (e.g., exhibitionism), we request the client to record each performance of the behavior as well. Information regarding self-monitoring procedures is provided elsewhere.[6]

Direct Observation. Direct observation of sexual arousal patterns in various stimulus settings is measured by a plethysmograph while the client either views or listens to prerecorded tapes. The stimulus tapes contain sexual scenarios in which we vary the degree of aggression employed to subdue the victim, as well as the victim's age and sex.

The client's tumescence reveals patterns of stimulus situations which elicit heightened degrees of sexual arousal. To the degree that a scenario containing sexual aggression or an inappropriate-age partner evokes arousal, the elements of the situation are considered to pose a risk of relapse.

Structured Interview. A structured interview devised by the authors[2] is conducted to analyze the circumstances associated with past offenses. The interview is used to discern both the high-risk events and the apparently irrelevant decisions (AIDs) that stimulated each aggressive act. At the conclusion of the interview, the concept of AIDs is formally introduced in the following manner.

Each of us make many decisions every day which seemingly are so minor in importance that they could have absolutely no significant effect on an individual's life. Yet regardless of the *apparent* irrelevance, each one of these decisions profoundly alters the range of behaviors that are subsequently available to us. The cumulative effect of all of these "apparently irrelevant decisions" has the potential to alter dramatically the final outcome of one's life.

An example may clarify the actual importance of even a single apparently irrelevant decision. Imagine a pedophile, who emerges from the front door of his home to take a walk along the tree-lined street of his suburban residence. Nearing the sidewalk, he decides to turn left. After a brief excursion, he notices a school playground brimming with gleefully playing children, a definite high-risk situation for a pedophile. Since the individual probably was familiar with his neighborhood, he would have been cognizant that going to the left would take him by the school, whereas turning right would have led him away from that high-risk area. So, an apparently irrelevant decision was his choice to turn left, rather than right, onto the sidewalk. Clearly, his decision to walk to the left was only an *apparently* irrelevant one.

If we look at the behavior you performed that got you into your current trouble, when did you make the *first* decision that started you toward your final decision to begin a sexual relationship with a female child?

At this point, the patient may provide any of a wide range of responses. In order to foster the atmosphere of cooperation that is critical to conducting therapy under the relapse prevention model, the patient's response should not be challenged severely or ridiculed. If the patient responds with a statement such as, "I didn't make a decision to do it, it just happened," the therapist could reply:

It is really kind of difficult for me to imagine how anyone can perform any behavior without first having decided at some point that he was going to do it. Consider the person who is an alcoholic, for example. Imagine him walking down a dimly lit city sidewalk close to midnight. As he walks, he reaches into his pocket for a cigarette and discovers that he's out. He anxiously looks around for a store where he can buy some more. A flashing red neon light catches his eye, and he begins walking briskly toward it. As he draws closer, he realizes that the red neon sign reads BEER. He pauses only a moment to deliberate, deciding that he really needs a cigarette so he'll go into the bar to get a pack. He enters the bar and goes to the cigarette vending machine. When he reaches into his pants pocket, he finds no coins. After asking two gray-haired men playing pool if they can change a dollar and seeing both heads shake no in unison, he turns toward the cash register near the bar to get change. Amid the clacking of billiard balls, he hears his name called, "George." Turning to the sound, he stares into drifting blue cigarette smoke and recognizes his foreman from the foundry. The foreman instantly turns to the bartender saying "Fill up a brew for George." Debating only a second, George sips his first taste of the foaming beer. That was only the first taste of many he had that night.

Now that you've heard this story, you may be able to see that George made a series of decisions which led up to his final decision to take a drink of beer. At each one of these choice points, George could have made a different decision that would have taken him away from a dangerous situation. Did he really *have* to have a cigarette? Did he have no alternative but to enter the bar? Could he have said no to the beer his foreman bought him? Instead, each decision that George made brought him closer to danger until he finally felt that he had no choice but to accept the drink that was offered. So you can see that George made a series of decisions, each of which contributed in some way to his finally taking the drink of beer.

Looking at your decision to have a sexual relationship with a female child in this way, can you tell me the earliest point at which you decided to seek out the relationship?

Another simple means of beginning to develop a framework of high-risk situations is to ask, "If you were to become sexually involved with a child in the future, how might it occur?" However, if the patient is still unable to state any decision he made that led to the offense, a suggestion should be made that he "may happen to think of one before we get together the next time."

Once the client begins to recall AIDs that he has made, the pace with which he remembers them will accelerate. By integrating information derived from the client's self-monitoring record, direct observation of his arousal patterns, a structured interview, and the AIDs that he recalls, a comprehensive picture of the situations posing a high risk of relapse may be obtained.

Coping Skills

Assessment of the client's repertoire of coping behaviors is important, since even minimal stress could precipitate the relapse of a sexual aggressive who lacks adaptive coping skills. Among the procedures used to evaluate the client's coping skills are the Situational Competency Test, self-efficacy ratings, relapse fantasies, and an autobiography.

Situational Competency Test.   The Situational Competency Test presents a series of narrative descriptions of high-risk situations and requires the client to verbalize coping responses.[7] The adequacy of the coping response, and the latency with which it is formulated, are evaluated. The Situational Competency Test has been shown to provide an accurate indication of the client's actual coping capacity in real-life situations. A problematic situation is considered to exist whenever the client is unable to formulate a coping response, verbalizes a strategy that is unlikely to be successful, or requires a long latency before responding. By employing descriptions of a wide range of risk situations, a profile of the client's coping skills is discerned.

Self-efficacy Ratings.   Self-efficacy refers to an individual's expectancy of being able to perform a specific task competently. Self-efficacy ratings are obtained by presenting the client with a list of specific high-risk situations and requesting him to rate (e.g., on a seven-point scale) how difficult it would be to cope with the situation without encountering any of the precursors to sexual aggression (i.e., negative emotional state, interpersonal conflict, substance use, and fantasies of aggressive sexual acts). This procedure may also be used to acquire information about the client's expected reaction to a first recurrence of unacceptable sexual fantasies.

Relapse Fantasies.   Relapse fantasies are useful assessment devices of coping behaviors. To develop relapse fantasies, the client is asked to create an imaginary account of the circumstances that could provoke a possible relapse sometime in the future. As an introduction to this guided fantasy, the therapist could state, "You and I both hope that a relapse will not occur in your case; we're working hard to enable you to prevent that. However, it would be very helpful to our work toward that goal if, for just the next few moments, you pretend that you're no longer involved in treatment and are having difficulty keeping yourself from performing a prohibited sexual act. I'd like you to sit back comfortably in your chair, close your eyes, and relax by breathing slowly, deeply. Pretend that it's the future; you're having difficulty not thinking about being with a child. Imagine a situation that would make it difficult for you to keep from acting on your desire. Allow yourself to actually see yourself in that situation. When you begin to imagine this scene vividly, just allow yourself to start describing your feelings and the situation as clearly as you can."

By reviewing the relapse fantasies with the client, the absence of adaptive coping responses and the use of maladaptive coping behaviors will be noted. The therapist and the client may then design coping behaviors that would better enable the client to avoid relapse in these situations.

Autobiography. Clients are asked to write an autobiography during the initial assessment period. The emphasis in these historical accounts is placed on the client's definition of his own psychological role. Certain types of role definitions (e.g., sex offender, victim of circumstances) reveal beliefs which lessen the likelihood that the client will employ adaptive coping responses, thereby predisposing him to relapse.

TREATMENT

In traditional treatment programs for sexual aggressives, the client is often asked to identify his "danger signal." The danger signal is considered to represent a warning to the individual that he is about to get into trouble and that psychological assistance should be sought.

The premise of the relapse prevention model is that the individual makes a series of apparently irrelevant decisions in high-risk situations that lead him either toward or away from sexual aggression. These apparently irrelevant decisions precede the "danger signal." Relapse prevention maintains that once an individual reaches his "danger signal," he is so far down the road to performing the forbidden behavior that, in essence, the decision to perform the behavior has already been made. The underlying notion is that it is easier to control the momentum of one's decision process at points that are more distant from the forbidden behavior (i.e., apparently irrelevant decisions) than at the point immediately preceding the problem behavior, which is when the traditional "danger signal" appears. The client and the therapist should view offending not as an all-or-none phenomenon that is due to uncontrollable sexual preferences and fate, but rather as an inappropriate coping behavior that results from a long series of decisions which slowly approach the final decision to perform a sexually aggressive act. Thus, the goal of relapse prevention is to interrupt as early as possible the sequence of changes in affect and behavior that are associated with sexual aggression.

Once assessment has yielded a comprehensive array of high-risk situations, the client can be taught to respond to those situational cues as discriminative stimuli which mandate immediate behavioral change. The cornerstone of the relapse prevention treatment program entails teaching the client adaptive coping strategies with specific skill training procedures, as well as instruction in general problem-solving procedures. Specific skill training remediates existing behavioral deficits or excesses, while a problem-solving orientation enables the client to have great flexibility in adapting to new problem situations rather than having to rely on rote learning of discrete skills which may not generalize across settings. Treatment components of the RP model are depicted in Figure 11-2.

Specific Skill Training

High-risk Recognition.   An important benefit of the emphasis placed on apparently irrelevant decisions (AIDs) and high-risk situations during assessment is that the client develops an increasingly rapid recognition of these events. A detailed delineation of the AIDs preceding past offenses removes the apparent irrelevance from these choices and alerts the client to the actual importance of each decision he makes, particularly those decisions made in high-risk situations.

Since the client becomes more vigilant for high-risk situations and develops the capacity to recognize dangerous circumstances rapidly, direct instruction in adaptive coping responses is conducted to enable the client to deal with these situations. By providing the client with prepared coping behaviors for specific risk situations, response to these situations may be more adaptive and may also be emitted more quickly. In essence, the client is programmed to emit adaptive coping responses. In this manner, the client escapes risk rapidly, thereby lessening his exposure to temptation, and performs the escape by using an appropriate coping response, thus eliminating the reduction in self-efficacy resulting from coping behaviors that may be ridiculed socially.

The most important advantage of programmed coping responses is that they enable the coping behavior to be emitted rapidly. The Situational Competency Test

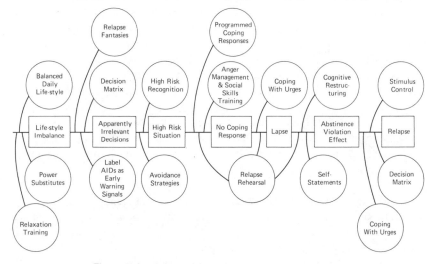

Figure 11-2.   Stages of intervention to prevent a relapse.

has been employed to identify which aspects of an alcoholic's decision making would be associated with relapse.[7] Adequacy and latency of verbalized coping responses were measured. Adequacy of the coping response was not related significantly to relapse. However, the faster the verbalized coping behavior was emitted, the less probable was relapse. The behavior employed as a coping response was not very important; the crucial factor in preventing relapse was simply getting out of the risk situation as quickly as possible by any means. By programming coping responses for specific risk situations, the likelihood of relapse is decreased by increasing the speed with which the individual can escape the situation.

In presenting the concept of programmed coping responses to the client, we sometimes use the following example to make the difference between a fast response and an optimal response clearer.

Imagine yourself alone in a room that contains a ticking time bomb. You have had no prior training in defusing time bombs, and there is no indication of when the bomb is set to explode. Two alternate coping responses come to your anxious mind. Ideally, you could remain in the room and attempt to defuse the bomb. This alternative is not very appealing, since it exposes you to a severe danger for an unnecessarily long time and potentially may lead to your demise. Immediately you enact the alternate coping behavior by dashing out of the room as fast as your feet will carry you. By leaving the room, you have saved your life and also will be able to warn others about the impending danger. Thus, your most productive and safest response is to leave the situation as quickly as possible rather than staying and trying to figure out how to defuse the situation.

If you had been trained in bomb disposal (a programmed coping response), you might have been able to function even more effectively in the situation. By successfully defusing the bomb, not only would you save yourself and others nearby, but you would prevent property damage in the room containing the bomb. Therefore, the programmed coping behavior would enable the optimal response to be emitted. If the optimal coping response had not been programmed, simply leaving the situation as quickly as possible would be the best behavior.

Since we've already identified a number of situations that pose a high risk of relapse to you, I want us to begin preparing you with optimal responses for those situations. Doing this will go a long way toward enabling you to prevent a relapse from happening.

Programmed Coping Responses. Since the client's responses to the assessment procedure reveal the use of maladaptive behaviors or the absence of coping behaviors, treatment may be used to design adaptive coping responses for risk situations. A general problem-solving process is employed to construct programmed coping responses.

The client initiates the problem-solving procedure by describing the risk situation *in detail*. Once the situation has been described fully, a brainstorming session is used to generate a large number of potential coping responses. During the brainstorming process, no criticism of any coping responses should be permitted. The important issue is to have the client generate as many behavioral alternatives as he can. After the list of alternatives has been completed, the potential consequences of each alternative are described to evaluate whether that coping response would have the desired effect of lessening the likelihood of relapse. The most effective, feasible coping response is then selected for performance. Focusing on the thought processes that the patient follows in performing the problem-solving strategy is important in providing clues suggesting additional problem areas for further elaboration (e.g., an unrealistic approach to life, grandiose expectations).

While instructing the client in problem-solving procedures, the therapist may enhance the client's learning by modeling both the problem-solving process and the selected coping behavior. If the high-risk situation and the selected coping response are interpersonal (e.g., disagreement with a spouse), role playing may be used to model the appropriate coping behavior. When the problem is intrapersonal (e.g., depression), an internal dialogue of self-statements may be modeled as a coping technique.

The client must then be given opportunity to practice the selected coping behavior and receive therapeutic feedback. Coaching on the behavior should continue until the client's performance matches the therapist's criteria for adequacy. If the client is unable to achieve criteria-level performance after repeated attempts with feedback, it may be necessary to return to the list of alternate coping responses and attempt to use the next best option that the client can enact successfully.

Continued practice of the behavior should be conducted throughout the client's treatment. Practice on these behaviors resembles the repetitive drills used by athletic coaches who strive to have their players respond "instinctively" in important situations. These "instinctive" reactions actually result from intensive programming. By practicing over time, the client will perform the behavior while in many situations and moods, enhancing generalization.

Stimulus Control.   The assessment procedure may reveal that the client's preferred fantasies of sexual aggression involve substances or weapons. This is particularly true of rapists. One study has reported that 83% of the rapists in their sample actually used a weapon to force victim submission.[8] Although we do not maintain that these rapes would not have taken place without a weapon, having a weapon available may increase the likelihood that an aggressor will act out his seething rage against women. Similarly, if an individual with aggressive sexual fantasies and marginally successful cognitive controls becomes intoxicated, the unacceptable behavior may erupt as the controls fail. To the extent that substances and weapons are related to sexually aggressive offenses, simply removing these materials from one's everyday environment may lessen the likelihood of an offense.

Coping with Urges.   Performance of indulgent behaviors receives immediate reinforcement, even for the sexual aggressor who may be satisfied momentarily by an explosive release of hostile emotions. Selectively recalling the positive aspects of past episodes of sexual aggression, while neglecting the negative aftereffects, increases the probability of a recurrence of the unacceptable sexual behavior. Positive outcome expectancies for the immediate effects become an especially potent force when the client is faced with a high-risk situation and is beginning to feel unable to cope effectively. Under such conditions the client may find his consciousness usurped by an urge to commit the sexually aggressive act.

In order to offset the influence of positive outcome expectancies, we educate the client that his overall response to sexual aggression is biphasic in nature: The initial rush of power and aggression is frequently followed by a delayed effect in the opposite direction (e.g., low self-efficacy and shame). We draw an analogy to the relapsing alcoholic who fondly recalls the pleasant relaxation induced by the first drink but who has forgotten about the torturous hangover produced by the tenth (until he has to live through it the next morning!). In order to provide a potent reminder for our clients that positive outcome expectancies are unrealistic, we refer to this phenomenon as the "problem of immediate gratification": the PIG phenomenon.

Individuals who yield to an urge may make the mistaken assumption that this craving will continue to increase in intensity until it overwhelms them, becoming impossible to resist. Therefore, an important point for the client to remember when an urge arises is that it will subside and pass away with time. If the individual is able to endure the fading of an urge without engaging in aggression, the internal pressure to respond may become weaker with each succeeding urge.

To increase the client's ability to recognize conditions that elicit urges, he can be asked to self-monitor the occurrence of all urges taking place within a selected time period. The client should include the following information in his observation of urges: a description of antecedent events or feelings, an estimate of the intensity and duration of the urge, and any coping response that could have been employed to reduce the likelihood of an urge developing.

As is true with high-risk situations, the first step in learning how to cope with an urge is being able to recognize one and label it as an urge. The client can then be taught to use self-statements to disrupt the urge. Statements such as "two minutes of power isn't worth the chance of prison" may be developed during treatment. Imagery may also represent a useful tool for coping with urges. During treatment, the client may be instructed to visualize himself feeling an urge and then successfully defeating it. The most effective image may be the picture we suggest clients develop as their self-image when they consider acting out an urge: that of an obnoxiously, grotesquely, fat PIG, waddling through a pen of odoriferous mud.

Avoidance Strategies.   Although it would be absurd to suggest that all high-risk situations can be avoided, some situations may be circumvented without unduly interfering with the client's life. A pedophile whose daily drive to work takes him by an elementary school can easily travel another route. A divorced man, previously convicted of incest, would be advised not to marry someone who has young children. Simply avoiding the high-risk situations to which one is exposed routinely may lessen the possibility of relapse.

Anger Management.   Since sexual aggression has been shown to be precipitated by anger, training in anger management is conducted. Clients receive a pamphlet describing the causes of anger (e.g., frustration, social abuse, injustices, unrealistic expectations, negative self-statements), the positive aspects of feeling angry (e.g., a descriminative cue indicating the need to begin coping with stress, release of tension, a source of energy), and the potentially negative functions of anger (e.g., unbridled expression can be destructive; anger can cause a disruption of thinking). We stress that anger can be expressed as an adaptive coping behavior. The goal of anger management is to enable constructive expression of anger, not to teach the client to inhibit it. Anger is viewed as a signal that it is time to employ a coping response and as a source of energy to enact the behavior. Anger is problematic, however, when it leads to aggression, when it is experienced too frequently or intensely, and when it lasts too long.

Since emotions and thoughts are intertwined, clients are shown how to use self-statements to modulate expression of anger.[9] Specific statements are prepared for the various sources and states of anger. Examples of self-statements for different situations include: frustration ("My muscles are getting tense, time to take some deep breaths . . . relax . . . and slow down"), social abuse ("I'm not going to let myself get pushed around, but I'm not going to go haywire either"), social injustices ("I can't expect everyone to act the way I'd like them to, but I can control my own reactions"), and arguments ("I'm not going to take this personally; I may feel angry but I know how to deal with it"). Self-statements are also developed for conflicts that are not resolved ("Forget about it and relax; thinking about it will only make me more angry"). When anger is handled successfully, self-statements are used as reinforcers to strengthen this coping response ("I'm getting better at this all the time; seeing myself handle anger successfully is almost getting to be fun").

A final element in the anger management program is assertiveness training. Assertive interactional skills enable the client to convey negative emotions without neglecting another individual's rights and also to enhance the expression of positive emotions.

Social Skills. Experience suggests that some sexual aggressives, particularly pedophiles, have deficient social skills. Some of the pedophiles with whom we work have no knowledge of how to initiate a conversation with another adult. Social skills training may improve the client's ability to interact and communicate effectively. Hopefully, these skills will enable the client to develop and maintain a satisfying relationship with another adult. The Personal Effectiveness Program is suggested as an excellent source for further information about social skills training.[10]

Relapse Rehearsal. Traditional forms of therapy fail to prepare clients for the possibility of relapse. The underlying assumption is that preparing the client for the possibility of relapse is tantamount to authorizing its occurrence. However, practice in dealing with possible crises occurs frequently in society. Children in school take part in fire drills; the Emergency Broadcast System interrupts communication airwaves to test their warning alert; life boat drills are held on cruise ships; and flight attendants outline emergency procedures prior to airline departures. Many of the training procedures for emergencies have proved so successful that they are no longer optional but are required by law. Preparing a sex offender for the possibility of relapse into deviant sexual fantasies is another means of instruction on how to act in order to prevent an emergency from turning into a catastrophe.

In treatment, the therapist should inform the patient that fantasies which appear unacceptable are probably going to recur occasionally. By accepting this belief, the negative influence of the abstinence violation effect (AVE) is lessened when fantasies later recur. Making this statement also impresses upon the patient the importance of learning how to deal effectively with a lapse into fantasy.

Relapse rehearsals may be staged in order to practice the behavioral skills needed to ameliorate the negative effect of the lapse into fantasy. Relapse rehearsals also enable the therapist and the patient to assess how well the patient has learned the importance of AIDs, programmed coping responses, problem-solving strategies for use when coping responses have not been programmed, and cognitive self-statements. In order to evaluate the patient's learning of these skills, the therapist may encourage the patient to "think out loud" how he would handle a lapse into unacceptable fantasies. Ideally the patient would state:

I've just recently been thinking of volunteering to serve as the supervisor of youth activities for my church group. The thought seemed really attractive to me. I'd be helping the church and the children; I'd be thought well of by the community; I'd be active and having fun. For some reason though, I felt uneasy about actually volunteering. I didn't know why—but finally, I realized that the decision was what we've been calling "apparently irrelevant." The decision didn't seem like such a big deal, but it sure would put me into an unnecessarily risky situation. I would be better off not volunteering.

Since I didn't have a coping response programmed for that situation, I used the problem-solving strategy I've learned. I figured out that as a supervisor I'd be alone with a lot of kids. We might even go on camping trips. I couldn't think of anyone who would volunteer to assist me on the job. My main alternatives seemed to be: (1) to go ahead and become a counselor; (2) to figure out another way I could be with kids in the company of other adults, like coaching little league baseball; or (3) to just turn down any job that might get me near kids. I knew I couldn't take the supervisor's position. It just had too many risks for me. I was tempted to think that I could handle the risks one at a time, but the risks would never end and one might occur when I'm feeling angry which would increase the risk. Coaching baseball seemed okay at first. Knowing that other adults are around would keep me in line. I wouldn't have to worry so much about what I might do. My one concern was that I could telephone one of the kids someday when I knew his parents weren't around. I might ask him to come over and play catch. No telling what that might lead to, but I'm afraid of the possibilities. So I think I'd better forget about coaching.

You know, for a second when I was thinking about the coaching job, I could almost see myself alone with a child from the team and could almost feel my hands rubbing slowly over his body. It terrified me. I've put so much work into my treatment only to be plagued by those fantasies again. Even though you said it was bound to happen, I guess I really didn't believe it until it did; but since I had heard that there was the possibility that the fantasies would come back, I wasn't decimated. The first thing I did was tell myself to relax. I started telling myself, "This doesn't mean you're still a sex offender—you didn't know how to stop yourself from acting out the fantasies before, but you do now, so do it. There's a lot of difference between having a fantasy like mine and doing it for real—everybody has unacceptable fantasies; the only difference between most people and sex offenders is that most people don't act out their unacceptable fantasies. I used to fantasize most when I was angry at someone, I'd better check to see if I'm angry now and deal with that. I'll have to be especially careful with my behavior when I'm angry, make sure to avoid places where children may be . . . ." These self-statements and ideas worked. I began to feel less anxious. I handled the crisis. I've learned the skills well enough to apply them once. I know I need to keep working on the skills so I can handle myself even better.

Decision Matrix.   A decision matrix is designed in order to help the client evaluate both the immediate and the delayed effects of performing another sexually aggressive act. In creating a decision matrix, the client is presented with a three-way table ($2 \times 2 \times 2$ matrix) in which the following factors are listed: the decision to perform a sexually aggressive act or to refrain from doing so; the immediate and delayed consequences of each decision; and, within each of the former categories, the positive and negative effects involved (see Figure 11-3). The client and the therapist work together to fill in each of the eight cells of the matrix, listing the effects which the client feels would have the greatest impact. The client should assign numerical ratings to each of the positive and negative outcomes listed to illustrate their relative importance. All effects that the client regards as important should be listed in the matrix, whether or not the therapist agrees with the client's choices. However, we demand that all decision matrices contain factors regarding the harm that a sexually aggressive act inflicts on the victim. We provide the client with a wallet-sized copy of his decision matrix and instruct him to review it, focusing on the delayed effects, whenever a fantasy or urge to perform a sexually aggressive behavior is detected.

Cognitive Restructuring.   The principal aim of cognitive restructuring is to counteract the self-deprecating cognitive and affective components of the abstinence violation effect (AVE) that are felt whenever the client lapses into a fantasy of sexual aggression. Instead of reacting to the first lapse as an indication of personal failure, characterized by guilt, conflict, and internal attribution (e.g., "This just goes to prove that I really am going to be a lifelong sex offender"), the client is taught to reconceptualize the episode as a single, independent event—to see it as a mistake rather than as a sign that he has permanently crossed over the border from being in absolute control to being absolutely out of control. Rather than viewing a slip as a disastrous failure in his self-control program, the client should regard a slip as an important indicator of progress: each lapse is a mistake, an event that teaches him something about how to handle similar situations in the future.

| | IMMEDIATE | | DELAYED | |
	POSITIVE	NEGATIVE	POSITIVE	NEGATIVE
TO REFRAIN	1. Increased Self-Efficacy 2. Social Approval 3. Respect of Children 4. Affection of Wife 5. No Harm to Another	1. Denial of Gratification 2. Momentary Anger 3. Frustration	1. Enhanced Self-control 2. Increased Social Approval 3. Affection of Wife 4. Enhanced Friendship 5. Avoidance of Jail 6. Freedom from Treatment	1. Denial of Gratification 2. Residual Anger (which becomes less in time)
TO PERFORM	1. Immediate Gratification 2. Release of Anger	1. Guilt 2. Social Censure 3. Loss of Self-respect 4. Harm to Victim 5. Risk of Injury 6. Possibly Getting Caught	1. Continued Gratification	1. Guilt 2. Social Censure 3. Loss of Self-respect 4. Identity of Offender 5. Lasting Harm to Victim 6. Loss of Children 7. Loss of Wife 8. Embarrassment of Relatives 9. Imprisonment

Figure 11-3.   Decision matrix.

The cognitive restructuring process is designed to lessen the negative aspects of the AVE which increase the likelihood of a single lapse into unacceptable fantasies precipitating a series of sexually aggressive behaviors. In addition to instructions to view each lapse as an independent event and an opportunity for increased success, the client is told to review the interacting forces of the environmental precursors (to detect high-risk factors) and the availability of an effective coping behavior; he is encouraged to employ problem-solving techniques to derive an effective coping response when his repertoire does not contain a situation-appropriate behavior.

The client is informed that he probably will experience at least some degree of guilt after the initial lapse. Guilt reactions are extremely dangerous since they exacerbate distress which may motivate the client to emit a sexually aggressive behavior in a maladaptive attempt to cope. Clients are taught that guilty feelings are to be expected after a lapse, that these feelings are natural consequences to a transgression, and that they will subside after a relatively short time (as long as clients do not reinforce them by relapsing). Knowing that the guilt will rapidly decay and eventually disappear makes it easier to tolerate the feelings without undue consequences.

Global Treatment Components

In addition to the very specific skills training such as programmed coping responses and cognitive restructuring in response to high-risk situations, there are also more global intervention techniques which a therapist may introduce in order to prevent relapse.

Life-style Intervention.   All of us at one time or another have experienced what can best be described as an unbalanced life-style: a seemingly endless list of demands which must be met, generally to the exclusion of more pleasurable activities. When the offender finds himself overburdened with various responsibilities and obligations at work and at home, the result is generally twofold: an insidious increase in stress and a nagging feeling that he is "losing control" or is a "victim of circumstances." This particular belief sets a devastating stage for the potential sexual aggressor. In his desperate attempt to release some of his pent-up feelings of anger and hostility or to prove that he can control some aspect of his life (e.g., the interaction with his victim), he strikes out in a sexually aggressive manner. Concomitant with these behaviors is a feeling of justification; the offender rationalizes his behavior by saying things such as, "I deserve a little satisfaction after all I have done for my boss, my wife, friends, kids . . . ."

It is necessary to keep an unbalanced life-style from getting out of control. One way to achieve this is through life-style intervention. The first step is to work with the client in assessing the level of deprivation he feels. To this end, the client is asked to keep a record of all his daily activities. How much of his time is spent doing obligatory chores, following orders, performing menial tasks at work, doing favors for friends? If a great deal more time is spent on these kinds of obligations than on activities from which the client derives satisfaction and pleasure, this could signal a potential risk for relapse. With this knowledge in mind, the therapist and the client can work together to create a more balanced life-style. The client should be encouraged to set aside time for himself to "indulge" in alternate behaviors which are socially acceptable.

Relaxation Training. It is important for the therapist to understand the distressful sense of powerlessness and the perceived lack of control which the sexual aggressor harbors. A second global intervention, relaxation training, can be used in conjunction with the life-style intervention to help the client cope with these feelings. Relaxation training diminishes stress responses, enhances one's sense of self-control, and facilitates utilization of several of the assessment and skill training procedures described previously (e.g., relapse fantasies, relapse rehearsal).

The issue of perceived self-control can be a prominent issue in conducting relaxation training with sexual aggressives. Since this may be the client's first exposure to relaxation induced by another's instructions, he may initially find the procedure and the concomitant alterations in somatic perception to be anxiety provoking. In order to circumvent the client's fears concerning lack of control, vulnerability, and perceptual changes, these issues should be discussed before attempting a relaxation induction. Stress that the procedure is simply a learning experience: he previously has learned to become anxious and tense, but he is now going to learn how to make himself relax. Emphasize that rather than signifying an inability to control himself, achieving relaxation will denote an increased skill of self-control. Describe the unusual sensations of floating and tingling that accompany the onset of relaxation. Assure the client that these feelings do not mean that he is losing control, but that he is making progress toward the goal of relaxation.

Since it is often difficult to practice novel behaviors in the real world, relaxation is used to facilitate covert rehearsal of newly acquired skills (e.g., relapse rehearsal). Once the client becomes relaxed, guided imagery may be employed to simulate high-risk situations and adaptive coping strategies. After developing relaxation skills in the treatment setting, the client should be encouraged to practice the procedure on his own as a safe and therapeutic way of managing stress and enhancing a sense of self-control over his behaviors.

Power Substitutes. For some of these individuals, the issue of power is paramount; for this group, power substitutes can provide a needed sense of mastery. It is important that these activities avoid competition with other individuals since the possibility exists that intense competition can result in a heightened sense of vulnerability, frustration, and lack of power. Activities such as jogging, body building, weight lifting, skiing, or sailing feature competition with oneself, gradual improvement, and exhilarating evidence that one is in command.

CONCLUSION

Relapse prevention is a systematic assessment and treatment program designed to provide sexually aggressive individuals with cognitive and behavioral skills which will reduce the probability of another offense. The model enhances maintenance of changes that have been induced by other treatments (e.g., antiandrogenic medication). By employing this approach, the short-term behavior changes occurring during therapy may finally last long enough to become old habits.

No final therapy session occurs under the relapse prevention model of treatment. Clients who believe that their treatment ends with the termination of formal therapy have never learned the premise underlying the relapse prevention model of maintenance. If the client has learned the component skills and applies them, he will continue his own therapy sessions every day of his life.

We currently are attempting to locate individuals who have performed sexually aggressive acts, but who have managed to avoid repetition of such behavior without benefit of treatment. By identifying common mechanisms which these people have used to prevent a relapse into sexual aggression, the relapse prevention maintenance model may be validated and refined.

REFERENCES

1. Marlatt, G.A. and Gordon, J.R. Determinants of relapse: Implications for the maintenance of behavior change. In Davidson, P., and Davidson, S. (Eds.) *Behavioral Medicine: Changing Health Lifestyles*. New York: Brunner/Mazel, 1980.
2. Pithers, W.D., Marques, J.K., Gibat, C.C., and Marlatt, G.A. Sexual aggression: just another bad habit? (submitted for publication).
3. Miller, W.R. The addictive behaviors. In Miller, W.R. (Ed.) *The Addictive Behaviors: Treatment of Alcoholism, Drug Abuse, Smoking, and Obesity*. New York: Pergamon Press, 1980.
4. Groth, A.N. *Men Who Rape: The Psychology of the Offender*. New York: Plenum Press, 1979.
5. Group for the Advancement of Psychiatry. *Psychiatry and Sex Psychopath Legislation: The 30's to the 80's*. New York: Group for the Advancement of Psychiatry, 1977.
6. Nay, W.R. *Multimethod Clinical Assessment*. New York: Gardner Press, 1979.
7. Chaney, E.F., O'Leary, M.R., and Marlatt, G.A. Skill training with alcoholics. *Journal of Consulting and Clinical Psychology* **46**:1092-1104 (1978).
8. Wolfe, J. and Baker, V. Characteristics of imprisoned rapists and circumstances of the rape. In Warner, C.G. (Ed.) *Rape and Sexual Assault: Management and Intervention*. Germantown, Md.: Aspen Systems Corporation, 1980.
9. Meichenbaum, D. and Cameron, R. The clinical potential of modifying what clients say to themselves. In Mahoney, M.J. and Thoresen, C.E. (Eds.) *Self-control: Power to the Person*. Monterey, Calif.: Brooks/Cole, 1974.
10. Liberman, R.P., King, L.W., DeRisi, W.J., and McCann, M.J. *Personal Effectiveness: Guiding People to Assert Their Feelings and Improve Their Social Skills*. Champaign, Ill.: Research Press, 1976.

12

Sequelae of Sexual Assault: The Survivor's Perspective*

Judith V. Becker, Ph.D.,
Linda J. Skinner, Ph.D.,
and Gene G. Abel, M.D.

Anecdotal reports and early research studies suggest that four areas of a woman's life which may be significantly affected by a sexual assault are depression level, fear level, sexual functioning, and interpersonal relationships. The goal of this study was to investigate the impact of a sexual assault by comparing samples of sexual assault survivors (n = 181) and women with no history of sexual assault (n = 79) in these four areas. In addition, the survivors' current levels of functioning in these areas were examined in relation to particular survivor characteristics and time elapsed since the most recent assault. The results indicated that compared to the nonassaulted women, the sexual assault survivors were significantly more depressed, had higher levels of fear, were more likely to have sexual problems, and reported greater dissatisfaction with their sexual partner relationships. Analyses of only the survivors revealed that the survivor characteristic of having sexual problems was significantly related to fear and depression levels, and dissatisfaction with partner relationships. The only significant change found in relation to time elapsed since most recent assault was the dissipation of some fears. Procedures for assessing depression and fear levels, sexual functioning, and satisfaction with partner relationship are discussed.

For the last 40 years, rape has had the greatest increase in comparison to all other crimes.[1] In 1979, almost 76,000 rapes were reported to the police,[2] and this statistic does not include the crimes of child molestation and incest. A retrospective survey of 1200 college-aged females revealed that 26% had had a sexual experience with an adult before they were 13 years old.[3] During a ten-year period in Hennipen County, Minnesota, there were almost four times as many reports of sexual abuse of children as reports of physical abuse.[4] Woodbury and Schwartz

---

*The term "survivor" rather than "victim" is used throughout this chapter in deference to the sensitivities of women who have already been made to suffer feelings of extreme helplessness. The authors do not want to risk, even remotely, contributing to the perpetuation of these feelings. The term is to be understood as having no implications whatever for a probability of death associated with sexual assault.

suggest that 10% of all Americans have been involved in incestuous experiences.[5] Yet, since sexual assaults are considered some of the most underreported crimes, the actual incidences of these offenses are unknown. These data demonstrate that the magnitude of the sexual assault problem is great. However, the effects of such an assault on a survivor are only beginning to be investigated. To date, the greater focus has been on the short-term effects of sexual assault. However, increasing attention is being directed at its long-term impact.

Regardless of the focus, many studies investigating the impact of an assault on a survivor share the following methodological problems: (a) sampling procedures are inadequately described; (b) small samples have been studied; (c) standardized tests have not been used; and (d) a comparison group of women with no history of sexual assault has not been included. Despite these limitations, existing research suggests that there are at least four major areas of a woman's life that may be significantly affected by a sexual assault. These areas are depression level, fear level, sexual functioning, and interpersonal relationships.

Depression Level

Depression is frequently noted in sexual assault survivors immediately following the assault.[6-13] Using the Beck Depression Inventory to assess depression level in 34 recent rape survivors, Frank, Turner, and Duffy found that 44% were moderately or severely depressed.[14] Furthermore, a closer examination of those 15 women indicated that 53% were experiencing a major depressive disorder.

While depression may be transient in nature, a long-term follow-up study of rape survivors conducted by Atkeson, Calhoun, Resick, and Ellis revealed that depression in sexual assault survivors may persist for months after the assault.[15] Depression levels of a group of survivors and a matched control group of non-assaulted women were significantly different up to four months following the assaults of the survivors. In addition, a number of the survivors continued to exhibit depressive symptoms 12 months after an assault.

As this study demonstrated, depression may be a long-term effect of sexual assault. To date, no study has focused on the presence of depressive symptomatology in sexual assault survivors more than one year following the assault.

Fear Level

Perhaps one of the most frequent sequelae of a sexual assault is fear.[6,10,11,13,16-19] A woman who experiences a life-threatening situation over which she has little or no control, such as a sexual assault, may develop phobic reactions or fears, and previous fears may be exacerbated subsequent to the episode. For some women, the new fears may be specific to the assault situation. A woman raped in a stairwell may fear public stairways, while a woman assaulted in a car may avoid riding in a car with male passengers. Other fears experienced subsequent to a sexual assault may be related to assault in general rather than to a woman's specific assault situation. While many women may be apprehensive about potential assault situations, sexual assault survivors may be particularly sensitive to the danger of such situations.

Kilpatrick, Best, and Veronen have proposed that fears of sexual assault survivors are learned through classical conditioning.[9] According to their social learning theory model, the assault itself is an unconditioned stimulus that evokes fear in the survivor. Cues or stimuli associated with the assault situation become conditioned to evoke similar fear in the woman.

Predictions following from this model include: (a) survivors have greater fear levels than nonassaulted women; (b) the greatest fears of survivors focus on assault-related cues; and (c) avoidance behaviors of survivors allow the fears to endure.[16] Support for these hypotheses has been reported. Kilpatrick, Veronen, and Resick found that sexual assault survivors had significantly greater fear levels than nonassaulted women.[10] These same authors reported that most of the elevated fears of survivors were related to the sexual assault situation or cues of potential assault.[16]

The results of a one-year follow-up study of rape survivors indicate that fear scores of survivors diminished somewhat as time since the assault increased.[20] However, even at one year postassault, the survivors had a greater level of self-reported fear than did a group of women with no history of sexual assault. Follow-up studies of the fears of sexual assault survivors, more than one year postassault, have not been reported.

Sexual Functioning

The sexual assault literature includes numerous comments on the actual or possible consequences that an assault may have on a survivor's sexual functioning.[6,9,11,21-26] The assault-related disruption in sexual functioning can be short- or long-term.

Studying rape survivors for up to 48 weeks after their assault, Ellis, Calhoun, and Atkeson found that some disruption of sexual functioning was experienced by 61% of the women immediately postassault.[27] While sexual activity had returned to normal for most of the women within four to six months after the assault, up to 20% of the survivors reported having sexual problems as long as one year following the assault.

Feldman-Summers, Gordon, and Meagher found that a group of sexual assault survivors, assaulted from two months to seven years previously, compared with a sample of nonassaulted women, did not differ in frequency of sexual activity or orgasms.[28] However, the survivors reported that their sexual satisfaction had diminished significantly since their assaults. Additionally, the postassault sexual satisfaction of the survivors was significantly less than that reported by the nonassaulted women.

Interviews with 81 rape survivors four to six years following their assaults revealed that 37% of the women felt that their sexual functioning had returned to normal within months of their assaults, while another 37% indicated that their length of recovery was years.[29] The remaining 26% felt they had not yet recovered sexually.

Only one study that categorized the types of sexual problems experienced by a sample of sexual assault survivors has been reported in the literature.[30] Of the 83 women interviewed, 34 indicated that they were experiencing sexual problems that were caused by their assaults. The most frequent types of sexual problems experienced were fear of sex, arousal dysfunction, and desire dysfunction. A study investigating the types of sexual problems experienced by sexual assault survivors versus nonassaulted women has not been reported to date.

Interpersonal Relationships

While the impact a sexual assault can have on the interpersonal relationships of a survivor has been overlooked somewhat, the results of one study indicate that survivors experience disruption in their overall social adjustment immediately postassault and that this disruption continues for several months.[31] One relationship that may be particularly vulnerable to such disruption is the sexual partner relationship. Partners who are told about the assault frequently find it difficult to offer support to the survivor.[32] The reaction of the partner is a combination of empathy, anger, guilt, and misunderstandings about sexual assault. Since a survivor may want to depend upon her partner for support in coping with the assault, a partner response that is less than supportive and empathetic may be viewed particularly negatively by the survivor and can result in severe disruption of the relationship.

Disruption of the partner relationship may occur even if a survivor elects not to disclose her assault to her partner. The emotional sequelae experienced by the survivor may interfere with her ability to interact with her partner, and lack of knowledge about the assault may cause the partner to respond negatively to the survivor's "mysterious" behavior.

To assist the survivor in recovering from her assault, it may be advisable to include her partner in postassault counseling whenever feasible.[32] However, it is first necessary to delineate the impact a sexual assault may have on a survivor's sexual partner relationship.

The purpose of this chapter is to examine the long-term consequences that a sexual assault may have on the four areas of a survivor's life discussed above. The results presented were drawn from work conducted at the Victim Treatment and Research Clinic at Columbia University in New York City.

THE VICTIM TREATMENT AND RESEARCH CLINIC

The Victim Treatment and Research Clinic was established to investigate the long-term impact of sexual assault on a survivor; it is open to women who are at least 18 years of age and have experienced at least one sexual assault involving physical contact between the assailant and the woman. A survivor's most recent assault must have occurred at least two months prior to her participation at the clinic. In addition, a sample of women who have no history of sexual assault is being seen to serve as a comparison group for the sexual assault survivors. The only requirements for the women serving as control subjects are that they be at least 18 years of age and never have been assaulted sexually.

When a sexual assault survivor or a nonassaulted woman is seen at the clinic, she participates in a three-hour testing and interview session. Tests administered assess depression and fear levels, sexual interests and activities, and quality of partner relationship. A structured interview format is followed to obtain information about a woman's personal background and sexual history. A narrative sexual assault history is obtained from each survivor. Each woman is paid $10 for her participation in the interview session.

To date, 200 sexual assault survivors and 80 nonassaulted women have been seen at the clinic. Preliminary data are available for 181 of the survivors and 79 of

Table 12-1. Referral Sources and Reasons for Participation for Sexual Assault Survivors and Nonassaulted Women.

	GROUP		
	ASSAULT SURVIVORS ($n = 181$)	NONASSAULTED WOMEN ($n = 79$)	χ^{2}*
Referral source			63.47[#]
Media	56.9%	26.6%	
Clinical	30.4%	13.9%	
Staff members	6.1%	17.7%	
Other	6.6%	41.8%	
Reason for participation†			
Help self‡	63.5%	33.3%	20.05[#]
Help others	40.9%	16.5%	14.74[‖]
Increase knowledge about			
sexual assault†	17.1%	9.9%	2.89
Sexual problems	0.0%	0.0%	—§
Other‡	16.0%	61.5%	54.06[#]

*For referral source d.f. = 3, and for reason for participation, d.f. = 1.
†Women could identify multiple reasons for participation.
‡For nonassaulted women, $n = 78$.
§χ^{2} cannot be computed.
‖$p < .005$.
#$p < .001$.

the nonassaulted women. Nineteen of the sexual assault survivors were excluded from the data analysis as they had been referred to the clinic specifically because of sexual problems.

The referral sources and reasons for participation for the sexual assault survivors and the nonassaulted women are presented in Table 12-1. Understandably, the two groups of women differed significantly on both of these variables. Sexual assault survivors were more responsive to media notices about the clinic and more likely to be referred by other clinical agencies, such as mental health clinics or rape crisis counseling programs. The nonassaulted women's participation at the clinic frequently was the result of hearing about the research project from friends who had participated in it. Similarly, the participation of the sexual assault survivors was most frequently prompted by a desire to receive help, whereas the nonassaulted women identified the money paid to all women who were interviewed as the primary reason for their participation.

A summary of the background characteristics for the sexual assault survivors and the nonassaulted women is presented in Table 12-2. The two groups did not differ significantly with regard to racial composition or partner status. However, the nonassaulted women were significantly older than the sexual assault survivors,

Table 12-2. Summary of Background Characteristics for Sexual Assault survivors and Nonassaulted Women.

	GROUP	
CHARACTERISTIC	ASSAULT SURVIVORS ($n = 181$)	NONASSAULTED WOMEN ($n = 79$)
Age		
Mean	29.59	32.06
Standard deviation	7.40	9.75
Range	18 to 67	19 to 74
Race		
Caucasian	79.0%	77.2%
Black	13.8%	19.0%
Hispanic	7.2%	2.5%
Oriental	0.0%	1.3%
Partner status		
Single	54.1%	46.8%
Married/living with partner	30.9%	43.0%
Separated/divorced/widowed	14.9%	10.1%
Years of education*		
Mean	14.96	16.24
Standard deviation	2.82	2.87
Range	9 to 24	10 to 24

*For sexual assault survivors, $n = 180$.

separate variance estimate t (118.88) $= -2.01, p < .05$, and had a significantly higher educational level, t (257) $= 3.36, p < .005$.

Sexual Assault Histories

The 181 survivors had experienced a total of 417 sexual assaults, with the number of assaults per woman ranging from 1 to 12. Fifty-nine percent of the women had experienced two or more assaults, $M = 2.30$. The actual number of assaults is underestimated since any series of three or more assaults perpetrated by the same assailant against one woman was counted as one ongoing assault. With 34.8% of the survivors experiencing ongoing assaults, multiple incestuous and marital assaults are not fully represented in the total number.

The length of time since the most recent sexual assault of each survivor ranged from 3 months to 40 years. A mean of 7.93 years had elapsed since the most recent assault, and at least 10 years had passed for 26.4% of the survivors.

A summary of assault characteristics for the 128 survivors of one or two assaults is presented in Table 12-3. For each characteristic, the data for women who had been assaulted twice were collapsed across both assaults. Women who had experienced more than two assaults were excluded as detailed information was collected for the first and the most recent assaults only.

THE IMPACT OF SEXUAL ASSAULT

A similar series of analyses was conducted to assess the long-term impact of a sexual assault on each of the four specified areas. The comparisons made and underlying hypotheses are presented below.

Sexual Assault Survivors versus Nonassaulted Women

To substantiate the negative impact of a sexual assault, 181 sexual assault survivors and 79 women with no sexual assault history were compared on the measures administered. It was hypothesized that the sexual assault survivors would be experiencing significantly more problems than the nonassaulted women.

Survivor Characteristics

Four specific sexual assault survivor characteristics were examined separately.

Number of Assaults Experienced.   If experiencing a sexual assault has a deleterious effect on the woman, it was hypothesized that being a survivor of multiple assaults would exacerbate any assault-related problems. To test this hy-

Table 12-3. Assault Characteristics for Survivors of One or Two Sexual Assaults.*

CHARACTERISTIC	
Age at first assault†	
Mean	14.39
Standard deviation	6.97
Range	1 to 29
Age at most recent assault‡	
Mean	21.38
Standard deviation	9.85
Range	1 to 57
Assault was first sexual experience	32.8%
Type of assailant	
Stranger	34.4%
Known	43.8%
Stranger and known	21.1%
Vaginal, oral, and/or anal penetration	88.3%
Ongoing assault	28.9%
Greatest degree of aggression used	
Verbal	16.4%
Physical	39.8%
Excessive physical	41.4%
Weapon used	43.8%
Assaulted in own home	53.9%
Reported at least one assault to the police	54.7%

*Relative percentages for an n of 128 are presented as information for some women is missing.
†Includes only women with two assaults, $n = 51$.
‡$n = 126$.

pothesis, the sexual assault survivors were divided into three groups: (a) those experiencing one assault, $n = 75$; (b) those experiencing two assaults, $n = 53$; and (c) those experiencing three or more assaults, $n = 53$.

Emotional and/or Psychiatric Problems Prior to Assault. Each survivor was asked if she had emotional and/or psychiatric problems in excess of the problems typically experienced by most people and if these problems predated her sexual assault. Of the 181 survivors, 59.7% reported that they had such preassault problems. Two women provided no information about prior problems. To investigate any possible relationship between preassault and postassault problems, survivors with and without emotional and/or psychiatric problems predating their sexual assault were compared.

Rape versus Incest versus Rape and Incest Survivors.   Since the assault characteristics and dynamics of rape versus incest may be very different, the two types of assault may have varying effects on the survivors. To test this hypothesis, rape ($n = 117$), incest ($n = 20$), and rape and incest survivors ($n = 39$) were contrasted. Some women were excluded from these comparisons since the necessary data for classification were not available.

Sexually Functional versus Dysfunctional Survivors.   Multiple problems following an assault are experienced by many sexual assault survivors. As noted previously and discussed in detail in a subsequent section, one problem common to many assault survivors is interference with sexual functioning. To test the hypothesis that assault-related sexually dysfunctional survivors ($n = 68$) experience additional problems of greater severity than do sexually functional survivors ($n = 80$), these two groups were compared.

Time since Most Recent Assault

Since some of the problems experienced subsequent to an assault may be transient in nature or dissipate as time since assault increases, the data were analyzed in relation to time elapsed since the most recent assault. The sexual assault survivors were divided into three groups according to the number of years since their most recent assault. The groups were: (a) less than one year, $n = 28$; (b) one to three years, $n = 42$; and (c) more than three years, $n = 111$. In the third group, the mean number of years since the most recent assault was more than 12.00, and ranged from 3 to 40 years.

DEPRESSION AND SEXUAL ASSAULT SURVIVORS

Cathy, a 30-year-old teacher, was waiting alone late one night at a bus stop when she heard a noise in some nearby bushes. She started to walk away from the source of the noise when an unknown man grabbed her and told her he would hurt her if she said anything. Cathy attempted to resist physically, but the man pushed her to the ground and knocked her unconscious. When she regained consciousness, she was cut and bruised. She found that she had been raped vaginally and robbed of her purse.

When she returned home, Cathy asked her uncle, a police officer, for advice about reporting the assault. The uncle indicated that he did not want it known at the precinct that his niece had been raped so she did not report the assault. Cathy did not seek medical attention until some small cuts on her chest, apparently inflicted during the assault by some kind of weapon, had become infected.

Cathy reports that since the rape she is extremely fearful and feels unable to cope. Interactions with men are particularly difficult for her and affecting her work, where she has a new male supervisor.

Cathy indicates that she is experiencing severe appetite changes marked by overeating and has gained over 50 pounds since the assault. She is having sleep disturbances and recurring nightmares in which people she knows change into monsters. She is uncomfortable around people and less assertive than she was prior to the assault. Feelings of helplessness permeate her daily activities. Cathy continues to feel rage, guilt, and shame about the rape. Additionally, she has a nervous stomach, feels extremely nervous, and is severely depressed.

Difficulty in coping with daily activities and feelings of helplessness, ineffectiveness, and guilt are symptomatic of the loss of control experienced by many sexual assault survivors. While other life experiences precipitate such reactions, these difficulties are particularly prevalent among sexual assault survivors, as evidenced in a comparison of the frequency of such symptoms in the sexual assault survivors and nonassaulted women seen at the Victim Treatment and Research Clinic. Each survivor was asked if she had continuously experienced particular symptoms since her most recent assault, while each nonassaulted woman was asked if she had had such symptoms in the six months prior to her interview at the clinic. Table 12-4 presents a summary of these data.

As can be seen, a greater number of sexual assault survivors were experiencing difficulties indicative of depression than were the nonassaulted women. The increased depression experienced by many sexual assault survivors was apparent in the finding that 54.5% of the 178 survivors, as compared to only 7.8% of the nonassaulted women, indicated that they were experiencing severe depression, $\chi^2 (1) = 48.69, p < .001$.

Table 12-4.   Frequency of Symptoms Associated with Depression in Sexual Assault Survivors and Nonassaulted Women.

| | GROUP | | | | |
| | ASSAULT SURVIVORS | | NONASSAULTED WOMEN | | |
SYMPTOM	n	%	n	%	$\chi^2(1)$
Headaches or other physical symptoms	178	36.5	79	22.8	4.72*
Appetite-changes	179	41.3	79	25.3	6.08*
Work-related difficulties	165	41.2	79	21.5	9.13†
Nervous stomach	164	38.4	79	16.5	11.96‡
Sleep disturbances	179	53.6	79	26.6	16.18‡
Guilt	167	52.1	79	24.1	17.20‡
Nightmares	180	51.7	79	19.0	24.12‡
Feelings of helplessness	167	59.3	79	19.0	35.02‡
Shame	165	53.3	79	11.4	39.24‡
Sexual problems	180	60.6	79	8.9	59.33‡

*p = .05.
†p = .01.
‡p = .001.

As these results illustrate, a sexual assault survivor may become depressed subsequent to her assault. Consequently, assessment of the problems experienced by a sexual assault survivor should include screening for possible depression.

The Assessment of Depression

An objective measure such as the Beck Depression Inventory can be used to assess depression level.[33] This self-administered, paper-and-pencil inventory has 21 items covering common symptoms of depression. Each item is followed by four statements reflecting increasing depression. A respondent is instructed to mark which of the four statements is indicative of how she/he feels at the present time. An overall depression score is obtained by adding the scores across all of the items. Higher scores indicate greater depression. The inventory requires only five minutes to complete.

The Impact of Sexual Assault on Depression Level

The Beck Depression Inventory (BDI) is included in the battery of tests administered to all women seen at the Victim Treatment and Research Clinic. In the series of analyses of BDI scores conducted and reported below, those who failed to answer all of the items on the inventory were excluded.

Sexual Assault Survivors versus Nonassaulted Women.   Since these two groups of women differed significantly in age and education level, and since BDI scores were significantly related to race, $r = -.27, p < .001$, adjustments for these variables were made in the comparison of depression levels for these two groups.

The distributions of assault survivors and nonassaulted women across severity levels of depression as determined by the BDI are presented in Table 12-5. More than 50% of the survivors were at least mildly depressed as compared to less than 12% of the nonassaulted women.

Table 12-5.   Severity Levels of Depression as Determined by the BDI for Sexual Assault Survivors and Nonassaulted Women.

| | | GROUP | |
| | | ASSAULT SURVIVORS ($n = 177$) | NONASSAULTED WOMEN ($n = 79$) |
SCORE	SEVERITY		
0–9	Normal	49.7%	88.6%
10–15	Mildly depressed	17.5%	6.3%
16–23	Moderately depressed	14.1%	3.8%
24+	Severely depressed	18.6%	1.3%

To determine if the assault survivors and nonassaulted women differed significantly in their depression levels, a hierarchical regression analysis with age, education level, and race as covariates was performed on the BDI scores to produce analysis of covariance results.[34] A significant educational level by group interaction was found, F (10,245) = 5.25, $p < .01$. BDI scores were negatively related to educational level for the survivors and positively related for the nonassaulted women.

Educational level was recoded as a deviation score from the grand mean, and the analysis was repeated. The subsequent overall F (5,249) = 8.30 was significant at the $\alpha = .01$ criterion level. Significant main effects were found for educational deviation scores, F (1,249) = 5.53, $p < .05$, and the group variable (survivors versus nonassaulted women), F (1,249) = 41.50, $p < .01$. Thus, these results indicate that the women who had been sexually assaulted experienced significantly greater levels of depression than did the women who had no history of sexual assault.

Analyses with Assault Survivors Only.   The BDI scores of the survivors were significantly related to educational level, $r = -.25$, $p < .001$, and race, $r = .19$, $p < .01$. To adjust for these relationships, hierarchical regression analyses with educational level and race serving as covariates were performed to produce analysis of covariance results in all comparisons of survivors' BDI scores.

Survivor Characteristics.   Of the four characteristics considered, one was found to be related to depression.

Sexually Functional versus Dysfunctional Survivors.   The distributions of sexually functional and dysfunctional assault survivors across severity levels of depression as determined by the BDI are presented in Table 12-6.

With adjustments made for educational level and race, a comparison of BDI scores for sexually functional and dysfunctional survivors resulted in a significant

Table 12-6.   Severity Levels of Depression as Determined by the BDI for Sexually Functional and Dysfunctional Assault Survivors.

		GROUP	
		FUNCTIONAL SURVIVORS ($n = 78$)	DYSFUNCTIONAL SURVIVORS* ($n = 67$)
SCORE	SEVERITY		
0–9	Normal	66.7%	35.8%
10–15	Mildly depressed	16.7%	16.4%
16–23	Moderately depressed	10.3%	14.9%
24+	Severely depressed	6.4%	32.8%

*These women reported that their sexual problems were related to their sexual assaults.

overall analysis of covariance, F (3,142) = 10.04, p < .01. Significant main effects were found for educational level, F (1,170) = 9.07, p < .01, and the sexual dysfunction variable, F (1,170) = 24.61, p < .01. These results indicate that the sexually functional survivors experienced significantly less depression, adjusted M = 8.85, than did the sexually dysfunctional survivors, adjusted M = 16.94, as measured by the BDI.

Time since Most Recent Assault.   While adjusted mean BDI scores decreased from 15.38 to 12.17 as the time since the most recent assault increased, the passage of time since the assault was not found to be significantly related to decreases in depression.

FEAR AND SEXUAL ASSAULT SURVIVORS

A 29-year-old attorney, Laura, was assaulted several years ago. She had just graduated from law school and was serving as a law clerk in a large city. One hot summer night she was alone in the house she shared with five other women when she went to bed wearing no clothes. At 1:30 A.M. she awoke to see a figure by her bed going through her wallet. Refusing to answer any of Laura's questions, the figure suddenly jumped on top of her. When Laura realized that the figure was not one of her roommates but rather a strange man, she began to struggle. However, when the man held a silvery metal object to her throat, Laura ceased resisting physically and attempted to talk her way out of the assault. The man told her to "shut up" with a foreign accent and then attempted unsuccessfully to penetrate her vaginally. After about 15 minutes he stopped and put her in the closet. When she could no longer hear the intruder and was certain he had left, Laura tried to call the police on the telephone in her bedroom but found that the cord had been cut. She did call the police on a second telephone in the house. The police escorted Laura to the hospital and told her where she could receive counseling.

The evening after the assault Laura flew home to stay with her parents and later moved to the Midwest. She tried to cut herself off from everything connected with the assault.

At the time of her interview, Laura indicated that she continues to experience great fears related to the assault and is very ashamed of her fears. She insists that she live on a high floor in a building with a doorman. She continues to feel compelled to check every room in her apartment before she locks the door. Every night she puts large boxes in front of her door to make it more difficult for an intruder to enter. Additionally, she insists upon having two telephones with lighted push-button dials in her apartment.

Laura said that all her activities are planned around safety issues. She feels she must be able to take taxicabs or she is unable to go somewhere. She has great difficulty sleeping alone in her apartment and continues to experience insomnia and nightmares. Additionally, regardless of how hot the weather, Laura is unable to sleep without clothes.

She has become very frightened of foreign men and is very uncomfortable passing them on the street. Laura continues to be more upset by street harassment than she has been in the past but finds it harder to respond assertively.

As the case history of Laura illustrates, a survivor of a sexual assault may develop numerous fears as a result of her assault. Such increased fear levels were apparent when sexual assault survivors and women with no sexual assault history seen at the Victim Treatment and Research Clinic were questioned as to whether or not they had fears frequently reported by sexual assault survivors. Table 12-7 presents a summary of these data.

Clearly, a greater number of sexual assault survivors than nonassaulted women reported having fears about situations in which a sexual assault may occur. The greater overall fear level of assault survivors was apparent in the finding that 63.7% of 179 survivors as compared to only 10.1% of the 79 nonassaulted women reported having significant generalized fears, χ^2 (1) = 63.08, $p < .005$.

These results indicate that a sexual assault survivor may experience one or more fears after her assault. Thus, a thorough assessment of an assault survivor should include the identification of fears she may be experiencing as a result of the assault.

The Assessment of Fear Levels

In addition to questioning a sexual assault survivor about any idiosyncratic fears she may have, an objective measure should be used to assess fear levels. One such measure is the Modified Fear Survey (MFS) reported by Veronen and Kilpatrick.[20] A modification of the Fear Survey Schedule developed by Wolpe and Lang[35] to

Table 12-7. Frequency of Fears for Sexual Assault Survivors and Nonassaulted Women.

| | GROUP | | | | |
| | ASSAULT SURVIVORS | | NONASSAULTED WOMEN | | |
	n	%	n	%	χ^{2*}
Walking on street at night	166	68.7	79	53.2	5.57†
Violence or harassment	168	72.6	79	51.9	10.28‡
Being alone	173	52.6	79	16.5	29.23‡
Men	170	64.1	79	15.2	51.69‡

*d.f. = 1.
†$p < .01$.
‡$p < .005$.

assess situations and items individuals find anxiety arousing or fear inducing, the MFS includes both rape-related and non-rape-related items and situations. Each item is rated on a scale of one to five reflecting the degree of fear produced by that item. A rating of one indicates that the item is not at all disturbing, while a rating of five indicates that the item is very disturbing. The 120-item survey can be completed in approximately 30 minutes.

Eight scores can be derived from the MFS. A total fear score is determined by summing the ratings for all of the items. In addition scores can be derived for the following subscales:

Animal Fears Subscale: Examples of the nine items on this subscale are crawling insects, dogs, and worms.

Tissue Damage Fears Subscale: Among the 19 items on this subscale are people who seem insane, human blood, and people with deformities.

Classical Fears Subscale: Examples of this 17-item subscale are automobiles, darkness, and sick people.

Social Fears Subscale: This 18-item subscale includes such items as speaking in public, tough-looking people, and being teased.

Miscellaneous Fears Subscale: Examples of this 11-item subscale are falling, strange shapes, and being in a strange place.

Fear of Failure Subscale: Among the 17 items on this subscale are being criticized, feeling disapproved of, and looking foolish.

Rape-related Fears Subscale: Examples of this 45-item subscale are parking lots, being in a car alone, and being on an elevator alone.

The Impact of Sexual Assault on Fear Levels

All women seen at the Victim Treatment and Research Clinic completed the Modified Fear Survey in order to assess their fear levels. Women who failed to answer all of the items on the MFS were excluded from the analyses of fear levels reported below.

Sexual Assault Survivors versus Nonassaulted Women.   Since these two groups differed significantly in age and educational level and the total fear score was significantly related to race, $r = .12$, $p < .05$, hierarchical regression analyses with age, educational level, and race serving as covariates were performed to produce analysis of covariance results.

The adjusted mean fear scores for the seven MFS subscales for the assault survivors and the nonassaulted women are presented in Figure 12-1. These two groups differed significantly not only in overall fear level, $F (1,232) = 38.78, p < .01$, but also on each of the subscales. These results indicate that the survivors had higher levels of rape-related fears, as well as non-rape-related, generalized fears than did the women with no history of sexual assault.

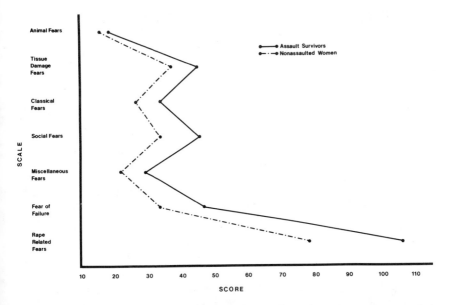

Figure 12-1.   Adjusted mean MFS subscale scores for sexual assault survivors and nonassaulted women.

Analyses with Assault Survivors Only.

The total fear scores of the survivors were significantly related to educational level, $r = -.21$, $p < .005$, and race, $r = .16$, $p < .05$. Thus, hierarchical regression analyses with educational level and race serving as covariates were performed to produce analysis of covariance results in all comparisons of survivors' MFS scores.

Survivor Characteristics.

Significant relationships were found between specific MFS subscales and all of the survivor characteristics considered. Additionally, overall fear level was related to the four characteristics.

Single versus Multiple Assault Survivors.   While the number of assaults experienced had no significant effect on overall fear level as measured by the MFS, this factor was related to the animal subscale. Women assaulted three or more times had a significantly greater adjusted mean score, $M = 19.80$, than did women who had been assaulted twice, adjusted $M = 15.99$, $F (1,156) = 7.07$, $p < .01$, but did not differ from women assaulted once, adjusted $M = 17.57$.

Prior Emotional and/or Psychiatric Problems.   As can be seen in Table 12-8, survivors with and without preassault emotional and/or psychiatric problems differed significantly on fear levels as measured by four of the seven MFS subscales and overall fear level. On each of these scales, women who reported experiencing

Table 12-8.   Adjusted Mean Fear Scores of Assault Survivors with and without Preassault Emotional and/or Psychiatric Problems.

| | GROUP | | |
SCALE	SURVIVORS WITHOUT ($n = 62$)	SURVIVORS WITH ($n = 97$)	F (1,154)
Animal fears	16.55	18.77	3.73
Tissue damage fears	40.74	47.06	9.65*
Classical fears	32.46	34.41	1.19
Social fears	41.52	47.59	7.03*
Miscellaneous fears	27.17	30.25	4.84†
Fear of failure	43.07	49.17	5.99†
Rape-related fears	100.42	110.26	3.79
Total	260.01	289.72	6.09†

†$p < .05$.
*$p < .01$.

emotional and/or psychiatric problems prior to their first sexual assault experienced greater levels of fear.

Rape versus Incest versus Rape and Incest Survivors.   This factor was related to two of the MFS subscales and the total fear score. As compared to the scores of rape survivors and rape and incest survivors, the scores of incest survivors were negatively related to educational level on the classical and rape-related fears subscales. Additionally, this same inverse relationship was found for incest survivors versus rape survivors on total fear score.

Sexually Functional versus Dysfunctional Survivors.   Comparisons of these two groups revealed that the sexually dysfunctional survivors experienced significantly greater levels of fear than the sexually functional survivors. Specifically, the dysfunctional survivors had more social fears, $F (1,127) = 6.32, p < .05$; a higher level of fear of failure, $F (1,127) = 6.86, p < .01$; and more rape-related fears, $F (1,127) = 4.31, p < .05$.

Time since Most Recent Assault.   Some of the fear levels as measured by the MFS were found to dissipate as time since the assault increased. While no such relationship was found for overall fear level, the passage of time had a significant effect on scores on the classical fears, $F (2,156) = 4.74, p < .01$, and rape-related fears subscales, $F (2,156) = 3.39, p < .05$. Women whose most recent sexual assault occurred more than three years ago had lower classical fear scores, adjusted $M = 31.60$, and rape-related fear scores, adjusted $M = 101.17$, than survivors who were assaulted less than one year ago, adjusted $M = 37.66$ and adjusted $M =$

117.56, respectively. However, the classical fear scores, adjusted $M = 36.36$, and the rape-related fear scores, adjusted $M = 111.57$, of women whose most recent assault occurred from one to three years previously did not differ significantly from the other two groups of survivors.

SEXUAL FUNCTIONING AND SEXUAL ASSAULT SURVIVORS

Alice, a 29-year-old administrative assistant, reported having a history of both physical and sexual abuse as a child. Her natural father was an alcoholic who physically abused her repeatedly. She was relieved when her mother divorced her father and she was free of his spankings and beatings.

When Alice was 11, her mother remarried and her stepfather began making sexual advances towards her. She eventually gained enough courage to tell her mother about the stepfather's behavior, but her mother refused to believe Alice. Unprotected by her mother, Alice was frequently abused by her stepfather. He repeatedly fondled her or forced her to perform fellatio on him. She was terrified by these assaults and relied on the most available means of protecting herself from them: she learned to withdraw her feelings and emotions.

This emotional withdrawal continued for four years. Her stepfather died when she was 15. However, by that age her withdrawal from people was well established. Never having been sexually involved with a male, Alice made the intellectual decision to have intercourse when she was 20. Lacking any dating skills, she elected to go to a bar to meet a man. She took him to her place. Initially, Alice wanted to have intercourse, but she changed her mind as she talked with the man. He refused to accept her saying no and raped her.

Three months later, Alice met the man she would eventually marry. Initially, she was quite aroused by him and engaged in sex with ease. However, she had no emotional feelings for him. They eventually married, and Alice began to develop warm feelings towards a man, her husband, for the first time in her life. Unfortunately, as their emotional closeness increased, she lost her sexual attraction to her husband. She began to realize that she could enjoy sex only with men for whom she had no feelings. Alice began withdrawing sexually from her husband, and fights about her lack of sexual responsiveness were frequent.

After three years of marriage, Alice began an affair that was purely physical and highly enjoyable for her. However, as time progressed, she developed stronger feelings for her lover and, as a result, she ended the affair. Shortly thereafter, the two began dating again but her partner maintained emotional distance from her. This lack of emotional attachment allowed Alice to continue a highly enjoyable sexual life with her lover.

Shortly before she was seen at the clinic, Alice separated from her husband. At that time she engaged in sex with a different man every night for a two-week period.

Alice describes herself as being the perfect sexual partner as she attends entirely to her partner's desires and does everything to make him happy. However, she does not focus on her own pleasure and what she likes. She is terrified and feels vulnerable when she even thinks about expressing caring feelings to her partner. Sex with unknown men poses no problem for her. With strangers she is able to perform easily and with much pleasure. However, Alice wants to be able to express caring and concern to men towards whom she has such feelings and also to enjoy sex with these same men.

Successful sexual activity requires a comfortable relationship with one's partner, low anxiety, skills at communicating to one's partner what is personally enjoyable and pleasurable, and comfort in providing for the sexual partner the type of sexual behavior he or she enjoys. However, as a result of her sexual assault, a survivor may feel that she no longer controls her own body. Fear may be associated with her genital organs, stimulation of genitalia, intimate contact with her body, sexual behavior, and sexual thoughts. It is not surprising, therefore, that a survivor's sexual functioning may be disrupted following a sexual assault.

The Assessment of Sexual Problems

Historically, the clinical interview has been the most frequently used method of assessing sexual problems.[36] Masters and Johnson were the first to propose the use of structured clinical interviews throughout the course of sexual dysfunction therapy.[37] The following guidelines for taking a sexual problem history preliminary to therapy were proposed by Annon.[38]

Description of Current Problem(s). The sexual assault survivor should be given the responsibility of determining what she considers to be a sexual problem and what is acceptable to her. For example, a survivor may indicate that she has no sexual desire but does not label this as a problem. While a lack of sexual desire may be perceived as a problem by others, the lack may be an important element in the recovery of the survivor.

The sexual problems reported by the women seen at the Victim Treatment and Research Clinic are placed in one of the following categories: fear of sex, desire dysfunction, arousal dysfunction, vaginismus, dyspareunia, primary nonorgasmia, secondary nonorgasmia, situational secondary nonorgasmia, or other sexual problems. A diagnosis of situational secondary nonorgasmia indicates that a woman is orgasmic in one situation, such as through oral sex, but not in another situation, perhaps through penile-vaginal intercourse. The other sexual problems category includes various sexual difficulties such as less frequent or intense orgasms or assault flashbacks during sexual interactions.

Onset and Course of Problem(s).   A woman should be asked when she began experiencing her sexual problem(s), and to delineate the onset and course of the problem(s).

Cause and Maintenance of Problem(s).   Treatment needs can be identified by having the survivor clarify what she sees as the causes of the problems and the factors that maintain her sexual difficulties.

Previous Treatment and Outcome.   It is important to have the woman explain the types of treatment that she has received for her sexual problems and the outcome of that treatment.

Current Expectations and Goals of Treatment.   Once again, the survivor should specify her treatment expectations and goals. Allowing the survivor to identify her needs is of paramount importance since she needs to gain a feeling of control over her life.

The Impact of Sexual Assault on Sexual Functioning

The guidelines described above are followed in obtaining a sexual problem history from each woman seen at the clinic. Each sexual assault survivor who is experiencing a sexual problem is asked if she believes that the problem is directly related to her assault. In the results presented below, sexually dysfunctional survivors who indicated that their sexual problems were not related to their assaults or were unable to identify any such relationship were excluded.

Sexual Assault Survivors versus Nonassaulted Women.   Nine of the women with no history of sexual assault and 68 of the assault survivors indicated that they were experiencing at least one sexual problem. Multiple sexual problems were more prevalent among the survivors. As compared to only 33.3% of the nonassaulted women, 60.3% of the survivors reported having two or more sexual problems.

The types and incidence of sexual problems reported by the two groups of women are presented in Table 12-9. With 89.7% of the survivors having at least one of the response inhibitory problems as compared to only 44.4% of the nonassaulted women, this category of sexual problems was significantly more common among the survivors, χ^2 (1) = 12.38, p < .001. In contrast, other sexual problems were more frequently reported by the dysfunctional nonassaulted women (66.7%) than by the assault-related dysfunctional survivors (7.5%), χ^2 (1) = 22.47, p < .001.

Table 12-9.   Types and Incidences of Sexual Problems of Sexually Dysfunctional Assault Survivors and Nonassaulted Women.*

| SEXUAL PROBLEM | GROUP | | $\chi^2(1)$ |
	ASSAULT SURVIVORS ($n = 68$)	NONASSAULTED WOMEN ($n = 9$)	
Response inhibitory problems			
Fear of sex	57.4%	11.1%	6.81‖
Desire dysfunction	55.9%	11.1%	6.37§
Arousal dysfunction	45.6%	22.2%	1.77
Orgasmic problems			
Situational secondary			
nonorgasmia†	10.4%	22.2%	1.05
Secondary nonorgasmia	7.4%	0.0%	.71
Primary nonorgasmia	4.4%	11.1%	.72
Intromission problems			
Dyspareunia†	10.4%	0.0%	1.04
Vaginismus	0.0%	0.0%	—‡
Other problems†	7.5%	66.7%	22.47#

*Percentages total more than 100% as some women had multiple sexual problems.
†For assault survivors, $n = 67$.
‡χ^2 could not be computed.
§$p < .05$.
‖$p < .01$.
#$p < .001$.

Survivor Characteristics.   No relationships were found between the presence of a sexual dysfunction and the survivor characteristics considered. However, rape, incest, and rape and incest survivors did differ in the types of sexual problems experienced.

Rape versus Incest versus Rape and Incest Survivors.   Primary nonorgasmia was significantly more prevalent among incest survivors (25.0%) than among rape (0.0%) or rape and incest survivors (5.9%), $\chi^2 (1) = 9.92, p < .01$. This finding suggests that compared to rape, an incestuous assault may have a greater impact on a woman's physiological response. Such an impact may be a consequence of being assaulted repeatedly by someone one should normally be able to trust rather than being assaulted one time by a nonrelated assailant.

Time since Most Recent Assault.   No relationship was found between the presence of a sexual dysfunction and time elapsed since the most recent assault. Thus, sexual difficulties may be experienced by sexual assault survivors not only immediately after an assault, but for months and even years later.

PARTNER RELATIONSHIPS AND SEXUAL ASSAULT SURVIVORS

A 27-year-old mother of four children, Debbie had a history of sexual abuse by an older brother. On numerous occasions, her brother would have Debbie and some of her female friends undress, and he and his male friends would insert sticks in the girls' anuses. Several years later, a 13-year-old Debbie had her first consensual intercourse with her boyfriend. Her brother was aware of this activity and used the knowledge to force her to submit to a vaginal rape. One night, he entered her room and threatened to tell their parents that she had had intercourse with her boyfriend if she refused to submit to his demands. Debbie told no one about this incident but felt great shame about it.

Debbie was married at the age of 20 and reported that the relationship was good. When she was 26, Debbie experienced yet another sexual assault. She was working as a night manager in a store where, one night, three men holding guns entered the establishment. They told her it was a robbery and proceeded to tie her hands together. While two of the men were getting the money out of the safe, the third man began rubbing against Debbie, fondling her breasts, and kissing her. He told her that they "would be really good together." Debbie attempted to prevent the assault by telling him that she was married and had three children. However, the assailant ignored her pleas and removed her pants. While talking about anal intercourse with her husband, the man instructed her to bend over. Before the assault proceeded further, the assailant was summoned by his fellow robbers and the three men left the store. Shortly thereafter, the assistant manager came upstairs and untied her hands. Debbie remained calm until her co-worker left the room, at which point she began crying.

The assault was reported to the police, and the three men were eventually caught and convicted of lesser charges than the sexual assault and robbery charges originally filed. The police referred Debbie to a clinic where she received good counseling.

Debbie told her husband about the assault and characterized him as being very understanding and concerned. He felt that the best way to deal with the assault was to forget about it.

The birth of Debbie's fourth child brought up the trauma again. She was uncomfortable seeing a male physician and did not want to be examined. Prior to this pregnancy, Debbie had not had a gynecological examination since the attempted rape. She had a very difficult labor due to her tension over being seen naked by others.

Debbie indicates that she has experienced many problems since the assault. She is uncomfortable with her body and dislikes being touched by her husband. She lacks trust in people in general and men in particular. She frequently is depressed and feels helpless.

These problems are having a significant impact on her relationship with her husband. The disruption is particularly related to her sexual problems. She feels little sexual interest and does not enjoy sex with her husband. Debbie particularly dislikes it when her husband caresses her body. She feels that her relationship with her husband has suffered greatly since her most recent sexual assault.

Not only may a survivor experience postassault problems, but significant others of the survivor may experience difficulties resulting from the assault. Mental health professionals working with sexual assault survivors should be sensitive to possible disruption in partner relationships in order to help survivors deal successfully with the assault experience.

The Assessment of Partner Relationships

A reliable instrument to assess marital adjustment has been developed by Locke and Wallace.[39] The test consists of 15 items that assess overall happiness; extent of agreement or disagreement on eight different issues, including handling of family finances, friends, philosophy of life, and ways of dealing with in-laws; accommodating behavior in disagreements; mutuality of leisure interests; desire to continue relationship; and shared confidentiality. Possible scores on this test ranged from 2 to 158. A score of 100 or more is generally indicative of a well-adjusted relationship as 96% of the persons in the well-adjusted relationship validation group scored 100 or better, whereas only 17% of the people in the maladjusted validation group had similar scores.

This test was modified for use at the Victim Treatment and Research Clinic so that its use would include women living with a partner or involved in an ongoing, committed relationship but not married to the partner. The modifications were restricted to the substitution of words such as "partner" for "husband" or "male," "committed relationship" for "marriage," and "relatives" for "in-laws." Retitled the Partnership-Relationship Adjustment Test (PRAT), this modified test can be completed by women in committed relationships regardless of legal marital status or sexual orientation.

The Impact of Sexual Assault on Partner Relationship

The PRAT is completed by all women in committed relationships seen at the clinic. Of the women seen to date, 75 sexual assault survivors and 48 nonassaulted women were involved in such a relationship when interviewed.

Sexual Assault Survivors versus Nonassaulted Women.   Because of significant differences in age and educational level, adjustments for these variables were made in the comparison of PRAT scores for these two groups of women. A hierarchical regression analysis with age and educational level as covariates was performed to produce analysis of covariance results. The sexual assault survivors were found to have significantly lower PRAT scores, adjusted $M = 101.97$, than the nonassaulted women, adjusted $M = 111.96$, $F(1,119) = 3.93$, $p < .05$. However, the difference between the two groups is even more striking when the distributions of the scores are examined. As compared to only 20.8% of the nonassaulted women, 41.3% of the survivors were classified by their PRAT scores as having maladjusted partner relationships, $\chi^2(1) = 5.54$, $p < .05$.

Analyses with Assault Survivors Only. The PRAT scores of the survivors were significantly related to number of children, $r = -.25$, $p < .05$. Thus, hierarchical regression analyses with number of children serving as covariates were performed to produce analysis of covariance results in all comparisons of survivors' PRAT scores.

Survivor Characteristics. Of the four characteristics, two were found to be related to partner adjustment.

Number of Assaults Experienced. As compared to the PRAT scores of single assault survivors, the scores of women who have experienced three or more assaults were negatively related to number of children.

Sexually Functional versus Dysfunctional Survivors. A comparison of PRAT scores for these two groups revealed that the assault survivors experiencing no sexual problems, adjusted $M = 113.42$, had significantly higher scores than did the dysfunctional survivors, adjusted $M = 94.40$, $F(1,73) = 10.12$, $p < .01$. Only 48.9% of the sexually dysfunctional women were involved in well-adjusted relationships, as compared to 75.9% of the sexually functional survivors, $\chi^2(1) = 5.38$, $p < .05$.

Time since Most Recent Sexual Assault. No relationship was found between PRAT scores and the time since the most recent sexual assault.

SUMMARY

It is difficult to design a scientific study investigating the impact of sexual assault on survivors. A controlled study would require obtaining data from a large sample of women, following these women over time, and later reassessing the sample to determine the incidence and impact of sexual assault. However, such a study is not feasible. Thus, investigations of the effect of sexual assault have been limited to evaluating women after they have been assaulted and drawing inferences that the assault and the observed symptoms are related at least in part. The inclusion of a sample of nonassaulted women in such studies, however, does add some strength to these inferences.

The results of this study strongly support the hypothesis that sexual assault can have a profound effect on a survivor. In fact, the four areas of a survivor's life investigated in this study were apparently permeated by the assault experience. When compared to the sample of nonassaulted women, the incidence of moderate to severe depression was seven times greater in the survivor sample and the survivors experienced significantly greater rape-related and general fear levels. In addition, depending upon the sexual problem being evaluated, sexual difficulties were up to six times more frequent among the survivors of sexual assault. Finally, twice as many survivors as nonassaulted women reported dissatisfaction with their partner relationships.

Further support for the hypothesis that the observed problems of the survivors were related to their assaults is the finding that only the development of some fears was related to the existence of self-reported emotional and/or psychiatric problems prior to being sexually assaulted. Even these problems were not related to the postassault development of significant rape-related fears.

A striking finding was the high incidence of sexual difficulties among the sexual assault survivors and, concomitantly, the significant other problems experienced by the assault-related sexually dysfunctional survivors as compared to the functional survivors. It may be that problems related to a sexual assault are exacerbated by developing sexual problems subsequent to the assault.

Previous studies indicate that postassault problems may persist for months to years,[16,20,22,25,27,28] and the results of this study support these findings. Only some of the fear levels measured by the MFS were found to diminish as time since assault increased. However, overall fear level did not decrease with the passage of time. Thus, these results indicate that mental health care providers working with sexual assault survivors should be sensitive to the possibility of observing such problems in survivors regardless of time since assault.

It is possible that the variety and the intensity of the postassault problems reported by the survivors seen at the Victim Treatment and Research Clinic are not representative of all sexual assault survivors. Survivors with few or minimal problems may have not been interested in participating in a study investigating the long-term impact of sexual assault. However, the findings reported here indicate that at least a large percent of assault survivors who come to the attention of mental health care providers are experiencing postassault problems. Additionally, professionals working with assault survivors should be particularly sensitive to possible increased levels of fear and depression, sexual problems, and disruptions in partner relationships in the survivors they see.

REFERENCES

1. Bowker, L.H. The criminal victimization of women. *Victimology: An International Journal* **4**:371-384 (1979).
2. Federal Bureau of Investigation. *Uniform Crime Reports-1979.* Washington, D.C.: U.S. Government Printing Office, 1980.
3. Gagon, J. Female child victims of sex offenses. *Social Problems* **13**:176-192 (1965).
4. Jaffe, A.C., Dynneson, L., and Ten Bensel, R.W. Sexual abuse of children: an epidemiological study. *American Journal of Diseases of Children* **129**:689-692 (1975).
5. Woodbury, J. and Schwartz, E. *The Silent Sin.* New York: New American Library, 1971.
6. Burgess, A.W. and Holmstrom, L.L. Rape trauma syndrome. *American Journal of Psychiatry* **131**:981-986 (1974).
7. Factor, M. A woman's psychological reaction to attempted rape. *Psychoanalytic Quarterly* **23**:243-244 (1954).
8. Katz, S. and Mazer, M.A. *Understanding the Rape Victim.* New York: Wiley, 1979.
9. Kilpatrick, D.G., Best, C.L., and Veronen, L.J. The adolescent rape victim: psychological responses to sexual assault and treatment approaches. In Kreutner, A.K. and Hollingsworth, D. (Eds.) *Adolescent Obstetrics and Gynecology.* Chicago: Year Book Medical Publishers, 1978.
10. Kilpatrick, D.G., Veronen, L.J., and Resick, P.A. The aftermath of rape: recent empirical findings. *American Journal of Orthopsychiatry* **49**:658-669 (1979).
11. Notman, M.T. and Nadelson, C.C. The rape victim: psychodynamic considerations. *American Journal of Psychiatry* **133**:408-412 (1976).
12. Nadelson, C.C. and Notman, M.T. Psychological responses to rape. *Psychiatric Opinion* **14**:13-15, 18 (1977).
13. Surtherland, S. and Scherl, D. Pattern of response among victims of rape. *American Journal of Orthopsychiatry* **40**:503-511 (1970).
14. Frank, E., Turner, S.M., and Duffy, B. Depressive symptoms in rape victims. *Journal of Affective Disorders* **1**:269-277 (1979).
15. Atkeson, B.M., Calhoun, K.S., Resick, P.A., and Ellis, E. Victims of rape: repeated assessment of depressive symptoms. *Journal of Consulting and Clinical Psychology* (in press).
16. Kilpatrick, D.G., Veronen, L.J., and Resick, P.A. Assessment of the aftermath of rape: changing patterns of fear. *Journal of Behavioral Assessment* **1**:133-148 (1979).
17. Queen's Bench Foundation. *Rape Victimization Study.* San Francisco: Queen's Bench Foundation, 1976.
18. Veronen, L.J. and Kilpatrick, D.G. *Conditioned fear and anxiety in victims of rape.* Paper presented at the meeting of the Association for the Advancement of Behavior Therapy, Atlanta, December 1977.
19. Veronen, L.J. and Kilpatrick, D.G. Self-reported fears of rape victims. *Behavior Modification* **4**:383-396 (1980).
20. Kilpatrick, D.G., Veronen, L.J., and Resick, P.A. *Aftermath of rape: one-year follow-up.* Paper presented at the meeting of the Association for the Advancement of Behavior Therapy, San Francisco, December 1979.
21. Bart, P. *Rape doesn't end with a kiss.* Unpublished manuscript, 1975.
22. Burgess, A.W. and Holmstrom, L.L. Recovery from rape and prior life stresses. *Research in Nursing and Health* **1**:165-174 (1978).
23. Gager, N. and Schurr, C. *Sexual Assault: Confronting Rape in America.* New York: Grossett and Dunlap, 1976.
24. Hilberman, E. *The Rape Victim.* New York: Basic Books, 1976.
25. McGuire, L. and Wagner, N. Sexual dysfunction in women who were molested as children: one

response pattern and suggestions for treatment. *Journal of Sex and Marital Therapy* **4**:11-15 (1978).

26. Holmstrom, L. and Burgess, A. *Sexual behavior of assailant and victim during rape*. Paper presented at the meeting of the American Sociological Association, San Francisco, September 1978.

27. Ellis, E.M., Calhoun, K.S., and Atkeson, B.M. Sexual dysfunction in victims of rape: victims may experience a loss of sexual arousal and frightening flashbacks even one year after the assault. *Women and Health* **5**:39-47 (1980).

28. Feldman-Summers, S., Gordon, P.E., and Meagher, J.R. The impact of rape on sexual satisfaction. *Journal of Abnormal Psychology* **88**:101-105 (1979).

29. Burgess, A.W. and Holmstrom, L.L. Rape: sexual disruption and recovery. *American Journal of Orthopsychiatry* **49**:648-657 (1979).

30. Becker, J.V., Skinner, L.J., Abel, G.G., and Treacy, E.C. Incidences and types of sexual dysfunctions in rape and incest victims. *Journal of Sex and Marital Therapy* **8**:65-74 (1982).

31. Resick, P.A., Calhoun, K.S., Atkeson, B.M., and Ellis, E.M. Social adjustment in victims of sexual assault. *Journal of Consulting and Clinical Psychology* **49**:705-712 (1981).

32. Silverman, D.C. Sharing the crisis of rape: counseling the mates and families of victims. *American Journal of Orthopsychiatry* **48**:166-173 (1978).

33. Beck, A.T., Ward, C.H., Mendelson, M., Mock, J., and Erbaugh, J. An inventory for measuring depression. *Archives of General Psychiatry* **4**:561-571 (1961).

34. Cohen, J. and Cohen, P. *Applied Multiple Regression/Correlation Analysis for the Behavioral Sciences*. Hillsdale, N.J.: Lawrence Erlbaum, 1975.

35. Wolpe, J. and Lang, P. A Fear Survey Schedule for use in behavior therapy. *Behavior Research and Therapy* **2**:27-30 (1964).

36. Bergler, E. The problem of frigidity. *Psychiatric Quarterly* **18**:374-390 (1944).

37. Masters, W. and Johnson, V. *Human Sexual Responses*. Boston: Little, Brown, 1966.

38. Annon, J. *The Behavioral Treatment of Sexual Problems*, Vol. 1. Hawaii: Kapiolami Health Services, 1974.

39. Locke, H.J. and Wallace, K.M. Short marital-adjustment and prediction tests: their reliability and validity. *Journal of Marriage and Family Living* **21**:251-255 (1959).

13
Procedures for Reducing Inappropriate Sexual Arousal: An Evaluation Review

Vernon L. Quinsey, Ph.D.
W.L. Marshall, Ph.D.

This chapter focuses upon research conclusions of numerous experimental investigations of inappropriate sexual arousal in which the "wrong" sorts of sexual activities and/or sexual partners are preferred.

Erectile assessments of sexual preferences are the crucial data in evaluating treatment procedures since they constitute the most satisfactory measurements for describing deviant sexual interests. The results of these numerous investigations form the basis for this chapter. The cumulative impact of these studies is evaluated. The authors conclude that developmental studies of the acquisition of sexual preferences should receive high priority, and ethically acceptable means of carrying them out should be developed.

INTRODUCTION

Over the past decade there has been increasing professional interest in the treatment of sex offenders. This has been occasioned in part by a perceived increase in the number of sex crimes and in part by changes in the attitude of society toward sexual behavior in general. Sex offenders can be, and are, viewed from a variety of perspectives, and their treatment has varied accordingly. From a clinical perspective, the most important treatment decision relates to the choice of a target for intervention. One could, for example, attempt to alter a sex offender's self-esteem, heterosocial anxiety, social skills, hormonal balance, attitudes toward women, etc. Most therapists would agree that treatment programs should be individualized and tailored to the particular pattern of problems which a sex offender presents (Abel, Blanchard, and Becker, 1976; Marshall and McKnight, 1975). Commonly, one of these problems is inappropriate sexual arousal in which the "wrong" sorts of sexual activities and/or sexual partners are preferred.

THE CONCEPT OF INAPPROPRIATE SEXUAL AROUSAL

Among behaviorally oriented clinicians, male sexual arousal is typically defined as penile tumescence and usually measured by a volumetric or circumferential device (see Chapter 15). Other methods of measuring sexual interest are often employed, but they are less standardized and open to criticism on various methodological grounds (Quinsey, 1973). Inappropriate sexual arousal is often reflected by increases in penile tumescence elicited by inappropriate stimuli. The stimuli are typically slides of persons who vary in age and gender, audiotaped stories describing various sexual practices, or movies (Abel, Blanchard, and Barlow, 1981). "Inappropriateness" is, of course, defined by social convention or legal statute, and varies over time, place, and circumstance.

There are several methods of scoring and reporting penile response changes. The simplest is raw response magnitude (i.e., the difference in millimeters or milliliters from stimulus onset to peak response). Raw response magnitude is often converted either (a) to percent of full erection, (b) to a z score (by dividing each raw response by the standard deviation of all of the subject's responses), or (c) to a ratio (by dividing the individual's average response to inappropriate material by his response to appropriate material).

Regardless of the method of measuring or scoring penile responses, the logic of interpreting sexual arousal patterns is the same. First, the sexual arousal patterns of a particular type of sex offender are measured, typically using both "normal" stimuli and stimuli that are relevant to the type of sexual offense which is of interest. Next, these arousal patterns are compared with those of non–sex offenders exposed to the same stimuli. Differences which the sex offenders exhibit from the patterns of non–sex offenders define inappropriateness, and it is these differences which are the focus of treatment. Because sex offenders typically show more arousal to inappropriate stimuli than normal individuals, one task of treatment is a reduction in inappropriate arousal; clearly, on occasion, another task is increasing appropriate arousal, but this is not the focus of the present chapter.

Note the complexity of the concept of inappropriate arousal. First, the differences among appropriate and inappropriate stimuli are considered within individuals; second, these differences are compared between sex offenders and "normals." It is insufficient to simply measure an individual's sexual arousal pattern to determine whether he responds to inappropriate stimuli. It is known, for example, that non–sex offenders show considerable arousal to slides of pubescent females (Freund, McKnight, Langevin, and Cibiri, 1972; Quinsey, Steinman, Bergersen, and Holmes, 1975) and to audiotaped descriptions of brutal rapes (Barbaree, Marshall, and Lanthier, 1979; Quinsey, Chaplin, and Varney, 1981). What differentiates child molesters and rapists from non–sex offenders are their penile responses to the relevant inappropriate material in relation to their responses to appropriate material.

Throughout this chapter we will be relying on erectile assessments of sexual preferences as the crucial data in evaluating treatment procedures. This is not only because the focus of this chapter is on the reduction of deviant interests, and erectile measures are the most satisfactory procedures for describing these interests, but also because the alternatives are quite unsatisfactory on their own although they may add to an overall evaluation of treatment. The three most popular alternatives to descriptions of penile responses as methods for assessing treatment changes are client's self-reports, therapist's judgments of improvements, and subsequent recidivism rates. Recidivism presents a problem as a measure of treatment success since it reflects not only repeated offending, but also police efficiency, the offender's luck or improved criminal skills, and a variety of other factors beyond experimental control (Quinsey, 1981). Furthermore, because of the noise inherent in such data due to the above-mentioned influences, large numbers are required for a convincing evaluation. This problem of numbers may be all but insurmountable in many treatment centers where the number of sexual aggressives is limited. In any case, estimates of recidivism require a long wait for the data to become available, which means that the program has to be continued without evaluation for several years.

Self-reports do not always correspond very well with objectively assessed sexual preferences (see Chapter 15) and are open to distortion more readily than erectile measures. Similarly, Quinsey and Ambtman (1978, 1979) have demonstrated that the clinical judgment of experienced clinicians is a poor predictor of outcome. We are, therefore, left with only one objective measure of treatment change—namely, erectile assessments of sexual interests—and we will examine the value of this method for predicting long-term outcome in the final section of this chapter. However, it is important to note that the goal of this chapter is to evaluate procedures for reducing deviant sexual interests so that erectile measures are appropriate and probably crucial to the goal of determining whether or not these within-treatment goals have been achieved.

REDUCING INAPPROPRIATE AROUSAL

Theoretically, two issues are important in clinical studies of inappropriate arousal reduction: (a) the degree of reduction in inappropriate arousal, and (b) the relation of these reductions to post-treatment sexual recidivism. It is possible, for example, for a treatment to affect recidivism but not sexual arousal; similarly, it is possible that researchers in this area have been mistaken and that reductions in sexual arousal can be achieved but not be related to recidivism. The focus of this section is on reductions in inappropriate arousal; a later section will relate these reductions to recidivism.

We will consider a range of approaches to the reduction of deviant arousal that includes aversive techniques, nonaversive procedures, and physical interventions.

Aversive Techniques

These approaches are based, at least procedurally, on an attempt to associate unpleasant experiences with the presently attractive, although unacceptable, stimuli or behaviors. Typically, these procedures have employed either electric shocks or imagined distress as the aversive event, but some therapists have used foul odors while others have used chemically induced nausea as the unpleasant stimulus.

Electrical Aversive Therapy: In electrical aversion therapy, shock is associated either with the stimuli thought to occasion the inappropriate arousal or with some aspect of the inappropriate behavior itself; for example, the behavior chosen to be punished could be penile responses to inappropriate stimuli. There is an extensive literature on aversive procedures employing electric shock, and several reviews have been written, particularly of the earlier research (Bancroft, 1974; Barlow, 1973; Feldman, 1966; Marks, 1976; Quinsey, 1973; Rachman and Teasdale, 1969). Marks has ably reviewed this early literature and has concluded: "Although the evidence suggests that aversion decreases deviance more than other methods, it is not absolutely conclusive and the overall effects are not startlingly large even when significant" (p. 280).

This section will examine research on the efficacy of electrical aversion therapy in terms of reducing inappropriate arousal to determine whether Marks' conclusions are still applicable. Research findings will be considered not only to determine the effects of aversion therapy, but also to explicate the processes underlying its effects. The focus of this section, therefore, is on studies which have employed measures of penile tumescence in evaluating electrical aversion therapy, particularly studies which have compared electrical aversion to other techniques.

In an early study which compared electrical aversion therapy to another method on the basis of tumescence changes, Bancroft (1970) treated 12 homosexuals with a signaled punishment paradigm and 11 with desensitization. In the signaled punishment procedure, subjects received a shock to the arm for increases in penile circumference elicited by a male slide. After the initial 15 sessions, subjects were shocked during a further 15 sessions for signaling when they had produced a homosexual fantasy. Desensitization involved relaxation training and graded exposure to a hierarchy of heterosexual situations over 30 sessions.

Penile circumference responses to homosexual and heterosexual slides were measured before and after treatment, and at the beginning of each treatment session. Responses to heterosexual slides were measured at the end of each session. No differences between groups were found over sessions, with the exception that post-treatment responses to heterosexual material were higher for the aversion group. Significant pre-post treatment increases in responsiveness to heterosexual slides were obtained in both groups, while a decrease in responsiveness to homosexual stimuli was significant only for the aversion group. Thus, in terms of reducing homosexual arousal, the aversion procedure was somewhat more effective, although the difference between groups was not significant.

McConaghy (1971, 1972) reported a series of studies which compared different aversive techniques in the modification of homosexual arousal patterns. Pre-post treatment measures included subjects' penile volume changes to 10-second slides of nude males and nude females which were inserted in a travelogue film and preceded by 10-second slides of a blue triangle and an orange circle, respectively. Prior to treatment, subjects showed penile volume increases to the male slides and decreases to the female slides. Subjects for whom treatment was delayed showed no change in this pattern of arousal at a second testing.

In the initial study, 20 homosexuals were given apormorphine aversion and 20 were given aversion relief therapy. In the former method 28 sessions were carried out over five days. In each session, nausea was paired with slides of males. In the aversion relief procedure (which was actually electrical aversion therapy combined with an aversion relief procedure), 14 slides of words and phrases related to homosexuality were read by the patient and followed by electric shock to the fingers. At the termination of the electric shock, a slide depicting heterosexual material was projected and this was not followed by shock. Patients were given 1050 shocks in five days of treatment. Penile responses to nude men were significantly reduced by both aversion techniques.

Using similar methods, McConaghy compared Feldman and MacCulloch's (1965) avoidance learning procedure with both classical conditioning and backward conditioning. Avoidance learning exposed subjects to a male slide with the instruction to leave it on for as long as they found it attractive. However, after 8 seconds a shock came on and continued until the subject turned off the slide. Later, the attempted removal of the male slide was made intermittently successful. Occasionally, the male slide was followed by a female slide. In the classical conditioning procedure, homosexual stimuli were associated with electric shock, the onset of which occurred toward the end of the exposure. Backward conditioning was simply the reverse order of the classical procedure in that shock preceded the onset of the homosexual slides. All three procedures reduced penile responses to male slides with no difference among treatments. Booster sessions, given post-treatment, had no appreciable effect.

Callahan and Leitenberg (1973) compared signaled punishment with covert sensitization using a within-subjects crossover design. The subjects were two exhibitionists, one transsexual, two homosexuals, and one homosexual child molester. Variable results were obtained with the erectile measures, and no clear superiority of either technique was evident.

Quinsey, Chaplin, and Carrigan (1980) compared biofeedback with signaled punishment in the treatment of 18 child molesters. The order of treatments was alternated across subjects. The biofeedback procedure consisted of signaling the patient with a red light (signaling an inappropriate response) when his penile response surpassed a preset criterion in the presence of a child slide, and with a blue light (signaling an appropriate response) in the presence of an adult slide. Patients were instructed to maximize blue and minimize red light time. In the signaled punishment (plus biofeedback) condition, shocks to the arm of an intensity selected by the patient occurred periodically as long as the subject was over criterion in the presence of a child slide.

Generalization probes were given before and after treatment, and in between each treatment type (usually of ten sessions' duration). These probes were conducted without shock electrodes attached and used slides which were not used in the treatment sessions. Data were analyzed by noting which individual subjects made significant improvements with each treatment type in the probe data. The signaled punishment plus biofeedback procedure was superior to biofeedback alone, with significantly more patients showing marked changes. This was true whether the punishment plus feedback procedure was given as a first or as a second treatment type. Overall, 13 of 18 patients exhibited significant improvement. The signaled punishment plus biofeedback procedure was also superior to a classical conditioning method used earlier in the same laboratory (Quinsey, Bergersen, and Steinman, 1976).

What can be concluded from these comparative studies? First, there has not been a great deal of research which compares electrical aversion to other techniques in reducing inappropriate arousal. Second, those studies which have been done indicate that electrical aversion is effective, but in some instances only marginally superior to other techniques. For instance, Bancroft found signaled punishment to be slightly superior to desensitization; McConaghy found classical conditioning aversion, backward conditioning aversion, avoidance learning, and apomorphine aversion to be equivalent; and Callahan and Leitenberg found no difference between covert sensitization and signaled punishment. On the other hand, Quinsey, Chaplin, and Carrigan (1980) found signaled punishment plus biofeedback to be superior to both classical conditioning and biofeedback alone.

These findings generally reflect an inconsistency both in terms of comparisons between techniques of treatment and in the amount of reduction achieved with individual subjects. These inconsistencies are difficult to interpret as the same electrical aversion procedures were not used in the various studies. It has been argued by both Bancroft and McConaghy that because widely different methods are equivalent in effectiveness, treatment results are due to nonspecific factors. However, this argument does not explain the differences among treatment types found by Quinsey, Chaplin, and Carrigan. Indeed the magnitude of reduction in inappropriate arousal was larger in this study than in any of the others. In addition, some investigators have found differences in effectiveness with different aversion therapy parameters. For example, Tanner (1973) showed that homosexuals altered their sexual arousal patterns more when higher shock intensities were employed. If there are differences in efficacy among electrical aversion therapy methods, then the results of comparative evaluations will often merely depend on which method is chosen for comparison.

Another problem in interpreting these studies results from differences in the patients selected for treatment. Sometimes homosexuals are used, sometimes a variety of sex offenders, and sometimes child molesters. It is altogether unclear whether these types of patients respond similarly to treatment. It has been found, for example, that transsexuals respond much more poorly than transvestites, fetishists, and sadomasochists to electrical aversion therapy (Marks, Gelder, and Bancroft, 1970). Thus, interactions between type of therapy and patient type may confuse comparisons of outcome across treatment studies.

The inconsistencies in the literature have unfortunately not spurred new efforts to resolve them, in part because electrical aversion has become unfashionable and in part because there is no acceptable theory to guide researchers in the area. Electrical aversion can indeed reduce inappropriate arousal but no one is sure why.

The procedures employed in aversion therapy are those of aversive conditioning in its operant or respondent forms. The most widely accepted explanation of the changes in sexual preferences associated with aversion therapy has been that inappropriate stimuli become conditioned suppressors of sexual arousal through their association with the unconditional stimulus of electrical shock (Rachman and Teasdale, 1969). This conditioned suppression formulation asserts that the inappropriate (conditional) stimuli come to elicit fear through a respondent conditioning process and this fear suppresses sexual arousal. Unfortunately, this theory has not fared well. As discussed in more detail elsewhere (Quinsey, 1973), what we know about aversion therapy does not match what we know about aversive conditioning. Aversion therapy is as effective with a backward as with a forward conditioning paradigm (McConaghy, 1971); the shock intensities employed are too low and the interstimulus intervals too long to establish conditioned suppression of arbitrarily selected operants on human subjects (Sachs and Keller, 1972); the subjects' self-reports are inconsistent with the idea of conditioned fear (Hallam, Rachman, and Falkowski, 1972); and finally, analog investigations using parameters from aversion therapy have produced no support for the conditioning interpretation (Quinsey and Varney, 1976).

Although it is conceivable that a variant of the conditioned suppression interpretation could be salvaged by invoking the special properties of the sexual arousal system, there is at present no independent evidence to support such a view. One could instead argue that operant processes are responsible for the changes, but it would be necessary to explain why such a variety of techniques, many of them respondent, work so well; in addition, one has to postulate impressively broad generalization gradients. Perhaps it would be more plausible to interpret these changes at least in part in terms of social influence or cognitive models (Bandura, 1969; Carlin and Armstrong, 1968; Quinsey, 1973), but none of these have been worked out in sufficient detail. In summary, it appears that Marks' (1976) conclusion, as it applies to electrical aversion, has been unaltered by subsequent research.

Covert Sensitization. Covert sensitization (or covert aversion) is essentially an analog of aversion therapy in which the stimuli and the aversive event, or responses and punishers, are elicited imaginally by the subject, usually as a result of carefully prepared prompts by the therapist. Several early descriptions of variations on this procedure were provided by Gold and Neufeld (1965), Cautela (1967), and Davison (1968), who reported reductions in interest in homosexuality and sadism. Barlow, Leitenberg, and Agras (1969) also successfully used covert sensitization with homosexual and a pedophile, and Harbert, Barlow, Hersen, and Austin (1974) were able to eliminate incestuous behavior using covert aversion. Unfortunately, all of these reports were based on uncontrolled observations in the absense of erectile measures of sexual preferences. Since that time, studies have appeared that meet the requirements of reasonable experimental control and objective measurement.

Barlow, Agras, Leitenberg, Callahan, and Moore (1972), for example, employed a controlled single-case design with three homosexuals in which they were able to effectively reduce erectile responses to male nudes by the application of covert aversion. Subsequently, Callahan and Leitenberg (1973), again using single-case experimental procedures with six clients (two of whom engaged in pedophilic behavior), demonstrated to their satisfaction the superiority of covert sensitization over contingent shock. However, closer examination of their data does not inspire confidence in Callahan and Leitenberg's conclusion, although subsequent reviewers (cf. Barlow and Abel, 1981) have accepted it. While they indicate that six clients took part in the program, data are presented for only two. Apparently in two other cases both procedures reduced deviant arousal, while for the remaining two patients neither procedure was effective. In the first case for which data are displayed, it is clear that covert aversion was more effective than electrical aversion, but neither method produced gains that were of clinical significance. For example, erectile responses to deviant stimuli were reduced to 70% of full erection which is hardly an encouraging change. In the second reported case, contingent shock markedly reduced deviant arousal, and this continued declining dramatically over the two sessions prior to the introduction of the covert procedure. Whether the subsequent reductions were due to covert sensitization or to the effects initiated by electrical aversion cannot be determined. This study, therefore, does little to strengthen claims for the effectiveness of covert sensitization.

McConaghy, Armstrong, and Blaszczynski (1981) point out that the electrical aversive procedure that provided the comparison in Callahan and Leitenberg's study had previously been shown by Bancroft (1969) to actually *increase* homosexual urges in two of ten patients. McConaghy et al. note that this is an unusual observation that was replicated by Callahan and Leitenberg in two of three homosexuals. This suggests that the electrical aversive treatment was far from optimal, so that any advantage for the covert procedure should not be understood as indicative of a general advantage over electrical aversion. In comparison with a more consistently powerful technique, McConaghy et al. found no differences between covert and electrical aversion, but unfortunately they did not employ erectile measures. In two other studies (Alford, Webster, and Sanders, 1980; Levin, Barry, Gambaro, Wolfinsohn, and Smith, 1977) although treatment was applied within appropriate experimental procedures, it turned out not to be possible to attribute positive changes in erectile responding to the specific effects of covert sensitization.

Despite these rather discouraging observations, Brownell, Hayes, and Barlow (1977) have produced clearly interpretable positive results using covert sensitization. They employed a multiple-baseline design with five patients, including a man who indecently assaulted women and man who sexually molested female children. These researchers were able to sequentially target different aberrant behaviors in their patients, and they found that in all but one patient, covert sensitization demonstrably reduced the targeted behavior (i.e., erectile responses to a particular deviance), while leaving the untreated ones intact. In the remaining patient, all deviant responses were reduced when covert sensitization was applied to just one behavior.

As a final note before ending this section, we would like to draw attention to the possibility of combining covert procedures with more direct, overtly explicit aversion. Laws, Meyer, and Holmen (1978) used valeric acid (which produces a foul odor) in the aversive treatment of a sadistic sexual offender, and they were able to reduce deviant arousal to almost zero. Although control by the olfactory aversion could not be held responsible for the benefits in this case, the results are consistent with earlier findings by Colson (1972) with homosexuals and by Marshall, Keltner, and Griffiths (1974) with two cases of fetishism. Maletzky (Maletzky, 1974, 1977; Maletzsky and George, 1973) has employed valeric acid to "assist" covert sensitization in the treatment of exhibitionists and in the reorientation of homosexuals. While he has found this procedure to be effective, he has relied on self-reports rather than erectile measures, and 11 of 30 patients required booster sessions at 12-month follow-up. However, this is an innovative approach worth pursuing.

In conclusion, support for the value of covert sensitization in reducing deviant sexual interests is not strong. In fact, there is only one study demonstrating effective changes of clinical significance that can be unequivocally attributed to the specific effects of covert aversion (Brownell et al., 1977). The combination of covert and overt aversive stimuli proposed by Maletzky (1974) has yet to be evaluated but appears to offer an alternative that may prove valuable.

Nonaversive Techniques

As we have seen, aversive techniques are not always effective. In addition, these procedures have brought their practitioners under attack from various sources on the grounds that they are coercive and threaten human dignity (Begelman, 1975), although it is hard to see how anything could be more threatening to one's dignity than an overwhelming desire to sexually attack a woman or child. In any case, researchers and clinicians have attempted to develop alternatives in order to avoid having to face controversy over the use of aversive therapy (particularly electrical aversion). To some extent, covert sensitization is seen as a more acceptable alternative, presumably because it does not involve the administration of externally delivered pain. Of course one option that has been proposed (cf. Barlow and Abel, 1976) is to focus on enhancing appropriate arousal first in the hope that deviant interest will reciprocally decline. Just exactly why we might expect deviant arousal to decrease as a result of increasing the valence of appropriate stimuli is not clear, and unfortunately the data are not adequate to confirm or deny this approach.

Limited alternatives to aversive therapy are available, although the evidence for their value is not extensive. Based on observations by numerous authors (Henson and Rubin, 1971; Laws and Rubin, 1969; Quinsey and Bergersen, 1976; Quinsey and Carrigan, 1978; Rosen, 1973; Rosen Shapiro, and Schwartz, 1975) that some males can exercise voluntary control over their erectile responses, Laws (1980) outlined a biofeedback-assisted procedure designed to train a bisexual pedophile to develop self-control over his sexual arousal. Earlier, Barlow, Agras, Abel, Blanchard and Young (1975) had obtained somewhat ambiguous results when providing homosexuals with feedback regarding their penile responses to heterosexual stimuli. Rosen and Kopel (1977) had attempted to use biofeedback to reduce deviant arousal rather than to enhance appropriate responses, and although their patient improved, at least initially, it was not clear that biofeedback was the crucial element. These authors argued that because heterosexual responses remained unchanged when transvestite-exhibitionist behavior was targeted, effects specific to biofeedback had therefore been demonstrated. Such an interpretation reveals a misunderstanding of the process of attribution of control in single-case analyses. If we hope to dismiss the role of nonspecific treatment factors in changing behavior, we must demonstrate in a design of this kind (i.e., multiple-baseline-across-behaviors) independence of effects over two or more *deviant* behaviors, rather than between one deviant and one appropriate response. After all, we would surely expect nonspecific factors to exert little influence on behaviors that are at best lower in priority in the patient's hierarchy of desire to change. To think otherwise would be to expect a degree of generalization from weak procedures (i.e., nonspecific factors) that we rarely get from far more powerful techniques.

In an attempt to demonstrate more direct control, Laws (1980) provided a patient with a video display of the polygraph tracing of his erectile responses to pedophilic material, within the context of a multiple-baseline design that targeted independent behaviors sequentially. This strategy demonstrated control by Law's procedure over the effective elimination of deviant sexual arousal. However, even when biofeedback was withdrawn, erectile responses to deviant stimuli continued to decline, which suggests it was not the feedback alone that was producing benefits.

Upon questioning, the patient revealed that he was using the biofeedback to assist him in conducting what was essentially a covert sensitization strategy of his own design. This suggests that feedback-assisted aversion might be an effective approach.

Quinsey, Chaplin, and Carrigan (1980) evaluated such a program in a comparative study involving signaled punishment that was described in detail earlier in this chapter. Biofeedback was for the most part unsuccessful (only 4 of 14 subjects improved), while contingent punishment was markedly effective (10 of 14 subjects significantly improved). Since Laws (1980) has provided data on only one subject, it is tempting to conclude, given discouraging data of Quinsey et al. and the earlier findings of Barlow and co-workers (Barlow, Agras, Abel, Blanchard, and Young, 1975), that biofeedback is of little value in altering deviant sexual preferences. However, it may be that the nature of the feedback is crucial to securing positive results, although Laws (personal communication) has noted that his procedure is rather cumbersome and requires equipment that may be beyond the financial means of most treatment programs.

Perhaps the problem here has to do with an assumption underlying the use of biofeedback. Laws (1980) makes this explicit when he suggests that the problem deviants have, and the reason they engage in their aberrant behavior, is that they are unable to control their sexual arousal to deviant acts. Now this may be true for those sexual agressors who display high levels of arousal in the laboratory to their preferred stimuli as did Law's subject, but it does not seem to be true for offenders who show lower levels of erectile responding. A group of incarcerated rapists were able to inhibit their responding to depictions of sexual aggression when so instructed, but most of these subjects showed rather low overall arousal during baseline assessment (Wydra, Marshall, Barbaree, and Earls, 1981). This low arousal may have been due to the kind of stimulus material used (standardized audiotapes), although the subjects were not instructed to control until they were already somewhat sexually aroused. For these low responders, then, the problem is not to train them to be able to control because clearly they can. Nor do we need to train them when to control their arousal since it has been demonstrated (Wydra et al., 1981) that rapists were accurate in their identification of inappropriate cues. Therefore, these low-responding rapists know when a woman is refusing, are aware of the inappropriateness of their behavior, and are able to control their sexual arousal, but they apparently choose not to do so.

We should point out a caution to this general line of argument. While the majority of rapists in Wydra et al.'s study were low responders, the few who showed higher arousal also were able to control their responses and were able to identify the inappropriateness of the rape cues. In addition to this, Abel, Blanchard, and Barlow (1981) concluded that the reason their subjects had difficulty in controlling was because the level of arousal elicited by their audiotapes was too low. Intuitively one would expect high arousal to be more difficult to control rather than low arousal, and it may be that Abel et al.'s subjects had difficulty because their audiotapes were individually tailored to each subject's preferences, whereas Wydra et al. used standardized, therefore less individually provocative, tapes.

Overall, we believe that these data suggest that the target in treatment for at least the low-arousal individuals should be to render inappropriate stimuli inert rather than to train these offenders to control their arousal. Marshall (Marshall, 1979; Marshall and Barbaree, 1978; Marshall and Lippens, 1977) described a procedure call "satiation" that was aimed at extinguishing the erotic value of deviant stimuli and acts.

The rationale for this technique is outlined in the original articles, and the reader is referred to those sources for the more complete theoretical derivation. Procedurally, satiation requires the subject to masturbate continuously for protracted periods (1 to 1½ hours) while verbalizing aloud every variation he can think of on the theme of his deviant interest (e.g., sex with children or forced sex with females). Whether or not the various components of this treatment (e.g., prolonged masturbation, verbalization of fantasies, etc.) are essential remains unexamined, but the evidence although limited encourages the use of satiation. In the most recent report (Marshall, 1979), two controlled single-case studies objectively evaluated the application of this procedure. A multiple-baseline-across-behaviors design demonstrated the power of satiation to reduce a series of sequentially targeted deviant interests in two pedophiles. The erectile responses of the first patient to two classes of children and several fetishisms were reduced to virtually zero only when satiation targeted each of the specific behaviors in turn. In the second case, erectile responses to children were unchanged by treatments that either enhanced self-esteem or employed electrical aversion. Satiation, however, effectively normalized the man's responses to young females.

In conclusion, then, the alternatives to aversive procedures are not supported by sufficiently convincing data. Biofeedback does not seem to be effective, although Law's approach seems to offer an encouraging alternative. While Marshall has used satiation with success, this procedure awaits independent evaluation.

Physical Procedures

The aim of physical treatments is to reduce sexual cravings so that deviant sexuality will be eliminated. Setting reduced sexual drive as the within-treatment goal requires the therapist to make at least two assumptions: (1) sexual aggressors have excessive libido, and (2) serum testosterone levels are highly related to the frequency and intensity of sexual urges, fantasies, and behaviors. It follows from these two propositions that reducing serum testosterone or blocking its action will eliminate deviant sexuality.

Contrary to the first assumption, several authors (Cohen, Garofalo, Boucher, and Seghorn, 1971; Cohen, Seghorn, and Calmus, 1969; Ellis and Brancale, 1956; Gebhard, Gagnon, Pomeroy, and Christenson, 1965; Glueck, 1956) have claimed that the commission of sexual offenses is a function of the offenders' sexual attitudes, particularly their feelings of sexual inadequacy, rather than high drive states. Record (1977) found that while sex offenders were more prudish, censorial, and sexually inadequate than non–sex offenders and normal individuals, the latter groups displayed greater sexual curiosity, higher general and specific sexual excitement, and stronger libido. Sex offenders were also found to have had their first sexual experience at a later age. In a subsequent study (Marshall, Christie, and Lanthier, 1977), pedophiles and rapists indicated a preference for a significantly lower rate of sexual activity than non–sex offenders. These observations are consistent with the conviction expressed by Schmidt and Schorsch (1981) that rapists do not have an enhanced sex drive.

All of these observations tend to deny the hypothesis that sex offenders are characterized by high sex drive. In addition, Rada, Laws, and Kellner (1976) found that only a small percentage of rapists had higher than normal levels of plasma testosterone, although these men were the most brutally violent offenders. Thus, lowering sex drive via reduced testosterone may be a valuable procedure for only a few very violent rapists. These findings agree with the opinions of Hardy (1964) and Whalen (1966) who claim that sexual behavior is controlled not by a biological drive but by experiential factors. Similarly it is well established that higher than normal levels of sexual activity more usually derive from nonsexual motives than as a result of somatic factors (Morgenthaler, 1974; Stoller, 1975).

As for the second assumption, Money, Wiedeking, Walker, Migeon, Meyer, and Borgaonkar (1975) provided anecdotal evidence that medroxyprogesterone acetate (Provera) could control the frequency of ejaculation, erection, and erotic behavior, and Pinta (1978) described changes in one patient's drive and fantasies that were linearly related to the dosage of Provera administered. Similarly, Rubin, Henson, Falvo, and High (1979) reported that plasma testosterone concentrations in normal individuals were positively and significantly related to the magnitude and speed of the erectile response. On the other hand, these same authors found a significant inverse relationship between testosterone levels and the frequency of orgasm, an observation that confirmed the earlier results of Kraemer, Becker, Brodie, Doering, Moos, and Hamburg (1976). According to Schiavi and White (1976) in their comprehensive review of the literature, the level of sexual activity is related not only to plasma testosterone but also to situational factors. Indeed, Laschet (1973), in her account of the use of antiandrogens, put this point quite clearly when she said: "Therapeutic failure is observed in heterosexual and homosexual pedophilia *when the manipulations have become independent*" (p. 315; italics added). By "manipulations," Laschet is referring to the deviant sexual behaviors of these offenders, and by "independent" she means independent of testosterone levels.

Clearly the assumptions of physical treatment procedures are questionable. However, the procedures may still be effective even though their rationale is unsound. Laschet (1973) points out that reductions in effective plasma testosterone may be achieved by one of four methods: (1) physical castration which involves surgical removal of the main production centers (i.e., the testicles); (2) surgical destruction of the hypothalamic receptors (hypothalamotomy); (3) inhibition of the gonadotropic function of the pituitary by the administration of medroxyprogesterone acetate; or (4) inhibition by antiandrogens (cyproterone acetate) of the androgenic action at the target organs.

Laschet's (1973) survey of the use of cyproterone acetate (CPA) certainly does not inspire confidence. We have already noted her rather circular observation that CPA does not benefit those offenders in whom the deviant behavior has become independent of testosterone levels, and it appears that she is referring specifically to sexual aggressors. Similarly, the results are far from encouraging with respect to the use of medroxyprogesterone acetate (i.e., Provera).

In a careful review of the literature, Lomis and Baker (1981) conclude that "little is known about the psychological effects . . . the long-term physical effects, or about its [Provera's] mode of action in human males" (p. 19). For the most part, evaluations of both Provera and CPA have been based on either recidivism or self-reports. As we noted earlier, these measures leave a lot to be desired. Erectile measures track the goals of treatment which presumably everyone agrees are to alter the deviant preferences of sexual aggressors. Unfortunately, only two studies have evaluated hormonal interventions by using penile response measures.

Bancroft, Tennent, Loucas, and Cass (1974) examined the merits of CPA and ethynylestradiol, and found that both reduced subjective deviant urges but neither had any effect on penile indices of deviant interests. Similarly Langevin, Paitich, Hucker, Newman, Ramsay, Pope, Geller, and Anderson (1979) obtained disappointing results with Provera. Administering Provera alone produced such high dropout rates that a proper evaluation was not possible, and indeed this seems to be a common problem with these hormonal procedures. Dropout rates vary from 30% (Walker and Meyer, 1980) to 100% (Langevin et al., 1979). In the treatment of patients at Johns Hopkins Hospital in Baltimore, Berlin and Meinecke (1980) provide data indicating that 9 of 20 patients dropped out of treatment: of the 13 child molesters in this study, 5 withdrew from treatment and 4 of these relapsed; an additional 4 child molesters who completed treatment also relapsed; only 2 patients of the total group were clear successes despite the poor quality of the assessment procedures.

Supplementing Provera with training in assertiveness increased the number of patients in the study of Langevin et al. who remained for the full course of treatment. However, despite the fact that this combined program produced noticeable decreases in the clients' self-reported arousal levels, there were no effects on erectile measures. Furthermore, a placebo procedure secured identical reductions in self-reported arousal.

Neither CPA nor Provera, then, seems to effect the kind of changes that are desirable in sexual aggressors. These procedures are plagued by high dropout rates and numerous unpleasant side effects (Lomis and Baker, 1981). If these methods have a place in the treatment of sex offenders, it must surely be only for those deviants in whom it can be demonstrated that sexual drive is excessively high. Such procedures can be seen as a way to dampen sexual ardor until behavioral methods can instill a more permanent state of self-control.

Heim (1981) and Heim and Hursch (1979) have reviewed the effects of physical castration on sex offenders, and have found the literature confusing and difficult to evaluate. Studies confuse differing populations of sex offenders, are methodologically poor, employ weak outcome measures, and fail to adequately assess long-term outcome. Unfortunately, no studies have evaluated sexual preferences by erectile measures either before or after castration. Despite these failings and the lack of demonstrated effects on either sexual misbehavior or sexual activity in general, somewhere in excess of 10,000 men were castrated in Zurich alone in the years between 1910 and 1961 (Plenge, 1961).

Heim (1981) was able to extract information on 39 castrates from various sources in West Germany. These patients included six men who were charged with offenses against adult males, but the rest met the criteria for sexual aggressives. The median time from release was 4.3 years. Sexual potency did not seem to be eliminated as a result of castration: 36% of the men Heim obtained data on still engaged in sexual intercourse (20% as frequently as one to three times per month), and 19% still masturbated. Some 70% had sexual thoughts at least occasionally, and although this is a bit higher than rates reported by others, independent researchers have nevertheless found that somewhere between 30 and 40% of castrates fail to show reductions in sexual potency after the operation (Cornu, 1973; Langeluddeke, 1963). For our purposes it is interesting to note that among Heim's patients, the rapists showed the greatest tendency to continue sexual activity after the operation: 73% of the rapists continued to engage in some form of sexual behavior, while 32% of the pedophiles and only 17% of the homosexuals remained sexually active. These rates are far too high to encourage optimism about the value of castration for eliminating sexual drive and thereby preventing future sexual offenses. In fact, Heim observed that these rates of sexual activity were highest among the younger offenders, which suggests that an age factor may be independent of treatment effects and may have confounded evaluations of castration by making it look more effective than it is.

For the purposes of evaluating outcome, given what we know about the independence of self-reports and actual behavior, particularly erectile responses, it is interesting to note that 89% of those castrates who considered their sexual drive to be reduced still engaged in sexual behaviors. This is consistent with Ford and Beach's (1951) claim that the effects of castration are dependent on the subject's attitudes rather than on his changed hormonal state. In any case, it appears that the body adjusts to castration by releasing androgens from the adrenal gland in order to compensate for the loss of testicular production (Egle and Altwein, 1975). Thus, if castration does reduce deviant sexual activity, it does so by processes other than those ordinarily claimed to mediate its effects.

Finally, surgical hypothalamotomy has been evaluated in a review of the literature by Schmidt and Schorsch (1981). Rieber, Meyer, Schmidt, Schorsch, and Sigusch (1976) had earlier concluded on the basis of a collaborative review that evaluation procedures were unsatisfactory, that undesirable effects of the surgery had been ignored, that the theoretical bases for the operation were questionable at best, and that treatment had neglected the valuable contribution which psychological therapies could make to the reduction of these problems.

Schmidt and Schorsch indicate that 75 patients were hypothalamotomized in the Federal Republic of Germany between 1962 and 1976. Of these patients 11 were rapists and 36 were pedophiles. Outcome was always judged by subjective and impressionistic means which it made difficult to evaluate changes. In most cases the operation did not affect hormonal levels, which were essentially normal two weeks after surgery, and the benefits for general functioning, including marital adjustment, were minimal. Unpleasant side effects were marked in a sufficient number of patients to justify extreme caution.

Although as Schmidt and Schorsch note there was a reduction in sexual activity and drive, the changes wrought by surgery were confounded by the fact that all offenders who had been operated on were released immediatedly thereafter. Thus a reduction in sexual feelings and behaviors might have been produced by environmental changes or, more likely as these authors point out, by the fact that all the subjects knew that release was contingent upon reduced sexual potency. This knowledge in fact may also have affected their pre-operation reports since they were only accepted for surgery if their reported sex drive was excessively high. As far as outcome is concerned, the results are again discouraging. Sexual orientation seemed unchanged, and only three patients appeared to be normalized by the procedure. Of the ten patients who were able to be contacted at follow-up, three refused to cooperate, one was deceased, two showed no change at all, and one was accused of murdering a young boy.

In summary, then, physical treatment procedures seem for the most part to be based on unfounded assumptions, and reports of their application rarely meet satisfactory standards of evaluation. In those cases where reasonable inferences can be made, the data are quite discouraging, and the only value of these procedures seems to be in the temporary suppression by CPA or Provera of excessive sexual drive in those rare offenders who show such a disposition.

FOLLOW-UP STUDIES AND CHANGE MAINTENANCE

This section will review studies which have related penile tumescence data to recidivism. If a reduction in inappropriate arousal is a suitable goal of treatment, then the amount of reduction should be inversely related to the probability of recidivism. The appropriate methodology for addressing this question is a group treatment study. Case studies can provide only ancillary information; in particular, they can address the issue of whether substantial reductions in inappropriate arousal preclude recidivism.

Follow-up data are obviously important for purposes of program evaluation, but they also serve to circumvent difficulties in the interpretation of changes in patterns of sexual arousal. Reductions in inappropriate arousal can usually be interpreted as a result of treatment or as a result of sexual response faking. Clearly, patients are often motivated to demonstrate improvement in order to secure their release from an institution, to please the therapist, etc. It is well known that many (but not all) sex offenders and non–sex offenders *can* voluntarily alter their sexual arousal patterns (see review in Chapter 15) but it is also clear that most sex offenders upon initial testing show inappropriate arousal even though they claim their preferences are normal (Quinsey, Steinman, Bergersen, and Holmes, 1975). The problem of faking is much more difficult with repeated testing. Although there have been a variety of attempts to eliminate faking as a problem, none of these methods is immune to criticism. Indeed, it could well be that patients who can "fake" improvement are demonstrating that they have acquired the ability to control their arousal and are therefore good risks. Follow-up studies which relate reductions in inappropriate arousal to outcome circumvent the faking problem: either the changes are related to outcome or not, and whether they are faked, voluntary, due to social influence, or whatever, is irrelevant. If the changes predict outcome, these changes are desirable, regardless of the mechanisms by which they are achieved.

A further methodological problem needs to be addressed with respect to outcome. As we noted in our introductory remarks, self-reported improvements, as well as therapist judgments of improvements and recidivism rates, represent poor outcome measures, although in a complete appraisal of treatment all of these should be added to the assessment of erectile responses.

The required methodological rigors are not met by any studies in the literature. Some of these issues have been addressed in the follow-up studies of released Oak Ridge sex offenders, but much more information is required for any definitive conclusion. In the first study (Quinsey, Chaplin, and Carrigan, 1980), 30 child molesters who had received biofeedback and/or aversion therapy were followed up for an average of 29 months. Post-treatment penile circumference data showed a small but significant relationship with whether the child molesters were convicted of a new child offense, returned to Oak Ridge because of a child offense, or committed a child offense which came to the notice of an Ontario psychiatric hospital. When this study was enlarged by adding new subjects (total $n = 132$) and extending the follow-up time (average $= 34$ months; s.d. $= 21$ months), no relationship between post-treatment arousal patterns and recidivism was found. However, the sexual arousal data taken from the initial testing of 100 treated or untreated child molesters, were significantly related to recidivism. One (of several) interpretations of these data is that changes in arousal patterns do not always persist through time. If such is the case, persons who have been treated and subsequently reoffend should show, upon reassessment, the same arousal pattern as before treatment.

Two Oak Ridge child molesters have recidivated post-treatment and been reassessed. The first of these patients showed marked arousal to slides of little girls. He made variable progress during the treatment sessions themselves and exhibited no improvement after biofeedback. Despite continued variability in the treatment sessions, the addition of a signaled punishment contingency resulted in a statistically significant improvement in his arousal pattern. Two weeks after treatment, this patient molested a young girl. In an assessment conducted after this reoffense, he showed the very same arousal pattern as before treatment. These results are of interest partly because faking was unlikely. This patient did not show any change in the biofeedback condition where faking would be expected and, in addition, did not appear to clearly understand what was expected of him as a result of treatment.

The other repeat offender was a child molester whom we had treated in 1973. Before treatment he showed high responsiveness to all female slides. Treatment results were not significant but indicated slight increases in responsiveness to adult female slides and decreases in responsiveness to child female slides. These benefits were maintained a month following treatment. Six years later he molested a 6-year-old girl, and we retested him in 1980. On that occasion he showed exactly the same pattern as he did on initial testing in 1973.

RECOMMENDATIONS FOR FUTURE RESEARCH

The most conspicuous problem in this literature is the lack of theory. With respect to the concept of inappropriate arousal itself, there are no theories of etiology which have other than laboratory demonstrations of plausibility or anecdotal support. We simply do not know how to account for individual differences in sexual arousal patterns. Clearly, developmental studies of the acquisition of sexual preferences should receive high priority, and ethically acceptable means of carrying them out should be developed.

The lack of theory carries over into the area of treatment intervention. We know that sexual arousal patterns can be altered, but we do not know what mechanisms are involved. Similarly we have no convincing theory of change maintenance, that is, why some persons "stay changed" and others do not. More extensive follow-up information on treated sex offenders is required.

It is, of course, difficult for theory construction to proceed independently of empirical investigation. Although it is apparent that some good individual studies have been done in this area, the various experiments have failed to produce a cumulative impact. Different experimenters and therapists have used too many different methods, patient populations, and measures to allow for strong inferences.

REFERENCES

Abel, G.G., Blanchard, E.B., and Barlow, D.H. Measurement of sexual arousal in several paraphilias: the effects of stimulus modality, instructional set and stimulus content. *Behaviour Research and Therapy* **19**:25-33 (1981).

Abel, G.G., Blanchard, E.B., and Becker, J.V. Psychological treatment of rapists. In Walker, M.J. and Brodsky, S.L. (Eds.) *Sexual Assault: The Victim and the Rapist*. Toronto: Lexington Books, 1976.

Alford, G.S., Webster, J.S., and Sanders, S.H. Covert aversion of two inter-related deviant sexual practices: obscene phone calling and exhibitionism. A single case analysis. *Behavior Therapy* **11**:15-25 (1980).

Bancroft, J.A. A comparative study of aversion and desensitization in the treatment of homosexuality. In Burns, L.E. and Worsley, J.L. (Eds.) *Behaviour Therapy in the 1970's*. Bristol: Wright, 1970.

Bancroft, J.A. Aversion therapy of homosexuality. *British Journal of Psychiatry* **115**:1417-1431 (1969).

Bancroft, J.A. *Deviant Sexual Behaviour: Modification and Assessment*. Oxford: Clarendon Press, 1974.

Bancroft, J.A. Tennent, G., Loucas, K., and Cass, J. The control of deviant sexual behavior by drugs. I. Behavioural changes following oestrogens and anti-androgens. *British Journal of Psychiatry* **125**:310-315 (1974).

Bandura, A. *Principles of Behavior Modification*. New York: Holt, Rinehart, and Winston, 1969.

Barbaree, H., Marshall, W., and Lanthier, R. Deviant sexual arousal in rapists. *Behaviour Research and Therapy* **17**:215-222 (1979).

Barlow, D.H. Aversive procedures. In Agras, W. (Ed.) *Behavior Modification: Principles and Clinical Applications*. Boston: Little, Brown, 1973.

Barlow, D.H. and Abel, G.G. Sexual deviation. In Craighead, W.E., Kazdin, A.E., and Mahoney, M.J. (Eds.) *Behavior Modification: Principles, Issues, and Applications*. Boston: Houghton Mifflin, 1976.

Barlow, D.H. and Abel, G.G. Recent developments in assessment and treatment of paraphilias and gender-identity disorder. In Craighead W.E., Kazdin, A.E. and Mahoney, M.J. (Eds.) *Behavior Modification: Principles, Issues, and Applications*, 2nd ed. Boston: Houghton Mifflin, 1981.

Barlow, D.H., Agras, W.S., Abel, G.G., Blanchard, E.B., and Young, L.D. Biofeedback and reinforcement to increase heterosexual arousal in homosexuals. *Behaviour Research and Therapy* **13**:45-50 (1975).

Barlow, D.H., Agras, W.S., Leitenberg, H., Callahan, E.I., and Moore, R.C. The contribution of therapeutic instruction to covert sensitization. *Behaviour Research and Therapy* **10**:411-416 (1972).

Barlow, D.H., Leitenberg, H., and Agras, W.S. The experimental control of sexual deviation through manipulation of the noxious scene in covert sensitization. *Journal of Abnormal Psychology* **74**:596-601 (1969).

Begelman, D.A. Ethical and legal issues of behavior modification. In Hersen, M., Eisler, R.M., and Miller P.M. (Eds.) *Progress in Behavior Modification*, Vol. 1. New York: Academic Press, 1975.

Berlin, F.S. and Meinecke, C.F. Treatment of sex offenders with antiandrogenic medication: conceptualization, review of treatment modalities, and preliminary findings. Unpublished study, Johns Hopkins Hospital, Baltimore, 1980.

Brownell, K.D., Hayes, S.C., and Barlow, D.H. Patterns of appropriate and deviant sexual arousal: the behavioral treatment of multiple sexual deviations. *Journal of Consulting and Clinical Psychology* **45**:1144-1155 (1977).

Callahan, E.I. and Leitenberg, H. Aversion therapy for sexual deviation: contingent shock and covert sensitization. *Journal of Abnormal Psychology* **81**:60-73 (1973).

Carlin, A.S. and Armstrong, H.E. Aversive conditioning. Learning or dissonance reduction? *Journal of Consulting and Clinical Psychology* **32**:674-678 (1968).

Cautela, J.R. Covert sensitization. *Psychological Record* **20**:459-468 (1967).

Cohen, M.L., Garofalo, R., Boucher, R., and Seghorn, T. The psychology of rapists. *Seminars in Psychiatry* **3**:307-327 (1971).

Cohen, M.L. Seghorn, T., and Calmus, W. Sociometric study of the sex offender. *Journal of Abnormal Psychology* **74**:249-255 (1969).

Colson, C.E. Olfactory aversion therapy for homosexual behavior. *Journal of Behavior Therapy and Experimental Psychiatry* **3**:185-187 (1972).

Cornu, F. Katamnesen bei kastrierten sittlichkeitsdelinquenten ous forensigch-psychiatrischer Sicht. Basel: Karger, 1973.

Davison, G. Elimination of a sadistic fantasy by a client-controlled counter-conditioning technique: a case study. *Journal of Abnormal Psychology* **73**:84-90 (1968).

Egle, N. and Altwein, J. Postpuberal castration and prostatic carcinoma. *Urology* **6**:471-473 (1975).

Ellis, A. and Brancale, R. *The Psychology of Sex Offenders*. Springfield, Ill.: Thomas, 1956.

Feldman, M.P. Aversion therapy for sexual deviations: a critical review. *Psychological Bulletin* **65**:65-79 (1966).

Feldman, M.P. and MacCulloch, M.J. The application of anticipatory avoidance learning to the treatment of homosexuality. 1. Theory, technique and preliminary results. *Behaviour Research and Therapy* **2**:165-183 (1965).

Ford, C. and Beach, F.A. *Patterns of Sexual Behavior*. New York: Harper and Row, 1951.

Freund, K. Assessment of pedophilia. In Cook, M. and Howells, K. (Eds.) *Adult Sexual Interest in Children*. London: Academic Press, 1980.

Freund, K., Chan, S., and Coulthard, R. Phallometric diagnosis with "non-admitters." *Behaviour Research and Therapy* **17**:451-457 (1979).

Freund, K., McKnight, C.K., Langevin, R., and Cibiri, S. The female child as a surrogate object. *Archives of Sexual Behavior* **2**:119-133 (1972).

Gebhard, P.H., Gagnon, J.H., Pomeroy, W.B., and Christenson, C.V. *Sex Offenders*. New York: Harper and Row, 1965.

Glueck, B.C. *Final Report: Research Project for the Study and Treatment of Persons Convicted of Crimes Involving Sexual Aberrations*. Albany, N.Y.: New York State Department of Mental Hygiene, 1956.

Gold, S.A. and Neufeld, I.L. A learning approach to the treatment of homosexuality. *Behaviour Research and Therapy* **3**:201-204 (1965).

Hallam, R., Rachman, S., and Falkowski, W. Subjective, attitudinal and physiological effects of electrical aversion therapy. *Behaviour Research and Therapy* **10**:1-13 (1972).

Harbert. T.L., Barlow, D.H., Hersen D.M. and Austin, J.B. Measurement and modification of incestuous behavior: a case study. *Psychological Reports* **34**:79-86 (1974).

Hardy, K. An appetitional theory of sexual motivation. *Psychological Review* **71**:1-18 (1964).

Heim, N. Sexual behavior of castrated sex offenders. *Archives of Sexual Behavior* **10**:11-19 (1981).

Heim, N. and Hursch, C. Castration for sex offenders: treatment or punishment? A review and critique of recent European literature. *Archives of Sexual Behavior* **8**:281-304 (1979).

Henson, D.E. and Rubin, H.B. Voluntary control of eroticism. *Journal of Applied Behavior Analysis* **4**:37-44 (1971).

Kraemer, H.C., Becker H.B., Brodie, H.K.H., Doering, C.H., Moos, R.H., and Hamburg, D.A. Orgasmic frequency and plasma testosterone levels in normal males. *Archives of Sexual Behavior* **5**:125-132 (1976).

Langeluddeke, A. *Die Entmannung von Sittlichkeitsverbrechern*. Berlin: de Gruyter, 1963.

Langevin, R., Paitich, D., Hucker, S., Newman, S., Ramsay, G., Pope, S., Geller, G., and Anderson, C. The effect of assertiveness training, Provera and sex of therapist in the treatment of genital exhibitionism. *Journal of Behavior Therapy and Experimental Psychiatry* **10**:275-282 (1979).

Laschet, U. Antiandrogen in the treatment of sex offenders: mode of action and therapeutic outcome. In Zubin, J. and Money, J. (Eds.) *Contemporary Sexual Behavior: Critical Issues in the 1970s. Baltimore: Johns Hopkins University Press, 1973.*

Laws, D.R. Treatment of bisexual pedophilia by a biofeedback-assisted self-control procedure. *Behaviour Research and Therapy* **18**:207-211 (1980).

Laws, D.R. and Holmen, M.L. Sexual response faking by pedophiles. *Criminal Justice and Behavior* **5**:343-356 (1978).

Laws, D.R., Meyer, J., and Holmen, M.L. Reduction of sadistic sexual arousal by olfactory aversion: a case study. *Behaviour Research and Therapy* **16**:281-285 (1978).

Laws, D.R. and Rubin, H.B. Instructional control of an autonomic response. *Journal of Applied Behavior Analysis* **2**:93-99 (1969).

Levin, S.M., Barry, S., Gambaro, C., Wolfinsohn, L., and Smith, A. Variations in covert sensitization in the treatment of pedophilic behavior: a case study. *Journal of Consulting and Clinical Psychology* **45**:896-907 (1977).

Lomis, M.J. and Baker, L.L. *Medroxyprogesterone acetate in the treatment of sex offenders: a literature review*. Paper presented at the 3rd National Conference on the Evaluation and Treatment of Sexual Aggressives, Avila Beach, California, March 1981.

Maletzky, B.M. "Assisted" covert sensitization in the treatment of exhibitionism. *Journal of Consulting and Clinical Psychology* **42**, 34-40 (1974).

Maletzky, B.M. "Booster" sessions in aversion therapy: the permanency of treatment. *Behavior Therapy* **8**:460-463 (1977).

Maletzky, B.M. and George, F.S. The treatment of homosexuality by "assisted" covert sensitization. *Behaviour Research and Therapy* **11**:655-657 (1973).

Marks, I.M. Management of sexual disorders. In Leitenberg, H. (Ed.) *Handbook of Behaviour Modification and Behaviour Therapy*. Englewood Cliffs, N.J.: Prentice-Hall, 1976.

Marks, I.M., Gelder, M., and Bancroft, J. Sexual deviants two years after electrical aversion. *British Journal of Psychiatry* **117**:173-185 (1970).

Marshall, W.L. Satiation therapy: a procedure for reducing deviant sexual arousal. *Journal of Applied Behavior Analysis* **12**:10-22 (1979).

Marshall, W.L. and Barbaree, H.E. The reduction of deviant arousal. *Criminal Justice and Behavior* **5**:294-303 (1978).

Marshall, W.L., Christie, M.M., and Lanthier, R.D. *Social Competence, Sexual Experience and Attitudes to Sex in Incarcerated Rapists and Pedophiles*. Report to Solicitor General of Canada, Ottawa, 1977.

Marshall, W.L., Keltner, A.A., and Griffiths, E. An apparatus for the delivery of offensive odors: a description and its clinical application. Unpublished manuscript, Queen's University, Kingston, Ontario, 1974.

Marshall, W.L. and Lippens, K. The clinical value of boredom: a procedure for reducing inappropriate sexual interests. *Journal of Nervous and Mental Disease* **165**:283-287 (1977).

Marshall, W.L. and McKnight, R.D. An integrated treatment program for sexual offenders. *Canadian Psychiatric Association Journal* **20**:133-138 (1975).

McConaghy, N. Aversive therapy of homosexuality: measures of efficacy. *American Journal of Psychiatry* **127**:141-144 (1971).

McConaghy, N. Aversive therapy of homosexuality. In Masserman, J.H. (Ed.) *Current Psychiatric Therapies*, Vol. 12. New York: Grune and Stratton, 1972.

McConaghy, N., Armstrong, M.S., and Blaszczynski, A. Controlled comparison of aversive therapy and covert sensitization in compulsive homosexuality. *Behaviour Research and Therapy* **19**:425-434 (1981).

Money, J., Wiedeking, C., Walker, P., Migeon, C., Meyer, W., and Borgaonkar, D. 47, XYY and 46, XY males with antisocial and /or sex-offending behavior: antiandrogen therapy plus counseling. *Psychoneuroendocrinology* **1**:165-178 (1975).

Morgenthaler, F. Die Stellung der Perversionen in Metapsychologie und Technik. *Psyche* **28**:1077-1098 (1974).

Pinta, E.R. Treatment of obsessive homosexual pedophilic fantasies with medroxyprogesterone acetate. *Biological Psychiatry* **13**:369-373 (1978).

Plenge, H. Die Behandlung erheblich ruckfalliger Sexualdelinquenten, vornehmlich der homosexuellen, unter Berucksichtigung der Kastration. *Monatsschrift Kriminologische Strafrechtsreform* **44**:15-41 (1961).

Quinsey, V.L. Methodological issues in evaluating the effectiveness of aversion therapies for institutionalized child molesters. *Canadian Psychologist* **14**:350-361 (1973).

Quinsey, V.L. The assessment and treatment of child molesters: a review. *Canadian Psychological Review* **18**:204-220 (1977).

Quinsey, V.L. Prediction of recidivism and the evaluation of treatment programs for sex offenders. Paper presented at Sexual Aggression and the Law: a symposium, Vancover, October 1981.

Quinsey, V.L. and Ambtman, R. Psychiatric assessments of the dangerousness of mentally ill offenders. *Crime and Justice* **6**:249-257 (1978).

Quinsey, V.L. and Ambtman, R. Variables affecting psychiatrists' and teachers' assessments of the dangerousness of mentally ill offenders. *Journal of Consulting and Clinical Psychology* **47**:353-362 (1979).

Quinsey, V.L. and Bergersen, S.G. Instructional control of penile circumference. *Behavior Therapy* **7**:489-493 (1976).

Quinsey, V.L., Bergersen, S.G., and Steinman, C.M. Changes in physiological and verbal responses of child molesters during aversion therapy. *Canadian Journal of Behavioural Science* **8**:202-212 (1976).

Quinsey, V.L. and Carrigan, W.F. Penile responses to visual stimuli: Instructional control with and without auditory sexual fantasy correlates. *Criminal Justice and Behavior* **5**:333-342 (1978).

Quinsey, V.L., Chaplin, T.C., and Carrigan, W.F. Biofeedback and signaled punishment in the modification of inappropriate sexual age preferences. *Behavior Therapy* **11**:567-576 (1980).

Quinsey, V.L., Chaplin, T.C., and Varney, G. A comparison of rapists' and non–sex offenders' sexual preferences for mutually consenting sex, rape, and physical abuse of women. *Behavioral Assessment* **3**:127-135 (1981).

Quinsey, V.L., Steinman, C.M., Bergersen, S.G., and Holmes, T.F. Penile circumferences, skin conductance, and ranking responses of child molesters and "normals" to sexual and nonsexual stimuli. *Behavior Therapy* **6**:213-219 (1975).

Quinsey, V.L. and Varney, G.W. Modification of preference in a concurrent schedule by aversive conditioning: an analog study. *Bulletin of the Psychonomic Society* **7**:211-213 (1976).

Rachman, S. and Teasdale, J. *Aversion Therapy and Behavioral Disorders: An Analysis.* Coral Gables, FL.: University of Miami Press, 1969.

Rada, R.T., Laws, D.R., and Kellner, R. Plasma testosterone levels in the rapist. *Psychosomatic Medicine* **38**:257-268 (1976).

Record, S.A. Personality, sexual attitudes and behavior of sex offenders. Unpublished doctoral thesis, Queen's University, Kingston, Ontario, 1977.

Rieber, I., Meyer, A.-E., Schmidt, E., Schorsch, E., and Sigusch, V. Stellungnahme zu stereotaktischen Hirnoperationen an Menschen mit abweichenden Sexualverhalten. *Sexualmedizin* **5**:442-450 (1976).

Rosen, R.C. Suppression of penile tumescence by instrumental conditioning. *Psychosomatic Medicine* **35**:509-514 (1973).

Rosen, R.C. and Kopel, S.A. Penile plethysmography and biofeedback in the treatment of a transvestite-exhbitionist. *Journal of Consulting and Clinical Psychology* **45**:908-916 (1977).

Rosen, R.C., Shapiro, D., and Schwartz, G.E. Voluntary control of penile tumescence. *Psychosomatic Medicine* **37**:479-483 (1975).

Rubin, H.B., Henson, D.E., Falvo, R.F., and High, R.W. The relationship between men's endogenous levels of testosterone and their penile responses to erotic stimuli. *Behaviour Research and Therapy* **17**:305-312 (1979).

Sachs, D.A. and Keller, T. Intensity and temporal characteristics of the CER paradigm with humans. *Journal of General Psychology* **86**:181-188 (1972).

Schiavi, R.C. and White, D. Androgens and male sexual function: a review of human studies. *Journal of Sex and Marital Therapy* **2**:214-228 (1976).

Schmidt, G. and Schorsch, E. Psychosurgery of sexually deviant patients: review and analysis of new empirical findings. *Archives of Sexual Behavior* **10**:301-303 (1981).

Stoller, R.J. *Perversion. The Erotic Form of Hatred.* New York: Pantheon, 1975.

Tanner, B.A. Shock intensity and fear of shock in the modification of homosexual behavior in males by avoidance learning. *Behaviour Research and Therapy* **11**:213-218 (1973).

Walker, P.A. and Meyer, W.J. Medroxyprogesterone acetate treatment for paraphiliac sex offenders. In Hayes, J.R., Roberts, T.K., and Solway, K.S. (Eds.) *Violence and the Violent Individual.* Jamaica, N.Y.: Spectrum, 1980.

Whalen, R. Sexual motivation. *Psychological Review* **73**:151-163 (1966).

Wydra, A., Marshall, W.L., Barbaree, H.E., and Earls, C.M. *Control of sexual arousal by rapists and nonrapists.* Paper presented at the 42nd Annual Convention of the Canadian Psychological Association, Toronto, June 1981.

Part IV

Building and Operating Behavioral Laboratories for Evaluating and Treating Sexual Offenses

14

How to Build and Operate a Behavioral Laboratory to Evaluate and Treat Sexual Deviance

D.R. Laws, Ph.D.
Candice A. Osborn

Concerned with applying a scientific approach to the assessment and treatment of sexual offenders, this chapter details the conditions under which sexual behavior occurs, what stimulates it, and what maintains it in strength. The core around which the authors pursue their major objective lies in the detailed description of how to build, operate, and staff a behavioral laboratory for those engaged in such research. They not only describe the devices they found of value but enumerate instrumentation, and staff training techniques they have found to be most effective. The limitations and values of a sexual behavior laboratory are discussed in addition to the initiation of treatment of sexual offenders, scheduling of sessions, evaluation of such sessions, and means of estimating their success or failure.

I. INTRODUCTION: WHY A LABORATORY?

From the behavioral point of view, the core of effective treatment lies not in what one believes about human nature or human behavior, but in how one identifies, describes, and assesses the problem to be treated. Effective assessment will, more often than not, structure effective treatment. Behaviorists have always downplayed unconscious and unobservable mental events, not asserting that they do not exist, but asserting that positing their existence is neither helpful nor necessary for adequate assessment or for effective and lasting behavior change to occur. If the focus is to be upon overt behavior, then one must seek not its wellsprings, but rather the conditions under which it occurs, what stimulates it, what maintains it in strength. Thus armed and guided by the data of assessment, one is in a good position to implement procedures, as directly and simply as possible, to effect the desired behavior change.

Given this position, how then do we apply this approach to the assessment and treatment of sex offenders? From the radical behaviorist point of view, the most straightforward way should be through the use of a contrived situation, called a "laboratory analogue." Barlow (1977) describes this approach:

The function of behavioral assessment in an ideal world would be the direct and continuous measurement of the . . . behavioral problem in the setting where the behavior presents a problem . . . Any procedure other than direct and continuous assessment of behavior in the natural environment is second best. Yet, in applied work these principles are constantly compromised for practical or ethical reasons. Thus, clinicians cannot or will not measure behavior in the natural environment that occurs in settings remote from the therapeutic setting, nor will they measure behavior such as aggressive behavior that occurs at very low frequencies. For ethical reasons, clinicians also will not observe some behaviors such as sexual interactions in the natural environment beyond the very beginnings of the chain of behavior (e.g., initial social approaches). To overcome these problems, contrived situations are devised to observe these behaviors at higher frequencies or in more convenient locations. In some cases the behaviors cannot be conveniently produced even in contrived situations. When this happens, as in the case of sexual behavior, clinicians move back down the behavioral chain and measure sexual arousal, presumably an earlier component in the chain of sexual behavior. (pp. 469-470)

There are a variety of ways to assess the components of sexual arousal. The early work of Masters and Johnson (1966) clearly showed that a number of physiological responses were associated with ongoing sexual behavior such as masturbation and sexual intercourse. However, sex offenders most frequently experience inappropriate sexual arousal which occurs prior to the commission of a deviant sexual act. Therefore, in assessing the arousal potential of sex offenders, one must be concerned primarily with those behaviors which form links in the chain of components that lead up to the performance of deviant sexual behavior. Any assessment should therefore identify those behaviors which are discriminative of sexual arousal from those which are not (see Tollison and Adams, 1979, pp. 37-44.)

Of the potentially relevant physiological responses, penile erection has been repeatedly demonstrated to be the single best index of male sexual arousal (Abel, 1976; Barlow, 1977; Freund, 1963; Masters and Johnson, 1966; Rosen and Keefe, 1978; Zuckerman, 1971) The erection response is highly specific, occurring in the presence of sexual stimuli and not in the presence of nonsexual stimuli. When the erection response has been measured concurrently with other relevant physiological variables (e.g., Bancroft and Mathews, 1971), it has been the only one which was discriminative of sexual arousal.

Given these findings, for purpose of the behavioral assessment of sexual arousal patterns in sex offenders, the best dependent variable will be the response of penile erection, although this may be supplemented by other subjective measures such as subjective estimates of arousal level, rating scales, self-reports of erotic value, interest, etc. (see Laws and O'Neil, 1981).

It therefore makes intuitive as well as practical sense to create a setting in which problems in deviant sexual arousal can be studied, preferably in isolation from the "noise" of the natural environment. Obviously this has the limitations of unreality typical of the contrived or laboratory analogue situation, but it also has considerable strengths, in particular the ability to deal with fundamental components of the problem. A sexual behavior laboratory is one of these contrived situations. Basically, it is an evaluation and treatment unit where patterns of sexual arousal to various classes of deviant and nondeviant stimuli can be measured in a laboratory environment, diagnostic/evaluative measures can be obtained, treatment interventions can be introduced, and observation can be made of any subsequent changes in sexual responsiveness. If one proceeds in this manner, working with single individuals at a time, it is possible to identify some of the components of both deviant and nondeviant sexual interests in any given individual, and develop specific treatment procedures to decrease the former and maintain the latter in strength or increase them if necessary. Once this is accomplished, the treatment person is in a position to assist the sexual deviant to develop additional behavioral and cognitive natural settings. Ideally, treatment should be continued in a long follow-up period and should include close monitoring of the use of the learned strategies in vivo, frequent self-reporting, and frequent laboratory measurement of ongoing deviant and nondeviant response levels.

A frequent complaint against this laboratory analogue approach is that it is the commission of deviant sexual acts, not sexual arousal, that is the "real" problem. Further, it is argued, because a direct causal relationship cannot be established between the two, it makes no sense to treat deviant sexual arousal. This objection ignores the rather obvious fact that deviant sexual arousal *is* deviant sexual behavior and is worthy of attention in its own right as a key link in the chain of behaviors leading to sexual offenses. The erection response is measured because it is the one behavior in the chain that *can* be objectively measured. Once again, Barlow's (1977) response to this objection summarizes the behaviorist position:

These procedures have in common a movement back down the behavioral chain to a point where earlier aspects of sexual arousal are measured. The assumption has been that sexual arousal is a necessary step in the chain leading to the consummation of sexual behavior. As such, changes in the strength or patterns of sexual arousal will have a direct relation to the strength or patterns of later behaviors in the chain . . . If satisfying (adult sexual) relationships are the goal, then events that precede intercourse, such as interest in social behaviors and sexual features of the partner, as well as fantasies of (adult sexual) interaction, are important targets of assessment and treatment. In view of these relationships, assessment (and treatment) of early events in the chain of the genital aspects of sexual behavior may be more important to long-lasting sexual satisfaction than assessments of the end-point of this chain. (pp. 473-474)

II. The Setting

A. Minimal Requirements

The most basic requirement of the laboratory setting is that the therapist must be able to send audiovisual information to the client and receive verbal communications and sexual response data from him. You will be dealing with information of a highly intimate nature, and you are asking the client to emit a response which he does not typically display openly to strangers, so privacy is essential. Whether you work in a hospital, prison, clinic, or private practice, you should seek a location that is secluded and quiet. It should be a location where clients can come and go easily and where your fellow workers are not likely to be continuously passing or intruding.

B. Effective Space Utilization

You do not need a lot of space. Our entire laboratory unit is situated in a 1500 sq ft area that has been partitioned to suit our particular needs. The actual laboratory section where we work with clients occupies an area only 15 ft wide by 25 ft long. Figure 14-1 shows a portion of the working area. In that area we have four client booths, a waiting area and access hallways, a polygraph, large stands for two slide projectors, a worktable, an equipment rack, a closed-circuit TV camera and monitor, a four-station intercom, all electronic control and switching equipment, and a rack to store all stimulus materials in use and all needed record-keeping forms. Within that area, two or three operators can comfortably work with three or four clients simultaneously.

Most beginning workers will not be afforded the luxury of building a laboratory exactly as they want it and, therefore, should maximize the use of what they *can* get. At minimum, we recommend two small rooms with an interconnecting door or a single room which can be partitioned. A variation of the latter would be a single room divided by a folding screen, the least desirable option. The more you can ensure privacy for your client, the more you maximize results.

C. Client Space

To the extent possible the client's area should be one free of distractions so that he is able to concentrate on the stimulus materials presented to him and/or perform other tasks assigned. In the two-room configuration described, these conditions are

Figure 14-1.   Portion of the working area showing front end of two client enclosures, back-projection screens, and interface panels.

met, but it is an inefficient use of space. In this set-up all clients must be seen consecutively, and with start-up, shutdown, and record-keeping time subtracted, one therapist will see only eight or so clients in a 6-hour working day. We have found that a single equipment operator can easily work with two clients simultaneously. Therefore, the more client space available, the greater the service capability.

In our arrangement, there are four client booths, each 4 ft × 6 ft and sharing common walls. Each has its own door opening to an access hallway. Ours are open at the top, but ideally each should have a ceiling with a ventilating fan. Each booth has an electronic interface panel in the front wall, with connectors to accommodate closed-circuit TV, intercom, signaling devices, and three physiological response inputs. The number of input-output jacks in these panels depends on the task at hand. All of the booths have TV receivers, and two are equipped with 2 ft × 3 ft back-projection screens for slide presentations. Commercial back-projection glass is very expensive; ordinary plate glass or Plexiglass that has been sand blasted works just as well. Finally, each enclosure is equipped with a comfortable chair and a headset with boom microphone for intercommunication and reception of audiotaped presentations. Figure 14-2 shows one of these client enclosures. Sound-proofing each enclosure would be desirable. In lieu of this, we play a "white noise" signal into small speakers installed in each room; this neutral, hissing noise covers up voices, audio presentations from other booths, sounds of telephone ringing, doors closing, etc.

Figure 14-2.   Typical 4 ft. × 6 ft client enclosure showing back-projection screen, interface panel and TV monitor.

We have described this setup at some length because we have found it to be adequate for the best type of laboratory needed to do the job. It seems more elaborate than it really is, and we recommend that you attempt to construct something similar. A 4 ft × 6 ft enclosure such as we have described could be built of ½-inch plywood, with multiple booths sharing a common wall. Used doors will also keep the price down. The interface panels are nothing more than aluminum or wooden plaques anchored to the wall with connectors; there is one on either side with interconnected female jacks. You can buy plate glass or Plexiglass, have it sand blasted at a glazier's, and install it yourself. If you have a plant operations department or maintenance shop in your workplace, they can construct this for you. If not, anyone who is handy with tools can do it.

At least two enclosures should definitely be constructed, and three would be preferable. Running three booths will not require duplication of expensive equipment since multiple stimulus presentations in a single booth are rarely required. With a single set of audiovisual equipment you could simultaneously run video into one booth, slides into a second, and audio into a third.

During the past year we have had the opportunity to test our service capacity. With three booths running, we can carry a working case load of about 50 clients. Of these, about 20 will be seen 3-4 times per week for treatment, and the remainder 3-4 times per week in some phase of assessment. With three assistants on the floor, we can see 20-24 clients per day; with one, we can see only 8-12 clients per day.

D. Operator Space

The operator does not require much space. In the two-room configurations suggested above all equipment and controls could be placed on a single table and cables run under the door to the client's room, for example, a videotape deck on the operator's side and the receiver on the client's. With portable equipment, this is the way it is done in our private practice, and it serves well for one operator working with one client at a time. In the hospital laboratory, the operator's space occupies a 5 ft × 15 ft area, still very small. Figure 14-3 shows the operator's working area. All of the equipment is arrayed 5 ft from the front of the booths, with the connecting cables strung overhead and down the booth walls to the interface panels. By taking just a few steps in either direction, a single worker can operate two slide projectors, two audiocassette players, two videotape decks, a closed-circuit TV camera, a videocamera switching panel, the intercom, and the polygraph. As the tasks performed are highly routinized, equipment operators quickly learn to be conserving of movement.

III. EQUIPMENT

A. Minimal Requirements

Whether for a single- or multiple-room laboratory, there are basic items of equipment needed for full evaluation and treatment capability:

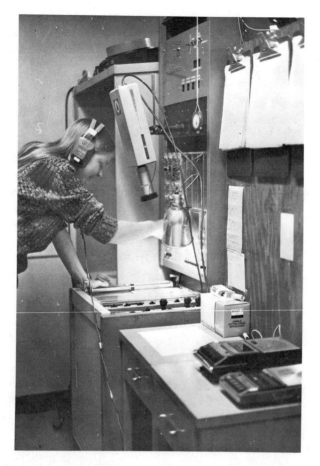

Figure 14-3.   Operator's work area.

1. A measurement device to record the erection response
2. A sensing device to pick up the response
3. A slide projector
4. An audiocassette recorder/player
5. A videocassette recorder
6. Stimulus materials in the form of videotapes, audiotapes, and slides.
7. Some sort of timing device such as a stopwatch.

B. Measurement Devices

The basic measurement system requires a sensing device, called a penile transducer, to detect the behavior and send an electronic signal to some type of recording device that can read out the minimum, maximum, and all intermediate values of the response. Preferably, to reduce operator error, the recording device should produce a hard copy record whether that be a pen tracing of the response or a digital readout in percentages. For this purpose, transducers are relatively cheap while recording devices are expensive.

1. Recorders. There are a wide variety of recorders. Some are multifunction, multichannel recorders which will record the erection response by adding the appropriate coupler. These machines, generally called, "polygraphs" or "physiological recorders," are the most flexible as they can record a variety of physiological responses (e.g., galvanic skin response, heart rate, pulse rate, respiration, etc.) and other events (e.g., stimulus on/off) concurrently with the erection response. They are available in tabletop and free-standing models. These units are the most expensive. If you are supported by extramural funds or have a generous equipment budget, you may wish to purchase one of these models. They are highly *non*portable and will only be useful in a fixed location such as a hospital, clinic, or research laboratory. Most workers will not be lavishly supported and will require a more modest recorder. If you are not interested in simultaneous recording of other responses or multiple recordings of erection responses from more than one location, choose a simpler recorder. The simpler models are portable and easy to operate. The best of these recorders will give you a hard copy readout of the behavior and produce a pen tracing of the behavior on a graduated chart. With this system, you can use a dual transducer hookup on a single person or two recordings from two locations. Figure 14-4 shows such a unit. The manufacturer states that the modular

Figure 14-4.   PRS-102 strip chart recorder (Medical Monitoring Systems, Inc.).

design permits changeover from one type of response to another and the custom modules can be built. There is also a highly portable machine, fitted into an overnight case and easy to operate which produces a single channel pen tracing. Figure 14-5 shows this machine. It has the added advantage of being able to accept a coupler to record female sex response as well.

It is our belief that a continuous record of the erection response is not necessary unless you are specifically interested in topographic characteristics of the behavior. Penile erection is a slow moving response, and samples obtained every 10-15 seconds give a complete picture of the behavior with no essential loss of information. Continuous records also require interpretation, which introduces observer error and adds extra steps to data retrieval. One unit is small, portable, very easy to operate, and produces a printed digital readout (e.g., 53 = 53%) on a calculator tape. Figure 14-6 shows such a digital monitor. It is designed to be calibrated for use with each individual client; two settings are made prior to each session and it is ready to use. An additional advantage is an adjustable sampling interval. It can be preset to print at intervals of 2.5, 5, 10, 20, or 40 seconds.

2. Pickup Devices. Choosing a sensor is an easy matter as there are only two in wide use. One, called the Barlow transducer (Barlow, Becker, Leitenberg, and Agras, 1970), resembles an oversized signet ring. It is a single piece of shaped steel, flat on top and open at the bottom. Figure 14-7 shows the Barlow transducer. An electronic strain gauge is attached to the flat section, and electronic leads run to the recorder. The transducer is fitted on the penis with the flat top on the dorsal surface, and a weak electrical current is passed through the strain gauge. When an erection occurs, the side sections of the ring are sprung outward, causing the strain gauge to bow, which creates electrical resistance. This resistance change is amplified by the recording unit and is read out as an analog signal to the recorder pen or the digital printer. This is a sensitive, perfectly adequate device, but it is fragile, easily broken, difficult to repair, and expensive. We do not recommend it to the novice worker.

A less fragile device is the Bancroft transducer (Bancroft, Jones, and Pullan, 1966), a mercury-in-rubber strain gauge. This is a loop of fine-bore silicone tubing filled with mercury and plugged at both ends with electrodes which run to the recording equipment. Figure 14-8 shows the mercury strain gauge. Electronically this device is identical to the Barlow unit except that the current is passed through the mercury. The unit is fitted around the penis like a rubber band. Erection strains the tubing and thins out the mercury column, creating a resistance change. The main advantage of this device is its low cost. It is reasonably durable and will last several months in daily use if carefully handled (Laws, 1977).

3. Audiovisual Devices. Three media are commonly used to produce stimuli in the laboratory setting.

Figure 14-5. Model SP-1N Sex Plotter, strip chart recorder (Farrall Instruments, Inc.).

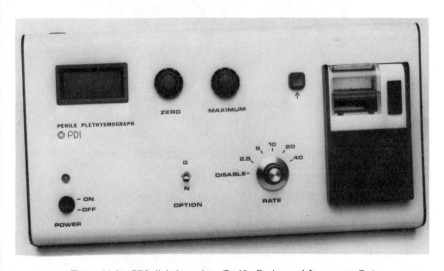

Figure 14-6. PDI digital monitor (Pacific Design and Instrument Co.).

Figure 14-7. Metal strain gauge, a circumferential transducer for recording penile erection (Farrall Instruments, Inc.).

Figure 14-8. Mercury-in-rubber strain gauge, a circumferential transducer for recording penile erection (Parks Electronics Laboratory, Inc.).

a. Video. Videotape and motion pictures are the most powerful medium of stimulus presentation (Abel and Blanchard, 1976). While somewhat expensive, a videocassette recorder (VCR) will more than pay for itself by greatly increasing the power of assessment and treatment evaluations. We recommend that you *do not*, if possible, use a reel-to-reel video deck. These are no longer state of the art machines, and they were never originally designed to take the beating they receive in presenting short tape segments and repeated fast forwarding and rewinding. This type of machine can break down rapidly and is expensive to repair. We recommend a ½-inch VCR that uses the VHS rather than Beta tape format. In terms of recording or picture quality, there is essentially no difference between the two types of VCR. In Beta format machines, however, the tape is constantly wrapped around the heads. This feature will increase the wear on heads and the tape transport from frequent fast forwarding and rewinding. In VHS format machines, the tape is unloaded from the heads before these functions occur (Klein, 1981). It is also preferable to purchase a machine that has solenoid-operated (called "soft-touch") controls rather than electromechanical controls; the latter will wear out more quickly in frequent use. Whether you buy a table model VCR or a two-unit portable depends upon your needs. The portable VCR has the tuner separate from the playback unit, which permits mobile recording with a fixed or hand-held camera. We recommend the top of the line Panasonic VCR as having all the desirable features mentioned.

b. Audio.   Therapist-constructed audiotaped descriptions of sexual activity may be tailored to each client's unique interests, and therefore a good quality audiocassette recorder-player is a must. You do not have to have a high-quality stereo machine, but you should get a top of the line monophonic unit from a name manufacturer such as Sony. It will not pay to buy cheap tape cassettes. You will find the C-60s or C-90s in the middle price range will be among the best. Any multiple-location, discount stereo dealer will have as good a price on recorders and tape cassettes as you will find.

c. Slide Projectors.   While slides are fairly weak stimuli for evoking sexual arousal (Abel, Barlow, Blanchard, and Mavissakalian, 1975), they are easy to make or obtain, easy to handle, and useful with perhaps two-thirds of the clients seen. We have used carousel projectors for years with excellent results. An auto focus machine is best but also the most expensive. A machine which could randomly access slides would be even better but still more expensive.

4. Intercommunication.   As we mentioned earlier, privacy for the client will produce the best results, and we recommended a two-room configuration for the laboratory. It is best to communicate with and make audio presentations to the client on some sort of intercom. Ours is more complex than necessary. Both our clients and our operators wear headsets with boom microphones. Our custom-built intercom allows us to switch back and forth through various modes of communication to the client rooms. This is desirable but not necessary. Inexpensive two- or multiple-station intercoms can be purchased ready to use.

IV. Stimulus Materials

A. Minimal Requirements

To measure sexual arousal. the stiumuli presented will have to be sufficiently erotic to evoke that arousal. With sex offenders, the best rule of thumb is that the more sexually graphic the material and the closer it comes to being representative of their professed or known sexual interests, the more likely arousal is to occur. Highly sexually explicit and pornographic material is needed. Lack of directness or euphemistic language will possibly defeat your efforts.

1. Video. It is not difficult to obtain erotic stimuli on videotape. Commercial sex shops will have the most explicit deviant materials (e.g., sadomasochism) but also the highest prices. An alternative source would be a mail-order dealer who has catalogues of commercial X-rated films. A feature-length film will be expensive to buy, and an alternative are the video clubs run by many video machine dealers. You usually must pay a membership fee, then they will rent feature-length films for one or two days. With your own plus a rented VCR you can then abstract only the very short sections needed for stimuli.

2. Slides. Pornographic slides can also be purchased from sex shops and by mail order. For some deviations (e.g., bondage, group sex, homosexuality), you will find these slides openly displayed. However, pornography dealers are frequent victims of sting operations, and they are naturally very wary of showing or selling certain materials such as pedophilic stimuli to unknown persons. Such material is probably in stock but under the counter and very expensive. There are several alternative sources. Police departments routinely pick up deviant sexual stimuli from arrested sex offenders. If you have police contacts, they may give or lend you material. You can also make your own. If you have the budget to purchase pedophile magazines (about $10 each), you can make your own slides with a 35-mm camera and a macro lens. If you cannot afford to purchase paraphiliac magazines or cannot find them, then purchase the freely available nudist magazines which have many pictures of naked males and females of all ages. Finally, it is possible to purchase some erotic slides intended for human sex research and therapy from companies which market only to bona fide therapists and researchers.

3. Audio. We have become increasingly impressed with the evocative power of audiotapes, especially when the scripts are about 4 minutes in length and highly graphic in content. The advantage of the audio approach is that stimuli can be tailored precisely to the client's interests. Our approach to this is to have the client write drafts of his own scripts as he is the best judge of what is erotic. This saves enormous amounts of therapist time. We review the scripts, edit or recommend changes, then record them. Sometimes the client records in his own voice: some-times we record in a male or female voice as he prefers. If you have very limited funds we recommend that you begin work with audiotapes. Consult Abel, Blanchard, Barlow, and Mavissakalian (1975) on how to proceed, but do not limit yourself to their suggestions.

V. EMPLOYEES

A. Minimal requirements

A small laboratory setup can be operated by a single person. That person need not be a Ph.D. in experimental or clinical psychology, and does not have to have extensive training in therapy, experimental design, and statistics, or any knowl-edge of electronics. However, that person *must* have experience in working with sex offenders in some modality, must have some appreciation of a behavioral approach to these problems, must be able to carry out the procedures rather strictly, and must be able to obtain, interpret, and report data.

B. Professionals

The availability of consultation from a Ph.D. level clinician or experimentalist would be desirable.

C. Paraprofessionals

A good choice for a lab director might be someone trained at the Master's level in one of the universities offering that degree in behavior analysis. Persons trained in these programs generally have a very good grounding in behavioral methods and could set up and supervise this sort of program.

1. Interns and Trainees.   Many institutions have clinical psychology interns employed on a yearly basis or trainees from other programs or institutions who are present "on rotation" to acquire skills in a new area. Since these persons generally already have some professional skills, administrators are often tempted to use them to set up new programs at low cost to the facility. This is false economy. Trainees are generally spread so thin that they will not give you the amount or kind of service required to set up a lab.

2. Graduate Students and Students Assistants.   Persons in these catego-ries can be a good buy. For senior positions, graduate students, especially predoc-toral candidates, make excellent lab managers. They are usually already trained to a competent skills level, and they can do evaluation and treatment planning, supervise all operations, organize and interpret all data, and write reports. We have hired graduate students for years with uniformly good results. Occasionally persons who have just completed doctorates are seeking a postdoctoral position to learn particular skills, and they also serve well as managers.

Once a lab is set up and operating, the day-to-day tasks can be handled by student assistants. These persons run all procedures, schedule clients, do data keeping, and write some reports. We hire students through the College Work Study Program in which they repay financial aid grants by working for program contractors.

3. Technicians.   If you use a lot of electronics, you will need a technician to keep them running. There is no substitute for continuous maintenance, on-the-spot trouble shooting, and construction of special equipment. We hire students from a university electronics engineering department on an hourly contract for services basis.

D. Consultants

In the early stages of setting up shop you may need a consultant. They are useful but, over the long haul, not as valuable as they are thought to be. They are also expensive, so use them sparingly. We recommend that you first attempt to find consultative help within your own organization or a related one in your community. If this does not suit your needs, hire a consultant but make certain first that he/she has the *specific* skills which you require. The Association for Advancement of Behavior Therapy maintains a consultant service and can assist you to make the best fit between your needs and the appropriate consultant.

VI. CLIENT SAFEGUARDS AND INFORMED CONSENT

A. Minimal Requirements

What you propose to do is ethical, humane, reasonable, and entirely defensible, and you need make no excuses. Be open, be honest, and share information about what you are doing with your colleagues. Our rule is that we will talk to anyone who will listen. Being open, however, does not mean sharing confidential information about clients with uninvolved others. You are dealing with very intimate information in a very critical area of behavior, and you will be asking people to give you samples of illicit behavior. If your clients do not believe that their rights are being protected and the data kept confidential, they will not comply and there is no reason why they should. Absolute confidentiality of data and informed consent are therefore essential. How one prepares an informed consent form depends upon the situation in which one works. The essential elements of informed consent and guidelines for evaluation and treatment of mental patients and prisoners may be obtained from the National Institute of Mental Health (Rockville, MD 20857). You should also consult a basic text in the area such as Schwitzgebel and Schwitzgebel (1980) for additional information.

B. To What Are They Consenting?

Reduced to essentials, clients are giving you permission to invade their privacy. The consent form that we use states very explicitly what we are about: we will ask detailed and possibly embarrassing questions about social and sexual history: we will present highly erotic materials: we will make measurement of the erection response: we will interpret the resulting data and write reports, and these will become part of a permanent record. We acknowledge that these procedures may create embarrassment, anxiety, shame, or depression, and we offer treatment for this. We state the benefits to be expected: learning more about one's sexual arousal patterns and problems associated with them, and the opportunity to participate in a behavioral treatment program to alter those patterns. We stress the voluntary nature of participation and the right to withdraw without reprisal. All reports are reviewed by the client and the staff for accuracy and fairness. No information is ever given to outside personnel without the explicit permission of the client and/or with him present.

C. Dealing with Client Apprehension

The best way to deal with client anxiety is to be very frank about what you propose to do. Many sex offenders expect rejection, and are often surprised to confront a treatment person who speaks their language and does not make a big deal of their unacceptable behaviors. We inform them that what we are doing is simply another form of assessment, not a "test" to which there are "right" and "wrong" answers. We stress that deviant sexuality is learned behavior, and so may be unlearned and other behaviors substituted. We indicate that our approach is simpler and more direct than talking about one's problems and that is why we do it in a laboratory situation. Many clients initially show fear of the penile transducer, apparently in the belief that we have a "sexual lie detector." This can be dealt with by explaining that it is impossible for us to make anyone become sexually aroused, that any information we obtain is being freely surrendered by them. A tiny minority of clients are offended by the mechanical nature of the procedures. Less than 1% of several hundred clients seen to date have expressed feelings of disgust, repulsion, or humiliation toward our approach. When this occurs, we urge the client to decline participation.

VII. ASSESSING SEXUAL DEVIANCE

A. Minimal Requirements

Minimally, any assessment must obtain therapeutically useful information about the behaviors which form links in the chain of components that lead to the performance of deviant sexual behavior. Traditionally the major avenues of approach to those components have been clinical interview, self-report, and psychological testing. More recently, physiological assessment has been added to the package. We will look at each of these approaches.

1. Clinical Interview. Sex offenders are notorious for their attempts to deny, minimize, and rationalize their deviant sexual behavior (Burgess, Groth, Holmstrom, and Sgroi, 1978; Cox and Daitzman, 1980; Groth, 1979). They will rarely present themselves for assessment unless collateral evidence is so overwhelming that they must to some extent acknowledge their deviant interests, and even then they remain defensive. Unless backed up by a large variety of unassailable collateral data, clinical interview will be the least valid measure of deviant sexual potential.

2. Self-report. Similarly, self-report inventories (e.g., Paitich, Langevin, Freeman, Mann, and Handy, 1977) on sexual practices or methods such as card sorts are wide open to influence by the client. Although recent evidence suggests that self-report data can be valid and useful measures (Hindelang, Hirschi, and Weis, 1981; Hirschi, Hindelang, and Weis, 1980), with sex offenders any such data should be viewed skeptically in the absence of other confirmatory measures.

3. Psychological Testing. Because of the directness of many of the items, much of the available psychological testing material is as open to influence as a self-report inventory. When these tests have been shown to demarcate sex offenders from normal individuals (e.g., Johnston and Anderson, Note 1), they have done so only in a global sense, without high specificity as to interests or activities. Projective testing is not the answer to this problem. If a client is willing to give frankly sexual responses to ambiguous stimuli, why not just ask him what you want to know?

4. Physiological Assessment. There has long been the hope that it would be possible to develop a multi-component physiological "signature" which would handily identify sex offenders. This hope has not been realized. However, as we stated above, the response of penile erection has consistently been demonstrated to be the best index of male sexual arousal, specific to preferred kinds of erotic stimuli and not to others. This is the minimal and most direct avenue to the components of deviant sexual behavior.

B. Measuring the Behavior.

With a physiological recorder and a supply of penile transducers on hand, you are now ready to measure the erection response. The instruction booklet accompanying each recorder will tell you how to attach the transducer to the subject and to the machine. You will see the response displayed by a pen tracing on a moving strip chart. On that you must be able to read the entire range of the response: minimum value (0% erection), the maximum value (100% erection), and all units in between. What this means is that you must calibrate your machine to each subject. This involves nothing more than making sure that the pen stays on the chart paper and is done by adjusting the sensitivity control of the coupler. What you want is to be able to use nearly the full width of the strip chart and still have a margin on either side. This will provide maximum information about the response. If the sensitivity is set too high, a very small response sensed by the transducer will cause the pen to go off the strip chart on the upper end. If the sensitivity is too low, a very large response or a full erection will result in a tracing with a very small elevation off the 0% baseline, which will be difficult to interpret. Since each machine is different, some trial and error will be necessary in order to discover how to get the response on the chart in a readable form.

If you are using a digital monitor, these problems can be handled in an easier fashion. Some models have two sensitivity controls called "zero adjust" and "full adjust," and each of these contains a three-digit counting dial. There is also a LED display that continuously shows measured values as a percentage. In order to calibrate this unit, the operator adjusts the zero control until the LED displays 0.000 when the client reports no erection. Whatever number is then shown on the counting dial represents his "zero sensitivity" or no-arousal setting. This operation is repeated with the full adjust, turning the control until the LED reads 1.000 when the client reports full erection. The number shown by the full adjust counting dial will represent his "100% sensitivity" or full erection or maximum arousal setting. By presetting the counting dials to these obtained numbers prior to any subsequent session, the monitor will automatically read all values between 0 and 100%, display them simultaneously on the LED, and print them out as percentage values on a continuous calculator tape. This is obviously simpler than interpreting a pen tracing.

Figure 14-9 shows a typical erection response tracing such as would be seen on a strip chart recorder. Reading the tracing is rather straightforward. You must first make the assumption that the erection response is distributed on an interval scale, that is, that each unit of change is equidistant from every other. This permits you to report the data as percentages of the maximum. For purposes of exposition, note that the response tracing shown in the figure covers five of the large divisions on the chart paper in its course from 0 to 100% and back to 0%. Each large division would represent 20% of the maximum, and each small division would represent 4%. These charts are usually printed on a millimeter scale, so if you knew that 25

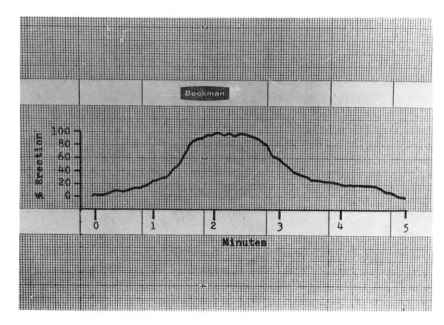

Figure 14-9.   Sample of a typical penile erection tracing on Beckman chart paper. In this example, each 5 mm of elevation = 20% of maximum erection.

mm of elevation = 100% or full erection, you could read any intermediate value immediately. That maximum can vary from subject to subject. What if it was 43 mm or 62 mm? In these cases, respectively, 4.3 mm or 6.2 mm would each equal 10% and roughly .5 mm would equal 1%. Obviously, counting up half millimeters invites observer error, but over a large series of observations a small error factor is not going to seriously affect any decisions.

C. Assessing the Rapist

1. Minimal Requirements.   Obtaining stimulus materials to assess sexual arousal to rape is not an easy matter. Perhaps the minimal requirements can best be stated by telling you what you should *not* do. Your quest for materials will probably not be furthered by asking the rapist, "Tell me what it is you find exciting about rape." You will very likely receive global and imprecise answers. Let us assume that you are able to measure the erection response. You might improve your assessment capability by showing your client a picture and requesting, "Imagine raping this woman." You will probably obtain a tracing, but unless he tells you what he imagines and you tape-record his verbal material, then match the tape sequences to elevations in the tracing, you still will not have any useful information. You might also say, "Tell me a rape fantasy," and then record his erection response as he speaks. Here again you need to tape his verbalizations and match the content to the tracing. Some commercial films such as *Straw Dogs* and *A Clockwork Orange* contain graphic rape sequences. This sort of stimulus is weak because it is contextually related to the film content and may or may not be representative of your client's interests. We therefore recommend that you not spend your time attempting to individualize assessment for each client. If you do, you will end up with broad variability in type and quality of data obtained, which will reduce your ability to evaluate the efficacy of your assessment package and make interclient comparisons impossible because every client received something different. What you want then is an assessment procedure that will apply to *all* rapists.

2. Stimulus Materials.   There are no commercially available packages for the physiological assessment of rapists. Accept the fact that you will have to construct your own.

a. Slides.   We recommend that you do not use slides. One can find multitudes of pictures of men abusing women (and other men) and apparently raping or otherwise humiliating them. As we mentioned above, this requires input from the client as to what he finds arousing and will vary tremendously from person to person. Slides are not particularly powerful stimuli (Abel et al., 1975a) and we have found them to be totally ineffective for assessing rapists.

b. Video.   Videotape is the most powerful medium for evoking sexual arousal, and we recommend it even it you must abstract sections from violent X-rated or commercial films. If you must do this, remember two things: make certain that each sequence is the *same* length, a minimum of 2 minutes, and also abstract sequences that appear to be examples of mutually consenting sexual activity so that you can compare arousal to conventional stimuli with arousal to rape stimuli.

For video assessment of rapists, we use a package that was developed for research purposes (Abel, Blanchard, Becker, and Djenderedjian, 1978). Clients view 2-minute silent segments in which a male and female simulate mutually consenting intercourse, a rape attack, and a physical assault without sexual activity. These are fast-moving, highly graphic sequences which reliably elicit large amounts of arousal. The client views these tapes under instructional conditions where he is sometimes requested to become sexually aroused and sometimes to suppress his arousal, and is additionally asked to give estimates of his peak arousal per presentation. With this procedure, data are obtained on (1) the client's uncontrolled arousal to one nondeviant and two deviant presentations (arousal instructions), (2) his potential for exerting self-control in the presence of the same types of stimuli (suppression instructions), and (3) his awareness of the magnitude of his arousal (estimates).

Although it might seem a formidable task, you could make a similar set of sequences using a home video system. The Abel et al. (1978) tape is far from a highly polished and professional product.

c. Audio.   If the video facilities are not available to you, the next best and far cheaper alternative is construction of audiotapes describing consensual intercourse, rape, and physical assault. We use a set originally developed by Abel, Blanchard, Barlow, and Guild (1977), which is essentially an audio version of the above described video sequences. If you are going to use audio, we would first recommend that you write scripts that will be at least 4 minutes long when recorded. We have found that with short audiotapes (about 2 minutes), subjects often begin to respond within the second minute so that substantial arousal is often just beginning as the tape ends. Information is lost, and when these data are plotted it appears that audio generates much less arousal than video. We have overcome this problem by lengthening the presentation to 4 minutes (e.g, Avery-Clark, Note 2). This produces substantially more arousal and is quite comparable to that produced with videotape.

3. What Do You Do with the Data?   You must find a way to summarize your information so that you can understand it, make judgments about it, and report it if necessary. The best way to do this is to prepare some sort of standard form which conveniently displays all the necessary information in a single place.

a. Data Sheets.   Figure 14-10 shows the data sheet we use to summarize rapist assessments for *both* video and audio procedures. The upper left-hand panel is divided into sections for video and audio data. As we read across the columns, "Stim" refers to the type of presentation: M = mutually consenting intercourse, R = rape, and A = assault; "Inst Set" refers to the instructional set given the client: A = arousal instructions, and S = suppression instructions; "Meas Vid" refers to the *peak* percentage measured in the video presentation; "Est Vid" refers to the peak percentage estimated by the client; and "Meas Aud" and "Est Aud" refer to measured values and estimates obtained for the audio presentations. There are two presentations for each type of stimulus, for example, two rape/arousal and two rape/suppression. These values are summarized as means and entered in the small table in the lower left panel.

   The obtained means are then plotted in the four graphs shown, the upper two for video and the lower two for audio. The filled circles represent the data obtained for the voluntary arousal conditions; the open circles, the data for the voluntary suppression conditions.

b. How to Evaluate the Data.   In data evaluation, we have adopted several conventions. We present them here, and they will apply to all assessment and treatment procedures to be described. We consider everything below 20% of maximum erection to be no arousal. Arousal between 0 and 20% is so low that one can hardly make an assessment judgment; 20% is far too low to make initiation of treatment worthwhile. We refer to the range from 20 to 40% as low arousal. Tentative assess-

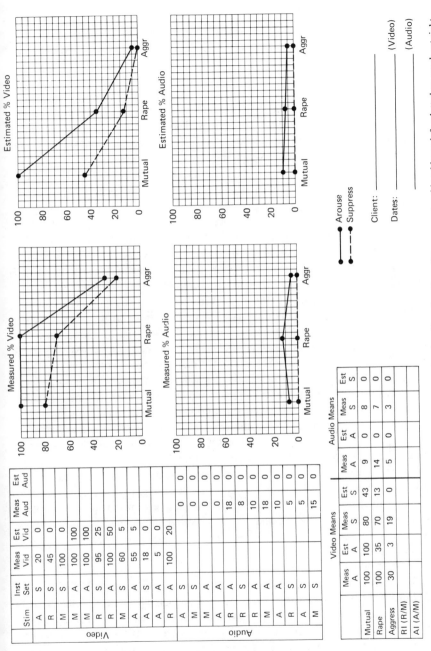

Figure 14-10. Sample data sheet for video and audio assessment of rapists. Data for all conditions are entered in tables at left, plotted on graphs at right (see text for details).

ment judgments can be made, but the amount of arousal does not justify treatment. We consider 40 to 60% to be moderate arousal. Assessment judgments can be clearly made, and if the peak arousal is between 50 and 60%, treatment intervention is feasible. The balance from 60 to 80% is considered high arousal; from 80 to 100%, very high arousal. Assessment judgments are quite clear-cut, and treatment is warranted.

In evaluating data such as those in Figure 14-10, we are asking several questions. First, how much does the client respond to deviant versus nondeviant stimuli? Second, how much self-control can he exert, and can he bring the response under control now or does he need training? Third, do his estimates match what we have measured: that is, how aware is he of his level of arousal? Let us apply these questions to the data of Figure 14-10.

Looking at the upper center panel, we see that this client responded at 100% to both consenting intercourse and rape, but only at 30% to physical assault. When asked to suppress his response to the same types of presentations, he was only able to reduce the behavior by 20-30%. First conclusion: he shows maximum arousal to consenting intercourse, a good sign. He shows an equal amount to rape stimuli and low arousal to aggression. Treatment will therefore focus on reducing arousal to rape stimuli while maintaining his nondeviant arousal in strength. Now examine the estimated data in the upper right panel. Under arousal instructions, he correctly estimated full arousal to consenting intercourse. His estimate of 35% to rape was grossly discrepant with the measured 100%, and he estimated no arousal to aggression while we measured 30%. Estimates for the suppression condition were similarly discrepant. Second conclusion: this client is denying that he becomes aroused to deviant material. This is typical of rapists and other deviants. Treatment will also have to focus on bringing his awareness into line with his measured values.

Look now at the audio data in the two lower panels. There is essentially no arousal in any condition, and the estimates are in reasonable agreement with the measured values. Several conclusions may be drawn from these data. First, had we used only audio stimuli we would have concluded that the client was a nonresponder and terminated him from the program. Lesson: always use more than one stimulus modality if possible. The data here seem to confirm the power of video, but you can always be wrong and you never know unless you try.

D. Assessing the Pedophile.

1. Minimal Requirements.
The same caveats stated previously about attempting to be too individualistic in preparing assessment materials apply equally to pedophiles. This group represents two-thirds of our referrals and may be the largest group seen. You will therefore need a set of general assessment procedures which will apply to heterosexual, homosexual, and bisexual pedophiles.

2. Stimulus Materials. There are some commercially available stimulus materials for assessing pedophiles, but we have found them to be somewhat ineffective and applicable to special cases rather than for general use. We recommend that you consider constructing your own stimuli.

a. Slides.   Slide sets of pedophilic stimuli are available to therapists only from Farrall Instruments (Grand Island, NB 68801). These are available sets of 15 each and usually show a single child dressed, undressing, and posing nude in different positions. The problem is that this single subject would have to be appealing to your pedophilic client. All of the subjects in these sets are in roughly the same age group, so you would additionally be unable to get a look at your client's arousal patterns across the age parameter.

Alternatively, we have already mentioned that slides of children of various ages, posing and engaging in sexual activity, are available from some sex shops and then only under the counter. In the event they could be purchased, you would pay a premium price. We also mentioned the possibility of obtaining slides, pictures, magazines, and movies from the confiscated stores of police departments. This is probably your best low-cost source for frankly pedophilic stimuli.

We constructed our own slide assessment several years ago by directly photographing pictures from nudist magazines, homosexual magazines, and confiscated pedophile magazines and pictures. We finally arrived at a 40-slide set, males and females in the age groups 1–7, 8–12, 13–17, and 18+, five slides per group. Each slide is presented to the client for 2 minutes under instructions to become sexually aroused if he finds the stimulus erotic. The peak arousal level per slide is extracted; a mean is computed for each age group; and a profile is plotted to show the average percent of full erection to each of the eight age groups. Sample data from this procedure are shown in Figure 14-11.

b. Audio.   In our experience, audiotaped assessments are very useful with pedophiles. You could construct audio scripts to examine any problem of interest in pedophilia, and we recommend that you try this. Thus far, audio assessments have been used primarily to separate pedophiles attracted to violence in sex from nonviolent ones (Abel, Becker, Murphy, and Flanagan, 1981; Avery-Clark, Note 2). In our laboratory's version (i.e., Avery-Clark's) there are six tapes in a series, five of which describe an escalating level of involvement in, and use of, violence to effect a sexual relationship with a child. The categories are: fondling, mutually consenting intercourse with a child, verbal coercion to accomplish intercourse, rape, and sadism. The sixth tape described mutually consenting intercourse with an adult partner. There are a homosexual and a heterosexual series. In constructing this series we followed our hunch, mentioned above, that scripts 4 minutes long would produce much more arousal than 2-minute scripts, and this was confirmed in use. Sample data from this procedure are shown in Figure 14-13.

c. Video. Videotapes or, more likely, motion pictures of children in sexual activity are not rare but they are difficult to obtain. Again, sex shops have them but do not display or sell them openly. Police stores are probably you best single source. Follow the suggestions given above if you plan to construct a video assessment from motion pictures.

3. What Do You Do with the Data?
As in the case of the rapist assessment, you need to construct a standard form on which to summarize your information for ease of handling and interpretation.

a. Data Sheets. Figure 14-11 shows the raw data summary form for the slide assessment and Figure 14-12 the resultant sexual interest profile graph.

On the raw data summary of Figure 14-11 you see the various age groups displayed across the top: MC = male child, MA = male adult, FC = female child, and FA = female adult. The slide numbers refer to the even-numbered bins of the slide tray, each stimulus slide separated by a blank. As may be seen by the placement of the slide numbers, they are presented in the order: 2, 4, 6, etc., but are randomized by age category. In each space the operator notes the *peak* value of arousal measured in a single presentation. These values are then summed (T = total) and a mean ($\bar{X}$) computed, and these means are plotted on the graph shown in Figure 14-12.

The sample data shown in Figure 14-12 display the profile of sexual interest. The four columns on the left show the data for response to males; the four on the right, response to females.

Figure 14-13 shows the data sheet used for audio assessment of pedophiles. The panels across the top half of the sheet show the raw data summary. There are two presentations per category designated "A Series" and "B Series." The capitalized letters refer to the type of presentation: MC = mutually consenting intercourse with a child, FA = female adult, MA = male adult, S = sadism, R = rape, F = fondling, and VC = verbal coercion. The column "SEQ" refers to the order in which the segments come up on the tape; "M" and "E" refer to measured and estimated values, and these are summed and computed as means in the boxes on the upper right. These means are then plotted on two or four of the graphs on the lower half of the sheet.

b. How to Evaluate the Data. We will examine the data from both of these assessments in turn. Look again at Figure 14-12. The profile is very straightforward. There was no response at all greater than 5% to males. On the female side, we see a classic picture of heterosexual pedophilia. There was no response to very young children (FC 1–7); response was in the high-arousal range to females from 8–12 years of age; and responses to teenagers and female adults were both in the moderate range. This is a not untypical profile of female pedophilia: very high

Raw Data Sheet
Slide Assessment Procedure

Date: _____

Client: _____

Operator: _____

MC 1-7	MC 8-12	MC 13-17	MA 18+	FC 1-7	FC 8-12	FC 13-17	FA 18+
#12 __2__	# 2 __2__	#14 __6__	# 6 __1__	#10 __4__	#18 __100__	# 4 __26__	# 8 __62__
#32 __5__	#22 __5__	#20 __4__	#30 __3__	#26 __2__	#24 __92__	#18 __44__	#28 __43__
#44 __0__	#34 __3__	#36 __3__	#40 __4__	#48 __2__	#46 __83__	#42 __38__	#38 __36__
#58 __1__	#60 __1__	#50 __2__	#52 __1__	#62 __1__	#64 __77__	#54 __32__	#56 __21__
#78 __4__	#72 __0__	#70 __2__	#66 __0__	#74 __1__	#80 __81__	#68 __47__	#76 __34__
T = __12__	T = __11__	T = __17__	T = __9__	T = __10__	T = __433__	T = __187__	T = __196__
X̄ = __2__	X̄ = __2__	X̄ = __3__	X̄ = __2__	X̄ = __2__	X̄ = __87__	X̄ = __37__	X̄ = __39__

COMMENT:

12/15/77
Rev
3/6/80

Figure 14-11.   Sample raw data summary for pedophile slide assessment. Data entered in each column are peak percentages of erection recorded for each 2-minute presentation.

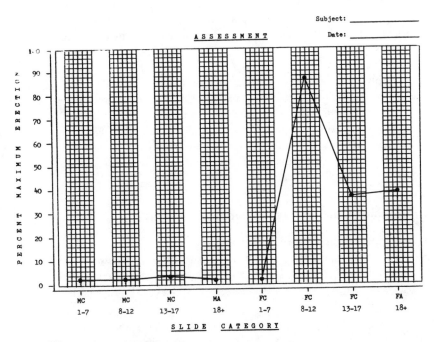

Figure 14-12.   Sample sexual interest profile from pedophile slide assessment. Four columns on left show average response to male stimuli; four on right, response to female stimuli. Data points are means from raw data summary sheet (Figure 14-11).

response to preteen females and rather modest arousal to more age-appropriate adults. Conclusion: treatment will have to focus on attenuating arousal to the preteen category and increasing arousal to the adult.

Figure 14-13 shows the data obtained from the pedophile audio assessment. The two left-hand panels show the measured arousal to the heterosexual and homosexual tapes; the right-hand panels, the client's estimates of his arousal to those stimuli. The curves of estimates almost exactly parallel those of measured arousal, indicating that his level of awareness was quite high and accurate. Evaluating the measured values is not as difficult as it might look. In the heterosexual series, this client responded in the high-arousal range to description of fondling, consenting intercourse with a child, and verbal coercion to accomplish intercourse. He showed no arousal (less than 20%) to descriptions of rape and sadism, and very high arousal to descriptions of consenting intercourse with a female adult. There are some differences in his homosexual profile. He responded to a description of fondling a male child in the low-arousal range and, as in the heterosexual series, had high arousal to descriptions of consenting intercourse with a male child and verbal coercion. There was essentially no arousal shown to descriptions of rape, sadism, or consenting relations with a male adult. Conclusions: this client may be a functional adult heterosexual who also molests both boys and girls. Although he may coercively use his influence as an adult to effect these relationships, he is likely to be benign in his activities and does not appear to be excited by the use of violence against his victims. Treatment would have to focus on reducing deviant arousal in the five categories where high responding was observed. However, his activities are probably all of a piece, so stimulus materials used in treatment could incorporate coercion, fondling, and intercourse in a single stimulus presentation, rather than treating each in turn. That would leave basically two categories to treat: arousal to young girls and arousal to young boys, and this could be done in a simple multiple baseline by treating each consecutively (see Hersen and Barlow, 1976, for details). No treatment appears warranted for his adult arousal, but it should be monitored continuously to ensure that it remains stable.

E. Assessing Other Sexual Deviants

1. Minimal Requirements. "Other sexual deviants" comprise about 5% of our case load in the sense that their deviant behavior is *exclusively* other than pedophilia or rape. You will see so few of these other exclusive types that it will probably be necessary to construct assessments on a case-by-case basis.

a. What Types Are You Likely to See? In this category we find such types as exhibitionists (by far the largest group), voyeurs, sadomasochists, transvestites, bestialists, fetishists, frotteurs, klismophiliacs, and similar "exotic" paraphiliacs. To be sure, rapists and pedophiles may have secondary or tertiary diagnoses of one

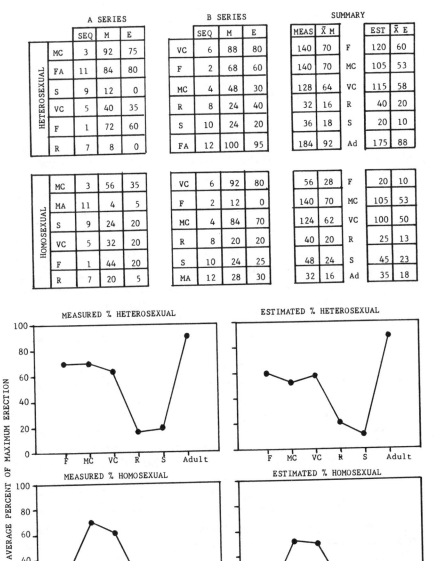

Figure 14-13.   Sample data sheet for pedophile audio assessment. Data for all conditions are entered in tables in upper panels, plotted graphs in lower panels (see text for details).

or more of these other deviations which should also be assessed and treated, but those having a primary diagnosis of exotic deviation, excepting exhibitionists, will be relatively rare.

b. Conserving Effort.   Your primary assessment efforts should be directed toward the two major deviant groups you are likely to see. Because we see so many clients who have a secondary diagnosis of exhibitionism, we constructed a special assessment for it. We did this also because exhibitionists appear to resemble each other, in terms of behaviors performed, more than they differ. The other deviations, however, are likely to be highly idiosyncratic in nature and difficult to subsume under a general assessment. In these cases, you should construct stimuli specific to your client's special interests.

2. Stimulus Materials.
There is a wide variety of stimulus materials which cater to exotic paraphilias.

a. Video.   Much is available on videotape and in motion pictures, for example, sadomasochism, fetishism, or klismophilia. We are aware, for example, of a supplier who offers a large catalogue of films devoted entirely to foot fetishism. Others cater exclusively to transvestites or to the bondage and discipline trade.

b. Slides.   Although slides depicting exotic paraphilias are undoubtedly available, a less expensive route is making your own from magazines. There are literally hundreds of magazines, freely available, which deal with paraphilias of every sort. These can be had from sex shops, general suppliers who offer a large variety, or specialty houses which cater to a single paraphiliac interest such as sadomasochism.

c. Audio.   Exotic paraphilias are instances in which audio descriptions are of particular value as you can very precisely target those behaviors of special interest to your client. These are also situations in which you will profit most from allowing the client to prepare drafts of his own scripts.

3. What Do You Do with the Data?
As recommended previously, you will need a standard form on which to record your raw data, summarize it, and make a graphic presentation.

a. Data Sheets.   We have already shown a sufficient number of sample data sheets for you to have an idea by now of what is required. In dealing with exotic sexual behaviors, we suggest that you do not prepare a special data sheet for each one. Prepare instead a general data summary form on which there is enough space to record as much raw data as you might conceivably collect on any single deviation (or multiple deviations), space for entering means values, and graphs on which to plot the data. This general sheet can then be labeled according to the behavior(s) with which you are dealing.

b. *How to Evaluate the Data.* We have presented a number of guidelines and examples so that you are now aware of the basics in making judgments from data obtained. You will find that those guidelines apply equally well to these other, less frequent behaviors.

F. How to Report the Data.

Reporting is tricky business and you must be extremely careful how you do it. *Never* make statements such as, "The video data confirm that this man is a rapist," or "The results of the audio assessment show that this man continues to be a danger to children." Both of these statements may well be true, but the data do not "say" that. The only thing that the data "confirm" or "show" is that under a set of very special conditions, the client produced some amount of penile erection to stimuli related to rape and pedophilia.

What *does* this mean, then? We may legitimately inquire what this small group of indices has to do with motivation or with the probability that a person will behave in a sexually deviant manner. Does the presence of high levels of arousal to rape, pedophilic, or other deviant stimuli in a laboratory mean that surely the person will rape, molest children, or otherwise disport himself in a deviant fashion? Of course, it does not. Undeniably, sexual arousal is considerably more than just penile erection. The erection response is not even present during the commission of some deviant sexual acts and, when present, the offender may or may not use his genitals in the act itself. Nonetheless, if in an assessment such as we have described, a male shows a very large erection response to a deviant sexual stimulus, and very little or no response to a nondeviant stimulus, this is more than presumptive evidence that he is more sexually attracted to the former than to the latter. This would be a particularly reasonable conclusion if the man had a known history of sexual deviance. Such data, however, *do not* mean that he will necessarily act upon this arousal; they *do* mean that he may be *at risk* to do so, and in the case of a known sex offender that is reason enough to justify therapeutic intervention. We say again: deviant sexual arousal *is* deviant sexual behavior. That is what the data show.

In reporting, we recommend that you limit yourself to what you know based on what *you* did; do not try to integrate your work with everything else in the record. Keep your report dry and matter-of-fact. Say exactly what you did and what you found. If data from a variety of procedures agree, report that. If the client cannot suppress the behavior and/or his estimates do not agree with measured values, report that. If the client comments on the procedure or says he believes that he needs additional treatment, report that. *Never* go beyond what the data tell you about his response to a particular procedure, and *never* make predictions about future conduct. We are not suggesting that you try to escape responsibility for what you find, but simply that you limit yourself to reporting what you *do* find. Many mental health professionals feel quite comfortable displaying "clinical judgement," "gut feelings," and various other modes of intuitive behavior; we suggest that these types of data do not justify that.

One day a client will be referred to you who has had literally hundreds of hours of verbal psychotherapy directed at his deviant sexuality. He will tell you how much his therapy treatment has meant to him, how it has helped as nothing before in his life to understand what sort of person he really is, and how certain he is that he will never, ever reoffend. Then you will assess him and he will absolutely blow the top off the chart responding to deviant stimuli. You will have to report this. Do the erection data show that psychotherapy has not "worked" for this client? Certainly not. Psychotherapy works very well with some problems, but sexual arousal problems do not seem to be among them. The behavioral data that you would present in this case simply suggest that there is unfinished business in this client's treatment program, nothing more. It would not be amiss to comment upon that.

VIII. Treating Sexual Deviance

A. Minimal Requirements

We are firmly convinced that successful treatment of sexual deviants must contain three essential components: the effort must be directed exactly to the problem; the operations should be as simple as possible; and any procedure should be portable in order that it may be used in a variety of settings, including the client's home.

1. Directness of Effort. Many, if not most, therapists believe that sexual deviants have "other" problems which are so overwhelming in importance that they are prevented from becoming fully functioning adults and, therefore, turn to sexual deviance as a compensation or a simpler, less demanding level of functioning. If this other problem could be cleared up, the argument goes, usually through the medium of intensive psychotherapy, the need to be a sexual deviant would also be cleared up. Many pedophiles, for example, are thought to fear and abhor social and sexual relationships with mature adults, and so turn to children who are "immature" and thus "less threatening." Treating this "other" problem is an example of a highly indirect approach. Pedophiles may well fear and abhor relationships with adults, but so do thousands of men who somehow do not become pedophiles. The fact is that pedophiles have learned, in whatever fashion, to endow children with erotic value, and they desire to have sexual relations with them. Their social behavior with children is certainly age-inappropriate, but the "real" problem is simply that they are sexually aroused by children and prey upon them for sexual purposes. This is the problem which should be directly treated.

2. Simplicity of Approach. Only the simple succeeds. Defining problems imprecisely encourages use of imprecise approaches. It is our belief that psychotherapy, while certainly useful in some respects, is the least direct way to treat sexual deviance. A man may spend years in psychotherapy learning why he became a sexual deviant and still maintain the same sexual feelings as when he began. Learning *why* one is a deviant is, it seems to us, considerably less productive than learning how to *stop* being one. The three treatments which we have chosen to present below all have these essential qualities of directness and simplicity. They are easy to do, require very little time per session, are so simple that they can be performed by a person with little training, and cut right to the heart of deviant sexual arousal.

3. Portability of Procedures. We have indicated that a laboratory may be in a fixed location or it may be portable. To measure the erection response, obviously the client must be present. He does not have to be present to carry out each treatment session. All of the treatments described below are such that they can be carried out in many different locations.

B. Will the Behavior Be Changed Permanently?

In relation to the stated requirements of directness, simplicity, and portability, it is necessary to emphasize that no psychological treatment, behavioral or otherwise, changes behavior irreversibly. The treatments to be described will change behavior and keep it changed as long as they continue to be practiced. If the treated person goes on to develop other, nondeviant and more reinforcing sexual behaviors, then this *may* eliminate deviant sexual interest and activity completely. Make no assumptions about that happening. We suggest that you consider sexual deviants as special types of junkies. Self-control will in every case be a full-time job, every waking hour for the rest of their lives. To accomplish that, they need direct, simple, and portable self-control procedures.

C. A Basic Handbook of Simple Treatments

1. Orgasmic Reconditioning. *a. What is it?* Orgasmic reconditioning, sometimes called masturbatory conditioning or reconditioning, is a counter-conditioning procedure (Laws and O'Neil, 1981; VanDeventer and Laws, 1978). The goal of the procedure is the reprogramming of the sexual deviant's masturbatory practices. The result of successful treatment is that nondeviant stimuli come to elicit sexual arousal but deviant stimuli do not.

b. When Do You Use It? Orgasmic reconditioning should be used with those clients whose assessment data reveal very low nondeviant arousal and very high deviant arousal. We have seen this configuration most often in pedophiles, but the treatment will be applicable to any client showing this arousal pattern. Some clients will tell you that they do not masturbate or do not like to, and others will refuse to masturbate in the laboratory. Do not force them to participate.

c. Steps in the Procedure.   See your client a minimum of three times per week in the laboratory. Tell him that on treatment days he should not masturbate after midnight and should limit his intake of fluids before appearing for treatment. Do not have him wear the transducer during treatment sessions as the tracing (or readout) will be disturbed by the masturbatory activity. In the first week (three sessions), have him masturbate to ejaculation using a *deviant* sexual fantasy. Prior to the third treatment session, conduct an evaluation in which you present audiovisual samples appropriate to his deviant and nondeviant interests. These can be audiotapes, videotapes, or slides, and they should be selected or constructed by the client. The data obtained in these evaluation sessions will be your main indices of success or failure in treatment, and it is absolutely essential that you obtain them. In the second week, have the client repeat the same procedure, except that he is now to use a *nondeviant* fantasy. In the third week, he should revert to *deviant* fantasy. Continue this alternation throughout treatment. Although it seems paradoxical, if the treatment is successful you will see deviant arousal (i.e., in the data from weekly evaluation sessions) begin to decline until it reaches a near-0 or 0% level. Nondeviant arousal should increase to a level above 50% at termination of treatment.

d. Data Sheets.   You will need two types of data sheet. One will summarize the data of treatment: client name, date, type of fantasy used, number and order of any supporting stimuli which may be presented, comments, etc. We use a standard treatment data sheet that is applicable to all treatments employed. You will be summarizing a small amount of data from each session so a separate sheet for each type of treatment is not necessary. The second data sheet is one on which you summarize your progress (or lack of it) in graphical form. If you use regular graph paper, for ease of plotting get the type which shows ten squares to the inch. These can be had in large sheets but are somewhat cumbersome. In addition you have to draw your axes on each sheet.

e. Evaluating Data.   Judgments about treatment data will be made using the same conventions described above for evaluating assessment data. In using orgasmic reconditioning, you will be starting out with levels of deviant arousal falling in the range from 50 to 100%; nondeviant arousal, if any, will be in the range from about 20 to 40%. You will see some variability in the evaluation data, but the general picture should be that deviant arousal will begin to fall to a much lower level and then nondeviant arousal will begin to rise, terminating at a fairly high level. If you do not observe this, the treatment has been unsuccessful (for more complete details, see Laws and O'Neil, 1981; VanDeventer and Laws, 1978).

2. Olfactory Aversion. *a. What is it?* This procedure is a type of aversive conditioning in which an unpleasant event is made to follow an undesired behavior. Olfactory aversion involves the pairing in time of extremely noxious but harmless odors with presentations of deviant sexual stimuli (Laws, Meyer, and Holmen, 1978). As the noxious agent we use crushable capsules of spirit of ammonia (Burroughs-Wellcome, Research Triangle Park, NC 27709). The effect of the treatment is to suppress deviant arousal. Concurrently maintained levels of nondeviant arousal will be largely unaffected by the intervention.

b. When Do You Use It? Olfactory aversion should be used with those clients whose assessment data reveal very high levels of *both* deviant and nondeviant arousal. You may see this pattern in any client.

c. Steps in the Procedure. See the client three times per week, and prior to the third treatment session conduct your weekly evaluation. You can have the client wear the transducer during treatment if you wish, but as treatment proceeds you will probably be measuring very little behavior. All stimulus presentations in this procedure will be deviant. You could, alternatively, have the client produce deviant fantasies. If you do this, make certain that he speaks them aloud so that you may periodically monitor them. The client controls the administration of the noxious agent. When the presentation (or fantasy) begins, have him crush the ammonia capsule between two fingers and inhale the fumes by passing the broken capsule back and forth about 6 inches *below* his nostrils. He should *not* place the capsule directly beneath his nostrils as the fumes can damage nasal membranes. He should also have a container in which to put the capsule between presentations. We use a small jar. The procedure reliably and completely suppresses deviant sexual arousal. Spirit of ammonia is a poison so do not use this treatment with suicide-prone clients.

d. Data Sheets. Follow the recommendations on data sheets given earlier under orgasmic reconditioning.

e. Evaluating data. Use the same conventions for evaluating these data as those described previously for assessment and treatment. In using olfactory aversion, you will begin with high levels of deviant *and* nondeviant arousal falling in the range from 50 to 100%. If you are measuring erection during treatment, you will initially see some deviant arousal which will be quickly suppressed as the agent is used. The evaluation data should show a fairly abrupt fall in deviant arousal from the first evaluation session onward; nondeviant arousal should be unaffected (see

Laws, Meyer, and Holmen, 1978, for details). In the unlikely event that olfactory aversion generalizes to nondeviant arousal, have the client masturbate to ejaculation using a *nondeviant* fantasy *following* the aversion session. This should restore nondeviant arousal to an acceptable level.

3. Verbal Satiation. *a. What Is It?* The well-documented observation underlying verbal satiation is that the continuous performance of a behavior in the same stimulus situation will eventually lead to a cessation of that behavior. The procedure requires the repetitive emission of deviant fantasies, with the result that the fantasies lose their power to elicit deviant arousal. Like olfactory aversion, the effect is specific to deviant arousal and nondeviant arousal is usually not affected by the treatment. See Marshall (1979) for a description of satiation therapy using masturbation as the behavior to be continuously repeated.

b. When Do You Use It? Verbal satiation may be used with any client who shows high entry levels of both deviant and nondeviant arousal. This pattern may be observed in any client. This procedure may be used with clients who decline to participate in olfactory aversion.

c. Steps in the Procedure. Again, see the client three times per week, and prior to the third treatment session conduct your weekly evaluation. It is useful to have him wear the transducer as the behavior will initially be somewhat more resistant to change by this method than with the use of a chemical agent, although you will see change fairly rapidly. Have the client simply verbalize deviant fantasies for periods of not less than 30 minutes. You must monitor his productions because the procedure becomes so boring that clients begin making long pauses and some go to sleep. Within three to four weeks the technique will exhaust his existing repertoire of fantasy material as it becomes more and more boring. It appears to have the ultimate effect of rendering newly created fantasy material useless before it can be elaborated into a functional form. In the optimum case, verbal satiation will selectively suppress deviant arousal. In some cases, it appears to have an attenuating effect on nondeviant arousal but does not suppress it.

d. Data Sheets. Follow the recommendations for data sheets given earlier.

e. Evaluating Data. Again, to evaluate data use the conventions described for assessment and treatment. Here, as well, you will begin with high levels of both deviant and nondeviant arousal. If you are measuring erection to deviant stimuli, you will see either an abrupt or a gradual suppressive effect on arousal. The data may show a smooth suppression like an extinction curve, or there may be more variability. The effect on nondeviant arousal is often to produce variability of about 20%. If this variability begins to show a serious downward trend or the variations become extreme, use the recommendations for instituting masturbatory conditioning given for olfactory aversion.

D. The Treatment Time Frame.

After completion of assessment, treatment is going to take from six to eight months. Very few clients will be in treatment over one year. Our usual estimate is 72 half-hour treatment sessions over six months. A few clients will finish in less time. These will be the best clients, highly motivated and highly responsive to procedures.

1. Establishing Baselines.

You need a point of reference against which to compare your treatment intervention, and for this reason you must establish pretreatment baselines of both deviant and nondeviant arousal. You do this by presenting the stimuli that you will eventually use in your weekly evaluation sessions for several days prior to initiating treatment. This will also tell you if those stimuli are going to be effective, and this is the time to make changes in them if necessary. Your baseline period ought to be about four to five days in length, and consecutive days would be best. What you are looking for is stability. If deviant arousal starts out at 80% in baseline, it should not vary wildly about that figure, but changes of plus or minus 5 or 10% are nothing to worry about. You will occasionally see deviant arousal begin to fall and/or nondeviant arousal begin to rise during baseline periods. If this happens, question the client about the stimuli and change them if necessary until you get a reasonably stable state before beginning (see Hersen and Barlow, 1976, for details).

2. Treatment and Evaluation Stimuli.

When you present stimuli in treatment and evaluation sessions, you must not present a small number of stimuli over and over or your client will become satiated and stop responding. You will need a relatively large pool of available stimuli, one category each for every behavior you are observing. Let us say that you are treating a bisexual pedophile with olfactory aversion. You decided on this because his assessment showed high arousal to two deviant and one nondeviant categories. You know that he is responsive to both slides and tapes, so you decide to use slides in treatment sessions and tapes for evaluation. At minimum you would need to assemble the following stimuli. In olfactory aversion treatment all presentations are deviant, so have the client select nine slides of attractive boys and nine of girls. In the treatment sessions, three slides from each group will be randomly selected and presented for 2 minutes each. Selection according to a table of random numbers will ensure that all slides are eventually presented an equal number of times. For evaluation sessions, have him write 18 scripts, 6 describing sexual activity with boys, 6 with girls, and 6 with an adult. In these sessions, again randomly select two from each category and present them. The data obtained here will be your indices of success or failure of treatment. Our experience indicates that clients do not become satiated if there are sufficient numbers of stimuli upon which to draw. If a client should become bored with a stimulus he believed to be effective, he will very likely tell you, and alterations and substitutions can then be made.

3. Initiating Treatment.   *a. Scheduling Treatment Sessions.* It does not really matter how you schedule treatment over a five-day week as long as you do not schedule more than one session on a single day. There appear to be no massed versus spaced trial effects in this work. Every other day is fine; three days in a row is just as good.

b. Scheduling Evaluation Sessions.   Your evaluation session *must precede* your third weekly treatment session. If the treatment is orgasmic reconditioning, the reason is obvious. If it is verbal satiation or olfactory aversion, scheduling evaluation after treatment may be subject to recency effects.

4. Evaluating Success and Failure.   *a. Altering Treatments.* There is nothing sacred about following a treatment regime to the letter because we tell you to do so or because you saw an article that described a particular method. Alter treatments when what you are doing is not producing the results you want. For example, you might be using free fantasy as the deviant stimulus presentation in a treatment, and it may not be producing the desired amount of arousal. Perhaps the addition of a slide presentation might make it more arousing to the client.

b. Changing Treatments.   Treatments are changed when they do not work. The descriptions we have given of the most common results suggest what to look for. For example, we had one client in verbal satiation whose verbalizations reliably produced 100% erections which were maintained for the entire 30-minute period. Obviously, he was not satiating. We changed the treatment to verbalization with olfactory aversion and it was effective. Use this rule of thumb: if deviant arousal remains at high levels or increases, and/or if nondeviant arousal is being suppressed from high levels or fails to increase from low levels, change the treatment. Do not be afraid to be imaginative.

c. How Much Is Enough?   We use specific exit criteria, and we offer them to you with the recommendation that you develop criteria specific to your needs and your situation. In our laboratory treatment is completed when weekly evaluation sessions reveal that:

1. measured deviant sexual arousal has been *less than 20%* of maximum erection (preferably 0%) for two months, and

2. measured nondeviant sexual arousal has been *greater than 50%* (preferably 80 to 100%) for two months.

These are criteria for termination of treatment only. If you can follow your client within your institution, or preferably in the community, you should by all means do so. If periodic evaluation shows a deterioration of treatment effects or if the client reports a recurrence of deviant arousal, reinstitute treatment on either a booster or a regular basis.

E. How to Report the Data

It is our belief that reporting of treatment data is a more sensitive business than reporting assessment data. Consumers are more accepting of assessment data if they believe that a man is a sexual deviant and the data seem to support that belief. Data from successful treatment, however, seem to say that the person is no longer a sexual deviant. This is not true, and you should not give the slightest hint that it is. As we said before, these are not irreversible effects by any stretch of the imagination. They are all procedures of self-management designed to bring undesired behaviors under control. If the procedures are not practiced by the client post-treatment, and in the absence of supervention of more positively reinforcing sexual experiences, there is no reason whatever to expect that deviant arousal will not reappear in full bloom. All you may legitimately report is that your client does (or does not) possess a skill for controlling his deviant sexual arousal which he did not display prior to treatment. Whether he uses it or not in the future is up to him. You may show concern for this, but you need not take the responsiblity for it.

In reporting treatment data, be brief and stick to the facts. Make no predictions, and do not speculate about the future. First summarize the original assessment data. Describe the treatment used, and give a rationale for applying it to this case. State what you did and what the results were. If you performed a post-treatment reassessment, compare those data with the original assessment. Finally, state your belief as to whether the treatment intervention was successful in assisting your client to gain self-control.

IX. Conclusion: Value and Limitations of a Sexual Behavior Laboratory

A. Value

The major values of having access to a sexual behavior laboratory are three:

1. Given a motivated and arousable client, a laboratory can provide rather precise information on the client's sexual arousal: (1) relative to the offense for which

he is being seen, (2) in areas possibly not associated with his presenting offense, and (3) relative to any nondeviant sexual arousal he may show. If additional measures on social history and social competence are obtained, these will serve to give a generally more comprehensive picture of deviant sexuality and competence in typical life situations than is usually available from most currently used means directed to the same ends.

2. Objective evidence of deviant sexual arousal is an incontrovertible fact. Verbal denials and rationalizations so frequently seen in sex offenders are difficult to maintain in the face of such evidence, although many continue to try. Coming to terms with deviant arousal means coming to terms with one's identity as a sexual deviant and has broad implications not only for behavior therapy but for any other therapeutic intervention. Few would deny that breaking down mechanisms of denial is a formidable task for any therapist.

3. In the treatment procedures, the client must confront what sort of sexual person he is. He is required, perhaps for the first time, to learn techniques which he can use in the natural environment to control his impulses and antisocial behavior, and so learn something about behaving as a responsible human being.

In summary, a sexual behavior laboratory can provide considerable information on a highly circumscribed area of human function, but one critical to successful, offense-free living for this clientele.

B. Limitations

While the data which you will obtain are objective, germane to the problem, and useful for assessment and treatment purposes, there are limitations to the interpretation which you may legitimately make of them.

1. The Setting.   Whether your laboratory is in a prison, a hospital, a clinic, or a private office, these are not measures obtained from an individual functioning at that moment in the real world. The situation is a laboratory analogue of the real world, and the client is not at that time being submitted to the natural environmental stimuli which elicit his deviant behavior. The data, therefore, are at best a good approximation of the client's real interests and behavioral propensities. In reporting such data, we constantly stress that they should *never* be used in isolation as clinical predictors.

2. The Data.   Human responsiveness varies from moment to moment and is constantly subject to many stimulus inputs. This is an assumption common to all psychometric and psychophysiological measurements. Thus the data obtained are from a single individual, at a particular time, in a very special place, under very special conditions. An hour later, a day later, under the exact same conditions, they might be somewhat different. In another setting, they might be very different indeed. This is not to say that the measures are unreliable, but only that human behavior varies from time to time and from place to place. One seeks consistency in measures varying somewhat from time to time, and trends in one direction or another over time.

3. Social Desirability, Attention, Demand, and Expectancy Effects.

These features are continuously present in *any* helping situation and probably cannot (or should not) be controlled. Clients in a laboratory setting such as we have described will receive very intimate and individualized attention from the staff, more than many would receive in other settings. This may contribute to some of the changes you will observe. The desire to look good (i.e., to appear nondeviant) or to please the therapist may have an effect on responsiveness. If your client is in the criminal justice system, he may see your laboratory as a make-or-break opportunity, and he may come to expect changes and thus produce some. To attempt to control experimentally for every aspect of these effects would turn an already rather cold and forbidding situation into one utterly barren of humanity. We decided years ago that this was an unacceptable price to pay. Instead we seek to mobilize client expectancies in the service of desired outcomes.

4. Misconception, Misconstruction, and Prejudice.

These are limitations imposed from outside, mainly by misinformed and uninformed critics. Several years ago we were accused of using a "technofix," implying that it was somehow debasing to use technology with human beings and that use of simple and direct procedures to accomplish treatment goals was inherently bad. If they speak of you at all, some of your more traditionally minded critics will call you naive and simple-minded to think that such simple procedures could possibly affect such complex and deeply rooted problems. Your work will be called cold, mechanical, inhumane, and humiliating. You will have to deal with this, and the manner in which you do depends upon how great a burden you are willing to shoulder, if indeed, you wish to respond at all. We recommended previously that you be open, forthcoming, and nonsecretive about what you are doing. You must be totally professional and ethical, and absolutely accountable for everything you do. You should by all means attempt to mesh your work with that of your more traditional colleagues. Say what you have to say, do not be defensive, do not apologize. If you appear as a supplicant with hat in hand, be assured that many will work most fervently to ensure that you remain in that role.

5. Where Do We Go from Here?

The horizon is apparently limitless, so what does the future hold? The answer is that we simply soldier on, following wherever the data take us. The theoretical physicist Robert Oppenheimer once said, "If you are a scientist you believe that it is a good thing to find out how the world works." Using the methods of science, we have found out a little about how the world of deviant sexuality works. So what does the future hold? We believe in the power of the scientific method to create useful knowledge, to throw light into some of the darker recesses of human behavior, to dispel ignorance. In those dark recesses, we will doubtless find that we resemble more than we wish those sexual outlaws whom we have scorned and labeled deviants. We will find that in matters sexual, the human being is a rather fallible and malleable organism, that in the end perhaps all of us have some capacity for loathsome acts. We have thus far successfully kept ourselves ignorant of many of the dimensions of human sexuality, and we have suffered for it. Ignorance is confining and ultimately crippling. Knowledge inevitably operates in the service of human understanding, even when we do not particularly wish to have that knowledge.

We have offered you here a sort of procedure manual, a kind of handbook for setting up shop in the human sexuality business. It may also be seen as a sort of progress report on the state of the art. We have undeniably made some progress, but we are nowhere near the end, or even the beginning of the end, of this labor. Rather we would suggest to you that the current status of the methods we have described for you in this chapter might more properly be seen as representing the end of the beginning.

REFERENCE NOTES

1. Johnston, S. and Anderson, R. *Development of scales to measure sexual psychopathology*. Paper presented at the 3rd National Conference on the Evaluation and Treatment of Sexual Aggressives, Avila Beach, California, March 1981.
2. Avery-Clark, C.A. *Differential erection response patterns of sexual child abusers to stimuli describing activities with children*. Doctoral dissertation, Department of Psychology, University of Southern California, Los Angeles, September 1980.
3. Abel, G.G., Becker, J.V., Murphy, W.D., and Flanagan, B. *Identifying dangerous child molesters*. In R. Stuart (Ed.) *Violent behavior*. New York: Brunner/Mazel, 1981, 116–137.

REFERENCES

Abel, G.G. Assessment of sexual deviation in the male. In Hersen, M. and Bellack, A.S. (Eds.) *Behavioral Assessment: A Practical Handbook*. Elmsford, N.Y.: Pergamon Press, 1976, p. 437-457.

Abel, G.G., Barlow, D.H., Blanchard, E.B., and Mavissakalian, M. Measurement of sexual arousal in male homosexuals: the effects of instructions and stimulus modality. *Archibes of Sexual Behavior* 4:623-629 (1975). (a)

Abel, G.G. and Blanchard, E.B. The measurement and generation of sexual arousal in male sexual deviates. In Hersen, M., Eislen, R.M. and Miller, P.M. (Eds.) *Progress in Behavior Modification;* Vol. 2. New York: Academic Press, 1976, p. 99-136.

Abel, G.G., Blanchard, E.B., Barlow, D.H., and Guild, D. The components of rapists' sexual arousal. *Archives of General Psychiatry* 34:895-903 (1977).

Abel, G.G., Blanchard, E.B., Barlow, D.H., and Mavissakalian, M. Identifying specific erotic cues in sexual deviations by audiotaped descriptions. *Journal of Applied Behavior Analysis* 8:247-260 (1975). (b)

Abel, G.G., Blanchard, E.B., Becker, J.V., and Djenderedjian, A. Differentiating sexual aggressives with penile measures. *Criminal Justice and Behavior* 5:315-332 (1978).

Bancroft, J., Jones, H.G., and Pullan, B.R. A simple transducer for measuring penile erection, with comments on its use in the treatment of sexual disorders. *Behaviour Research and Therapy* 4:239-241 (1966).

Bancroft, J. and Mathews, A. Autonomic correlates of penile erection. *Journal of Psychosomatic Research* 15:159-167 (1971).

Barlow, D.H. Assessment of sexual behavior. In Ciminero, A.R., Calhoun, K.S., and Adams, H.E. (Eds.) *Handbook of Behavioral Assessment.* New York: Wiley, 1977, p. 461-508.

Barlow, D.H., Becker, R., Leitenberg, H., and Agras, W.S. A mechanical strain gauge for recording penile circumference change. *Journal of Applied Behavior Analysis* 3:73-76 (1970).

Burgess, A.W., Groth, A.N., Holmstrom, L.S., and Sgroi, S.M. *Sexual Assault of Children and Adolescents.* Lexington, Mass.: Lexington Books, 1978.

Cox, D.J. and Daitzman, R.J. *Exhibitionism: Description, Assessment, and Treatment.* New York: Garland Press, 1980.

Freund, K. A laboratory method for diagnosing predominance of homo- or hetero-erotic interest in the male. *Behaviour Research and Therapy* 1:85-93 (1963).

Groth, A.N. *Men Who Rape.* New York: Plenum Press, 1979.

Hersen, M. and Barlow, D.H. *Single Case Experimental Designs: Strategies for Studying Behavior Change.* Oxford: Pergamon Press, 1976.

Hindelang, M.J., Hirschi, T., and Weis, J.G. *Measuring Delinquency.* Beverly Hills: Sage, 1981.

Hirschi, T., Hindelang, M.J., and Weis, J.G. The status of self-report measures. In Klein, M.W. and Teilmann, K.S. (Eds.) *Handbook of Criminal Justice Evaluation.* Beverly Hills: Sage, 1980, p. 473-488.

Klein, E.M. An audiophile's guide to videocassette recorders. *Stereo Review* 46:52-62 (1981).

Laws, D.R. A comparison of the measurement characteristics of two circumferential penile transducers. *Archives of Sexual Behavior* 6:45-51 (1977).

Laws, D.R., Meyer, J., and Holmen, M.L. Reduction of sadistic sexual arousal by olfactory aversion: a case study. *Behaviour Research and Therapy* 16:281-285 (1978).

Laws, D.R. and O'Neil, J.A. Variations on masturbatory conditioning. *Behavioural Psychotherapy* 9:111-136 (1981).

Marshall, W.L. Satiation therapy: a procedure for reducing deviant sexual arousal. *Journal of Applied Behavior Analysis* 12:377-389 (1979).

Masters, W.L. and Johnson, V.E. *Human Sexual Response.* Boston: Little, Brown, 1966.

Paitich, D., Langevin, R., Freeman, R., Mann, K., and Handy, L. The Clarke SHQ: a clinical sex history questionnaire for males. *Archives of Sexual Behavior* 6:421-436 (1977).

Rosen, R.C. and Keefe, F.J. The measurement of human penile tumescence. *Psychophysiology* 15:366-376 (1978).

Schwitzgebel, R.L. and Schwitzgebel, R.K. *Law and Psychological Practice.* New York: Wiley, 1980.

Tollison, C.D. and Adams, H.E. *Sexual Disorders.* New York: Gardner Press, 1979.

VanDeventer, A.D. and Laws, D.R. Orgasmic reconditioning to redirect sexual arousal in pedophiles. *Behavior Therapy* 9:748-765 (1978).

Zuckerman, M. Physiological measures of sexual arousal in the human. *Psychological Bulletin* 75:297-329 (1971).

EDITORS' NOTE: Lists of equipment suppliers may be obtained by writing on letterhead stationery to Dr. Greer.

15
The Current State of Technology in the Laboratory Assessment of Sexual Arousal Patterns

C.M. Earls, Ph.D.
W.L. Marshall, Ph.D.

To treat a sexual offender, one must understand the process through which he arrived at the level of sexual arousal that motivated the act. This includes not only varieties of stimuli but levels of responding penile tumescence as well. There is a growing body of experimental literature revolving around measuring the sexual components of erectile responses to arousal. Such measurement techniques not only have been found to be reliable indices of early stages of such sexual arousal, important in considering treatment approaches, but also permit differentiation between appropriate and deviant arousal. The authors carefully detail a variety of measurement technologies and the validity of the conclusions derived from them. They also review in depth a number of unresolved issues in this type of research which it is hoped will result in more effective treatment.

INTRODUCTION

Over the past 20 years or so it has become increasingly popular to assess male sexual arousal using procedures which directly monitor penile tumescence. This popularity stems, in part, from a growing body of experimental literature indicating that as a "response," erection appears to be the single most reliable index of the early stages of sexual arousal (Barlow, 1977; Rosen and Keefe, 1978; Zuckerman, 1971). Also, this response system permits us to discriminate between heterosexual arousal and (a) homosexual arousal (Barr and Blaszczynski, 1976; Barr and Mc-Conaghy, 1971; Freund, 1961, 1963, 1967a; Mavissakalian, Blanchard, Abel, and Barlow, 1975; McConaghy, 1967); (b) fetishism (Marks and Gelder, 1967); (c) transsexualism (Barr and Blaszczynski, 1976); (d) transvestism (Marks and Gelder, 1967); (e) exhibitionism (Langevin, Paitich, Ramsey, Anderson, Pope, Pearl, and Newman, 1979); (f) pedophilia (Freund, 1967a, 1967b; Freund, Chan, and Coulthard, 1979; Quinsey, 1977); and (g) rape (Abel, Barlow, Blanchard, and Guild, 1977; Abel, Blanchard, Becker, and Djenderedjian, 1978; Barbaree, Marshall, and Lanthier, 1979; Kercher and Walker, 1973; Kolarsky and Madlafousek, 1972). As a further advantage, erectile responses are relatively easy to measure, occur rapidly to a variety of types of sexual stimulation, and can easily be reversed, all of which allow the successive presentation of a variety of stimuli within short time periods.

As Zuckerman (1971) notes, other approaches to the description of sexual preferences have been tried but without much success. For instance, early research (Hess, 1968; Hess and Polt, 1960) examined the value of pupillary responses to various sexual stimuli on the assumption that these would vary according to the interest of the subject. While Hess and his colleagues found data to support their hypothesis, subsequent research revealed contaminating influences from various sources (e.g., brightness levels, experimenter influence, etc.) that cast serious doubt on the value of this approach (Zuckerman, 1971). Recently, however, Abel (personal communication, 1981) has developed a computer-based technology for describing moment-to-moment eye movements that permits the assessor to record the amount of time the subject spends looking at various parts of a visual display. Abel has had subjects view slides of naked bodies of adult males and females as well as of children, in the hope that this technology will provide more accurate descriptions of the visual preferences of deviants and nondeviants. There are many possible applications of this approach, once the initial technical problems have been solved.

In addition to these approaches, investigators routinely ask subjects to report their levels of subjective arousal or, in some other manner, report their preferences for various sexual stimuli and behaviors. There are numerous indications in the literature that we cannot rely on the self-reports of sexual deviants. Although Abel and his colleagues (Abel et al., 1977; Abel, Blanchard, Murphy, Becker, and Djenderedjian, in press; Mavissakalian et al., 1975) found that rapists reported attraction to deviant acts that matched their erectile-assessed preferences, other researchers have found marked discrepancies, with self-reports reflecting normal desires (Farkas, Sine, and Evans, 1979; Hinton, O'Neill, and Webster, 1980; McConaghy, 1969; Wincze, Venditti, Barlow, and Mavissakalian, 1980). Rosen and Kopel (1977) report data dramatically demonstrating the unreliability of self-assessed sexual preferences. Their patient continued to tell them throughout a two-year follow-up period that he was free of transvestite desires when he was, in fact, continually engaging in such behaviors. No doubt, self-reports are easier to distort than erectile measurements of sexual arousal, but some of the distortion may be the result of inadequate measurement procedures rather than deliberate dissimulation. For instance, it has been observed in other problem areas that the correspondence between self-reported and physiologically assessed arousal can be increased by increasing the descriptive detail of both the stimuli and what the subject is required to do (Lick, Sushinsky, and Malow, 1977) and by employing magnitude estimation procedures (Grossberg and Grant, 1978). It is, therefore, possible to improve methods for obtaining estimates of subjective arousal, but more objective procedures will still remain the keystone of the assessment of sexual preferences.

Despite the obvious value and popularity of measures of erectile strength, there are some clear disadvantages. For instance, investigators must make the assumption that repeated measurements of an individual's penile responses allow the specification and prediction of some global aspect of sexual behavior. Zuckerman (1971) views the situation as similar to the distinction between states and traits in psychometric testing, such that a measure of the current level of sexual tension (i.e., state) is related in some way to the overall level of sexual arousability or responsiveness (i.e., trait). Behavioral researchers have not, however, neglected to concern themselves with this relationship. In fact, a large portion of the work conducted in the area of male sexual arousal is aimed precisely at this distinction, that is, how well a particular series of observations aids in the prediction of general sexual behavior.

Farkas (1978) has recently identified *three* specific threats to the internal and external validity of experiments and treatment assessments which use penile measures (see also replies by Levin, Gambaro, and Wolfinson, 1978; Rosen and Kopel, 1978). The first of these threats concerns the fact that some males can exert voluntary control over their erection (Abel, Blanchard, Barlow, and Mavissakalian, 1975; Freund, 1971; Freund et al, 1979; Henson and Rubin, 1971; Laws and Holman, 1978; Laws and Rubin, 1969; Quinsey and Bergersen, 1976; Quinsey and Carrigan, 1978; Rosen, 1973; Rosen, Shapiro, and Schwartz, 1975). This ability to control erectile responses casts some doubt on the degree to which the assessment accurately reflects the individual's preferences, and we will return to this issue later. However, it is important to note here that this cause for concern arises only when a supposedly deviant individual shows a "normal" profile, whether at initial testing or after treatment. If treatment has been conducted in a controlled manner allowing for appropriate inferences regarding treatment effects, then the problem may not be as significant. Of course, whenever a deviant profile is obtained, there should be no doubt about the validity of the measure, since someone would hardly fake aberrant interests. Nevertheless, the problem still remains with respect to an initial evaluation that reveals responding within the normal range. Several methods have been suggested to offset the tendency to fake (Laws and Holman, 1978). However, as pointed out by Rosen and Kopel (1978), none of these methods is entirely satisfactory. The fact remains that voluntary response control poses a threat to the internal validity of any assessment.

The second criticism raised by Farkas also addresses the issue of internal validity. Specifically, the relationship between self-reported arousal and arousal assessed by circumferential measures is not, as we have seen, always congruent and is often surprisingly low. At this point more data are required. If a measure is claimed to assess sexual arousal, one would expect it to correlate highly with perceived arousal. The fact that it does not, reflects on the value of the methodology. Errors in methodology may inhere in the erectile assessment or, more likely, in the approach to the description of subjective arousal.

The final issue addressed by Farkas concerns external validity, that is, how well laboratory assessments of sexual preferences predict behavior outside of the testing situation. As Rosen and Kopel (1977), found, sometimes not very well. These authors submitted a report on the successful treatment and two-year follow-up of a transvestite-exhibitionist. The article was accepted for publication; however,

> On the eve of publication of this case study, 2½ years after the original treatment program, the authors received an urgent telephone call from the client's wife. When Mr. and Mrs. W. arrived at the clinic on the following day, Mrs. W., in a highly emotional state, immediately confessed that her husband had deceived the therapists for more than a year. (p. 915)

While this course of events may not be typical of therapy outcome, it does highlight the fact that physiological assessment of penile responding may bear little relationship to behavior outside the laboratory. Actually, the issues are somewhat more complicated than this. The tactics of assessment and treatment employed by Rosen and Kopel, and no doubt by many other researchers and therapists, reflect several assumptions. In the first place, it is assumed that evaluations of sexual preferences using erectile measures are stable across time, so that there is no need for subsequent reappraisals after the immediate post-treatment or short-term follow-up assessment. This is a question of both the reliability of the measurement procedures and the stability of altered sexual preferences. Although Farkas (Farkas, Evans, Sine, Eifert, Wittlieb, and Vogelmann-Sine, 1979) demonstrated reliability with repeated measures for the mercury-in-rubber strain gauge, these measures were taken only seven days apart. For estimating longer-term effects, such as those following treatment, we need to repeat assessments over more extended periods.

Secondly, it is assumed that the laboratory description of sexual preferences predicts past, present, and future extralaboratory behavior. This is a question of validity, and although, as we have seen, data are available indicating correspondence between erectile assessments and past behavior, we do not have a satisfactory basis for determining the power to predict current or future sexual acts. In an examination of different methods for describing the changes in erectile patterns that best predicted long-term outcome in a mixed group of sexual deviants, Marshall (1975) based his judgments on data collected in an earlier study (Marshall, 1973). He found that the most accurate predictions of success or failure at follow-up involved changes in the relative magnitudes of circumferentially measured erections to deviant and nondeviant cues. By adding data on patients treated in the year after his earlier report, Marshall predicted success for 15 of 17 cases on the basis of *either* reductions in deviant arousal *or* increases in arousal to appropriate cues. All but one of these patients abstained from deviant acts during follow-up which was extended to between three and five years. Two additional patients did not show satisfactory changes in the relative magnitude of their erectile responses to deviant and appropriate cues, and were consequently considered failures in treatment; however, only one of these subsequently reoffended, while one of those for whom success was predicted also failed. Thus this method of using penile assessments to predict future behavior was inaccurate in 2 of 17 instances: one for whom assessment predicted success actually failed, and one who was considered a failure appeared to succeed.

Quinsey (1981) has summarized data from his laboratory which indicate that penile circumference assessments conducted before treatment predict later recidivism, while post-treatment sexual preferences described by erectile measures are related to short-term recidivism but not long-term outcome. This suggests that the procedures Quinsey employed to alter deviant arousal patterns (i.e., signaled punishment) have transitory effects that must be capitalized upon if lasting reorientation is to be achieved. Since those patients who did subsequently recidivate had reverted to their original pattern of sexual preferences upon retesting, it seems likely that repeated assessments throughout follow-up would have revealed an increasing reversion to deviant interest.

Rosen and Kopel's (1977) data do not reflect on the issue of predictive validity as seriously as one might expect from an initial consideration, in that they only assessed the erectile responses of this patient at four months follow-up, relying thereafter on the patient's self-reports. According to the patient's wife, the aberrant behavior did not reappear until after this four-month post-treatment assessment. Again we see that penile assessment predicted immediate behavior change but not long-term outcome. As we saw with Quinsey's data, this type of outcome encourages two appropriate responses. First, as Rosen and Kopel suggest, repeated evaluations of erectile-determined preferences are needed throughout follow-up to detect reversions to deviant interests before this interest converts into aberrant behavior. Second, it is clear that changes in sexual preferences can be produced by various procedures but these changes are not long-lasting unless other changes occur in the individual. Just what these other changes need to be is not clear at the moment, although we suspect that they have to do with social functioning (Murphy, Quinsey and Marshall, 1981; Whitman and Quinsey, in press), probably with the sexual aggressor's control over his behavior when intoxicated (Barbaree, Marshall, Lightfoot, and Yates, 1979) or angry (Yates, Barbaree, and Marshall, 1980), and with his attitudes both toward women (Malamuth, personal communication, 1981) and to the specifics of his sexual attack (Malamuth, 1981).

All of these issues call into question the present state of our technology and possibly the deployment of this technology. The intent of this chapter is to briefly review the status of our current response measurement technology and to point out, with reference to work done in our laboratory, how our limited understanding of the operating characteristics of the penis places constraints on our potential ability to make accurate behavioral predictions based on these responses. The argument which we will develop here is that investigators and clinicians concerned with the physiological measurement of male sexual arousal are employing procedures which have reasonable degree of face validity but have yet to be adequately defined, validated, or tested for reliability.

MEASUREMENT TECHNOLOGY

The most notable feature of penile tumescence is that blood flow into the various corpora causes a change in penile volume. Obviously enough, since the penis is cylindrical in shape, the volume change can also be thought of as a change in both length and circumference (diameter).[1] To date, the measurement of penile changes can be divided into two distinct technologies: one is concerned with the assessment of complete volume changes (Freund, Sedlacek, and Knob, 1965; McConaghy, 1967); the other focuses on circumferential changes (Bancroft, Jones, and Pullen, 1966; Barlow, Becker, Leitenberg, and Agras, 1970). To this date, penile length changes have been neglected.[2]

Rosen and Keefe (1978) have provided the most comprehensive review to date of the currently available measurement technology. They critically evaluated the two existing methods of volume measurement (Freund's and McConaghy's) and five of the most popular methods of circumferential measurement. Each device was considered in light of its electrical specifications (ac versus dc measurement capabilities), degree of sensitivity, reliability, ease of use, and a variety of both technical and clinical considerations such as durability and portability. Based on these considerations, Rosen and Keefe concluded that the transducer of choice in a clinical setting, where portability and client comfort are high priorities, is either the Barlow electromechanical strain gauge or the Parks mercury-in-rubber strain gauge. When extremely sensitive and precise measurement is desirable, Rosen and Keefe recommended the volumetric device.

The advantage of portability and client comfort is easy to understand. Vol-

---

1. Throughout this chapter, the terms circumference and diameter are used interchangeably. While the measurement transducers are usually referred to as "circumferential," it has become procedurally easier in many laboratories to express data in terms of diameter change.

2. Penile tumescence has also been assessed in terms of temperature change (Fisher, Gross, and Zuch, 1965; Hammer and Webster, 1980; Seeley, Abramson, Perry, Rothblatt, and Seeley, 1980). However, the popularity of temperature assessment devices will, for the time being, remain limited. One of the chief drawbacks to this type of measurement is that once the penis undergoes an erection, the surface, and undoubtedly the deeper tissue, retain a certain amount of heat. This means that a return to the prearousal surface temperature of the penis is extremely slow, which limits the number of stimuli that can be presented during a single session. The same problem presents serious limitations to the use of thermistors to measure labial temperature changes during the assessment of female sexual arousal (see Henson and Rubin, 1978; Henson, Rubin, and Henson, 1979a, 1979b).

umetric devices take up a large amount of laboratory space and consist of a complex network of apparatus, while the tranducer itself represents a bulky intrusion on the subject's anatomy. On the other hand, the entire measurement and recording apparatus of circumferential devices (when a digital voltmeter rather than a polygraph is employed) can easily be carried in a briefcase, with the actual transducer weighing less than a gram. However, the conclusion that the volumetric device is more sensitive and precise requires elaboration.

To date, only two experiments have directly compared volumetric and circumferential measures. McConaghy (1974) examined the relative merits of a mercury-in-rubber strain gauge and his volumetric device in a classical conditioning paradigm. His results indicated that there was some concordance between the two measures, but at times the two devices recorded changes in opposite directions. This difference was attributed to an initial blood flow into the cavernosa, which McConaghy claimed forced the penis to immediately lengthen and narrow somewhat. This longitudinal response would, of course, be recorded by the volume device as an increase, while the circumferential gauge would respond as though a decrease had occurred. Unfortunately, this observation was one of the few useful aspects of McConaghy's article. He presented no data to allow the determination of absolute changes in penile dimension and no statistical description of the correlation between the two devices.

Freund, Langevin, and Barlow (1974) presented a somewhat more interesting comparison between a circumferential and a volumetric device. They used a Barlow electromechanical strain gauge and Freund et al.'s (1965) version of a plethysmograph to compare the responses of males to neutral slides, female nude slides, and male nude slides (each of the sexual slides was also divided into four age categories). The results indicated that volume changes discriminated between each of the various age categories of females, with only the youngest age category being nondifferentiated from neutral or male slides. The circumferential measure, on the other hand, allowed only for the discrimination between mature and child females. On the basis of these results, Freund et al. concluded that volume changes provided the most accurate description of specific preferences because of the greater sensitivity of this measurement device. However, these data must be viewed with some caution since the technical problems of attaching both instruments to the same individual resulted in a loss of data from 34 of the 48 subjects.

In spite of the methodological and technical limitations of the studies of both McConaghy and Freund et al., it is generally accepted in the literature that the assessment of penile volume is, in fact, a more sensitive description of sexual preferences. From an empirical perspective this conclusion seems premature, although intuitively it has the ring of truth to it since the volumetric method assesses the total physiological penile change, whereas circumferential assessments record changes in a single direction at a single discrete point along the shaft of the penis. Furthermore, observation of a penis during the erectile response reveals that although diameter changes may occur, they are not readily observable while volume changes are dramatic and obvious. However, the issue of sensitivity and precision has yet to be adequately addressed empirically.

Along with the acceptance of the superior sensitivity of the volumetric device, there also appears to be a general acceptance of the claim that circumferential measures falling below 10% of maximal tumescence are due to random fluctuations (Abel, Barlow, Blanchard, and Mavissakalian, 1975; Abel and Blanchard, 1976). Indeed Laws (1981) disregards changes below 20% of full erection. It seems to be the case that if an experimenter is interested in minimal (<10%) levels of arousal, volume measurement is the procedure of choice, with the circumferential device being reserved for arousal levels greater than 20%. Why this should be so is not clear. Mercury-in-rubber strain gauges are commonly used in both animal and human surgery to measure extremely small physiological changes (e.g., pulse). In fact, there is no empirical support for the notion that arousal below 10% is attributable to random variation. Nevertheless, this view appears to be entrenched and to have dissuaded researchers from focusing on low arousal levels. To further confuse the issue, reports on the use of the volumetric transducer express penile changes in terms of cubic centimeters of air displacement; circumferential responses are reported in millimeters of diameter change or as some percentage of the total diameter change during erection. Given the available data, therefore, there is no convenient way to compare these measures.[3] Thus, even if the volumetric device is more sensitive, it is impossible to specify or quantify any meaningful comparison between the two assessment methodologies in terms of the range of this sensitivity.

As we have noted, the mercury-in-rubber strain gauge is commonly used in the general detection of small physiological changes. Given that the purchase or construction of a volumetric device is generally beyond the resource or patience of most investigators, it is important at this time to determine whether or not mercury gauges can be adapted to the measurement of similar small penile changes. It certainly appears that the common restriction on the use of circumferential measures to the assessment of penile changes larger than 10 to 20% of full erection is the result of convention rather than of careful experimentation.

The need to describe early and minimal changes in erectile responding to depictions of various sexual acts concerns not only the need to more accurately detail the entire erection but also the need to examine the possibility that early changes may be under less voluntary control than later more substantial levels of arousal. These early minimal responses may not be as readily detectable by the subject, and of course if he cannot detect them, it is unlikely that he can control them. Despite the fact that it is some 12 years since Laws and Rubin (1969) first demonstrated that some subjects could exact some degree of control over their erections, very little progress has been made in determining when as individual is exerting voluntary

---

3. The most convenient method would appear to be to express volume changes as a percentage of total change since this is the way diameter changes are typically described.

control, or whether there is an aspect to penile responding which is not influenced by volition. It seems reasonable to assume that if there is a reflexive and thus uncontrollable component to erection, it occurs in the early stages of erection. Therefore, if the processes of control are to be adequately elaborated and over- come, we must first describe in greater detail the characteristics of penile respond- ing during these early stages. Recently we have undertaken a series of experiments which have begun to explore penile responding at levels well below 10%. How- ever, before describing this work, we must consider some recent findings regarding the mercury-in-rubber strain gauge.

Mercury-in-rubber Strain Gauges

The mercury-in-rubber strain gauge is usually considered to be one of the better methods of measuring penile circumferential changes. As we noted, this type of gauge has many advantages in that it is inexpensive, easy to use, unobtrusive, and available in various diameters. It has also been shown to respond in a linear fashion at room temperature over a wide range of values (Davidson, Malcolm, Lanthier, Barbaree, and Ho, 1981), and has been demonstrated to be reliable over repeated measures during penile flaccidity and tumescence (Farkas et al., 1979). Based on their experience with the gauge, Farkas et al. concluded that "the mercury-in- rubber strain gauge can be used with some confidence, especially if its limitations are carefully considered" (p. 555). These authors claimed that there were three specific limitations to these gauges: "(a) it is expandable over only 10% of its resting length; (b) the mercury tends to separate at the upper ranges of expansion; and (c) the gauge is temperature sensitive" (p. 555). However, as Earls and Mar- shall (1980) noted, Farkas et al. did not "carefully consider" any of these "limita- tions." The first limitation was true of the early homemade gauges (e.g., Bancroft et al., 1966; Whitney, 1949), whereas with the currently available commercial gauges something like the opposite is true. The gauge *must* be stretched 10 to 15% of its resting diameter while in use (Parks Electronics Limited). The second limita- tion is subject to experimenter vigilance. If the mercury does separate, it is imme- diately evident by a large and sudden voltage increase which is well beyond the plethysmograph's normal output. Farkas et al. were correct in noting that the gauge is subject to temperature variation, and this is specifically recognized by the manu- facturer (Parks Plethysmograph Model 270 manual). Unfortunately, Parks (per- sonal communication, 1980) has no data to determine the limits of this sensitivity. Experimenters using the gauge must make the assumption that when a room tem- perature gauge (22 to 26°C) is placed on a human body (surface temperature 33 to 35°C), the gauge adjusts to the higher temperature and retains the linear voltage output function reported by Davidson et al. (1981). Given the penis changes in surface temperature during tumescence (Fisher, Gross, and Zuch, 1965; Hammer and Webster, 1980; Seeley, Abramson, Perry, Rothblatt, and Seeley, 1980), users must further assume that these changes exert little effect.

In order to reduce experimenter uncertainty, Earls and Jackson (1981) conducted two experiments to determine the effects of temperature on the mercury gauge. In the first study, temperature was held constant at 0, 24, and 33°C while diameter was systematically increased. During the second experiment, diameter was held constant while the ambient temperature was changed from 50 to 0°C. The results of both experiments indicated a temperature sensitivity so slight that it can be ignored when monitoring penile tumescence (i.e., in the "worst case" during experiment 2 the plethysmograph voltage changed 007 mV per °C). With respect to the temperature-responsive features of the mercury gauge then, there appear to be no difficulties that stand in the way of its routine use.

Unfortunately, there is another important aspect to the measurement of penile tumescence that has so far been overlooked. In the studies of both Davidson et al. and Earls and Jackson, the linearity of plethysmographic output was determined by placing the strain gauge over variable sized cones. Providing the strain gauge with these physically determined linear increases resulted in corresponding linear changes in the output of the plethysmograph, which of course is essential to the veridical functioning of the measurement procedure. Whether or not the changes that occur in the penis during tumescence correspond to the changes that were produced by gradually increasing cone sizes remains open to question, and can only be answered by a detailed description of the operating characteristics of the penis itself. Furthermore, we do not know if equivalent proportions of change described by plethysmographic output, represent equivalent proportions of the attractiveness of the stimulus. That is, supposing the penis does physically change in a linear fashion throughout erection (which seems unlikely), do these changes reflect a linear increase in the erotic value of the eliciting stimuli? An answer to this question requires a careful comparison between penile responses and subjective arousal, although at present, as we have noted, our procedures for accurately describing subjective arousal leave a lot to be desired. In any case, in order to address either of these issues (i.e., the correspondence between penile changes and plethysmographic output on the one hand, and erotic attraction on the other), we need a more precise account of the actual physical changes that occur in the penis during erection.

Concerning the issue of the linearity of changes in the penis during erection, unfortunately there are no data available to address the topic. When reporting magnitude of erectile responses, investigators have sought a method of data expression which allows comparability both within and between individuals. As it turns out, the easiest method to achieve such comparability is to express penile circumferential changes as a percentage of the total possible change during a full erection. The adoption of such a ratio scale has required, in the absence of any evidence, the assumption that the response strength at 50% of a full erection is approximately half maximal response strength and, therefore, that a stimulus which generates 50% erection is only half as appealing or sexually exciting as one which results in a full erection. If erection does, in fact, occur in a linear fashion circumferentially, such an assumption may be warranted. However, it seems likely that a linear model of erection is too simplistic and that various magnitudes of responding will play a more complex role in the discrimination and eventual prediction of sexual behaior.

Low-level Erectile Responses

An experiment by Laws (1977) provides some evidence not only that mild levels (<10%) of circumferentially measured arousal include an interpretable response but also that when the penis changes during an erection it does not do so in a linear fashion. Rosen and Keefe (1978) recommended the use of either the Barlow-type strain gauge *or* a mercury-in-rubber strain gauge for measuring penile circumference change. Laws, therefore, considered it useful to determine how the two circumferential devices compared, and he addressed this question in an experiment using a single subject. The results indicated no significant differences between the measurement capabilities of the two devices, and based on this lack of difference, Laws favored the use of the mercury-in-rubber strain gauge because of its durability, commercial availability, and reduced cost. However, the important observation for our present problem was that Laws, like McConaghy (1974) before him, observed an initial circumferential *decrease* in the penis (recorded by both transducers) following the onset of an erotic stimulus. Laws noted that this decrease in penile diameter occurred with enough regularity that the electromechanical device (Barlow's gauge) had actually been observed to slip and change position on some subjects tested in his laboratory. This apparent decrease in penile diameter is also evident in the data presented by several other investigators (Abel, Blanchard, Barlow, and Mavissakalian, 1975, Figures 1 and 4; Laws and Bow, 1976, Figure 2; Rosen, Shapiro, and Schwartz, 1975, Figure 3).

Based on these observations, we have recently completed a series of experiments which demonstrate that penile responses below 10% of maximal tumescence do, in fact, contain an interpretable component which is not consistent with the generally assumed linearity of erection. Both Laws and McConaghy independently hypothesized that the apparent penile decrease in their polygraphic records was a result of an initial arterial blood flow which forced the penis longitudinally before manifesting itself as a circumferential increase. In the first experiment, we demonstrated that this polygraphic decrease could be reliably observed (Earls and Marshall, 1981a). Briefly, we used a mercury-in-rubber strain gauge to track penile circumferential changes in six subjects. Responses were recorded at two levels of sensitivity: one which allowed the full circumferential change to be recorded on the paper width of a single polygraph channel (the usual approach), and a second in which the voltage input was magnified by a factor of 25.

Figure 15-1 is a section of the polygraphic record obtained from one subject in this experiment: the data for this subject are representative of the effects observed in the other five subjects. The line designated "Channel 3" indicates the onset and

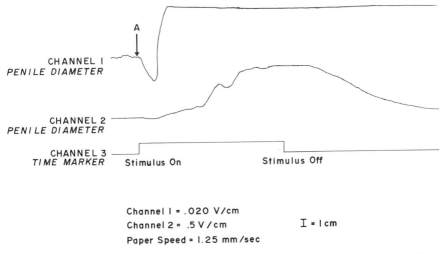

Channel I = .020 V/cm
Channel 2 = .5 V/cm   I = I cm
Paper Speed = 1.25 mm/sec

Figure 15-1.   A polygraphic record of the data obtained for subject 2 (experiment 1) during a 30-second baseline, stimulus introduction, tumescence, and a return to baseline.

offset of the stimulus. For the purposes of clarity, the arrow at point A also indicates stimulus onset. The function labeled "Channel 2" shows the voltage output that is typically described by polygraphic displays of plethysmographic voltage output during penile tumescence. The subject reported that he had achieved a full erection in the presence of the stimulus. The datum of chief concern, however, is the voltage change immediately following the stimulus introduction. As can be seen from an inspection of the "Channel 2" function, there was a slight decrease in voltage when compared to the preceding baseline level of responding. This decrease corresponds exactly to that shown in the data presented by Laws (1977).

The function labeled "Channel 1" in Figure 15-1 shows the voltage output of the plethysmograph magnified 25 times. As indicated in this function, baseline responding was relatively stable for the 30-second period preceding the presentation of the stimulus. When the stimulus was presented, there was a brief time period (2.0 seconds for this subject) before the voltage output began a smooth monotonic decrease. The function reached its minimal value (a pen deflection of 1.6 cm or .032 volt) before it began a rapid increase which continued well past the baseline level until it reached the limits of the excursion of the polygraph's pen. This course of events was the characteristic pattern of all subjects tested. It is also noteworthy that in those instances when a stimulus was introduced before a complete return to baseline, no decrease in voltage occurred.

To determine whether the post-stimulus decrease was, in fact, a result of penile lengthening, a second experiment was conducted in which penile responding to an erotic stimulus was videotaped throughout the entire erection cycle. The results

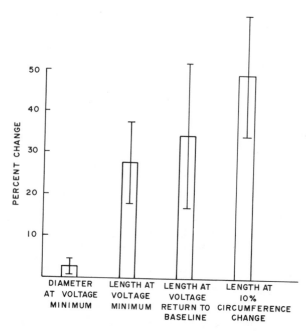

Figure 15-2. A bar histogram showing the mean diameter and length changes in experiment 2 immediately following stimulus introduction and at 10% of full erection (diameter).

indicated, once again, that during the initial stages of arousal, the penis appears (polygraphically) to decrease in diameter. However, the videotaped recordings clearly showed that during this post-stimulus decrease, the penis was undergoing a substantial length change (Earls, 1981). For the purposes of data presentation, there are three discrete points during the early stages of erection in which the results can be easily compared across subjects: at the minimum value of the polygraph decrease curve, at the time when the curve returns to its baseline level, and at the (conventionally accepted) 10% level. In addition, there are two measures which can be quantified at these points: diameter and length. Figure 15-2 is a bar histogram describing both diameter and length (as percentages of the total change in each variable during full erection) at the minimal value of the circumferential voltage curve, at the return to diameter baseline, and at 10% of the diameter of full tumescence.

As indicated by the figure, the diameter change during the plethysmographic voltage decrease represented a mean of approximately 2.5% of the total change that occurred during erection (s.d. = 1.14%, range = 0.8 to 3.8%). However, length at the same point had already increased by a substantial portion of its total change (mean = 28.05% s.d. = 9.85%, range = 13.3 to 41.3%). By the time diameter had reattained its baseline level, length had increased even further (mean = 34.5%, s.d. = 17.5%, range = 16.0 to 58.1%). Finally, when penile diameter had increased to 10% of its maximal value, an average of 49.2% (s.d. = 14.2%, range = 26.7 to 61.3%) change had occurred in length. To place these changes in some perspective, the point at which the plethysmographic voltage returns to baseline is, in standard penile assessments using standard measurement sensitivities, the point in time when erection is usually thought to begin. As we have seen, very little diameter change had taken place by this time. In fact, it could easily be, and usually has been, ignored as "random variation." However, the length change that had taken place at this point already represented an average of more than one-third of the total change that took place during the erection. At 10% of diameter-assessed arousal, almost half of the total length change had already occurred.

It would appear than that Laws (1977) and McConaghy (1974) were correct in claiming that the plethysmograph voltage decrease is accompanied by a lengthening of the penis, and it seems reasonable to assume, as these experimenters did, that an influx of arterial blood produces the longitudinal movement. It also seems that the penile body is constructed such that this longitudinal movement results in a circumferential decrease until the point where the cavernosa are saturated; then the elastic erectile tissue begins to expand, resulting in diameter increases. However, apparently neither Laws nor McConaghy suspected that this lengthening was of such magnitude and significance as we have found. If the lengthening can be considered "sexual arousal," and there seems little doubt that it can (no similar decrease in diameter was observed in the absence of an erotic stimulus), it is apparent that circumferential measures do not completely, or even satisfactorily, describe sexual responsivity.

Encouraged by the magnitude of the lengthening response, we have recently developed a working, albeit cumbersome, transducer which is capable of detecting length changes throughout the erectile sequence (Earls and Marshall, 1982). Using this device, we have been able to show that penile lengthening can be measured without the necessity of videotaping the penis. In its simplest form, this transducer consists of two mercury-in-rubber strain gauges: one formed into a closed loop (standard circumferential gauge). and a second, open gauge which is attached longitudinally to the penis. Using this arrangement of gauges, we have conducted a series of pilot studies which suggest that males can detect the early stages of penile lengthening (i.e., circumferential tumescence below 10%) but are unable to control its occurrence. Furthermore, our preliminary studies have indicated that attempts to control penile responses can be accurately identified on the basis of polygraphic tracings of both penile diameter and length. At this point, more data are required; however, it seems abundantly clear that penile lengthening responses (or circumferential changes below the usually accepted levels) have the potential to yield important assessment and treatment outcome data.

We view the value of these experiments as twofold. First, the data collected to date suggest that with the appropriate instrumentation it may be possible to increase measurement precision and sensitivity beyond that offered by the usual approaches. We have already noted the advantages of measuring changes in length over changes in diameter but in addition, lengthening responses may represent an advantage over volumetric assessments. Since the penis simultaneously decreases in diameter *and* increases in length, the total volume displaced by the organ may remain relatively constant during the very early stages of arousal. In keeping with the point made earlier, if there are both reflexive and voluntary components to erection, it is likely that they can only be distinguished at these early stages. Therefore, it is necessary that we continue to develop instrumentation which is sensitive to the true changes that the penis undergoes during the full cycle of erection.

Second, these data underline how little we know about the nature of the response we are measuring. Investigators have arbitrarily agreed among themselves that the penis is roughly cylindrical in shape and maintains approximately this shape throughout erection, so that all that is needed is some method of tracking the circumferential changes of this cylinder to make an accurate determination of both current and future sexual arousal. Furthermore, this assumption has led to the adoption of a convention which states that since there is an upper limit to the enlargement of an individual's penis (a full erection), partial changes in penile circumference can be accurately expressed as a ratio percentage of this full erection.

The data we have collected concerning arousal below "10%" of full erection show that initial arousal is actually a circumferential decrease which can be expressed, in conventional terms, as a negative percentage value. It has also been a consistent observation in our laboratory that when a subject is asked to report 100% erection, the polygraph curve describing diameter changes rises, reaches a maximal value, and remains at that value for some time *before* the subject declares he is in a state of maximal arousal. This observation suggests that circumferential measures are not accurately tracking physiological changes in the region of 85 to 100% of full erection. What needs to be determined at this juncture is whether this lack of linearity, most certainly at the initial stages of arousal and perhaps at the later stages, seriously affects clinical and empirical judgments regarding sexual preferences. Whether this criticism of current methodology will prove to be important is, in some sense, not the issue. What is important, however, is that investigators recognize some of the limitations of the data available to date. To this end, the remainder of this chapter will be devoted to a discussion of several issues, including those raised by Farkas (1978), which will have to be experimentally addressed in order to improve the validity of penile assessments.

Unresolved Issues

As mentioned earlier, one of the initial questions which arose in the assessment of penile tumescence was whether an erection was a voluntary or an involuntary response. Several writers view erections as primarily reflexive: that is, given the appropriate somatogenic or psychogenic stimulation, an erection *will* occur (see, for example, Houssay, 1955; Masters and Johnson, 1966; Weiss, 1972). The observations that erections occur with a high degree of regularity during sleep and are not always related to erotic dreams would seem to provide some support for this stance (Karacan, Williams, Thornby, and Salis, 1975; Weiss, 1972). This view has generated a spate of studies which have attempted to condition penile responses. The implicit assumption in these efforts is that since tumescence is reflexive in nature it should be amenable to modification through a conditioning process. In fact, a large majority of the behavioral treatments available use procedures which are clearly based on assumptions that at least originally derived from a conditioning framework.

The alternative hypothesis, that erection is subject to voluntary control, has also resulted in numerous studies. The issue of voluntary control is one which is central to the interpretation of penile tumescence. If erection is not solely reflexive and is in some part determined by whether or not the subject allows himself to become aroused, then the validity of the measure is called into serious question. For example, it is generally assumed that one of the goals of treatment for sexual deviance is to reduce arousal to the deviant sexual cues and to increase arousal to socially acceptable heterosexual cues. In this instance, a heavy reliance is often placed on the results of physiologically measured tumescence to determine treatment progress. If it is the case that males can successfully suppress or generate erections, then the effects of treatment will almost invariably be confounded with practice in controlling arousal.

In the next two sections we will outline the current status of experimentation concerning penile conditioning and voluntary control. Within these sections it is important to note that almost all of the work done has been with arousal above 10% of circumferentially measured erections. Our point here is that erection may be comprised of both a reflexive and controllable component. However, given the focus on arousal above 10%, there has been no opportunity to examine or separate these components.

Conditioning Erectile Responses

Investigations of penile conditioning fall into one of two categories: (a) attempts to condition tumescence by pairing two stimuli in time or (b) pairing a visual or fantasized stimulus with reinforcement.

There have been numerous attempts to investigate the effects of classical conditioning on penile tumescence, most of which have used circumferential measures (Beach, Watts, and Poole, 1971; Herman, Barlow, and Agras, 1974; Rachman, 1966; Rachman and Hodgson, 1968), while two have used a volumetric device (Langevin and Martin, 1975; McConaghy, 1974). Each of these studies has reported some change in tumescence which was attributed to conditioning. However, all experiments failed to include the appropriate control conditions generally associated with a demonstration of conditioning (Rescorla, 1967). In addition, with the exception of the study by Herman et al., none of the reports included sufficient data to allow the reader to make an independent evaluation of the experimental effects. In one experiment (Langevin and Martin, 1975), there were two levels of CS intensity, but this factor exerted no experimental effect. The failure to find an effect of CS intensity casts serious doubts on any claim that the observed effects were the result of classical conditioning (Mackintosh, 1974). In the only report that clearly failed to find a conditioning effect, Marshall (1974) exposed four subjects to 324 CS-UCS pairings, resulting in "little or no treatment change in the rated sexual attractiveness of the stimuli" and changes in penile responding that "were inconsistent and of no clinical significance" (pp. 298-299).

It is evident that before any firm conclusions can be drawn regarding the classical conditioning of penile responses, it will be necessary to devote some attention to the use of appropriate control procedures. It would also be worthwhile to consider what is meant by a "response." Since there is little information concerning the exact nature of mild levels of penile erections (i.e., below 10%), it is not clear whether experimenters using classical conditioning procedures have, in fact, identified an appropriate conditioned response.

The second category of experiments which have attempted to condition penile tumescence is, in fact, concerned with reinforcing erectile responses to appropriate stimuli, with the supposed reinforcer being sexual arousal or orgasm. Work done in this context generally assumes that sexual arousal has already been conditioned, via masturbation, to some inappropriate stimulus; that is, the reinforcing effects of genital stimulation and orgasm in the presence of deviant fantasies are said to result in deviant arousal patterns and often in sexually deviant behavior (Marquis, 1970; McGuire, Carlisle, and Young, 1965).

Numerous authors have reported successful results using either orgasmic reconditioning alone (Jackson, 1969; Marquis, 1970) or masturbatory conditioning in conjunction with other treatment strategies (Abel, Barlow, and Blanchard, 1973; Davison, 1968; Evans, 1968; Lo Piccolo, Steward, and Watkins, 1972; Marquis, 1970; Marshall, 1973; Thorpe, Schmidt, and Castell, 1964). However, as Conrad and Wincze (1976) have pointed out, all of these studies have been either uncontrolled clinical trials or case studies often with only a single subject. The use of more than one treatment intervention at a time, lack of physiological measures, reliance on self-report, and limited follow-up data make it difficult to evaluate the efficacy of orgasmic reconditioning. In addition, there are possibly important procedural differences across studies that might affect outcome. For example, although most therapists instruct patients to conduct orgasmic reconditioning as homework (Marquis, 1970), others have implemented the procedures within a laboratory setting (Marshall, 1979). Furthermore, while some researchers employ orgasm as the reinforcer (Marquis, 1970), others use preorgasmic arousal for the same purpose (Annon, 1973).

In an experiment designed to exert more experimental control, Conrad and Wincze (1976) used four subjects in a single-case experimental design to assess the effect of reconditioning alone. They found a notable lack of treatment effects in all patients. Similarly, Abel and Blanchard (1976) have reported only limited success in four subjects using orgasmic reconditioning. Like Conrad and Wincze, they concluded that the results of studies using this treatment procedure "are far from impressive" (p. 125), with controlled studies showing more negative than positive results (see also Keller and Goldstein, 1978). However, again, there is insufficient information regarding the nature of penile responding to determine what constitutes a response which will be sensitive to reinforcement contingencies. It may be reasonable to suppose that initial, and thus far unexplored, low levels of arousal may require shaping by successive approximations before they attain sufficient strength to be monitored using circumferential measures.

In general, experimental efforts to condition penile responses using either classical or orgasmic conditioning have not been very successful. If, as earlier writers maintain, erection is a reflexive response to sexual stimulation, it is reasonable to suppose that some form of conditioning would be effective. However, the lack of persuasive results with conditioning procedures does not allow a conclusive choice between the reflexive and the voluntary nature of penile erections. A more direct answer to this question can be found in experiments in which subjects are explicitly asked to control their erections.

Control over Erections

Freund (1963), using a volumetric measure, was the first to suggest that penile tumescence could be brought under voluntary control. His primary interest was directed toward detecting patients who were faking erections in order to appear sexually "normal." However, the results also indicated that when instructed, subjects were able to produce penile responses by fantasizing in the presence of the stimulus.

Laws and Rubin (1969) employed a circumferential transducer to investigate the extent to which subjects, when asked, could inhibit a penile response in the presence of an erotic stimulus. Subjects were instructed either to do nothing to inhibit arousal or to inhibit arousal deliberately. Three of the seven subjects originally used were rejected because they failed to produce a full erection to the stimulus film. The remaining four subjects demonstrated that they could substantially reduce penile tumescence when so instructed. When asked what method they used to inhibit arousal, all subjects reported engaging in cognitive activities which were essentially diversionary in nature. The findings reported in this experiment have been confirmed by numerous other studies with both volumetric measures (Freund, 1971; Freund et al., 1979) and circumferential measures (Henson and Rubin, 1971; Laws and Holman, 1978; Quinsey and Bergersen, 1976; Quinsey and Carrigan, 1978; Rosen, 1973; Rosen et al., 1975).

Geer and Fuhr (1976) specifically investigated the role of cognitive activities in the inhibition of penile responding. They presented subjects with an erotic audiotape in one ear and a series of single numerical digits in the other. The results of this procedure clearly indicated an inverse relationship between penile tumescence and the level of difficulty in attending to the digits. These authors interpreted their findings as indicating that the erotic value of a particular stimulus is dependent on the extent to which the subject attends directly to that stimulus. Based on these results, Abel and Blanchard (1976) have suggested that *whenever* voluntary control is exerted over penile responding, it may be a result of the subject shifting his attention away from the stimulus. Regardless of the accuracy of this suggestion, it seems clear that erection is not simply a reflexive response but is also dependent on higher cortical activity.

Abel et al. (1975) have extended the work on the control of penile responses by assessing the ability of 20 homosexual subjects to suppress their responses to stimuli presented within three modalities: audiotapes, slides, and videotapes. Subjects were instructed either to deliberately become aroused or to suppress arousal in the presence of the erotic cues. Their results showed that these subjects were able to significantly reduce penile tumescence to both videotape and slide depictions; there were no significant reductions in arousal to the audiotaped material. Abel et al. hypothesized that suppression of response to auditory stimuli may be more difficult because these stimuli may compete with distracting thoughts or images. However, since audiotapes characteristically result in low levels of arousal, Abel et al. advanced an alternative hypothesis that suppression can occur only when the potential for arousal is high.

Wydra, Marshall, Barbaree, and Earls (1981) conducted an experiment which allows a choice between these two hypotheses. Convicted rapists and normal college-aged males were asked to suppress their arousal to audiotaped episodes of both mutually consenting sex and rape (see Barbaree et al., 1979). Both groups were able to significantly reduce their arousal when instructed to. Since Wydra et al.'s subjects showed arousal levels comparable to those of Abel et al.'s subjects, it is clear that arousal levels do not have to be high before voluntary control can be exerted.

One advantage of the evidence bearing on the control of erection is that researchers have become increasingly wary of interpreting results that show no tumescence. In these cases there are two interpretations: either the stimulus is genuinely not arousing, or the subject is suppressing arousal. The problem of distinguishing between no sexual interest and suppression has led to a number of recommendations, including using only cooperative subjects (Abel and Blanchard, 1976), use of a stimulus detection task (see Henson and Rubin, 1971; Laws and Rubin, 1969), providing a task to occupy the subject's hands so that potential interference with the measurement devices is minimized (Laws and Holman, 1978), and employing a surveillance camera (Freund, personal communication, 1980; Laws and Holman, 1978). One of the recommendations made by Abel et al. (1975), although possibly sound, was in fact based on an error in interpretation. These authors suggested that investigators place more faith in erections than nonerections since "it has been shown that subject's ability to generate erections voluntarily is much poorer than their ability to suppress erections" (p. 259). Now this suggestion is appropriate when applied to deviant arousal patterns identified by assessment. Clearly no one is going to fake deviant interests unless asked to. However, if a subject displays arousal to appropriate stimuli, are we to take that as accurately reflecting such an interest because individuals find it difficult to generate arousal? In fact, it is doubtful that men do find it all that difficult to generate erections.

Abel et al. based their claim on data presented by Laws and Rubin (1969) in which four subjects were asked to generate arousal in the absence of any erotic stimulation. Under these conditions, the levels of arousal generated were relatively low with no subject attaining a full erection. In addition, the polygraphic curves during this procedure indicated that patterns of arousal were substantially different from those obtained when subjects were aroused by erotic material. The problem in drawing conclusions from these data is that while Abel et al. were making claims about arousal in response to an actual stimulus, Laws and Rubin's observations were based on arousal in the absence of any specific stimuli. Since most faking is done when an actual stimulus is presented, the comparison which is necessary to determine the validity of Abel et al.'s assumption concerns arousal to a stimulus that has low or neutral erotic value for the subject versus arousal deliberately generated to that stimulus.

Such a comparison has been made by Quinsey and Bergersen (1976), and Quinsey and Carrigan (1978). These investigators asked heterosexual subjects to respond as they normally would to stimuli depicting adult females and female children. Subjects were also requested to respond so as to make it appear they preferred small children, that is, to inhibit arousal to the adult stimuli and generate an erection to the child stimuli. The results indicated significant concordance with the instructions in two of five subjects in the Quinsey and Bergersen study, and seven of nine subjects in the Quinsey and Carrigan study. Unfortunately, neither of these published reports included samples of the polygraphic records when faking instructions were in effect. The absence of such records makes it impossible to directly compare the faked arousal in Laws and Rubin's experiment with the faked patterns in the experiments of Quinsey and his colleagues (see also Laws and Holman, 1978). Nonetheless, Quinsey's data indicate that it may not be all that difficult for some males to present deceptive arousal by *both* inhibiting and generating erection.

Self-reported versus Physiologically Assessed Arousal

As mentioned earlier, penile tumescence is usually recognized as the most reliable index of male sexual arousal (Zuckerman, 1971). One would expect that if physiological measures are detecting sexual arousal, these measures would correlate highly with subjects' self-reported arousal. As we noted earlier, some investigators have found a reasonable agreement between these two indices (Abel et al., 1977; Abel et al., in press; Mavissakalian et al., 1975), while others have found the relationship to be quite low (Farkas et al., 1979; McConaghy, 1969; Wincze et al., 1980). The results of our two experiments described above may help explain this discrepancy.

Just to remind our readers, these experiments demonstrated that the penis expands substantially along its longitudinal axis before any circumferential increase is observed. We found that by the time a 10% circumferential increase had occurred, length had already increased to 49.2% of its total change. Since we cannot expect subjects to report tumescence on a dimension of circumference alone, it may not be reasonable to expect self-reports to consistently correlate highly across subjects with circumferentially determined tumescence. Of course, it does seem more likely, given the actual physical magnitude of changes that occur in the penis during tumescence, that subjects base their estimates of arousal more on length changes than on increases in diameter. We might, therefore, expect self-reported arousal to correspond more accurately to changes in penile length. What is required is an experiment which compares self-reported arousal with physiological changes measured by either a volumetric device or, preferably, the circumferential/length transducer. At the time of writing, such an experiment is being conducted. We have hypothesized that the correlation between self-reported arousal and circumferentially assessed erection will be low in the early stages of penile change (i.e., 10% of full erection) and high in the later stages. We expect consistently high correlations throughout the cycle when erection is defined in terms of length changes. If these hypotheses are supported, it will further strengthen the validity of the circumferential/length transducer and at the same time dispel one of Farkas' criticisms concerning the internal validity of erectile measures.

However, the discrepancy in the literature as to the correlation between self-reported and physiologically assessed arousal may, as we noted earlier, be a result not only of noncircumferential penile changes but also of the measurement methodology. In addition to our earlier remarks, it is important to note that those authors reporting a good correlation have generally asked their subjects to simply indicate the highest percentage of erection achieved during a particular stimulus presentation. Experimenters reporting low correlations, on the other hand, have most often employed a continuous or moment-to-moment self-report measure (e.g., Wincze's "cognitive lever").[4] It seems likely that at least some of the between-experiment discrepancies may be due to these differing procedures. It may be the case that it is easier and more accurate for a subject to report a single

---

4. It should also be noted that the experimenters computing a correlation coefficient on moment-to-moment penile changes are not using this statistic in an entirely appropriate manner. The use of the Pearson product-moment correlational statistic requires the assumption that observations within each variable (x and y; self-report and penile tumescence) are independent. When a subject is asked to report arousal at time N, his report as well as his level of tumescence, is dependent on his report and tumescence at time $N - 1$. The effect of this particular dependence is to spuriously inflate the value of r. Therefore, the r statistic is appropriate in terms of a *descriptor* of a particular relationship but cannot be interpreted as an *exact* numerical representation of covariance and, most importantly, cannot be justifiably used within an inferential statistical model.

estimate of maximal arousal than to maintain a precise tracking of moment-to-moment changes in either tumescence or "perceived arousal" (however, see Wincze et al., 1979). Therefore, we are asking our subjects for an estimate of maximally attained arousal as well as for moment-to-moment estimates. In this way, any discrepancies between measurement methodologies should be revealed. Our expectation at this time is that single-point estimates will be more accurate than the overall continuous measure, but that the accuracy of the continuous measure will improve after the initial stages of tumescence have occurred.

Predictive Validity

When Farkas (1978) questioned the validity of strain gauge measures, he was clearly referring to the ability to predict extralaboratory behavior on the basis of penile tumescence assessment. However, there are two aspects to this issue. One involves the complexity of human behavior in the absence of laboratory control. In the natural setting, many factors other than simple sexual preferences determine behavior. For instance, we have already seen that social competence, alcohol intoxication, anger, and attitudes toward both women and sexual aggression all affect the probability that a man will sexually attack women or children. Thus the accurate prediction of who will or will not rape or engage in sex with children will, in all probability, never be possible using the unitary measure of penile tumescence. Any generalizations regarding such complex behavior will require an analysis which includes a wide variety of physiological, behavioral, and self-reported variables.

On the other hand, prediction in the sense of determining sexual orientation or behavioral proclivities that may put men at risk for offending may be possible on the basis of penile measurement alone. Indeed, a good number of experiments cited earlier have delineated response patterns which serve to differentiate groups of men who, for one reason or another, have known sexual histories (e.g., convicted rapists versus nonrapist; Abel et al., 1977; Barbaree et al., 1979). A potential difficulty arises when an individual's sexual history is unknown; that is, given a randomly chosen male, can we identify his sexual orientation based on no other information than his penile responses? The answer, at present, is no. The reason is simply that we can never be sure he is not faking either tumescence or flaccidity. The issue of predictive validity, in this form, brings us back to the issue of voluntary control. When voluntary control can be adequately taken into account, the validity of penile assessment measures will be vastly increased. In addition, as a final note, we consider that the accurate description of any individual male's sexual orientation will only be possible when we have data on a representative sample of the population that includes deviants and nondeviants. The adequate collection of data on the erectile preferences of nondeviants has been neglected and represents a serious inadequacy in our knowledge.

REFERENCES

Abel, G.G., Barlow, D.H., and Blanchard, E.B. *Developing heterosexual arousal by altering mastur-batory fantasies: a controlled study.* Paper presented at the 7th Annual Convention of the Association for the Advancement of Behavior Therapy, Miami, December 1973

Abel, G.G., Barlow, D.H., Blanchard, E.B., and Guild D. The components of rapists' sexual arousal. *Archives of General Psychiatry* **34**:895-903 (1977).

Abel, G.G., Barlow, D.H., Blanchard, E.B., and Mavissakalian, M. Measurement of sexual arousal in male homosexuals: effects of instructions and stimulus modality. *Archives of Sexual Behavior* **4**:623-629 (1975).

Abel, G.G. and Blanchard, E.B. The measurement and generation of sexual arousal in male sexual deviates. In Hersen, M., Eisler, R., and Miller, P. (Eds.) *Progress in Behavior Modification*, Vol. 2. N.Y.: Academic Press, 1976.

Abel, G.G., Blanchard, E.G., Barlow, D.H., and Mavissakalian, M. Identifying specific erotic cues in sexual deviations by audiotaped descriptions. *Journal of Applied Behavior Analysis* **8**:247-260 (1975).

Abel, G.G., Blanchard, E.B., Becker, J.V., and Djenderedjian, A. Differentiating sexual aggressive-ness with penile measures. *Criminal Justice and Behavior* **5**:315-332 (1978).

Abel, G.G., Blanchard, E.B., Murphy, W.D., Becker, J.F., and Djenderedjian, A. Two methods of measuring penile response. *Behavior Therapy* (in press).

Annon, J.S. The therapeutic use of masturbation in the treatment of sexual disorders. In Rubin, R.D., Brady, J.P., and Henderson, J.D. (Eds.) *Advances in Behavior Therapy*, Vol. 4. New York: Aca-demic Press, 1973.

Bancroft, J.H.J., Jones, H.G., and Pullen, B.R. A simple transducer for measuring penile erection with comments on its use in the treatment of sexual disorder. *Behaviour Research and Therapy* **4**:230-241 (1966).

Barbaree, H.E., Marshall, W.L., and Lanthier, R.D. Deviant sexual arousal in rapists. *Behaviour Research and Therapy* **17**:215-222 (1979).

Barbaree, H.E., Marshall, W.L., Lightfoot, L, and Yates, E. *The effects of alcohol on sexual aggres-sion.* Paper presented at the 2nd National Conference on the Evaluation and Treatment of Sexual Aggressives, New York, May 1979.

Barlow, D.H. Assessment of sexual behavior. In Ciminero, A.R., Calhoun, K.S., and Adams, H.E. (Eds.) *Handbook of Behavioral Assessment*. New York: Wiley, 1977.

Barlow, D.H., Becker, R., Leitenberg, H., and Agras, W.S. A mechanical strain gauge for recording penile circumference change. *Journal of Applied Behavior Analysis* **3**:73-76 (1970).

Barr, R. and Blaszczynski, A. Autonomic responses of trans-sexual and homosexual males to erotic film sequences. *Archives of Sexual Behavior* **5**:211-222 (1976).

Barr, R.F. and McConaghy, N. Penile volume responses to appetitive and aversive stimuli in relation to sexual orientation and conditioning performance. *British Journal of Psychiatry* **119**:377-383 (1971).

Beech, H.R., Watts, F., and Poole, A.P. Classical conditioning of a sexual deviation: a preliminary note. *Behavior Therapy* **2**:400-402 (1971).

Conrad, S.R. and Wincze, J.P. Orgasmic reconditioning: a controlled study of its effects upon the sexual arousal and behavior of adult male homosexuals. *Behavior Therapy* **7**:155-166 (1976).

Davidson, P., Malcolm, P.B., Lanthier, R.D., Barbaree, H.E., and Ho, T.P. Penile response measure-ment: operating characteristics of Parks plethysmograph. *Behavioral Assessment* **3**:137-143 (1981).

Davison, G.C. Elimination of a sadistic fantasy by a client-controlled counterconditioning technique: a case study. *Journal of Abnormal Psychology* **73**:84-90 (1968).

Earls, C.M. Erectile responding below 10% in the human male. Unpublished doctoral dissertation, Queen's University, Kingston, Ontario, 1981.

Earls, C.M. and Jackson, D.R. The effects of temperature on the mercury-in-rubber strain gauge. *Behavioral Assessment* **3**:145-149 (1981).

Earls, C.M. and Marshall, W.L. A limitation of the mercury-in-rubber strain gauge? *The Behavior Therapist* **3**:3-4 (1980).

Earls, C.M. and Marshall, W.L. *A new dimension in the assessment of male sexual arousal.* Paper presented at the 15th Annual Convention of the Association of the Advancement of Behavior Therapy, Toronto, November 1981.(a)

Earls, C.M. and Marshall, W.L. The simultaneous and independent measurement of penile circumference and length. *Behavior Research Methods and Instrumentation* **14**:447–450 (1982).

Evans, D.R. Masturbatory fantasy and sexual deviation. *Behaviour Research and Therapy* **6**:17-19 (1968).

Farkas, G.M. Comments on Levin et al. and Rosen and Kopel: internal and external validity issues. *Journal of Consulting and Clinical Psychology* **46**:1515-1516 (1978).

Farkas, G.M., Evans S.M., Sine, L.F., Eifert, G., Wittlieb, E., and Vogelmann-Sine, S. Reliability and validity of the mercury-in-rubber strain gauge measure of penile circumference. *Behavior Therapy* **10**:555-561 (1979).

Farkas, G.M., Sine, R.F., and Evans, I.M. The effects of distraction, performance demand, stimulus explicitness, and personality on objective and subjective measures of male sexual arousal. *Behaviour Research and Therapy* **17**:25-32 (1979).

Fisher, C., Gross, J., and Zuch, J. Cycle of penile erection synchronous with dreaming (REM) sleep. *Archives of General Psychiatry* **12**:29-45 (1965).

Freund, K. Laboratory differential diagnosis of homo- and heterosexuality—an experiment with faking. *Review of Czechoslovak Medicine* **7**:20-31 (1961).

Freund, K. A laboratory method for diagnosing predominance of homo- and hetero-erotic interest in the male. *Behaviour Research and Therapy* **1**:85-93 (1963).

Freund, K. Diagnosing homo- or heterosexuality and erotic age-preference by means of a psychophysiological test. *Behaviour Research and Therapy* **5**:209-228 (1967). (a)

Freund, K. Erotic preference in pedophilia. *Behaviour Research and Therapy* **5**:339-348 (1967).(b)

Freund, K. A note on the use of the phallometric method of measuring mild sexual arousal in the male. *Behavior Therapy* **2**:223-228 (1971).

Freund, K., Chan, S., and Coulthard, R. Phallometric diagnosis with "nonadmitters." *Behaviour Research and Therapy* **17**:451-457 (1979).

Freund, K., Langevin, R., and Barlow, D. Comparison of two penile measures of erotic arousal. *Behaviour Research and Therapy* **12**:355-359 (1974).

Freund, K., Sedlacek, F., and Knob, K. A simple transducer for mechanical plethysmography of the male genital. *Journal of the Experimental Analysis of Behavior* **8**:169-170 (1965).

Geer, J.H. and Fuhr, R. Cognitive factors in sexual arousal: the role of distraction. *Journal of Consulting and Clinical Psychology* **44**:238-243 (1976).

Grossberg, J.M. and Grant, B.F. Clinical psychophysics: applications of ratio scaling and signal detection methods to research on pain, fear, drugs, and medical decision making. *Psychological Bulletin* **85**:1154-1176 (1978).

Hammer, D. and Webster, J.S. *Relative utility of thermistor versus Barlow strain gauge in assessing male sexual arousal.* Paper presented at the 14th Annual Convention of the Association for the Advancement of Behavior Therapy, New York, November 1980.

Henson, C., Rubin, H., and Henson, D. Women's sexual arousal concurrently assessed by three genital measures. *Archives of Sexual Behavior* **8**:459-469 (1979).(a)

Henson, D.E. and Rubin, H.B. Voluntary control of eroticism. *Journal of Applied Behavior Analysis* **4**:37-44. (1971).

Henson, D.E. and Rubin, H. A comparison of two objective measures of sexual arousal of women. *Behviour Research and Therapy* **16**:143-151 (1978).

Henson, D.E., Rubin, H.B., and Henson, C. Analysis of the consistency of objective measures of sexual arousal in women. *Journal of Applied Behavior Analysis* **12**:701-711 (1979).(b)

Herman, S.H., Barlow, D.H., and Agras, W.S. An experimental analysis of classical conditioning as a method of increasing heterosexual arousal in homosexuals. *Behavior Therapy* **5**:33-47 (1974).

Hess, E.H. Pupillometric assessment. *Research in Psychotherapy* **3**:573-583 (1968).

Hess, E.H. and Polt, J.M. Pupil size as related to interest value of visual stimuli. *Science* **132**:349-350 (1960).

Hinton, J.W., O'Neill, M.T., and Webster, S. Psychophysiological assessment of sex offenders in a security hospital. *Archives of Sexual Behavior* **9**:205-216 (1980).

Hooker, C.W. Reproduction in the male. In Ruch, T.C. and Patton, H.D. (Eds.) *Physiology and Biophysics*. Philadelphia: Saunders, 1966.

Houssay, B.S. *Human Physiology*. New York: McGraw Hill, 1955.

Jackson, B.T. A case of voyeurism treated by counterconditioning. *Behaviour Research and Therapy* **7**:133-134 (1969).

Karacan, I., Williams, R.L., Thornby, J.I., and Salis, P.J. Sleep-related penile tumescence as a function of age. *American Journal of Psychiatry* **132**:932-937 (1975).

Keller, D.J. and Goldstein, A. Orgasmic reconditioning reconsidered. *Behaviour Research and Therapy* **16**:299-300 (1978).

Kercher, G.A. and Walker, C.E. Reactions of convicted rapists to sexually explicit stimuli. *Journal of Abnormal Psychology* **81**:46-50 (1973).

Kolarsky, A. and Madlafousek, J. Female behavior and sexual arousal in heterosexual male deviant offenders. *Journal of Nervous and Mental Disease* **155**:110-115 (1972).

Langevin, R. and Martin, M. Can erotic responses be classically conditioned? *Behavior Therapy* **6**:350-355 (1975).

Langevin, R., Paitich, D., Ramsay, G., Anderson, C., Pope, S., Pearl, L., and Newman, S. Experimental studies of the etiology of genital exhibitionism. *Archives of Sexual Behavior* **8**:307-331 (1979).

Laws, D.R. A comparison of the measurement characteristics of two circumferential penile transducers. *Archives of Sexual Behavior* **6**:45-51 (1977).

Laws, D.R. *Evaluation of sexual aggressives*. Paper presented at the 3rd National Conference on the Evaluation and Treatment of Sexual Aggressives, Avila Beach, California, March 1981.

Laws, D.R. and Bow, R.A. An improved mechanical strain gauge for recording penile circumference change. *Psychophysiology* **13**:596-599 (1976).

Laws, D.R. and Holman, M.L. Sexual response faking by pedophiles. *Criminal Justice and Behavior* **5**:343-356 (1978).

Laws, D.R. and Rubin, H.B. Instructional control of an autonomic response. *Journal of Applied Behavior Analysis* **2**:93-99 (1969).

Levin, S.M., Gambaro, S., and Wolfinsohn, L. Penile tumescence as a measure of sexual arousal: a reply to Farkas. *Journal of Consulting and Clinical Psychology* **46**:1517-1518 (1978).

Lick, J.R., Sushinsky, L.W., and Malow, R. Specificity of fear survey schedule items and prediction of avoidance behavior. *Behavior Modification* **1**:195-203 (1977).

Lo Piccolo, J., Steward, R., and Watkins, B. Treatment of erectile failure and ejaculatory incompetence of homosexual etiology. *Journal of Behavior Therapy and Experimental Psychiatry* **3**:233-236 (1972).

Macintosh, N.J. *The Psychology of Animal Learning*. New York: Academic Press, 1974.

Malamuth, N.M. Rape fantasies as a function of exposure to violent sexual stimuli. *Archives of Sexual Behavior* **10**:33-47 (1981).

Marks, I.M. and Gelder, J.L. Transvestism and fetishism: clinical and psychological changes during faradic aversion. *British Journal of Psychiatry* **113**:711-729 (1967).

Marquis, J.N. Orgasmic reconditioning: changing sexual object choice through controlling masturbation fantasies. *Journal of Behavior Therapy and Experimental Psychiatry* **1**:263-271 (1970).

Marshall, W.L. The modification of sexual fantasies: a combined treatment approach to the reduction of deviant sexual behavior. *Behaviour Research and Therapy* **11**:557-564 (1973).

Marshall, W.L. The classical conditioning of sexual attractiveness: a report of four therapeutic failures. *Behavior Therapy* **5**:298-299 (1974).

Marshall, W.L. The prediction of treatment outcome with sexual deviants based on changes in erectile responses to deviant and nondeviant stimuli. Unpublished report, Queen's University, Kingston, Ontario, 1975.

Marshall, W.L. Satiation therapy: a procedure for reducing deviant sexual arousal. *Journal of Applied Behavior Analysis* **12**:10-22 (1979).

Marshall, W.L. and Barbaree, H.E. The reduction of deviant arousal: Satiation treatment for sexual aggressors. *Criminal Justice and Behavior* **5**:294-303 (1978).

Masters, W.H. and Johnson, V.E. *Human Sexual Response*. Boston: Little, Brown, 1966.

Mavissakalian, M., Blanchard, E.B., Abel, G.G., and Barlow, D.H. Responses to complex erotic stimuli in homosexual and heterosexual males. *British Journal of Psychiatry* **126**:252-257 (1975).

McConaghy, N. Penile volume change to moving pictures of male and female nudes in heterosexual and homosexual males. *Behaviour Research and Therapy* **5**:43-48 (1967).

McConaghy, N. Subjective and penile plethysmograph responses following aversion relief and apomorphine therapy for homosexual impulses. *British Journal of Psychiatry* **115**:723-730 (1969).

McConaghy, N. Measurement of change in penile dimensions. *Archives of Sexual Behavior* **3**:381-388 (1974).

McGuire, R.J., Carlisle, J.M., and Young, B.G. Sexual deviations as conditioned behavior: a hypothesis. *Behaviour Research and Therapy* **2**:185-190 (1965).

Murphy, W.D., Quinsey, V.L., and Marshall, W.L. *Social skills of sexual aggressives*. Paper presented at the 3rd National Conference on the Evaluation and Treatment of Sexual Agressives, Avila Beach, California, March 1981.

Quinsey, V.L. The assessment and treatment of child molesters: a review. *Canadian Psychological Review* **18**:204-220 (1977).

Quinsey, V.L. *Prediction of recidivism and the evaluation of treatment programs for sex offenders*. Paper presented at Sexual Aggression and the Law: a symposium, Vancouver, Canada, October 1981.

Quinsey, V.L. and Bergersen, S.G. Instructional control of penile circumference in assessments of sexual preference. *Behavior Therapy* **1**:489-493 (1976).

Quinsey, V.L. and Carrigan, W.F. Penile responses to visual stimuli. *Criminal Justice and Behavior* **5**:333-342 (1978).

Rachman, S. Sexual fetishism: An experimental analogue. *Psychological Record* **16**:293-296 (1966).

Rachman, S. and Hodgson, R.J. Experimentally-induced "sexual fetishism": replication and development. *Psychological Record* **18**:25-27 (1968).

Rescorla, R.A. Pavlovian conditioning and its proper control procedures. *Psychological Review* **74**:71-80 (1967).

Rosen, R.C. Suppression of penile tumescence by instrumental conditioning. *Psychosomatic Medicine* **35**:509-514 (1973).

Rosen, R.C. and Keefe, F.J. The measurement of human penile tumescence. *Psychophysiology* **15**:366-376 (1978).

Rosen, R. and Kopel, S.A. Penile plethysmography and biofeedback in the treatment of a transvestite-exhibitionist. *Journal of Consulting and Clinical Psychology* **45**:908-916 (1977).

Rosen, R.C. and Kopel, S.A. Role of penile tumescence measurement in the behavioral treatment of sexual deviation: issues of validity. *Journal of Consulting and Clinical Psychology* **46**:1519-1521 (1978).

Rosen, R.C., Shapiro, D., and Schwartz, G.E. Voluntary control of penile tumescence. *Psychosomatic Medicine* **37**:479-483 (1975).

Seeley, T.T., Abramson, P.R., Perry, L.B., Rothblatt, A.B., and Seeley, D.M. Thermographic measurement of sexual arousal: a methodological note. *Archives of Sexual Behavior* **9**:77-85 (1980).

Thorpe, J.G., Schmidt, E., and Castell, D. A comparison of positive and negative (aversive) conditioning in the treatment of homosexuality. *Behaviour Research and Therapy* **1**:357-362 (1964).

Weiss, H.D. The physiology of human penile erection. *Annals of Internal Medicine* **76**:793-799 (1972).

Whitman, W.P. and Quinsey, V.L. Heterosocial skill training for institutionalized rapists and child molesters. *Canadian Journal of Behavioural Science* (in press).

Whitney, P.J. The measurement of changes in human limb volume by means of a mercury-in-rubber gauge. *Journal of Physiology* **109**:5-6 (1949).

Wincze, J.P., Venditti, E., Barlow, D., and Mavissakalian, M. The effects of a subjective monitoring task in the physiological measure of genital response to erotic stimulation. *Archives of Sexual Behavior* **9**:533-545 (1980).

Wydra, A., Marshall, W.L., Barbaree, H.E., and Earls, C. *Control of sexual arousal by rapists and non-rapists*. Paper presented at the 42nd Annual Convention of the Canadian Psychological Association, Toronto, Canada, June 1981.

Yates, E., Barbaree, H.E., and Marshall, W.L. *The effects of "anger" on sexual arousal to rape cues*. Paper presented at the 14th Annual Convention of the Association for the Advancement of Behavior Therapy, New York, November 1980.

Zuckerman, M. Physiological measures of sexual arousal in the human. *Psychological Bulletin* **25**:297-327 (1971).

Appendix
Treatment Programs in the
United States and Canada

Listed below are many of the treatment programs mentioned in the text, as well as others which may be geographically closer to the reader. Persons interested in organizing a treatment program or in expanding an existing one would profit greatly from corresponding with or visiting one or more of the following sites.

California

Sexual behavior Laboratory
Atascadero State Hospital
Atascadero, CA 93422; (805) 461-2305
Richard Laws, Ph.D., Dir.

Child Sexual Abuse Treatment Program
Solano County Mental Health
1408 Pennsylvania Ave.
Fairfield, CA 94533; (707) 429-6521
Henry Raming, Ph.D., Dir.

Neuropsychiatric Institute
University of California at Los Angeles
750 Westwood Blvd.
Los Angeles, CA 90024; (213) 825-0102
Dr. Gloria Powell, Dir.

Child Sexual Abuse Treatment Program
6950 Levant St.
San Diego, CA 92111; (714) 560-2371
Gerald Vernon, Ph.D., Dir.

Paul A. Walker, Ph.D.
1952 Union St.
San Francisco, CA 94123; (415) 567-0162

Parents United
P.O. Box 952
San Jose, CA 95108; (408) 280-5055
Harry Giarretto, Ph.D., Dir.

Child Abuse Treatment Program
P.O. Box 4160, Rm. 2161D
Civil Center Br.
San Rafael, CA 94903; (415) 499-7172
Carol Johnston, Adm.

Napa County Mental Health Service
2344 Old Sonoma Road
Napa, CA 94558; (707) 253-4561
James Featherstone, M.S., Dir.

Colorado

Darrow Clinic
1635 Pearl St.
Denver, CO 80203; (303) 831-4160
Dr. James Selkin, Dir.

Behavior Therapy Laboratory No. GAPS
Colorado State Hospital
Pueblo, CO 81003; (303) 543-1170, ext. 2798
Wayne Smyer, Dir.

Connecticut

Connecticut Sex Offender Treatment Program
Correctional Institute—Somers
P.O. Box 100
Somers, CT 06071; (203) 749-8391, ext. 36
A. Nicholas Groth, Ph.D., Dir.

District of Columbia

St. Elizabeths Hospital
2700 Martin Luther King, Jr. Ave., SE
Washington, DC 20032; (202) 574-7162
Dr. Vallory G. Lathrop, Dir.

Florida

Avon Park Correctional Institute
P.O. Box 1100
Avon Park, FL 33825; (813) 453-3174
Michael T. McCrocklin, Ph.D., Dir.

North Florida Evaluation and Treatment Center
P.O. Box NFETC
Gainesville, FL 32601; (904) 375-8484
Mike McAnaney, Dir.
Dr. Geraldine Boozer Rehabilitation Program
for Sex Offenders

South Florida State Hospital
1000 SW 84 Ave.
Hollywood, FL 33023; (305) 983-4321
William R. Samek, Ph.D., Dir.

Hawaii

Queen's Physicians' Building
Suite 909, 1380 Lusitana St.
Honolulu, HI 96813; (808) 533-1711
Jack S. Annon, Ph.D., Dir.

Illinois

Vienna Correctional Center
P.O. Box 275
Vienna, IL 62995; (618) 658-2081
Jim Rouse, Dir.

Maryland

Special Offenders Clinic
Psychiatric Institute of Maryland
Room M609
Baltimore, MD 21202; (301) 528-6475
Jonas R. Rappeport, M.D., Dir.

Biosocial Psychohormonal Clinic
Johns Hopkins Hospital
235A Phipps Clinic
Baltimore, MD 21205; (301) 955-6292
Fred S. Berlin, M.D., Ph.D.

Massachusetts

Massachusetts Treatment Center
P.O. Box 554
Bridgewater, MA 02324; (617) 727-8929
Richard J. Boucher, Dir.

Norfolk County Sexual Assault Unit
614 High St.
Dedham, MA 02026; (617) 326-7829
Patricia Nigrelli, Dir.

Minnesota

Anoka County Child Sexual Abuse Treatment
  Program
Anoka Court House
Anoka, MN 55303; (612) 421-4760, ext. 1630
Gerald Keeville, Coordinator

Family Sexual Abuse Program
6545 France Ave. S.
Edina, MN 55435; (612) 920-4400, ext. 435
Miriam Ingebritsen, Dir.

Minnesota Correctional Institution
7525 4th Ave.

Lino Lakes, MN 55014; (612) 786-2800
Nancy M. Steele, Ph.D., Dir.

Alpha House, Inc.
2712 Fremont Ave. S.
Minneapolis, MN 55408; (612) 872-8218
Gerald T. Kaplan, Dir.

Port of Olmsted County, Inc.
2112 East Center St.
Rochester, MN 55901; (507) 288-3385
Ronald Amdahl, Dir.

Minnesota Security Hospital
Intensive Treatment Program for Sexual
  Aggressives
St. Peter, MN 56082; (507) 931-7150
Richard K. Seely, Dir.

Minnesota Correctional Facility
Box 55
Stillwater, MN 55082; (612) 439-1910
Marvin L. Rosow, Psychiatric Social Worker

Mississippi

Maximum Security Unit
Fulton St. Hospital Program II
Fulton, MS 65251; (314) 642-3311, ext. 205
David A. Jannick, Dir.

Missouri

Missouri Sexual Offender Program
Division of Corrections
P.O. Box 236
Jefferson City, MO 65102; (314) 751-2389
Constance A. Avery-Clark, Ph.D., Dir.

New Jersey

Adult Diagnostic and Treatment Center
P.O. Box 190
8 Production Way
Avenel, NJ 07001; (201) 574-2250
Ira Mintz, Ph.D., Dir.

Sexual Counseling Service
College of Medicine
Rutgers Medical School
P.O. Box 101
Piscataway, NJ 08854; (201) 463-4273
Sandra Leiblum, Ph.D., Dir.

New Mexico

Alternative Inc.
P.O. Box 1280
Albuquerque, NM 87103; (505) 247-0173
Linda Winter, Program Coordinator

New York

Sex Clinic, Dept. of Psychology
State University of New York—Albany
1400 Washington Ave.
Albany, NY 12222; (518) 457-3999
David H. Barlow, Ph.D.

Sexual Behavior Clinic
New York State Psychiatric Institute
722 W. 168th St.
New York, NY 10032; (212) 568-4000, ext. 303
Gene G. Abel, M.D., Dir.

North Dakota

Sex Offender Program
North Dakota State Penitentiary
Box 1497
Bismarck, ND 58501; (701) 224-2980
Jack Paul, J.D., Dir.

Ohio

Department of Psychiatry
Wright State University
Box 927
Dayton, OH 45401; (513) 276-3934
Abraham Heller, M.D., Dir., Community and
    Forensic Psychiatry

Pennsylvania

Joseph J. Peters Institute
112 S. 16th St.
Philadelphia, PA 19102; (215) 568-6627
Elaine P. Bencivengo, M.A., Dir.

State Correctional Institution at Dallas
Dallas, PA 18612; (717) 675-1101
Edward J. Klem, Dir.

Rhode Island

Adult Correctional Institutions
Box 8273
Cranston, RI 02920; (401) 464-3317
John DiLorenzo, Dir.

Tennessee

Special Problems Unit
University of Tennessee
Psychiatry, 4 East
865 Poplar Ave.
Memphis, TN 38104; (901) 528-5490
William Murphy, Ph.D., Dir.

Memphis Correctional Center
6000 State Rd.

Memphis, TN 38134; (901) 372-2080
Joseph Krisak, Ed.D., Dir.

DeBerry Correctional Institution (DCI)
3250 Ezell Pike
Nashville, TN 37211; (615) 833-9415
David T. Shefrin, Ph.D., Dir.

Texas

Family Sex Abuse Counseling Program
Family Service Association
230 Pereida
San Antonio, TX 78210; (512) 226-3391
John Dauer, Coordinator

Vermont

Behavior Therapy and Psychotherapy Center
Department of Psychology
University of Vermont
Burlington, VT 05405; (802) 656-2661
Harold Leitenberg, Ph.D., Dir.

Virginia

Stanton E. Samenow, Ph.D.
4921 Seminary Rd. #104
Alexandria, VA 22311; (703) 931-0004

House of Thought
North Housing Unit
Powhattan Correctional Center
State Farm, VA 23160; (804) 784-3551
Tim Hodges, Coordinator

Sexual Abuse Treatment Program
3432 Virginia Beach Blvd.
Virginia Beach, VA 23452; (804) 486-7223
Frances Elrod, Dir.

Washington

Sex Offender Program
Western State Hospital
Ft. Steilacoom, WA 98494; (206) 756-9573
Maureen Saylor, Dir.

Wisconsin

Wisconsin Division of Corrections
Bureau of Program Resources
Box 7925
Madison, WI 53707; (608) 266-2789
Eugene H. Strangman, Dir.

Winnebago Mental Health Institute
Box H
Winnebago, WI 54985; (414) 235-4910
John Juettner, M.S.W., Dir.

Canada

Forensic Clinic
701-805 W. Broadway
Vancouver, BC, Canada V521K1;
  (604) 873-8561
Dr. D. Eaves, Dir.

Oak Ridge Division
Mental Health Center
Penetanguishene, Ontario, Canada LOK1PO;
  (705) 549-7431
Dr. V.L. Quinsey, Dir.

Forensic Services
St. Thomas Psychiatric Hospital
P.O. Box 2004
St. Thomas, Ontario, Canada N5P3VP;
  (519) 631-8510
P.D. Gatfield, M.D., Dir.

Geller and Shedletsky
188 Eglinton Ave., Suite 704
Toronto, Ontario, Canada M4P2X7;
  (416) 482-4311
Dr. S.H. Geller

Clarke Institute of Psychiatry
250 College St.
Toronto, Ontario, Canada M5T1R8;
  (416) 979-2221, ext. 320
Dr. S. Hucker, Dir.

W.J. Saunders
130 Clinton St., Unit 17
Toronto, Ontario, Canada M6G2Y3

INDEX